TRADE UNION FOREIGN POLICY

Jeffrey Harrod

Trade Union Foreign Policy

A Study of British and American Trade Union Activities in Jamaica

Doubleday & Company, Inc., Garden City, New York
1972

Library of Congress Catalog Card Number 77–175381

Printed in the United States of America
First Edition

CONTENTS

PART I
INTERNATIONAL ACTIVITIES OF TRADE UNIONS

PART II
A SPECIFIC CASE: JAMAICA

PART III
ANALYSIS AND CONCLUSIONS

FOREWORD

It is the author's hope that certain aspects of the substance, approach, and presentation will allow this book to have an importance beyond that part of it which may be termed a case study. Firstly, it is intended to contribute to the growing awareness of the means and processes by which one society exerts power over another. Secondly, it has been designed to suggest a method for other in-depth examinations of such links between societies, and, finally, the presentation, with its extensive use of subtitling, has been specifically developed to facilitate efficient selection of sections of the work by the specialised reader.

The book was completed in 1969, and that portion of it which is historical thus finishes in mid-1967. Some events have taken place in Jamaica, and within the foreign unions involved in Jamaica, since that time which have at least a superficial importance, but no attempt has been made to add to or revise the text in the light of these occurrences. In general, they affect neither the account up to 1967 nor the overall analysis.

This book is mainly the result of an individual research project and has not been financed by any government, foundation, international organisation, university, corporation, or any other person or organisation. It was originally presented to the University of Geneva for the degree of Ph.D., through the Graduate Institute of

International Studies. During a short preparatory stage and an equally short writing stage, a standard student living grant was received from the Graduate Institute, which at that time derived a large part of its funds from American sources. The research and travel during the years 1965–68, pursued in five countries and on two continents, including a year in Jamaica, were financed exclusively from personal earnings.

Inputs into the writing of a work such as this come from many sources, and in this way my gratitude is extended to all those important persons in my life. Special thanks, however, I must give to Professor Robert W. Cox, as my thesis supervisor, for his patience in answering letters for nearly five years and for making pertinent and profound comments on the work. At a later stage, Professor Roy Prieswerk made exceptionally valuable suggestions in the construction of the book. The finished work is, of course, entirely my responsibility. Professor Jacques Freymond, Director of the Graduate Institute, has also earned my gratitude for his personal involvement in my earlier difficulties in pursuing Ph.D. studies. My greatest thanks, however, must go to Paddy Summerfield for her intellectual contribution.

Geneva, 1971 *Jeffrey Harrod*

TRADE UNION FOREIGN POLICY

CHAPTER I

INTRODUCTION

In general this book is concerned with the methods and processes by which societies shape and control other societies, whether it be within the framework of colonialism, imperialism, or the neo varieties of either. Likewise, it generally examines the nature and effects of the activities of non-governmental organisations in international relations as well as the problems relating to transfers of organisations from one society to another.

Specifically it is the study of the involvement of British and American trade unions in the growth and development of trade unions in Jamaica.

Non-Governmental Organisations in International Relations

Non-governmental organisations have existed as long as the nation-state system and, in the case of the church, even before the creation of that system, but interest in them as international actors did not develop in a serious manner until the last two decades.

It is difficult to construct an adequate legal definition of a non-governmental organisation.[1] At present they are mainly characteristic of societies in which non-governmental, or private, concentrations of power are not only permitted but are both legitimate and institutionalised. These latter aspects enable them to be described as organisations with a degree of autonomy in action and policy from the legally constituted or *de facto* accepted state government power.

Two factors, one academic and one historic, have caused non-governmental organisations to become of special interest to students of international relations. The first was the rise of academic studies of decision-making and policy-making in state foreign policy. In these it was shown that non-governmental organisations, or interest groups, exercised a varying, but often important, influence on the final form of state foreign policy and actions.[2]

The second factor arose from the establishment of the United Nations (UN) and the creation of the intergovernmental specialised agencies immediately after World War II. International associations or federations of churches, trade unions, and other such organisations were given special recognition within the UN as consultative organisations to the Economic and Social Council. The structures, functions, and policies of these in-

[1] See J. Lador-Lederer, *International Non-Governmental Organisations*, Leyden, 1963, pp. 59–70.

[2] See B. Cohen, *The Influence of Non-Governmental Groups in Foreign Policy-Making*, Boston, 1959; F. Chambers, "Interest Groups and Foreign Affairs," *Yearbook of World Affairs*, Vol. 8, 1954, pp. 220–41; and, more recently, J. Frankel, *The Making of Foreign Policy*, London, 1963.

ternational non-governmental organisations thus became of academic and practical interest.[3]

Coupled with this growth of inter-governmental organisations was the development of the Functional theory of international integration which assigned an important role to non-governmental organisations.

The basic tenet of the theory is that there exists in most societies certain practical or "functional" requirements and that international cooperation on these problems will be more successful as it avoids divisive nationalism and politics.[4] The theory sees the nation-state as essentially artificial and preventing the full flowering of a latent unity which exists among the populations of the world. Thus, David Mitrany, considered the founder of the modern Functionalist school, complained in 1943 that: "Our social activities are cut off arbitrarily at the limit of the state and, if at all, are allowed to be linked to the same activities across the borders only by means of uncertain and cramping political ligatures."[5]

Non-governmental organisations thus satisfy two aspects of the theory—they are presumed not to be infected by the politics and nationalism arising from the governments of the nation-state and also, in their cross-national actions, they promote cooperation on the basis of the particular functions for which they were created. For these reasons, knowledge of the exact nature of in-

[3] See B. Pickard, *The Greater United Nations: an Essay Concerning the Place and Significance of International Non-Governmental Organizations,* New York, 1956; and L. White, *International Non-Government Organizations, Their Purposes, Methods and Accomplishments,* New Brunswick, 1951.

[4] For a thorough discussion of the Functional theory see E. Haas, *Beyond the Nation-State,* Stanford, 1964, pp. 3–126; J. Sewell, *Functionalism and World Politics,* Princeton, 1966, pp. 29–72; and R. Dowse, "A Functionalist's Logic," *World Politics,* Vol. 18, No. 4, July 1966, pp. 607–23.

[5] D. Mitrany, *A Working Peace System,* London, 1943, p. 42.

ternational contacts among non-governmental organisations and whether they fulfill the expectations of the theory has become of some importance.

AS INDEPENDENT ACTORS

For students of international relations the interest in non-governmental organisations has thus been in their role in the making of state foreign policy and in their cooperative ventures within international associations.

The main interest of this study, however, is in the independent activities of non-governmental organisations in international relations. The emphasis is on the cases where non-governmental organisations from one society are directly involved in another, without the intermediary of the state foreign policy-making process or an international association. The latter may have to be considered, but only in cases where they are clearly used as an instrument for the execution of one member's policy.

The contemporary importance of this aspect of non-governmental activities has resulted from changes in the number and type of states extant on the international scene and in the disparity of economic wealth among them. A large number of states have been created, usually from colonies, which are often small in size, and almost all are economically weak. At the same time, the advanced industrialised countries have increased their levels of affluence and technological capability, both of which facilitate ease of international travel and communication.

Thus, with relatively limited resources a non-governmental organisation from an industrial country can launch a project in a less-developed country. In such countries, non-governmental organisations, sometimes with a budget as large as that of the host state, find independent action has greater impact, meets less-organised resistance, is superficially less complex and is certainly less expensive than similar actions in an industrial country. Thus the power of a non-governmental organisation to act independently is augmented simply by the size, economy, and conditions found in the majority of the newer states.

This situation is reflected in the number of non-governmental organisations directly involved in programmes for less-developed countries. A European directory lists over 200 such organisations offering development assistance in various forms.[6] In Britain, for 1962–63, over 100 organisations spent £15 million and maintained 6000 employees (nationals) abroad; one organisation had £1.4 million committed to 140 projects in 33 countries.[7]

Factors which enable a non-governmental organisation to act independently are multiple, but it is sufficient to point to a few important conditions without which an independent role would be virtually impossible.

Apart from an independence of governments, implicit in the name and definition, the organisation must also have some international freedom to enable its officials to travel, transfer funds, and communicate internationally. Secondly, it must possess the organisational capability, in terms of financial power, information, and staff resources, necessary to execute its policy. Thirdly, it must have at its disposal the means and channels for executing international policy which would usually mean contacts

[6] Centre for Labour and Social Studies: *Directory of Non-Governmental European Organisations Offering Assistance in the Developing Countries*, Rome, 1964.

[7] P. Williams and A. Moyes, *Not by Governments Alone: the Role of British Non-Government Organisations in the Development Decade*, London, 1964, p. 9 and pp. 48–50.

abroad, counterpart groups in other societies, international associations, and individual and organisational associates. Organisations with these characteristics can then become independent actors in international relations directly affecting the political, economic, and social conditions of states and nations in which they are involved. They have, in effect, their own developed and implemented foreign policy.

THE PERSONAL DIMENSION

The involvement of an organisation in the society of another state is based on the existence of a cross-national group of similar origin, name, or formal structure and the accepted legitimacy of contacts between such groups.[8] The agent, or actor, from a non-governmental organisation is therefore more often involved at the participatory level and consequently has an impact on the growth, development, and operation of the social organisation concerned. Furthermore, he is often the policy-maker for his own organisation, or at least the principal supplier of information for policy-makers. The result of organisational policies and programmes, as well as their formulation, is thus directly dependent on the performance of the in-field actors. Because such performances are cross-cultural, the personal and cultural dimension in the study of organisational policy and impact is of paramount importance.

[8] Governments may, of course, regulate or forbid such international contacts with the groups in their jurisdiction. See regulation effected by Brazil in relation to international trade union organisations; USA Department of Labor: *Labor Developments Abroad,* Vol. 14, No. 3, p. 19.

The greatest body of literature concerning the behavioural characteristics of persons in cross-cultural circumstances has arisen either from the colonial administrative, the corporate or, more recently, technical assistance experiences.[9]

From the management studies and the work of some anthropologists, some aspects of the behaviour have been identified. One of the most noticeable of these is cultural shock, a phenomenon which results from a psychological inability to deal with a new environment and is manifested, in extreme cases, by severe emotional disintegration.[10] Cultural shock is only the observable extreme of a range of reactions to the disturbing impact of cross-cultural experience, especially when that experience has come from attempts to perform specific tasks. Many of the behavioural characteristics of persons operating in a cross-cultural situation can, in fact, be seen as a variety of attempts to dampen and mitigate cultural shock and its less-spectacular manifestations.

[9] On the colonial experience see A. Burns, *The Colonial Civil Servant*, London, 1949; and J. S. Furnival, *Colonial Policy and Practice*, Cambridge, 1948; on corporate experience see J. Fayerweather, *The Executive Overseas: Administrative Attitudes and Relationships in a Foreign Culture*, New York, 1959; and T. Brannen and F. Hodgson, *Overseas Management*, New York, 1965; and on technical assistance see W. Sharp, *Field Administration in the United Nations System*, New York, 1962, pp. 119–68; and S. Lundsfeldt, "The Interpersonal Dimension in Technical Assistance: Statement of a Problem," *Mental Hygiene*, Vol. XLV, No. 8, July 1961, pp. 374–82.

[10] The cultural shock of Europeans in Africa is described in M. Herskovits, *The Human Factor in Changing Africa*, London, 1963, pp. 113–19; see also S. Lesser and H. Peter, "Training Foreign Nationals in the United States," in R. Likert and S. Hayes, eds., *Some Applications of Behavioural Research*, UNESCO, 1957; its effects are noted in A. Willner, "The Foreign Expert in Indonesia: Problems of Adjustability and Change," *Economic Development and Cultural Change*, Vol. II, No. 1, April 1953, pp. 71–80.

The first of these is the conscious (and sometimes unconscious) denial that there is a difference in the structures, values, and processes between the actor's culture and the host culture. A second method is a psychological or conscious attempt to re-create the home environment which then shields and dampens the impact of a totally alien environment. Such action is sometimes supported by ideologies in which the actor's culture is considered superior to the host culture and thus a mandate, as in the colonial situation, is given for such re-creations. More recently, the colonial mandates have sometimes been succeeded by those coming from social scientists, thus Rottenberg can say as late as 1952, in relation to the economic development of "backward peoples," that "Our traditions must become theirs, or they must remain poverty-stricken, or the world's well-to-do must move a never ending flow of gifts to them. There is no other way out."[11] Another attempt, less important to performance but very important to information, is a cross-cultural projection in which, on the rational level, similarities of structures or functions are perceived between the actor's culture and the host culture and the normal attributes of such structures from the actor's culture are then assumed to exist.[12]

Some writers have argued that the greater degree of cultural relativity possessed by the person concerned, the less need to resort to these practices. A lack of cultural relativity has been defined as a basic failure to recognise

[11] S. Rottenberg, "Income and Leisure in an Underdeveloped Economy," *Journal of Political Economy,* Vol. 60, No. 2, April 1952, fn. 8, p. 97.

[12] See W. Hurh, "Imitation: Its Limitations in the Process of Inter-Societal Cultural Diffusion," *International Journal of Comparative Sociology,* Vol. 10, Nos. 3–4, September and December 1969, pp. 263–85; and R. Edgerton, "Some Dimensions of Disillusionment in Cultural Contact," *South West Journal of Anthropology,* Vol. 21, Autumn 1965, pp. 231–43.

that one's own culture is merely one among many and that it will never be exactly duplicated in another environment.[13]

Historically, the results of these behavioural characteristics can be woven into an explanation for the collapse of empires and large international conflicts, but the importance of them in this study is that they clearly impair the ability to deal with the operational environment which is important to the success or failure of non-governmental policies and programmes. Also the presence or absence of a degree of cultural relativity will determine the nature of the information gathered and the feedback received, both of which are important to decision-making at the organisational level.

Less-Developed Countries and Organisational Transfer

Since World War II, a large number of states have entered the international system which have been known collectively as the third world, developing or less-developed countries. These collective descriptions have been based on the common characteristic of low per capita income and national product when compared with the industrial states of the world. But there are other equally important common phenomena, one of which is that most of the states have been colonies and have subsequently continued to have a wide range of foreign involvements in their societies.

[13] See R. Benedict, *Patterns of Culture*, New York, 1961; M. J. Maquet, "Objectivity in Anthropology," *Current Anthropology*, Vol. 5, 1964, pp. 47–55; and M. Herskovits, *Man and His Works*, New York, 1948.

The importance of this last factor to this study is that they have been subjected to attempts to transfer organisations, originally from the colonial metropolitan power, and more recently from other industrial countries.

Organisational transfer is a complex task and theory concerning it is not well advanced; as one writer remarks, ". . . the adaptation of the salient features of human organisations from one environment to another is so difficult and the results so unpredictable that the key elements—structural form, technologies, hierarchical systems, functions and goals—are often exported in their original form."[14]

It is obvious that such an original and imported form may be dysfunctional in its new setting as the new social ecology may demand different or additional functions.[15] Any movement towards a more functional or adapted form will depend on a number of variables, one of which is the strength and nature of foreign elements in the growth and operation of the organisation.[16]

An attempt to identify, isolate, and assess all the foreign involvements in the transfer, growth, and operation of social organisation in a society presents problems of definitions. The usual phrase "foreign influences" is too precise and indicates a teleological attitude. For this

[14] J. Windmuller, "External Influences on Labor Organizations in Underdeveloped Countries," *Industrial and Labor Relations Review*, Vol. 16, No. 4, July 1963, pp. 569–70; see also W. Robson, "The Transplanting of Political Institutions and Ideas," *The Political Quarterly*, Vol. 35, No. 4, October–December, 1964, pp. 410–19; and R. Farmer, "Organisational Transfer and Class Structure," *Academy of Management Journal*, Vol. 9, No. 3, September 1966, pp. 204–16.

[15] See comment on viability of imported organisations in K. Boulding, "Social Dynamics in West Indian Society," *Social and Economic Studies*, Vol. 10, No. 1, March 1961, p. 33.

[16] See H. Lasswell, "Foreign Influences on American Labor," in J. Hardman, ed., *American Labor Dynamics*, New York, 1928, pp. 360–66.

reason the phrase "foreign elements" has been used as it can include a wide range of phenomena, such as an identifiable promotion of a foreign model by a local group or person, a conception of organisation derived from foreign experience, a foreign person or funds from foreign organisations. The use of the word "element," however, has not solved the problem completely and, as with some of the other more conventional words, it necessarily remains a vague collective noun used to cover a heterogeneous group of phenomena, attitudes, organisations, and persons.

Although the phrase could be stretched to encompass a whole range of subjective matter (for example: Could education be considered a foreign element?) it is generally unnecessary to do so as it is usually applied to the clearer and more tangible aspects of involvement as foreign financial aid and personnel from foreign governments and non-governmental organisations.

Foreign means foreign to the geographic situation of the society but, more important, it also means foreign to the local conditions and culture. In ex-colonial societies it could be claimed that, as the whole society was based on exports of the metropolitan powers, the metropolitan derived models, concepts, or policies could not be considered alien. In most ex-colonies, however, there in fact exists an indigenous culture exclusive to the society with distinct psychological, sociological, and political attributes, and, in relation to these, metropolitan exports continue to be foreign.

Trade Unions

There are three main non-governmental groups which have traditionally been involved in international activities—the church, the corporations, and trade unions. Unlike the church and corporations, trade union foreign involvement has not been subjected to thorough investigation, partly because the more important of them are of recent origin and partly because they have been considered as relatively unimportant.[17]

For these reasons, and also the more practical one of availability of source materials, trade unions were selected as the non-governmental organisations for this study. To avoid the more traditional structural and formal conception of trade unions and to ensure the emphasis on the social ecology of the organisations, trade unions are considered here as social organisations. Two social psychologists have described a social organisation as "specific groupings of actual people, which are characterized by the possession of the following: (1) cultural products (such as buildings, robes, prayers, magic formula, songs), (2) a collective name or symbol, (3) distinctive action patterns, (4) a common belief system, (5) enforcing agents or techniques."[18]

[17] As with most non-governmental organisations, the role of trade unions in state foreign policy-making has been investigated. See, for example, M. Hardy, *The Influence of Organized Labor on the Foreign Policy of the United States*, Liège, 1936.

[18] D. Krech and R. Crutchfield, *Theory and Problems of Social Psychology*, New York, 1948, p. 369; and see also P. Blau and S. Scott, *Formal Organisations: a Comparative Approach*, London, 1963, pp. 2–5.

The functions of such organisations are usually revealed by the behaviour pattern or belief systems of the membership or its leaders. Thus functions may be basic or accessory and they may or may not conform to those formally stated by the leadership. These are important considerations in this study as international activities are usually an accessory function for trade unions and in less-developed countries the union's social and psychological functions are often as important as the economic functions.

An examination of the making and implementation of trade union foreign policy requires access to both documents and field actors and for this reason British and American unions were selected for the study. While policy-making is centralised, the success or failure of it will depend on the particular locale in which it is exercised, especially when the importance of the personal dimension is considered. The selection of a country where a detailed examination of British and American trade union foreign policy could be made was thus confined to one in which there was prima facie evidence of British and American union involvement.

Jamaica's history as a British colony and the known interest of United States' trade unions in Latin America and the Caribbean would indicate that both British and American unions had been involved in that country. It was with only this general knowledge that Jamaica was selected as a suitable country for a case study, although as always, practical factors also interceded.

The selection of Jamaica and its somewhat isolated consideration therefore does not imply that its experience in this respect is unique. Neither is it necessarily typical but it may be representative, as there are indications that the Jamaican experience with foreign unions may be shared with other nations and territories in the

Caribbean and also by other less-developed countries in Latin America, Asia, and Africa.

TRADE UNIONS IN LESS-DEVELOPED COUNTRIES

As a result of either a colonial experience or other more recent contacts with industrial countries, most less-developed countries have groups which are generally known as trade unions.[19] These organisations, however, may have functions which don't conform with their formal structure or with the functions associated with trade unions from industrial countries.[20]

Because of a degree of autonomy from governments, their origins as imports, and their nominal, if not substantive, imitation of their industrial country counterparts, trade unions in less-developed countries have been readily open to foreign involvement. The group-to-group nature of non-governmental activity has meant that one of the most important foreign involvements in such unions has been from foreign trade unions.

Foreign trade unions have not been the only foreign actors, however, and new trade unions have been created and the leaders of existing ones subjected to the advice, urgings, and pressure to pursue policies which are in

[19] See S. Sufrin, *Unions in Emerging Societies*, New York, 1964; W. Galenson, ed., *Labor and Economic Development*, New York, 1959; B. Millen, *The Political Role of Labor in Developing Countries*, Washington, 1963.

[20] See S. Gosh, *Trade Unionism in the Underdeveloped Countries*, Calcutta, 1960, pp. 322–26; A. Mehta, "The Mediating Role of the Trade Union in Underdeveloped Countries," *Economic Development and Cultural Change*, Vol. VI, No. 1, October 1957, pp. 16–23; and A. Sturmthal, "Unions and Economic Development," *Economic Development and Cultural Change*, Vol. VIII, No. 2, January 1960, pp. 199–205.

accordance with the wishes and perceptions of foreign governments, individuals, or organisations. Furthermore, the structure and functions of social organisations are also determined by other organisations and groups in the society, especially if they stand in symbiotic relationship, and these other organisations would also be affected by their own foreign elements.

The impact of British unions, for example, in an ex-colony such as Jamaica is obviously not only the work of the British national trade union centre but also that of the metropolitan government as well as an assortment of British educators, members of parliament, organisations, literati and their local supporters, all of whom might urge trade union leaders to adopt "the British way." Thus this study has to be total in the sense that all aspects of foreign involvement have to be described and assessed. Nevertheless, within this framework, primary emphasis is placed on uncovering and assessing the role of foreign trade unions.

Approach

Greater emphasis than usual is perhaps being placed on discussing the basic approach and research problems associated with this study. The reason for this is that so much research on less-developed countries, especially dealing with trade unions, is presented by the researcher, and therefore apprehended by the reader, as if it were not cross-cultural.[21] The studies are presented, and pos-

[21] See for example the approach adopted in B. Roberts, *Labour in the Tropical Commonwealth*, London, 1964. The approach used in this book is presented in schematic form as an appendix.

sibly the research conducted, exactly as if it were a study of an industrial country. Rarely does the researcher indicate whether he is aware of the bias which may enter his writing by virtue of his own culture or that statistics, newspapers, magazines, and other sources cannot be viewed in the same light as their same-name counterparts in other societies.

In this and the following section the basic approach and problems of research are discussed at length to indicate the differences between research in industrial and in less-developed countries.

For several decades scholars have attempted to segment the arc of human activity into exclusive domains which, although in accord with western intellectual tradition and culture, has in practice resulted in the building of isolated organisational and disciplinary empires. Specialisation, fragmentation, and isolation have tended to deny the concept of interrelatedness of scientific, social, and psychological phenomena and prevent a discussion of totalities. In more recent times, the desire to inhibit conflict and confrontation of all kinds has amplified this practice as discussions of parts and means are less disruptive and more convenient than discussions of wholes and ends.

While the moral and political implications of this are vast, intellectually it has brought into question some of the investigations and descriptions made by social scientists. As one author notes: "No adequate diagnosis or realistic predictions are possible when events and human behavior are viewed as influenced by one factor or a particular group of factors rather than in relation to the total context. Such inquiry arrives at conclusions which provide neither substantive and significantly correct predictions nor relevant criteria for the formulation of social policy. In short, a specialisation which neglects the intrinsic interdependence of social events and processes must ultimately fail as an instrument of policy designed to cope with social problems."[22] In other words, the exclusion of interrelatedness by fragmentation and specialisation brings the accuracy of results into doubt.[23]

RE-INTEGRATION OF SOCIAL SCIENCE

Recent developments in theory and approaches in social science are, however, undermining the rigid divisions of specialisation. In particular, systems theory and decision-making theory emphasise the notion of interrelatedness rather than diminish it.

These theories and the increasing recognition of interrelatedness arise partly from the impact of new subject matter in natural and social sciences. The development in natural sciences has been the growth of environmental studies which has incorporated the older concept of ecology. In arguing that natural scientists were becoming less, rather than more, narrow, a leading medical scientist, Dr. D. P. Medawar, pointed out that: "Each one tries to achieve a synoptic grasp of all disciplines pertaining to his chosen plane of analysis. A modern ecologist, for example, tries to make himself fa-

[22] K. Kapp, *Toward a Science of Man in Society*, The Hague, 1961, pp. 10–11.

[23] For example, the pure economic theories of wage and price determination were brought into doubt many years ago by works stressing "non-economic behaviour." See S. Lipset and M. Trow, "Reference Group Theory and Trade Union Wage Policy," in M. Komarovsky, ed., *Common Frontiers of Social Science*, Glencoe, 1957, pp. 391–411.

miliar with genetics, population dynamics, ethology and environmental physiology."[24] In social sciences the concept of ecology has a central place in such theoretical propositions as the Sprouts' *The Ecological Perspective on Human Affairs.*[25] In other theories and approaches, ecology, as the Sprouts adequately point out, appears in the disguised form of "setting," "environment," or "foundations."[26] Human ecology has been, for some time, a branch of social psychology dealing with the man/physical-environment relationship rather than with the broader concept of ecology developed by the Sprouts.

The new subject matter in the social sciences which has assisted the retreat from fragmentation is the study of less-developed countries. This subject was only new inasmuch as social scientists were asked to view these societies for the first time from the standpoint of economic development. Thus, it was from the tortuous attempts of economists to fit their theories and panaceas, based on unquestioned notions of the nature of man and society, into the context of a strange and non-western environment that it became clear that a comprehensive approach could not be avoided. In the study of a western industrial country some case for fragmentation and specialisation could be made; functionally specific organisations and groups do, to some extent, exist, data used by researchers is often developed and presented with reference to disciplinary divisions and the relationship between cultural patterns and organisational forms is not readily recognised.

[24] Dr. D. P. Medawar, "Anglo-Saxon Attitudes," Tizard Memorial Lecture at Westminster School, London, 1965. Reprinted in *Encounter*, Vol. XXV, No. 2, August 1965, p. 53.

[25] H. Sprout and M. Sprout, *The Ecological Perspective on Human Affairs,* Princeton, 1965.

[26] *Ibid.*, p. 6.

But in less-developed countries, even in 1952, there was already a realisation of the need for economists to have a different approach. In that year Belshaw claimed that economic development was more than a response of individuals to material incentives, that the standard equilibrium analysis was inadequate and that: "There is a need for a wider, if less tidy, approach by economists, which draws on the resources of other social sciences or applied arts–anthropology, sociology, political science, education, law or public administration–and sets economic motivation, not austerely apart but in its proper place in complex systems of responses, beliefs, organizations and institutions."[27] To satisfy this demand the researcher would not only have to acquire a wider technical competence but also behave as a good anthropologist and question the relevance of every value, every assumption and marginal bias which had been derived from his own culture. It has become increasingly clear, therefore, that a meaningful interpretation of economic or social phenomena can only be made with a substantial knowledge of the total environment and culture.[28]

The growing realisation of the necessity for an integrated approach has led more quickly to reform in policy-making than it has academically. As one author, in 1968, notes in relation to policy-making in international organisations: "The technical international officials concerned are nearly all advocates of a comprehensive planned approach. 'Comprehensive planning' is the key

[27] H. Belshaw, "Economic Development as an Operational Problem," *Civilizations*, Vol. II, No. 2, 1952, pp. 159–60, as quoted in L. Shannon, *Underdeveloped Areas*, New York, 1957, p. 196.
[28] This point is made in G. Kavadias, "Assimilation of the Scientific and Technological 'message,'" *International Social Science Journal*, Vol. 18, No. 3, 1966, p. 371; and is also implicit in the approach of I. Davies, *African Trade Unions*, Harmondsworth, 1966.

phrase in the revision of official ideology now going on within the technical departments of international agencies where there is awareness of the dysfunctional effect of earlier simplistic enthusiasm."[29]

Some branches of social science have recently made significant contributions to the re-integration of the various disciplines and approaches, the most notable being social psychology and social or cultural anthropology.[30] Although no social science can avoid the necessity of accepting a concept of culture operating between man and environment, it is only these two branches, and especially anthropology, which have placed culture in a central position. The contemporary application of procedures and frameworks of anthropology to industrial societies and the consequent examination of the cultural determinants of their political and economic systems are a substantial advance over the previous methods of investigation.

Culture for Tylor is "that complex whole which includes knowledge, belief, art, morals, law, custom and other capabilities and habits acquired by man as a member of society."[31] A more modern view is that "culture, as a term used by sociologists and cultural anthropologists, is the totality of group ways of thought and action which are widely accepted and followed by a group of

[29] R. Cox, "Education for Development," *International Organization,* Vol. XXII, No. 1, Winter 1968, p. 326.

[30] There are some semantic difficulties with this nomenclature. Often the same subject matter is called social anthropology in Britain, cultural anthropology in the USA, and ethnology in France. See C. Lévi-Strauss, *Anthropologie Structurale,* Paris, 1958, p. 5. Other authors would designate any approach utilizing these subjects as the "sociological approach." See G. Schwarzenberger, *Power Politics,* 3d ed., London, 1964, pp. 8–14.

[31] E. Tylor, *Primitive Culture,* London, 1891, Vol. I, pp. 1–6, as reprinted in L. Coser and B. Rosenberg, eds., *Sociological Theory,* New York, 1957, p. 17.

people."[32] It is only in the light of a knowledge of this "complex whole" or "totality" that more specific institutions or organisations can be properly considered. Without a knowledge of the basic culture it is impossible to assess the full range of consequences, both manifest and latent, positive and negative of any social organisation or institution. This is especially true in the case of trade unions which carry with them implicit notions of structure and function derived from other cultures.

For these reasons extensive use is made of the concepts and approaches of both social psychology and anthropology. But this study involves international economics, development economics, law, political science, and individual psychology, so the quality of the work will ultimately depend on how well the researcher has mastered and connected the substance of social knowledge currently found in these compartments of social science.

Cross-Cultural Research

The basic methods of research for this study have been the traditional ones of examination of written material, interviews, and field observations. The dangers of these methods are well known[33]—the nominal or formal view derived from documents and the subjective nature of interviews and personal observation.

In cross-cultural research these dangers are increased because they usually cannot be offset by the insights, such as the ability to detect "freudian slips," to make

[32] P. Walter, *Race and Cultural Relations*, New York, 1952, p. 17.

[33] See M. Duverger, *Méthodes des Sciences Sociales*, Paris, 1961.

meaningful projections from documentary evidence, and to appreciate the nuances of social stratifications, which a good researcher will have developed in relation to his own culture. The development of insights into a strange culture may be complicated by three factors: first, the lack of cultural awareness on the part of the researcher; second, divisions between the researcher and the host society created by class, race, nationality, and language differences; and third, in some cases the general lack of existing knowledge of the culture which would be of assistance in solving these problems.

THE PERSONAL DIMENSION IN RESEARCH

The problems for the cross-cultural researcher are somewhat similar to those of the representative from a non-governmental organisation described above, except that the effects will be on the information gathered rather than on operations performed. Lack of cultural relativity on the part of the researcher and cross-cultural projection can render research meaningless.[34]

This is particularly true in the case of trade unions, as often their names and formal structure are cross-cultural, leading researchers to assume, seek, or create informal processes and functions which correspond to their own environment but which may not be warranted in the new conditions.[35]

[34] The problem of information and understanding is dealt with in E. Hall, *The Silent Language*, New York, 1959; see also F. Northrop and H. Livingston, eds., *Cross-Cultural Understanding*, New York, 1964.

[35] For an examination of the cultural bias which exists in major works on trade unionism, see V. Allen, "The Study of African Trade Unionism," *Journal of Modern African Studies*, Vol. 7, No.

The development of the mental equipment of an anthropologist is a personal factor which can be solved to a lesser or greater degree according to the personality of the individual and the training he receives.[36] The fragmented nature of western social science, however, and the tendency to accept that expertise within one culture or one type of society is, even without reconsideration of method and approach, qualification for cross-cultural studies, presents problems concerning the existing body of research.

As Margaret Mead points out, ". . . if the observer is untrained, he gives more data about his own cultural position than about the other upon which he is reporting: but in a trained social scientist there will be a sharp difference in level in the abstractions which he finds relevant between the order of material he presents about another culture and that which he includes on his own."[37] Many of the general or specific works on Jamaica could be placed in the category of those which reveal more about the culture and political bias of the writers than the conditions which exist in Jamaica. For example, the only published work on the specific issue of trade unionism in the Caribbean, Knowles's *Trade Union Development and Industrial Relations in the British West Indies,*[38] brought this comment from another student of Jamaican trade unionism, "this author is inclined to make extreme generalizations. It is possible that as a North

---

2, 1969, pp. 294–97. An approach designed to overcome some of these problems is outlined in G. Almond and G. Coleman, eds., *The Politics of Developing Areas,* Princeton, 1960, pp. 3–64.

[36] A. Wilson, "Recruitment and Selection for Work in Foreign Cultures," *Human Relations,* Vol. 14, No. 1, 1961, pp. 3–21.

[37] M. Mead, "The Study of National Character," in D. Lerner and H. Lasswell, eds., *The Policy Sciences,* Stanford, 1951, p. 77.

[38] W. Knowles, *Trade Union Development and Industrial Relations in the British West Indies,* Berkeley, 1959.

American anxious to see indications of a drift towards North American business unionism the existing pattern in the West Indies presents a vivid contrast."[39]

More obvious difficulties arise from differences in class, race, and language. In countries in which the managerial and educated class is distinctly segregated from the majority of the people by values, experience, aspirations, income, and life-style, the researcher from an industrial country will always be viewed as a member, and possibly an agent, of that class. In Jamaica the race or colour of the researcher (in this case white) is identified with the Jamaican managerial, clerical, and administrative groups, especially as the latter have often adopted some of the attitudes of superiority towards country people, the unemployed and working class, previously held by the British colonialists.[40] It must also be mentioned that recent disclosures of covert foreign government sponsorship of academic research for military purposes has further complicated the responses a foreign researcher receives from groups or persons whose suspicions have been aroused.[41] Thus, a researcher, when in contact with any group or class, is confronted by either deference, suspicion, an over-willingness to say what he might be expected to want to hear, or a latent and sometimes overt antagonism. No criticism of these attitudes is here implied, for they no doubt perform a necessary and justifiable protective function, but they also clearly present a problem for a seeker of accurate information.

[39] G. Eaton, *The Development of Trade Unionism in Jamaica, W.I.*, unpublished Ph.D. dissertation, McGill University, Canada, 1961, p. 22.

[40] See K. Norris, *Jamaica, the Search for an Identity*, London, 1962, pp. 61–65. It should also be noted that Jamaican creole, even though partly based on English, is not readily understood without study and practice.

[41] See statement of Professor K. H. Silvert, *The New York Times*, February 26, 1967, Section IV, p. 1.

KNOWLEDGE OF CULTURE

The final problem associated with cross-cultural research is the general lack of information about the culture and environment to be studied. The problem could not be better stated than by a group of West Indians in a paper which, after describing the nature of the plantation society, its transitory elite and culturally diverse slaves and indentured labourers, continued, "with these features, no society could ever have fixed any of its own points of reference. It was natural to see the world through outside eyes and never did it become urgently necessary to organise a fund of knowledge about the home environment or even about the wider world. It is out of this background that has emerged what we describe as the Afro-Saxon culture which puts its highest premium on achievement by mimicry . . ."[42] Thus, the authors continue, the "task is to observe our environment, to find out about the circumstances in which we live, to discover who we are and what is our history . . . In other words, to develop a consciousness of our own humanity in relation to our natural habitat."[43] Ortega y Gasset places such knowledge as one of the two primary dimensions of human life without which all must be chaos.[44]

[42] Authors anonymous, "Intellectual Tradition and Social Change in the Caribbean," *New Word Pamphlet,* Kingston, Jamaica, no date, p. 11 (originally appeared in *New World Fortnightly,* Nos. 27 and 28, November 12, 1965); see also comment by M. Herskovits, *The Human Factor in Changing Africa,* Preface, pp. VIII–IX.

[43] *Ibid.*

[44] J. Ortega y Gasset, *Man and Crises,* London, 1959, pp. 24–27; and see L. Pye, *Politics, Personality and Nation Building, Burma's Search for Identity,* New Haven, 1962; and E. Erikson, *Young Man Luther,* London, 1958, especially pp. 248–55.

These quotations not only illustrate the problem presented by a basic lack of pre-existing knowledge but also an equally difficult problem. A society characterised by "achievement by mimicry" and a tendency to view the environment through "outside eyes" obviously presents, for the outside observer, the greatest difficulty in distinguishing the nominal from the real.

Sources

In order to make effective use of the source materials it is necessary to counter, or at least be aware of, the general problems of cross-cultural research. Source materials from less-developed countries (other than from participant observation), even though similar in structure to those from industrial countries, cannot be given the same evidential weight. Examples from source materials from Jamaica used in this study will indicate the caution with which they must be considered.

WRITTEN MATERIAL IN JAMAICA

Firstly, it must be remembered that Jamaica, as with many other less-developed countries, is a verbal society which means there is neither the habit nor the inclination to record events in writing. As with most verbal societies, communication of the historic kind is found in the social practice of story telling and in folk songs.

In the modern period, the reluctance of colonial governments to invest in primary education has kept functional literacy low, even though government statistics, using school attendance as a base, put it much higher.

For these reasons, throughout most of the period of this study (1935–67) the only persons with the ability or interest to record events, write pamphlets, and produce magazines were usually in leadership positions. The intellectuals, normally recorders of current history, were engaged in a large number of activities which prevented them from writing studied, historical accounts of their times. The intellectual in Jamaica is, and has to be, multi-functional. In the mid-thirties, the early period of this study, the intellectual would often be leader, organiser, accountant, and publication editor of any group or organisation and would not be able to delegate these tasks owing to the lack of such skills in the society.

The result of these aspects of Jamaican life is that the already scarce written material will tend to be written by the same people. Richard Hart, an early actor in Jamaican trade unionism, has produced some of the most important documents relating to the nature of Jamaican trade unions, regional trade union organisations, trade union education and history, and news sheets and bulletins for the organisations. Most of this was achieved while he was Vice President of the Trades Union Congress of Jamaica (TUCJ), General Secretary of the Caribbean Labour Congress, and a working lawyer. Many such documents do not bear the author's name and it is only through extensive research that they are revealed to have a common source. The dangers of acquiring a mono-interpretation of events from such sources are obvious.

There is only one publisher in Jamaica producing daily newspapers, one morning and one evening. The morning newspaper, the *Daily Gleaner*, is thus the only source of continuous and current news on the island, a fact which makes the orientation of the paper an essential factor in assessing its usefulness as a source. It has, for example, been argued that it was "anti-labour" in the sense that it opposed the trade union movement. Norman Manley, leader of the People's National Party and opposition leader in the House of Representatives, claimed in 1966 that the Jamaican Employers' Federation views were "expressed in the Press [sic] from time to time and get far more notice than anything expressed in favour of the working class movement . . . there was no large circulation newspaper in Jamaica which supports the working class cause, because the only mass daily newspaper as well as a lot of columnists invariably take an anti-trade union attitude."[45] While there is little evidence that substantial distortion exists in the news stories there have, however, been many instances in which general articles have been uncompromising in their anti-union tone. In 1961, for example, one year before Jamaican independence, a series of articles was published and prominently placed—"Syndicalism, Sabotage and Anarchy" by H. S. Burns (May 16, 1961), "Trade Unions Have Ruined the Island Economy" by Gladstone Burke (May 20, 1961), and "Our Trade Unions—Stifling and Sabotaging Production" by W. A. Sinclair (June 3, 1961).

Apart from a possible anti-union bias in news selection, perhaps the greatest problem with the *Gleaner* as a research source is that before the mid-fifties the paper showed no interest in local events and trends. European and Korean war news dominated throughout the 1940s and was then replaced by general news from Britain and the USA. The important events in the Jamaican trade union movement which occurred between 1949 and 1952 go virtually unrecorded in the *Gleaner*. It may have been the European orientation of the paper rather than de-

[45] *Public Opinion*, December 16, 1966, p. 1.

liberate censorship which caused Ken Hill, an early activist in Jamaican unions, to complain of "censorship of strikes."[46] As a source for trade union affairs, then, the *Gleaner* has to be treated with reserve.

Interviews with persons who have played a role in the development of the Jamaican trade union movement help to supply the missing information. However, the problem here is similar to most contemporary historical work in that the major actors are still alive and often in important political positions. Thus on the most controversial and sensitive issues the interviewees have collectively arrived at an interpretation which causes the least pain and embarrassment but which is often not completely in accord with other evidence.

PROBLEMS OF STATISTICS

Many statistics from official and unofficial sources cannot be considered in the same manner as they would be in industrial countries.[47] In Jamaica, a statistic which in an industrial country might be merely an interesting and verified fact becomes a factor upon which political lives and material fortunes may depend.[48]

On the international level, social and economic statistics are often the key to continued or increased economic aid. The USA Food for Peace Act of 1966, for example, directs the President to take into account what recipient countries are doing to be self-sufficient. A small increase

[46] From a letter published in the *Worker and Peasant*, Vol. 1, No. 1, April 1940.

[47] On reliability of data, see V. Allen, *op. cit.*, pp. 297–307.

[48] Statistics from industrial countries are not always above suspicion. See O. Morgenstern, *On Accuracy of Economic Observations*, Princeton, 1963, especially p. 21.

in crop output, statistically evidenced, qualifies one country for surplus food sales and denies them to countries with less satisfactory statistics.[49] Further, any country wishing to maintain a satisfactory image, for whatever reason, be it national pride, to attract tourists, or to placate demands of another power, must have statistics to support that image. The incentives for arranging the most favourable statistic are, therefore, readily apparent.

On the domestic level, statistics are used, as they are in other countries, to support political claims and counter claims. In conditions of less-developed countries, however, there is rarely a countervailing force with sufficient finance, personnel, or expertise to be able to confirm or refute politically produced, distorted, or adjusted statistics.

In Jamaica, professors of economics, government officials, and trade unionists argue over unemployment statistics—not over a fraction of a percentage point, or a small percentage of total work forces, but over estimates ranging from 7 to 20 per cent of the total work force. As mentioned above, government and private estimates of literacy vary widely. In the 1967 general election, the People's National Party (PNP) claimed that through deliberate government mismanagement some 300,000 electors were disenfranchised while, naturally, the figure given by the ruling Jamaica Labour Party (JLP) is much lower, yet this occurred in the framework of known past election statistics and a supposedly sophisticated voter registration system which required, among other things, a photograph of the voter on the registration card.[50]

In the case of unions, the obvious incentives to inflate membership have always been well known and in the

[49] See N. Balfour, "America in the War on Hunger," *World Today*, Vol. 22, No. 12, December 1966, pp. 529–34.
[50] *Daily Gleaner*, March 4, 1967, p. 1.

close union-political party system in Jamaica the membership statistic becomes even more important. In 1964 a special audit, after accusations of corruption, of the National Workers Union (NWU) showed that of the 130,964 members 40 per cent were not dues-paying.[51] No such audit has been possible with the Bustamante Industrial Trade Union (BITU). The conflicting reports and claims about union affliation among workers at various enterprises has been eased somewhat by the Ministry of Labour provisions for a secret poll, but in other areas the statistical claims continue unabated.

It is only with extreme caution and mental reservations that social statistics can be used as evidence of power or reality.

[51] *Daily Gleaner,* December 12, 1964, p. 1.

Part I

International Activities of Trade Unions

CHAPTER II

INTERNATIONAL ACTIVITIES: THE INCENTIVES

The interest in cross-national organisational contact and cooperation, from which the whole phenomena of trade union foreign policy arises, appeared almost at the inception of trade unionism in Europe. As early as 1834 the workers of Nantes wrote to the workers of London: "Brothers and Friends! Do not let our Union be stopped by the seas or rivers that mark the boundaries of States. Let us put into communication . . . all the great centres of industry in the world."[1]

From that time trade union involvement in international relations has taken three basic forms; first, participation in the domestic political process as a foreign policy pressure group; second, in cooperation with the state in the exercise of its foreign programmes; and third, independent international activities.

While each of these forms are part of a total trade union foreign policy, it is only the last which can approximate the foreign policy of a state, for it is only in

[1] R. Postgate, *The Workers International*, London (no date), p. 13, as quoted in L. Lorwin, *Labor and Internationalism*, New York, 1929, p. 16.

the independent activities that trade unions have control over originating, making, and execution of the policy.

The independent aspect of trade union foreign policy itself has three basic forms, the participation in international trade union associations, direct involvement in state diplomacy, and direct involvement in other societies. The activity in the so-called Internationals has been well documented.[2] The direct interventions in diplomacy have been rarer, the attempt of the British TUC, in association with the Labour Party, to send delegates on a mission to the Russian and Polish authorities in the 1934 boundary disputes being one example.[3]

It was not, however, until after World War II that direct involvement of trade unions from one society in a foreign society became prevalent. No doubt arising from cooperation with state diplomacy, in 1945, the American Congress of Industrial Organizations (CIO) and the American Federation of Labor (AF of L) began extensive independent activities and by 1950 the AF of L was spending approximately $500,000 annually on international affairs and maintaining bureaux with full-time staff in Brussels and Latin America.[4] An author writing in 1948 described this as "a new kind of diplomacy, a kind of free enterprise diplomacy."[5]

From that time to the present, there has been a considerable expansion of independent activities and, although the British have never been quite as extensive as

[2] See for example, W. Foster, *History of the Three Internationals*, New York, 1955.

[3] B. Hennessy, "British Trade Unions and International Affairs 1945–1953," unpublished Ph.D. dissertation, University of Wisconsin, 1955, p. 71.

[4] F. Peterson, *American Labor Unions*, New York, 1952, pp. 218–19.

[5] J. Anderson, "The Power of American Unions Abroad," *World Review*, November 1948, p. 41.

the American, both trade union movements spend considerable time and money on their international activities.

Reasons for International Activities

Most of the reasons given for trade union involvement in international society are derived from the formal explanations of the leadership and from trade union ideological attachments. The result of this is that much trade union international activity is ascribed to idealistic reasons, even by groups not usually inclined to credit trade unions' leaders with such sentiments. Thus the British Conservative Political Centre notes: "But there has usually been an idealistic side to their [trade unions'] activities which has made them internationalists."[6] Explanations which concentrate on a single causative factor, such as these, have been the rule rather than the exception.

In order to place conventionally stated reasons for trade union involvement in better perspective as well as to suggest some less well-known reasons, an approach can be adopted which views international action in relation to the needs and functions of social organisations and their leaders.

Social organisations come into existence to perform primary functions in society which relate to the specific welfare and needs of the membership. In the course of performing these functions leaders will promote or defend group ideology and identity, oppose antagonist groups,

[6] Conservative Political Centre: *Trade Unions and International Activities*, London, 1963, p. 1.

support cooperating groups, oppose or defend governments, serve their own personal needs, and so on.

In all of these functions and tactics, existing or proposed international action can be useful, and it is in this use that incentives for international involvement can be found, however weak they may be.

CATEGORIES OF INCENTIVES

Five categories of functions, needs, and tactics of social organisations in which international involvement can be used may be identified. These are rarely single causes in themselves; some categories have such weak incentives that international activity occurring in them more often arises from one or several of the other categories. International activity used in such functions or tactics is thus a convenience supplied by incentives from other categories.

Bearing this in mind, it may be said that incentives and impetus for involvement in international society arise from social organisations when they:

(1) have basic functions in international society;
(2) are increasing or maintaining power in pursuance of performing primary domestic functions;
(3) are acting in support of the nation;
(4) are promoting or defending a political movement or group ideology;
(5) have a leadership which uses accessory functions for internal political and personal reasons.

These categories can now be examined in relation to trade unions, using examples mainly from the British and American experience.

Performing Basic Functions

Incentives arising from the first category are the most obvious as involvement in international society is the result of direct international links with the welfare of union members. While primary functions connected with wages and employment are normally performed within the domestic environment, some industries and trades, and therefore unions, are affected by events abroad.

The connecting factors are international trade, international migration, and international investment.

INTERNATIONAL TRADE

The classic case of involvement of these issues is the attempt of trade unions in one state to raise the wages in another state and so offset a competitive threat from that foreign industry. Hamilton, after interviewing AF of L leaders concerning the membership of the USA in the International Labour Organisation (ILO), reported, "the leadership continues to recognize that ILO membership is of little direct value to American workers in terms of their domestic aspirations, but emphasis has been put on American labor's stake in raising living standards throughout the world, particularly the problem of raising wage standards in competing industries."[7] The same sentiment

[7] W. Hamilton, "The Development of Foreign Policy Attitudes in Certain American Pressure Groups," unpublished Ph.D. dissertation, Yale University, USA, 1955, p. 278; see also "Unions' Foreign Policy; Raise Overseas Wages," *Nation's Business* (USA), Vol. 50, April 1962, p. 33–35.

has been ascribed to the British trade unions' promotion of trade unions in the Indian cotton textile industries. In cases such as these, the trade unions will often find allies in the business groups affected by the growth of low cost industries abroad.[8]

The "low-wage" issue is one that unionists face whenever their industries are involved in international trade with countries of differing levels of economic and social development.

It is thus an issue which has its most important impact on relations between unions of industrial countries and unions of less-developed countries.[9]

It should be noted that economic analysis does not confirm in every case that a low wage-cost factor is the cause of competitive production.[10] More important is the productivity of labour and therefore claims of "unfair" competition by unionists may or may not be real in the economic sense. The claim, however, retains its political potency, for the causes of international competition are not necessarily relevant to its effects and if a union seeks to suppress the competitive threat, the low-wage issue is a useful legitimizing reason. Likewise the raising of labour-costs abroad can reduce the competitive advantage even if labour productivity is higher.

[8] See H. Lasswell, "Foreign Influences on American Labor," in J. Hardman and associates, *American Labor Dynamics*, New York, 1928, p. 363.

[9] See A. Braunthal, "Economic and Social Aspects of International Trade Union Work," *Annals of American Academy of Political Science*, Vol. 310, March 1957, p. 21–30.

[10] See USA Government: *Commission on Foreign Economic Policy, Report to the President and Congress*, Washington, 1954, pp. 62–63, and for importance of wage-cost see dissenting view of Senator E. Millickin at p. 85.

INTERNATIONAL MIGRATION

Trade unions have also been involved in international society in attempts to stem the inflow of foreign labour. In the last century the issue was often one of imported foreign strikebreakers and it was their use in the 1850s which spurred British trade union international activity.

In more recent times, the problems have arisen in relation to economic integration and migration. While paying lip service to the universality of labour aspirations, trade unions in the countries of the European Common Market sometimes have opposed free movement of foreign workers. This is not unique but "merely a restatement of the deep seated fear of organised labour everywhere that unorganised foreign workers will depress wage standards and make for unemployment."[11]

INTERNATIONAL INVESTMENT

The inflow of investment funds, whether direct or portfolio, has not been an important issue for American and British unions, partly because the exact effect has not been fully realised and partly because direct investment has not (as in less-developed countries) been accompanied by overt foreign management and control. In Britain, however, as USA investment increases, more attention is being paid to direct investment problems as evidenced by a resolution passed by the 1964 TUC congress,

[11] E. Haas, *The Uniting of Europe*, London, 1958, p. 221; see also R. Beever, *European Unity and the Trade Union Movements*, Leyden, 1960.

"whilst not deprecating bona fide foreign investment in British firms, Congress deplores the infiltration of foreign capital into British industry for the purpose of acquiring control of key sectors of the British economy."[12]

The outflow of investment, especially direct investment in foreign subsidiaries, has recently become of special interest to unions and has prompted considerable international activity. This has occurred as a result of an increase in the number and size of corporations which have extensive operations abroad. These operations, permitting the international transfer of production, for example, have been used to reduce the bargaining power of unions. As a counter-measure the unions have sought contact with their counterparts abroad, especially those established at the subsidiary plant or organisation of the international corporation concerned. The new involvement has so far taken the form of increased activity by international trade secretariats, the despatching of union negotiators from the corporate headquarters-based to the subsidiary-based union, or attempts at absorption of unions at the subsidiary by unions at headquarters.

As the operations of these corporations (sometimes inaccurately described as multi-national corporations) increase, trade union involvement, in attempting to perform a prime function for membership at international level, will likewise increase.

Increasing or Maintaining Domestic Power

In this second category of incentives, international activity is used to acquire domestic prestige, acceptance, and

[12] TUC: *96th Annual Congress, Report of Proceedings*, 1964, p. 491.

power, or conversely, to diminish the effectiveness of antagonistic groups, organisations, or publics.

The nature of the organisation's domestic social ecology is particularly important here for it will determine whether international action will be useful or necessary. In this category, however, the selection of international action as a useful means of achieving domestic objectives will also depend greatly on the inclination of the leadership.

One example in this category has been the attempts to gain public acceptance by responding to popular demands for wider participation in state foreign policy-making. Another is the use of international activity in relations with other groups and organisations, whether it be for antagonistic or status seeking purposes.[13]

The first example arose from the historic development of demands for democratic control of foreign policy and although this development did not come exclusively from trade union members, trade union leaders were prepared to translate these demands into organisational action.

Until World War I, foreign policy had been basically the exclusive province of government, diplomats, and merchant organisations while public opinion and other groups had no significant influence. However, the "rapidly growing labour force began to insist on popular control of foreign policy as a key to liberal peace"[14] and this insistence was eventually rewarded. The later de-

[13] See, for example, the use of accessory functions for status seeking by Canadian unions as outlined in D. Kwavnick, "Pressure Group Demands and the Struggle for Organizational Status: the Case of Organized Labour in Canada," *Canadian Journal of Political Science*, Vol. 3, No. 1, March 1970, pp. 54–72.

[14] A. Mayer, *Political Origins of the New Diplomacy, 1917–18*, London, 1959, p. 14, as quoted in Frankel, *Making of Foreign Policy*, London, 1963, p. 71.

velopment of the mass labour movement in the USA meant the stringent demands for inclusion in foreign policy were made mostly after World War II. In 1947 the International Ladies Garment Workers' Union argued: "To be effective democratic foreign policy requires that its application and the nation's foreign services should not be left exclusively in the hands of diplomatic and financial technicians and former military leaders, although in some cases their services may be exceptionally useful. We totally disapprove the policy of the United States Government in failing to call into its foreign services representatives of the labour movement . . . above all the drawing in the representatives of the trade union movement, which is the largest body of voluntary organisations in the community."[15]

Demands such as these lead to the involvement of trade union officials in the post-war international programmes of the USA as it had done in the earlier period for the British unions.[16] These arguments concerning participation have been widely recognised, as illustrated by a statement by Dean Rusk, ex-Secretary of State for the USA: "Foreign policy is the total involvement of the American people with peoples and governments abroad."[17]

The second example of the use of international activity

[15] Quoted in W. Hamilton, "The Development of Foreign Policy Attitudes in Certain American Pressure Groups," p. 338.

[16] For American union participation in government international programmes, see D. Heaps, "Union Participation in Foreign Aid Programs," *Industrial and Labor Relations Review*, Vol. 9, No. 1, October 1955, pp. 100–8.

[17] Informal remarks to State Department policy-making officers in *Department of State Bulletin*, March 20, 1961, p. 395, as quoted in C. Lodge, *Spearheads of Democracy*, New York, 1962, p. XI; see also J. Windmuller, "Labor: a Partner in American Foreign Policy," *Annals of the American Academy of Political and Social Sciences*, Vol. 350, 1963, pp. 104–14.

to mitigate pressure from antagonist groups or win public support is illustrated by the actions of West German trade unions concerning the European Economic Community (EEC). The trade unions acted internationally in support of the proposals but, according to a study made, the support was not an expression of internationalism but more the result of "labor's search for social responsibility and equality *within* Germany."[18] In similar manner the AF of L used its anti-communist activities in Europe immediately after World War II to oppose the Taft-Hartley Laws, the National Association of Manufacturers, as well as the rival national centre, the CIO. Since the mid-1950s, trade union aid to less-developed countries has been used to demonstrate the moral superiority of trade unions vis-à-vis other groups.

It should be noted that the choice of international activity as a means of increasing or maintaining domestic power is not always completely voluntary. This is particularly true of a national centre, such as the AFL-CIO, which has limited opportunity to be effective in national economic domestic matters owing to government reluctance and the power of other interest groups. In contrast the government may welcome trade union international involvement and other interest groups are less likely to be concerned with or opposed to such activities. International activity thus presents an attractive method of acquiring status within the national policy-making elite and also perhaps within the public at large.

[18] E. Haas, *The Uniting of Europe*, p. 224, and D. Kwavnick, "Pressure Group Demands and the Struggle for Organizational Status: the Case of Organized Labor in Canada," especially pp. 59–61. (This author's italics.)

Serving the Nation

This incentive for trade union international involvement has been subjected to considerable examination in the course of arguments and counter-arguments concerning the claimed international orientation of trade union movements. The Marxist theory of the cross-national identity of interests of workers under capitalism, echoed to some extent in the Functional theory of integration, plus the idealist strain sometimes attributed to trade union leaders, have contributed to the notion that there is an inherent internationalism within trade unions.[19]

Arguments concerning the internationalism of unionists do not, however, eclipse the fact that unions have served the nation both knowingly and unknowingly in the exercise of its foreign policy through cooperative as well as independent activity. This arises from two aspects of the nation-state. First, it evokes the emotional response of nationalism which itself is derived from the state as the organisational expression of ethnocentricity, group loyalty, and security drives. Second, tangible benefits and assistance in performing basic functions can come from assisting the state in foreign policy.

Incentives arising from nationalism may be very close to those associated with ideology. The elevation of nationalism to a universal ideology, sometimes known as "universalistic nationalism,"[20] means that supporting the

[19] See H. Collins, "Karl Marx, the International and the British Trade Union Movement," *Science and Society*, Vol. 26, No. 4, 1962, pp. 400–21.

[20] H. Morgenthau, *Politics Among Nations*, 3d ed., New York, 1961, pp. 244–59.

nation may arise from ethnocentricity as well as belief systems. The discussion here is of incentives rising from ethnocentricity and the division is merely one of convenience as often nationalism and ideology are completely integrated.

In general, support of the nation arises from the supremacy of attachments to it over other group loyalties. In two world wars trade unions have demonstrated, or at least trade union membership has demonstrated, that national loyalties override class, and group loyalties, and that any national crises, whether real or perceived, will subvert internationalism or universalism.

The idea that for self-preservation purposes unions must assist in the exercise of state foreign policy receives the strongest promotion in times of national crisis. But leaders also sometimes justify their peace-time involvement by appeals to self-preservation; thus an AFL-CIO staff member argued in 1957 that "the American labor movement for reasons of self-preservation must devote some of its time, manpower and resources to what is happening in the world of which we are a part."[21] More often, support of the nation is evidenced by such phrases as "union members know that what's good for America is good for American labor."[22]

The latter sentiment expresses the vested interest in the actions of the state which organisations and groups have by virtue of their domicile. Borkenau pointed out in 1942, when countering the claims of a labour internationalism, that "the labour movement . . . had over and over again to bow to nationalist trends not only because

[21] G. Brown, "Why Should We Be Interested in International Affairs," *American Federationist*, Vol. 64, March 1957, p. 13.
[22] AFL-CIO: *Why Unions?*, Washington, D.C., 1962 (no page nos.).

it was not strong enough to counter them, but because they coincided with its own most urgent interests."[23]

Other writers have argued that as the state has taken greater control of economic policies, especially those of migration and trade, the trade unions must look more to national rather than international action in performing basic functions.[24] In this way labour movements and socialism became nationalised as the nation became socialised.

These considerations are among those which make serving the nation an important category of incentives for trade union international activity.

Supporting Ideologies

The fourth category, promoting or defending an ideology, is the one which receives the most attention from both unionists and commentators on labour affairs. Apart from a general tendency to ascribe much of human political behaviour to ideological causes, the situation is confused because trade unionists invariably describe their international activities in ideological terms, even when they are obviously pragmatic and for reasons of tangible self-interest.

The possession of an ideology will, as with any other possession, result in its defense upon attack. The reverse case, of promoting, rather than defending, an ideology is not so easily explained. It is not the place here to discuss the causes of the crusade or evangelical nature of ideol-

[23] F. Borkenau, *Socialism, National or International*, London, 1942, p. 157; see also D. Langley, "The Colonization of the International Trade Union Movement," *New Politics*, Vol. 5, Winter 1966, pp. 52–56.

[24] For example, E. Carr, *Nationalism and After*, London, 1945.

ogies, but if it is accepted that the possession of an ideology results in its dissemination, then trade unions can be seen defending or championing three types of ideology: political ideology, movement ideology, and group ideology.

POLITICAL IDEOLOGY

Political ideologies promoted by trade unions have usually been associated with capitalism, democracy, socialism, communism, and, to a lesser extent, christianity.

The political ideologies held and promoted by trade union leaders do not always coincide with the ideology propagated by the state government. Since World War II, however, in the USA the statements of national ideology and those of the trade unions have been almost identical.

The American trade unionists have consistently championed the cause of "democracy and freedom" in much the same manner as the USA government and political leaders. The constitution of the AFL-CIO, written in 1955, states, "we pledge ourselves . . . to the strengthening and *extension* of our way of life and the fundamental freedoms which are the basis of our democratic society,"[25] and that one of the objectives of the organisation is "to give constructive aid in promoting the cause of peace and freedom in the world."[26]

Such support of an ideology is most frequently stated in negative terms, that is, as the defeat of an opposing ideology, usually communism and sometimes fascism. Here the association with the state is most complete, as

[25] AFL-CIO: *Constitution as Amended 1961*. (This author's italics.)

[26] *Ibid.* "Article II, para. 7," p. 3.

evidenced by the following statement, "the AFL-CIO considers it a duty to help the United States meet its heavy world responsibilities at this critical juncture of history when the Communist threat to democracy is so acute."[27] It is support of such broad ideologies, expressed negatively, which has meant that, at least formally, many of the AFL-CIO international programmes have been based on stated anti-communism. The American Institute for Free Labor Development (AIFLD) was created by the AFL-CIO Executive Council in 1960 "to assist democratic trade unions of Latin America in their struggle to grow stronger and remain free by resisting Communist and other totalitarian operations."[28]

Despite the basically socialist declarations in the British TUC constitution, British trade unionists have not internationally promoted broad political ideologies in the manner of the American leaders. Nor have they claimed to support the state in pursuance of such an ideology. The latter circumstance may be accounted for by the differing political ideologies held by trade unionist and government leaders—especially when the Conservative Party is in power; it could not be expected that a Conservative government would promote trade union socialism abroad. Nevertheless, the British unions have on occasions shown a willingness to assist trade unions abroad which are professedly socialist. Such was the case of the interest free loans, amounting to £145,000, extended to the socialist-led General Federation of Belgium Workers in 1961.[29] This loan was granted after almost

[27] "AFL-CIO Work Is World Wide," *New York Times*, November 17, 1963, section II (Special Advertisement Supplement for the AFL-CIO), p. 7.

[28] AIFLD: *The American Institute for Free Labor Development*, Washington, D.C., 1965 (no page nos.).

[29] *Keesings Contemporary Archives*, Vol. XIII, 1961–62, p. 17969A.

two weeks of anti-government riots in Belgium and although the TUC claimed the loan was politically neutral, under the circumstances such a claim was difficult to support.[30]

MOVEMENT IDEOLOGY

The movement ideology, promoted or defended, by trade unionists is identified by the claims made that organised labour is essential to industrial society and that only through it will come social and economic betterment for society as a whole. One author describes the movement ideology in relation to USA unions as "the notion that organized labor should be the standard bearer of reform; that wage earners because of their preponderant numbers and consciousness of need for reform, are best able to bring about world-wide social and economic reorganization."[31] It is, in effect, the "trade union remedy" for the world's ills.[32]

Within this ideology is the most substantial claim to a labour universalism. It is from this ideology that phrases such as "brotherly interest," "solidarity," and "fraternal aid" are derived. Much of the trade union activity abroad is clothed in this ideological garb; the Belgian loan of the TUC mentioned above was said to be made because of the solidarity of the trade union movement; aid and as-

[30] See "TUC: Disinterested Loan," *Economist*, Vol. 198, January 14, 1961, p. 116; for the effects of the international promotion of an ideology on domestic politics see K. Deutsch, "External Influences on the Internal Behaviour of States," in R. Farrel, *Approaches to Comparative International Politics*, Evanston, 1966, pp. 5–26.

[31] F. Peterson, *American Labor Unions*, New York, 1952, p. 189.

[32] W. Hamilton, "The Development of Foreign Policy Attitudes in Certain American Pressure Groups," p. 290.

sistance, even when arising from self-interest, is said to be "brotherly aid." Many writers attribute most of trade union international activity to a movement ideology calling it "idealism," "labour internationalism," and "international group loyalty." Thus, like all ideologies, true incentives arising from the movement ideology are difficult to discern.

GROUP IDEOLOGY

Not all trade unions can be said to be possessed of a group ideology. Group ideology, in the international sense, arises from trade unions claiming to have attributes (other than nationality) which make them unique. It is the narrowest of the three labour ideologies specified, because it relates to one group in society and to unique factors which are said to separate it from other such groups in other societies. Two of the most important examples of group ideology defended or promoted by trade unionists are the business unionism of the USA and the co-determination system in Western Germany. The use of international activity to promote these ideologies is most pronounced in the case of the trade unions of the USA although, in relation to European integration, the Western German unions have demonstrated similar behaviour.[33]

The affiliation of the AF of L to the International Secretariat of National Trade Union Centers (ISTUC) in 1910 was, according to one authority, because it "would obtain a forum from which 'pure and simple' trade unionism might effectively counterpose its proven ideas and methods to the false and misleading schemes of the

[33] E. Haas, *The Uniting of Europe*, p. 224.

apostles of a new society."[34] The promotion of American "business unionism" from that date has been international and the argument that other movements must be saved from their aberrations well evidenced, especially in relation to less-developed countries.[35]

Leadership Needs

The fifth category concerns incentives for international action arising from personal inclinations of leadership and requirements of intra-organisation politics.

It is clear that a leadership unencumbered by rank-and-file interest may, if it feels so inclined, take its organisations into international society. Here the emphasis is on personal benefit, the satisfaction of vanity, or fulfillment of an interest arising from family, rather than organisational, background. It has been said that trade unionists from less-developed countries sometimes see trade unions from industrial countries as "travel agencies."[36] The same may be said of trade union leaders of industrial countries in regard to their organisations' activities abroad. This author was made very much aware, in numerous interviews with trade unionists, of the personal pleasure they acquired from expenses-paid trips abroad, especially as, until recently, such activities would be outside of the normal scope of their lives.

The use of international affairs in the course of internal

[34] J. Windmuller, *American Labor and the International Labour Movement, 1940–53*, New York, 1954, p. 7.

[35] B. Millen, *The Political Role of Labor in Developing Countries*, Washington, 1963, p. 3.

[36] J. Windmuller, "External Influences on Labor Organizations in Underdeveloped Countries," p. 560.

organisational political disputes must not be overlooked. Although all interviewees in relation to the British TUC stated that no special status could be obtained by being a member of the International Committee, all agreed that it was a senior committee and that membership of it, and involvement in international affairs, could assist in gaining support within the leadership. Sometimes internal power struggles are fought in terms of a foreign policy issue, as was the case, at least to some extent, in the "unilateralism" battle in the British TUC in 1961.[37] The split in 1966 between the two American labour leaders, George Meany of the AFL-CIO and Walter Reuther of the UAW, was dramatised in terms of foreign policy issues although the underlying reasons are more obscure.[38] However, such dramatisation means that each contestant will be affected by events abroad which prove or disprove the positions adopted; the incentive for involvement here is thus obvious.

There has been no attempt to describe the general policy of British and USA trade unions or assess the role of these incentives within it. That the incentives discussed above are present, is no guarantee that actions in international society are derived from them, nor has anything been said concerning their relative importance. The various disguises of international action have also not been mentioned; for example, while it is certain that the "brotherly spirit" of the movement ideology supplies an incentive, it does not mean that international action taken in its name is, in substance, in accordance with it. Original incentives sometimes get lost as the action takes on an impetus of its own.

It is one of the purposes of the Jamaican case study

[37] See *Keesings Contemporary Archives*, Vol. XII, 1959–60, p. 17698A.

[38] See *The New York Times*, June 19, 1966, p. 73.

to see how strong these incentives, impulses, and motivations are in a specific case.

Means of International Involvement

National labour organisations acting independently and directly in the international system have several means by which they can extend their influence and become involved in other societies. The most common of these are money grants, loans, gifts, project financing, education of foreign trade unionists, supplying advisers to foreign unions, and propaganda.

The financial aspects are the most important of the direct means. Financial involvement can take such forms as building a union headquarters, gifts of office equipment, paying for staff additions, loans to strike funds, and outright operating grants. The means of direct and independent involvement are the prime interest of this study.

However, there are several indirect means of foreign involvement which may complement or, when used by opposing organisations, disrupt the existing direct action. In general and as already briefly noted the three principal indirect means by which trade unions attempt to secure international objectives are: first, acting as a pressure group on state governments or other influential groups; second, by operating in direct association with governments or government agencies; and third, by acting through, or with, international, regional, or occupational groupings of trade unions as well as intergovernmental international organisations.

In many societies, and certainly in Britain and the USA, trade unions are accepted as a legitimate pressure group in relation to state foreign policy as well as acting in opposition to, or in conjunction with, other important groups. In this manner an attempt is made to see that trade union objectives are incorporated in state foreign policy and for this reason, as well as the specialised nature of the pressure group, such actions are more noticeable in the areas of international trade, investment, and migration.

Seeking international objectives by direct association with governments rather than by pressure group action first arose in connection with joint government and trade union programmes connected with educational and technical assistance. It resulted in the appointment by governments of trade unionists as advisers both to foreign visitors and in foreign countries.

For British trade unions such cooperation began during the 1930s when trade unionists were appointed as Labour Advisers for the colonies, although the practice was not, at that time, very widespread.[39] Likewise, after World War II, American trade unionists were appointed as advisers for the European Recovery Program and, subsequently, such programmes were vastly expanded, mainly in relation to less-developed countries. By 1959 such cooperation between unionists and government had assumed the proportions of a new statecraft, as was pointed out by George C. Lodge, Assistant Secretary of Labour for International Affairs: "The day has long since gone when relations with other countries can be effectively carried on solely in the traditional 'diplomatic way' at the usual 'diplomatic' levels. The power of

[39] For the view that such advisers were part of general British imperial policies, see J. Woddis, *The Mask Is Off: an Examination of the Activities of Trade Union Advisers in the British Colonies*, London, 1948, p. 48.

Africa and Asia is often not in the hands of government officials, but rather in the hands of relatively obscure native leaders who first appear on the national scene as leaders of workers' organisations."[40]

It was no doubt such observations as these which led to another type of government-union association which was recently revealed by the publishing of evidence that certain USA trade unions had served the Central Intelligence Agency (CIA) of the USA government. In some cases the Agency used the facilities of the union, both domestic and foreign, without the knowledge of the leaders: in other cases the leadership is believed to have known about the operations. One such case was that of the American Federation of State, County and Municipal Employees, AFL-CIO, whose recently elected president announced that prior to his election, two CIA men were in the union's international affairs department and on behalf of the department dispersed $60,000 abroad.[41] On the appointment of the new president, these men were dismissed and the operation stopped.[42] Victor Reuther, head of the United Auto Workers of America (UAW) international affairs department, has charged that the AFL-CIO international operations were "involved with the CIA."[43] This accusation, and similar ones from other sources,[44] have been rejected by the AFL-CIO. So far, there have not been similar disclosures concerning any covert association between government and British trade unions.

[40] G. Lodge, "Labor's Role in Newly Developing Countries," *Foreign Affairs,* Vol. 37, July 1959, p. 66; and see "US Pushes Unions to Hurt Viet Cong," *Denver Post,* October 13, 1965, p. 3.
[41] *The New York Times,* February 21, 1967, p. 46.
[42] *Ibid.*
[43] See *The New York Times,* June 19, 1966, p. 73.
[44] See, for example, D. Kurzman, "Lovestone's Cold War," *New Republic,* June 25, 1966, pp. 17–22; and G. Morris, *CIA and American Labor,* New York, 1967.

The most widely known and most thoroughly investigated means of trade unions indirectly acquiring international objectives is through international trade union organisations. International associations of trade unions have characterised the movement since the beginning of the century. The International Federation of Trade Unions (IFTU), founded in 1919, lasted until 1945 when a new organisation was created, the World Federation of Trade Unions (WFTU). By 1949, however, disputes with communist trade unions led to the withdrawal of the British and American delegations[45] and to the creation of the International Confederation of Free Trade Unions (ICFTU). The WFTU remained in existence with membership drawn mainly from communist countries while a smaller organisation, the International Federation of Christian Trade Unions (IFCTU), existed throughout the whole period.[46]

These internationals represent, for this study, instruments for individual national labour organisations pursuing their policy in international society. They are not, however, always captive organisations and the manner in which they can be used will vary according to the political power of the different national trade union organisations. The same may be said concerning regional organisations, and the International Trade Secretariat (ITS), the former basing membership on geographic regions and the latter on occupation or industry. The International Labour Organisation, through the seating of labour delegations, also provides at least a forum through which the policies of national trade union organisations can be publicised.

[45] See further, L. Lorwin, *The International Labor Movement*, New York, 1953, pp. 238–61.

[46] This organisation changed its name to World Confederation of Labour (WCL) in October 1968.

CHAPTER III

BRITISH AND AMERICAN TRADE UNIONS

Domestic problems and activities are usually much more important to unions than their international activities. For this reason, the making and implementing of trade union foreign policy can be considered as an accessory function of the organisation which receives only a small proportion of funds available and is rarely a subject of interest for the general membership.

The lack of membership interest in the international activities of interest groups has been described by one writer as the "Law of Marginality of Interest in Foreign Policy Issues."[1] Trade unions are no exception to this Law, and studies have consistently shown that rank-and-file interest is slight or non-existent.

A researcher who investigated the development of foreign policy attitudes in the American Federation of Labor and other non-governmental organisations in 1955, concluded: "Attitudes were developed and articulated by a small, identifiable group at the apex of the hierarchy in each organisation. The characteristic federal structure and the passivity of the membership on matters normally considered subordinate to central groups

[1] E. Fagerberg, *The "Anciens Combattants" and French Foreign Policy*, Geneva, 1966, p. 19.

objectives enabled opinion leaders to modify agreed statements of principle in the direction of personal policy preferences."[2] More recently, Windmuller has noted: "With only few exceptions concentrated at regional and local leadership levels, there is no articulate 'public opinion' in labor's ranks on foreign policy. Foreign competition aside, ordinary members simply do not consider their organizations to have a vital stake in such issues in comparison with bargaining, grievances, and other more mundane services."[3]

Few specific studies have been made concerning the rank-and-file participation in foreign policy issues in British unions but the evidence that exists suggests that the pattern does not vary substantially from the American. A British trade union leader who was active in international affairs noted, 'international affairs are regarded as important only by a limited number of people at the top. The problem has always been to involve the general membership for it is difficult to interest them in anything else but the most immediate affairs.'[4] Likewise, and despite the sometimes extensive debates of foreign affairs at the annual conference of the TUC, a scholar who studied British trade unions and international affairs for the period 1945 to 1953 concluded that policy was nevertheless mainly determined by a few men on the TUC General Council.[5]

[2] W. Hamilton, "The Development of Foreign Policy Attitudes in Certain American Pressure Groups," unpublished Ph.D. dissertation, Yale University, USA, 1955 (from the abstract attached, no page no.).

[3] J. Windmuller, "The Foreign Policy Conflict in American Labor," *Political Science Quarterly*, Vol. 82, No. 2, June 1967, pp. 226–27.

[4] Statements made by interviewees, who are to remain unidentified for reasons previously stated, will be enclosed in single quotation marks.

[5] B. Hennessy, "British Trade Unions and International Affairs, 1945–1953," unpublished Ph.D. dissertation, University of Wisconsin, 1955, pp. 6–15.

The result of this situation is that in international activities, trade union leadership is virtually unencumbered by membership interest or demands and can therefore exercise greater control in this area than in the domestic or primary functions. It would appear therefore that in the making and implementing of trade union foreign policy the importance of individual personality, idiosyncrasy, and caprice would be greater than the organisational structure and its social ecology.[6] Without denying this basic orientation, for several reasons in the study of the independent international activities of trade unions some emphasis must be placed on the organisational background.

First, studies have shown that social organisations develop their accessory functions as a result of their interaction with other groups, organisations, and publics, rather than from membership demands.[7] Second, the organisational background and ecology forms a major part of the basic experience for any trade union decision-maker. Finally, in cross-cultural circumstances trade union actors are likely to use notions of structures and processes derived from their own organisational experience in formulating directives for the host organisation or society.[8]

The use of the social ecology of trade unions to develop a more complete explanation of the reasons for trade union involvement in international relations has been demonstrated in a previous chapter. The importance of the social ecology here is its relevance in relation

[6] See, for comment on the importance of the individual, D. Easton, *The Political System*, New York, 1953, p. 202.

[7] D. Krech and R. Crutchfield, *Theory and Problems of Social Psychology*, New York, 1948, p. 306.

[8] For general discussion of these issues see J. Kunkel, "Some Behavioral Aspects of the Ecological Approach to Social Organization," *American Journal of Sociology*, Vol. 73, No. 1, July 1967, pp. 12–29.

to leadership decision-making and the individual performance of the in-field actor.

Decision-making theory in general deals with the identification and weighing of variables which affect a person selecting a course of action from a number of alternative courses. One authority has defined decision-making as a process in which the decision-maker confronts his values with the image of his environment[9]; the Sprouts have called this the meeting of the psychological and operational environments.[10] The operational environment may inhibit or expand possible action and may be observed by persons other than the decision-maker.

Normally the operational environment of a trade unionist is the domestic environment, or social ecology of the trade union, where the primary functions of trade unions are performed, while the international aspect of the operational environment usually arises only in relation to an accessory function. Strictly, an operational environment must be a whole and to make rigid divisions in it is theoretically false and diminishes the interrelatedness of all the factors in it. Without denying this, however, it is useful to view the operational environment in which the trade union performs its primary domestic function as its *domestic* operational environment and the environment of the accessory international function as its *international* operational environment.

The psychological environment is the accumulated experience of the decision-maker which sets psychological limits to his decision. The contents of such an environment are obviously more difficult to determine, although knowledge of the culture of the decision-maker would give some important directives. More usually, theorists

[9] J. Frankel, *The Making of Foreign Policy,* London, 1963, p. 9.
[10] H. Sprout and M. Sprout, *The Ecological Perspective on Human Affairs,* Princeton, 1965, pp. 11–12.

have included such factors as personality characteristics, values, social background, and general experience.[11]

Unlike the politically or technically qualified state decision-maker, trade unionists are involved in international relations simply by virtue of their domestic leadership of unions. Their social experience is intimately related to their role as union leaders, their general experience has come from performing the primary functions of trade unions domestically, their values and ideologies relate to groups and movements, as well as nations and social philosophies.

In terms of this decision-making model then, the domestic operational environment encountered by the trade unionist in performing primary functions is the greatest source of experience, values, and ideologies for the psychological environment. In this way the social ecology of the organisation becomes important for policy-making relating to the accessory function of international involvement.

At the highest level of policy-making there are therefore two partially conflicting characteristics—the freedom gained from the structure and membership of the organisation in performing an accessory function and the constraints of the psychological environment which is derived from the organisational experience.

The ability to think in different terms when dealing with international relations rather than the domestic environment will again depend on the personality of the individual. However, the recognition of the possibility of such conflict means the domestic environment cannot be overlooked. At least one author has noted the transposition of actions and processes from the domestic environ-

[11] J. Robinson and R. Snyder, "Decision-Making in International Politics," in H. Kelman, ed., *International Behaviour*, New York, 1966, pp. 443–48.

ment into international relations. According to Hamilton, in the AF of L "references to the problem of negotiating with the Soviets suggest a projection of the environment of the collective bargaining situation with relatively little conception of the inherently different problems involved in international diplomatic discussions."[12]

At the lower level of policy-making and at the operational level the social ecology of the organisation of which the actor is a representative becomes even more important. Models are derived from it, it forms the substance of cross-cultural projection and the basis from which organisational transfers are attempted. A knowledge of the social ecology and organisational background is therefore necessary to understand the nature of the policies developed as well as their operational success or failure. For all these reasons the social ecology and organisational background of British and American trade unions becomes of paramount importance in understanding their foreign policy, both in general and in the specific case of Jamaica.

Functions

SOCIOLOGICAL ORIGINS

The sociological conditions which resulted in trade unions as, to use a definition of the Webbs, "a continuous association of wage earners for the purpose of maintaining and improving the conditions of their work-

[12] W. Hamilton, "The Development of Foreign Policy Attitudes in Certain American Pressure Groups," p. 286.

ing lives,"[13] are a matter of controversy. Marx (the theorist as opposed to the activist) saw the labour movement as revolutionary and arising out of the concentration of capital and the increasing impoverishment of the masses. The movement thus began as a response to increasing material misery and became revolutionary upon the realisation that this process could not be stopped without replacing the system of capital ownership. The Webbs, more inclined to the equilibrium theories, claimed that unions would secure the maximum wage from a perfect market (marginal product of labour) and would thus equalise wages and conditions, but they also believed that unions would become at least political, if not revolutionary.

In the more modern period, American scholars have developed theories concerning the basis of unionism. Using information from Russian, German, British, and American experiences with unions, Selig Perlman argued that although unions were reactive to material economic conditions, they started as political movements and subsequently found their optimum function as economic interest groups.[14] Kerr and associates concurred that labour movements were reactive, but suggested that they were reactive to industrialisation rather than capitalism and that their diverse forms resulted from the types of political systems or elites through which industrial society is governed.[15] A similar view, although more firmly based in sociology, has been that of Tannenbaum, who feels that unions are an attempt by workers in an industrial society to regain social security

[13] S. Webb and B. Webb, *The History of Trade Unionism*, rev. ed., London, 1920, p. 1.
[14] See S. Perlman, *A Theory of the Labor Movement*, New York, 1949, and R. Lester, *As Unions Mature*, Princeton, 1958.
[15] C. Kerr and others, *Industrialism and Industrial Man*, Cambridge, Mass., 1960.

which has been lost through the destruction of the agrarian societies.[16]

NON-POLITICAL AND POLITICAL UNIONISM

Consciously or unconsciously many of these contemporary theorists seek to explain what is perceived to be a lack of political ideology or "political" action in the American trade union movement. They seek to find "proper" functions of a trade union which would then supply a criteria for use in foreign policy or development planning. Interestingly, for this study, it is claimed that the dichotomy between "political" and "non-political" unionism is well illustrated by the British and American trade unions.

At the practical level it is unlikely that substantial differences can be found between British and American trade unions' functions in relation to their respective political systems. Both use the political system for attempts at achieving group goals as opposed to one or other of them being political in the sense that they are factors in an ideological system intent on reshaping the society in accordance with the goals of the ideology.

Thus many studies have shown that the claim that American trade unions are not political depends on the definition of politics. American unions have always been involved in assisting individuals and parties to acquire political power and influencing the course of social and economic legislation.[17] Likewise, the political activities

[16] F. Tannenbaum, *The True Society*, London, 1964.

[17] For an examination of American unions in politics see J. Hutchinson, "Labour and Politics and America," *Political Quarterly*, Vol. 33, April 1962, pp. 138–49; and AFL-CIO: *Union Political Activity Spans 230 Years of US History*, Washington, D.C., 1960.

of British unions may not always be as they seem.[18] One student of comparative unionism has pointed out that "the fact that the British trade union movement declares itself in favour of nationalisation of land, mines, minerals and railways and the American trade union movement does not, does not necessarily stamp the latter as the more 'backward' movement. A revolutionary programme is no evidence of revolutionary intentions, neither is the absence of such a programme evidence of reactionary intentions. The real character of a movement is to be found in its activities and what it attempts to do."[19] The difference between the unions arises more in the means and formal structure by which unions attempt to use the political system to achieve their goals. It is this difference which gives rise to the perception of British unions as political and American unions as non-political. As the construction of models is derived from the perceptions and common beliefs of the leaders rather than from theoretical considerations it is the former which is of interest in the analysis of foreign policy.

The most common statement of the differences between the two union movements is that the British unions have an intimate connection with the British Labour Party and that many leaders claim adherence to a socialist ideology, while American unions concern themselves solely with increasing wages and improving working conditions of their members. In the course of research for this study at least nine names have been discovered to describe the nature of American unions: business unionism, economic unionism, no-ultimate-ends unionism, philosophy-of-no-philosophy unionism, non-

18 For the "business unionism" of British unions see J. Cole, "The Non-Philosophy of the Unions," *New Society*, August 29, 1963, p. 20.

19 B. Roberts, *Trade Unions in a Free Society*, 2d ed., London, 1962, p. 22.

political unionism, pragmatic unionism, practical unionism, pure-and-simple unionism, and bread-and-butter unionism. Business unionism is the term most widely used within the USA by academics as well as trade unionists.

In sum, it can be said that, at the formal level, it is clear that American union leaders have not as a rule verbally professed an attachment to any of the common and *named* political ideologies which have been supported by many British and European trade unionists.

The effect of this is that any political functions performed by American trade unions are never seen to be in a framework of an over-all ideology. The non-political aura is also enhanced by the basically pragmatic policies pursued by the two major American political parties, thus, whether or not the political functions of the American trade unions are similar to the British there is a widespread belief to the contrary. Business unionism, that is the narrowest definition of the functions of trade unions in society, is therefore widely accepted as the most accurate description which also supports the claim of the uniqueness of the American trade union movement.[20]

GENERAL FUNCTIONS

There is more agreement on the other functions of trade unions in Britain and the USA. Both bargain with employers on behalf of their members on questions of wages and work conditions, both recruit and train workers to hold positions within the industrial relations

[20] B. Millen, *The Political Role of Labor in Developing Countries*, Washington, D.C., 1963, p. 3.

system. The British unions, however, can also be viewed as having a recruiting function in relation to constitutional political power, as union leaders often move into the legislature and sometimes into government positions.

On the more sociological functions the differences are matters of degree. Which union movement more readily supplies security or group morale to offset the isolated individualism of industrial society does not concern us here, except to recognise that such functions of trade unions do exist and, as we shall see, are more noticeable in other cultures than in Britain and the USA.[21]

Structures

There are several recognised union structures of which the craft, industrial, and general are the most common. In fact, few unions are pure in type and most merge into each other, creating a large number of intermediate varieties.

Craft unions, the oldest and most original variety, unite by membership all persons engaged in a single craft or occupation and, although originally local in nature, have in both the USA and Britain become national in operation. Industrial unions arose from the new methods of mass production which were established in this century and they seek to secure membership from all workers in an industry, regardless of their particular skill or occupation. General workers' unions, as the name implies, gather into one union workers in a number of

[21] One writer suggests that, in the British case, joining a trade union satisfies a "group sense" and organises the "them-us" divisions. See R. Hoggart, *The Uses of Literacy*, Harmondsworth, 1957, pp. 80–81.

trades, crafts, industries, and occupations, although the bulk of the membership is usually unskilled or semi-skilled workers.

Both Britain and the USA have craft unions and they represent the oldest structural form for both countries. The USA has industrial unions, but as an ILO mission noted, "there are few truly industrial unions in the United Kingdom."[22] On the other hand, the general workers' union has been described as "primarily a British institution."[23] Thus, in general, USA unions are craft and industrial and British unions are craft and general.

STRUCTURAL PROBLEMS

Both national movements have witnessed difficulty in formulating or adjusting to new trade union structures. Disputes over structure usually disguise struggles, fought between the established hierarchy and the new centres of power, arising from production methods which require new organisational structures.

Such was the case with the American labour movement which was divided for almost twenty years on the prima facie issue of craft versus industrial unions. The division was most noticeable at the national level, although obviously it reached into all areas where trade unions were active. The split was epitomised by the dual existence of the American Federation of Labor, which was basically a loose federation of craft unions and the Congress of Industrial Organizations, a federation of industrial unions. The AF of L had been founded in 1886

[22] International Labour Office: *The Trade Union Situation in the United Kingdom, Report of a Mission*, Geneva, 1961, p. 65.
[23] International Confederation of Free Trade Unions: *Glossary of Trade Union Terms*, Brussels, 1964, p. 52.

and had remained the undisputed organisation representing the American labour movement as a whole until the CIO challenge in 1938, when a group of already organised industrial unions refused to respect the jurisdiction of craft unions with members in their industry. The division lasted until December 1955, when the two organisations merged into the American Federation of Labor and Congress of Industrial Organizations (AFL-CIO).

The difficulties in the British labour movement with structure have not had such clear manifestations as in the USA. The British national centre, the Trades Union Congress (TUC), did not have to deal with industrial unions and absorbed the emergence of the multi-craft unions as well as the general unions. The general unions, of which the Transport and General Workers' Union is the most well known, have as a result of their size played a major part in the British trade union movement. While the TUC was able to absorb without disruption the new unions, the power struggle has taken place with regard to the older, almost ancient, small craft and local unions whose leaders have been unwilling to amalgamate, merge, or disband in favour of the industrial or multi-craft unions. This fragmentation has been called "the tribal system in operation, with all the little chieftains"[24] and has remained a problem of trade union organisation for the last fifty years.

The structural background against which policy, foreign or domestic, is made thus differs significantly between the USA and Britain, as does the historical background to disputes involving structural issues.

Because of the need for national, rather than individ-

[24] Noah Ablett in 1932 with reference to the numerous county unions which eventually became the National Union in Mineworkers, quoted in H. Pelling, *A History of British Trade Unionism*, London, 1963, p. 220.

ual, trade union representation in international society, trade unions' international activities have traditionally been the formal responsibility of the national trade union centres. Although this responsibility has recently fragmented under the impact of powerful individual unions the national centres are still the most important bodies dealing with international matters.

The National Centres

THE BRITISH TUC

The British TUC has been in existence since 1868 and is described as "a permanent association of trade unions . . . constituted by the affiliation of trade unions."[25] According to the 1962 constitution its objects are "to promote the interests of all or any of its affiliated organisations . . ." and "generally to improve the economic and social conditions of workers in all parts of the world and to render them assistance . . ."[26] It also lists, under seven headings ranging from wages to education and housing, the steps that should be taken to achieve these broad objectives, one of which is "public ownership and control of natural resources and of services–Nationalisation of land, mines and minerals. Nationalisation of railways."[27] Unions of all types may affiliate to the TUC,

[25] Trades Union Congress: *The ABC of the TUC*, London, 1964, p. 3.
[26] TUC: *Rules and Standing Orders of Trades Union Congress*, London, 1962, "Objects," para. (a), p. 3.
[27] *Ibid.*

although federations of unions do not normally do so as their individual members are often already affiliated.

The main importance of the TUC is that it has the ability and prestige to be able to speak for the whole trade union movement. It has won "the unchallengeable right and authority to speak for the organised workers of Britain."[28] The TUC has provisions for settlement of disputes between affiliated unions and for suspension of unions considered to be following practices "detrimental to the interests of the Trade Union Movement."[29] But the power of control over individual unions is not great and union autonomy is left virtually unaffected. Certainly the TUC cannot be considered in form or in practice as an organisation created primarily for keeping good order or enforcing established principles within the trade union movement.

Apart from the annual congresses, which have important deliberative functions, the main body in which constitutional power is vested is the General Council. This executive committee is composed of thirty-four delegates from nineteen different trade groups within the TUC and a General Secretary, all elected by the annual congress.

The General Council divides itself into committees of which the three most important are considered by trade unionists to be the Finance and General Purpose, Economic and International.[30] These committees are served by an administration of about eighty persons appointed by the General Secretary. The importance of the administration, and particularly the General Secretary, must be emphasised, as he and his staff represent the

[28] TUC: *The ABC of the TUC*, p. 3.
[29] TUC: *Rules and Standing Orders, etc.*, Rule 13, para. (b) and (c), p. 10.
[30] According to British unionists interviewed.

only continuous application of time and effort to the problems of the whole trade union movement. Members of the General Council are usually leaders of their own unions and are required to service the more specific demands arising from that position.[31]

THE AMERICAN AFL-CIO

Unlike Britain, the USA has had more than one national centre throughout the history of the trade union movement. From 1886 until 1938, the American Federation of Labor (AF of L) was the national centre; from 1938 to 1955, there were two, the AF of L and the Congress of Industrial Organizations (CIO); finally these two merged in 1955 to create the AFL-CIO, the current national centre. In 1968, however, the United Auto Workers of America (UAW) withdrew from the AFL-CIO and joined with other non-affiliated unions to create the Alliance for Labor Action (ALA).[32]

The AF of L and CIO merger in 1955 basically joined two federations of unions into one federation of national and international unions.[33] The constitution of the AFL-CIO mentions broad aims such as "the attainment of security for all people"[34] but specifies only narrow objectives of trade unions such as "to aid workers in securing improved wages, hours and working conditions . . ."[35]

[31] E. Wigham, *What's Wrong With the Unions,* Harmondsworth, 1961, p. 30.
[32] *The New York Times,* July 24, 1968, p. 51.
[33] USA domestic unions are often called "international" as they have branches in Canada.
[34] AFL-CIO: *Constitution as Amended 1961,* Washington, D.C., 1962, "Preamble," p. 1.
[35] *Ibid.,* "Objects and Principles," para. 1, p. 2.

Most of the other eleven articles pertaining to objectives and principles deal, on the one hand, with union autonomy and, on the other, with undesirable practices associated with corruption and communism; thus one of the objects, which later became a base for action against several unions, is "to protect the labor movement from any and all corrupt influences and from undermining efforts of communist agencies and all others who are opposed to the basic principles of our democracy and free democratic unionism."[36] Unions not living up to these ideals may be expelled from the federation but, as in the British case, this may not make a substantial difference for if the union is large enough and strong enough it can continue to exist outside the national centre, as many unions have done.

The bi-annual conferences of the AFL-CIO elect the officers of the organisation, which include a President, Secretary-Treasurer, and twenty-seven Vice-Presidents, which together constitute the official governing body, known as the Executive Council. There is also a General Board which consists of the Executive Council plus officers of each of the affiliated unions and of the seven trade and industrial departments into which the organisation is divided. By far the most important body is the Executive Committee composed of the President, the Secretary General, and nine Vice-Presidents elected by the Executive Council. Clearly, the most important officers are the President and the Secretary-Treasurer. But the weight of the original CIO is felt through the Industrial Union Department (IUD) of the organisation and the head of that department is also considered an important personality in the policy-making process of the AFL-CIO. After the withdrawal of the UAW, with mem-

[36] *Ibid.*, para. 6, p. 3.

bership of 1.5 million, the IUD still represented five million workers in fifty-nine unions.[37]

Both the TUC and the AFL-CIO have the bulk of trade union members within their affiliated unions. With a total USA work force of 67,762,000 in 1963, the AFL-CIO had 12,407,000 members in approximately 135 unions; unaffiliated union membership was approximately 3,000,000. In 1966 with a total British work force of 24,974,000 the TUC had 8,867,552 members in 170 unions with approximately 1,000,000 unaffiliated trade union members.[38]

While the numerical superiority of the American unions is not great, compared with the British unions, the different economic levels of the two countries are reflected in the budgets of the national centres. In 1963 the AFL-CIO recorded an income of over $19 million while three years later, in 1966, the TUC managed with just under $2 million.[39]

The budgetary differences between the organisations obviously affect the staff complements. It has been estimated that American unions have one paid official for every 300 members while the British have one for every 900.[40]

[37] *International Union of Food and Allied Workers Bulletin,* Vol. 39, Nos. 5 and 6, May–June 1968, p. 13.

[38] Work force statistics from International Labour Office: *Yearbook of Labour Statistics,* Geneva, 1967, pp. 279–92; membership statistics from AFL-CIO: *Proceedings of the 5th Constitutional Convention,* 1963, pp. 37–40, and TUC: *98th Annual Congress 1966, Report of Proceedings,* p. 63.

[39] Financial data from AFL-CIO: *Proceedings of 5th Constitutional Convention,* 1963, p. 10, and TUC: *98th Annual Congress 1966, Report of Proceedings,* p. 65.

[40] Estimate by B. Roberts as quoted in E. Wigham, *What's Wrong With the Unions,* p. 32.

Social Ecology

GROWTH OF UNIONS

Relations between trade unions and other groups and organisations in society have varied greatly since the beginnings of the movement in the last century. While the most important period for this study is 1940 to the present, a significant difference between British and American trade union growth means that the experience of the 1930s is also important.

The experiences of many American trade unionists differ greatly from the British because of the recent and rapid rise of the mass trade union movement in the USA. As an International Labour Office Mission in 1959 to investigate the trade union situation in the USA noted, "a mass labour movement has existed for less than a generation in the United States."[41] The British trade unions, on the other hand, had won legal acceptance and widespread industrial participation since pre-World War I. Both movements experienced a decline in existing membership between 1920 and 1935, but in the British case this reflected economic conditions rather than government or employer hostility. In the 1930s, the American trade unions had to make up losses sustained in the previous decade and also, unlike the British, establish unionism, often accompanied by violence, in previously

[41] International Labour Office: *The Trade Union Situation in the United States, Report of a Mission*, Geneva, 1960, p. 26.

un-unionised industries such as steel, automobile, and mining. This difference is reflected in all aspects of the social ecologies of the two union movements.

TRADE UNIONS AND PUBLIC OPINION

The nature of relations between trade unions and other groups in society is governed, to some extent, by the general acceptance of trade unions in society. Differences in culture and in the history of trade union movements have produced a substantial difference in the level of general acceptance of trade unions in Britain and the USA. The ILO mission observed, "it would seem as if the trade unions in the United States operate in a social system which they accept, but which does not yet fully accept them."[42] This, they believed, was because "the individualistic attitude of Americans generally, including many union members themselves, often leads to a suspicion and distrust of trade unionism, which is by its very nature a collective activity."[43] This conflict between basic attitudes and trade unionism is clearly not so prevalent in Britain, where there is no identifiable cultural trait precipitating antagonism, distrust, or opposition to the concept of trade unionism. Some evidence of this phenomena is available from public opinion polls taken on the subject of trade unions in both societies. According to polls taken in 1963 and 1964, the public accepted overwhelmingly the principle

[42] *Ibid.*

[43] *Ibid.* See also S. Lipset, "Trade Unions and Social Structure: I," *Industrial Relations* (University of California), Vol. 1, No. 1, October 1961, pp. 78–89.

of unionism, although a greater proportion of Americans were totally opposed to unions than were the British.[44] But the greatest indications of the differences are found in the reasons for disapproval of trade unions. The British public polled felt that unions lost favour over specific issues such as, "(a) disagreement between unions or union leaders, (b) failure to maintain discipline, in particular, to contain wildcat or unofficial strikes, (c) squabbling over political issues, (d) weakness in pursuing the legitimate industrial aims of the union members."[45] The USA poll, in contrast, showed that opposition to unions was the more generalised one that unions "are becoming much too powerful."[46] Thus in 1959, 1961, 1962, and 1965, over 40 per cent of people polled felt that laws restricting unions were not strict enough."[47] The ILO commission noted that such criticisms arose from basic attitudes rather than a true assessment of the situation because "the proportion of union membership among workers is no higher, and the resources of industry and its ability to resist exaggerated demands by the unions would seem to be greater, than in a number of other countries."[48]

[44] "Opinion of Labor Unions," *Public Opinion News Service*, Princeton, American Institute of Public Opinion, January 30, 1963; and Gallup Poll: *Trade Unions and the Public in 1964*, London, 1964, Section 1, Table 1 (no page no.).

[45] Gallup Poll: *Trade Unions and the Public in 1964*, p. 2.

[46] G. Gallup, "Many Say Laws Curbing Unions, Business, . . . Not Strict Enough," *Public Opinion News Service*, October 22, 1961. For a trade unionist's reply to this criticism, see G. Meany, *Power for What*, Washington, D.C. (no date, 1962?).

[47] Gallup Poll: *Public Opinion News Service*, February 14, 1965.

[48] ILO: *The Trade Union Situation in the USA, etc.*, p. 26.

TRADE UNIONS AND EMPLOYERS

This basic difference between mass attitudes towards unions is reflected in the style, if not substance, of union relations with other groups, especially employers. Throughout the 1930s in the USA, many unions had to struggle for recognition in major industries. As late as 1937, ten people were killed in the "Memorial Day massacre" while attempting to win union recognition in the steel industry. Unionists now at the top of their unions have often experienced personal violence. The late leader of the UAW, Walter Reuther, for example, was beaten by company security guards in 1937 at Ford Motor Company while organising in the company.[49] Despite these events, trade unions rapidly gained power, prestige, and legal acceptance. But a considerable residue of employer hostility remains and when cooperation breaks down, union-management relations are often expressed in antagonistic and volatile language.

The British trade unionists' experience with employers has been different. They have not had to deal with violence, at least not at the same level as that resulting from American employer-union clashes, and the residue of hostility is not so high towards them.

TRADE UNIONS AND POLITICAL PARTIES

Relations with political parties has been a factor which, more than any other, is said to distinguish British and

[49] *Life*, Vol. 61, No. 9, August 1966, p. 31.

American unionism. The British trade union movement has a clear formal and financial association with the British Labour Party. Trade unions can affiliate themselves to the Labour Party and pay dues to the party in accordance with membership, but trade union members of an affiliated union can contract out of the party levy which is otherwise automatically taken with union dues. In 1959 there were eighty-seven unions, representing 5,564,010 members, affiliated with the Labour Party and this force is represented on the National Executive of the party by twelve trade union members out of twenty-seven.[50] Trade unions also pay expenses of candidates for election to Parliament, who are then often known informally as "trade union MPs."

The association between the trade unions in the USA and the Democratic Party is much more loosely defined, although, in substance, as has been mentioned above, the relationship may not be as different from that of the TUC and the Labour Party as it appears. Trade unions support the election of candidates through money as well as publicity. But their influence on party policy is not so direct and trade unions must compete with other interest groups to promote their policies within the party.

TRADE UNIONS, GOVERNMENT, AND LAW

Relations with governments obviously differ widely in accordance with the party or president in power and with the time period. It should be pointed out, however, as it is a widespread misconception, that there is no his-

[50] ILO: *The Trade Union Situation in the United Kingdom, etc.*, p. 106.

torical evidence that trade unions in Britain enjoy easier relations with a Labour Party government than with a Conservative Party government. Indeed, the reverse may be the case, for the Labour Party's attempts at economic planning have frequently brought them into conflict with the trade unionist conception of freedom of action in wage demands.[51]

Relations between unions and governments are evidenced by the various legislation which has affected unions. The British unions gradually and successfully won legal rights with respect to recognition and bargaining while the main legislation for American unions came in the 1930s. In the Trade Disputes Act of 1906, the British movement gained rights which were not achieved fully by the USA unions until the Norris-LaGuardia Act of 1932.

For trade unions in the USA, government legislation has, until the 1930s, been restrictive. As one writer noted, "it would be difficult to exaggerate the influence of legal weapons on the relations between capital and labour in the United States during the first quarter of the twentieth century. It strengthened the employers' hands and encouraged them in their refusal to recognise unions and to accept collective bargaining."[52] While the British experience was of progressive and incremental legislation easing the trade union into an industrial relations system, the American experience was one of spasmodic pro- and anti-labour legislation. The New Deal era saw much pro-labour legislation and an argument

[51] See V. Allen, *The Trade Unions and the Government*, London, 1960; R. Mackenzie, *British Political Parties*, London, 1963; and the statement in *Tribune*, September 1968, p. 1.

[52] E. Davies, *American Labour, the Story of the Trade Union Movement*, London, 1943, p. 33.

can be made that the modern trade union movement dates from that time. Following this spate of permissive and favourable legislation towards the trade unions, the 1947 Taft-Hartley Act, claimed by unionists as being anti-labour, can be seen as a reaction to the preceding legislation. The existing laws of industrial relations are complex but a brief description is necessary.

Following various acts of Congress, it is now standard practice in the USA that trade unions are recognised as bargaining agents between workers and employers after a statutory body, the National Labor Relations Board, has designated the bargaining unit and also often supervised elections of the bargaining agent. There is legislation in many states forbidding closed shop, although Federal law allows union shop agreements between union and employers providing that a worker not a member of the trade union may continue to work as long as he pays union dues. Collective bargaining results in a contract which is enforceable by law, although court action over labour contracts is rare.[53] There are minimum wage laws and laws affecting the absolute right to strike.

In the British case, trade union representation rests on "tradition and common sense"[54] and rarely becomes an issue. On the same basis there is no closed or union shop, although employers in general agree to encourage 100 per cent trade union membership which in practice nearly operates as a closed shop. There are provisions for compulsory arbitration and some affecting the right to strike, although the latter restrictions are considerably fewer than in the USA. One noticeable difference exists between the results of collective bargaining—in Britain the

[53] ILO: *The Trade Union Situation in the USA, etc.*, p. 109.

[54] ILO: *The Trade Union Situation in the United Kingdom, etc.*, p. 65.

result is not a contract as in the USA but a "collective agreement" which does not have the binding force of law.

These, then, are the broad lines of structure, function, and social ecology within which trade union leaders of both countries operate. It remains to consider union leadership and some aspects of internal union government.

Trade Union Leadership

LEADERS AND RANK-AND-FILE

Unions in Britain and the USA are characterised by oligarchic tendencies. There is a degree of difference, however, because the British unions are held to be less oligarchic than those in the USA.

Lipset suggests that the cause of oligarchy in American unions is a "functional interrelationship" between corporations and trade unions, the centralisation of the former creating oligarchy in the latter.[55] Kerr argues that the reasons lie in the necessity for unity in face of antagonist groups and in the lack of ideological conflicts.[56] An American admirer of the "democracy" which exists in the British Amalgamated Engineering Union concludes that necessary changes in American union government to achieve such democracy are difficult because "in short,

[55] S. Lipset, "The Political Process in Trade Unions," in W. Galenson and E. Lipset, *Labor and Trade Unionism. An Interdisciplinary Reader*, New York, 1960, p. 220.

[56] C. Kerr, *Unions and Union Leaders of Their Own Choosing*, Santa Barbara, 1957, pp. 12–13.

the spirit and content of the reforms needed are largely absent from, or in contradiction to, American culture."[57] The less oligarchic tendencies of British unions and any lack of centralisation is more the result of history and tradition than deliberate attempts to involve the rank-and-file. The trade union movement is divided into a number of jealous units and even the large unions, in the course of their amalgamations, have had to give constitutional recognition to the pre-existing and firmly established local units. Simple factors such as the differences in geographic distance between any national headquarters and locals must also be taken into account.

Regardless of the degree of oligarchy, both countries' unions show marked divisions, and even hostility, between leaders and rank-and-file. Lipset notes, "the members of union officialdom, who share far more in common with each other than they do with the rank-and-file, develop a self-consciousness regarding their common interests which finds expression in their use of the organization machinery for defense of their individual tenures and group retention of power."[58] The divisions in the USA tend to be in power and consequently in life-style; in Britain, divorce between rank-and-file is expressed socially, possibly because of a greater class consciousness in the society and because trade union leaders are "working class, who lead middle-class lives and wield upper class power."[59] At the annual congresses of the TUC, hostility is expressed towards what is called the "platform" (a reference to the leaders who sit on the platform at the conference hall).

Oligarchy is often associated with gerontocracy. Here

[57] J. Edelstein, "Democracy in a National Union: the British AEU," *Industrial Relations*, Vol. 4, No. 3, May 1965, p. 124.
[58] S. Lipset, "The Political Process in Trade Unions," p. 222.
[59] A. Sampson, *An Anatomy of Britain*, London, 1962, p. 554.

there is a marked difference between unions in the USA and Britain. The prevailing gerontocracy in the USA is not hard to recognise; in 1965 the twenty-nine members of the AFL-CIO Executive Council had an average age of 63½ years and included President of the AFL-CIO, George Meany (70), and other such notable labour leaders as David Dubinsky (73), Jacob Potofsky (70), O. A. Knight (62), A. Philip Randolph (75), and Joseph Moreschi (80).[60]

It is obvious that most USA unions do not have compulsory retiring ages and this is especially the case of the AFL-CIO. In Britain the gerontocracy is not so prevalent because, firstly, there is a widespread rule that leaders must retire at sixty or sixty-five and, secondly, that trade unionists remove themselves into other areas, particularly Parliament and government or quasi-government agencies. The British unions provide a recruiting function for society which the American unions do not. A union career in the USA means, with few exceptions, a commitment for life to union work, whereas in Britain it does not.

The leaders of the national centres are usually the same body of men who lead the individual unions but there are two important exceptions. In the case of the AFL-CIO, the President does not hold other union positions and in the TUC it is the General Secretary who has no other responsibilities. These two men play an important role in policy-making.

[60] "The Tired Old Guard," *Time* magazine, March 5, 1965, p. 47; there are, however, occasional leadership election battles such as that experienced by the United Steelworkers of America in 1964.

LEADERS AND IDEOLOGY

Before attempting a comparison between the ideologies of British and American trade union leaders it should be pointed out that such ideologies depend as much on conditions and culture in the two societies as they do on the individuals' position as trade union leaders. Any two individuals from British and American societies might well show the same basic differences in attitudes and ideologies as two trade unionists.

It has been noted that American trade unions claim to be "non-political" or "business" unions in relation to their functions. In ideological terms "non-political" has meant the denial of adherence to any political ideology. It is not surprising that a largely immigrant society with a conception of Europe being divided into jealous monarchies at best and squabbling "isms" at worst, brought forth the notion that trade unions associated with a political ideology were "foreign." Consequently, employers and governments were not opposed when they demanded that trade unions, as an entrance fee, should be non-political and, in particular, non-socialist.

For these reasons, and many others, American trade union leaders have consistently associated political ideologies as foreign and prevented their entry into union politics. John L. Lewis, President of the CIO, commenting on the resolution passed by the organisation to stay out of World War II, claimed "without question this action should refute and silence those critics who are wont to slander the CIO as adhering to a philosophy foreign to Americans. Our movement is committed to no policy or ism that is imported from abroad."[61] The tradition of opposition to political ideology has persisted and the CIO, which was originally considered by some to be a vehicle for opposition to the tradition of ideological conservatism of the AF of L, soon followed the accepted norm.

Under the leadership of Phillip Murray, one reporter observed, "the unspoken rule around the CIO headquarters is that 'ideology' must not be mentioned in meeting; discussions stick to specific issues."[62] Opposition to political ideology and advocacy of business unionism are clearly related and one follows logically from the other. One commentator has suggested that such practices now have power uses, that "diffuse" ideologies disrupt oligarchic control and that "business unionism as a set of ideas, justifying the narrowest definition of a union's role in society and area of service to its members, discourages widespread membership participation and legitimates oligarchic leadership."[63]

The power consolidation theory would seem to have some justification in the 1940s and 1950s where anti-communism was a convenient tool to use in seeking or retaining power.

Almost every American labour leader can be quoted as opposing political ideology and promoting business unionism; persons said to be holders of political ideologies have been suspect and opposed throughout the history of the trade union movement. Two factors arise from this experience. First is the importance given to trade union leaders' role in defeating holders of political ideologies; and second, the consequential inability to

[61] *Steel Labor*, October 27, 1939, p. 5.
[62] *Life* magazine, February 11, 1946 (no page no.), as reprinted in *Steel Labor*, December 1952, p. 9.
[63] S. Lipset, "The Political Process in Trade Unions," p. 236.

appreciate political ideologies or to criticise society in a fundamental way. As the ILO mission of 1961 noted, "the Mission was struck in its discussions with union leaders by the almost total absence of any questioning of the bases of the American economic system. Unlike many Labour movements in Europe and elsewhere, the trade unions in the United States do not appear to even consider, still less advocate, any major changes in the system in which they operate, in spite of the many bitter battles that have occurred between unions and capital."[64]

The British trade union leaders are less homogeneous and it is here that the great differences lie. Clearly, not all British trade union leaders are adherents to a political ideology but a proportion of them are, and their presence is accepted without question. The TUC, like the AF of L and CIO, has expelled unions which have had communist leaders, but trade unions with properly elected communist leaders are present and accepted.

The British trade union movement, then, has not sought to exclude all holders of political ideologies from its ranks and this leavening has resulted in at least a verbal examination of some of the broader issues relating to society.

Other ideologies, notably movement and group ideology, are more pertinent to trade unions' role in international society and have been discussed in that chapter.

[64] ILO: *The Trade Union Situation in the USA, etc.*, p. 26.

The Models

The models of unionism and industrial relations which are derived from the domestic environment can now be briefly sketched.

AMERICAN MODEL

The American model is of craft or industrial unions, with narrowly defined aims and functions, no formal political affiliation, and no professed adherence to a named ideology. Trade unions are oligarchic and gerontocratic in nature, centralised in administration, and experience only minimal participation from the rank-and-file. Despite some government regulation and historical restriction, the presence and limited aims of the unions have been accepted by the society and may be pursued legitimately.

The national centre does not compromise union autonomy with respect to collective bargaining but appropriates policing functions concerning internal union government and politics. The complexity of the federal structure and the differing conditions and laws within the various states have prevented the national centre from becoming the authoritative voice on industrial and economic matters for labour and for the whole society.

The legal framework of industrial relations includes statutory machinery for the recognition of bargaining units and the election of a union agent, restrictions on the right to strike, minimum wage laws, and legally enforceable contracts concluded between unions and employer.

The American trade union leaders have acted within a society in which there is a considerable generalised hostility to the concept of trade unions, and most of them have encountered extreme employer resistance to unions. They have consistently opposed, on the individual and organisational level, adherence to political ideologies.

BRITISH MODEL

The British model is of craft or general unions which encompass both the narrow aims of unions and also participate actively in the broader and more diffuse issues. They have formal and intimate connections with a political party and are prepared to associate officially with a named ideology. There are a large number of individual trade unions, some with a very limited membership. Trade union government has oligarchic tendencies but traditional local autonomy mitigates trends towards a high degree of central authority. Rank-and-file participation in union government varies but is never very great. Government regulation is minimal and procedures and issues which have been contentious in the past have been solved by voluntary understanding rather than by precise statutory legislation and bodies. The unions have been accepted as legitimate entities and have been able to pursue both the narrow industrial aims as well as the broader objectives.

The national centre, by virtue of its position as unified spokesman for the labour movement and the integration of union leadership with national leadership, can affect, but not substantially, individual unions in industrial negotiation.

The legal framework of industrial relations is not extensive, many issues being solved by procedures established without legal codification. Minimum wage laws exist, there are no general or easily invoked laws mitigating the right to strike, there is no legal compulsion for union recognition, and collective bargaining agreements cannot be enforced by law.

The British trade union leaders have acted within a society in which they are criticised mainly on specific, rather than general, issues. Widespread hostility towards unions does not exist. Relations with employers have not been characterised by extreme hostility and rarely have the leaders encountered violence from any private groups.

These are then the models which trade unionists and others take with them and sometimes attempt to duplicate in less-developed countries. It is clear that model is used in its narrowest sense, describing an organisation, its formal structure, processes, and functions, and consequently the model described may not be real, in the sense that the processes so described or the structure so drawn correspond to the real or actual structure and processes. The reason for this narrow definition is clear; it is usually only the formal structure and processes which are sufficiently well known to be proposed as a model for imitation. Many politically active persons in Jamaica in the late 1930s and early 1940s made it their business to know the broad lines of the British model. They knew the relationship of the Labour Party with the trade unions and the structure of the British TUC and attempted to duplicate it. The same may be said about the perceived functions of trade unions, although here the model is never clear and the difficulties of duplication more obvious.

The model of a trade union movement may not, when involved in transference to another society, coincide with the concept of trade unionism. While models are derived from formal descriptions and are usually rooted in culturally and geographically specific areas, a concept is more generally derived. Thus some actors conceive trade unions as merely pressure groups, others as political organisations, and yet others as grievance-alleviating structures, and so on. It is obvious that it would be possible to advocate the "American model," for example, but at the same time have a conception of a trade union which has functions far beyond those, formal or real, of the actual American unions.

These models may be neither precise nor accurate but when viewed relatively, as a trade unionist in a foreign environment must do, they provide a guide for policy and action and their importance is therefore considerable.

CHAPTER IV

POLICY TOWARDS LESS-DEVELOPED COUNTRIES

Before considering the relevance of the incentives for foreign involvements and the actions of foreign trade unionists in Jamaica it is necessary to describe the policy-making structures and general policies of the relevant foreign unions involved.

The general policy of interest here is the one in which Jamaica would be included and this would be the policy concerning the colonies, or less-developed countries as they were called after receiving their formal independence. Although such a policy would be related to the general international policy it is sufficiently distinct to permit separate examination. This is largely because less-developed countries present a cluster of situations and problems which have no parallel in the industrial countries, a fact which caused some union organisations to create special policy-making structures and designate special staff for this area of international policy.

The record of foreign union involvement in Jamaica will reveal that the two most important organisations were the British TUC and the United Steelworkers of America (USWA). As regards their general policy these two organisations must be treated differently as the British TUC is a national centre with a mandate for the representation of the individual unions in most international matters, while the USWA is an individual industrial union which has been affiliated to its own national centres. Further, the USWA, while having a general international policy and executing its own policy in Jamaica, did not concern itself with a specific policy towards less-developed countries. For this reason, in the case of the USWA, the policies of the AF of L, CIO, and AFL-CIO must be considered.

THE BRITISH TRADES UNION CONGRESS

Decision-Making in International Affairs

The formal structure of decision-making in international affairs in the British TUC is the same for other matters: the annual congress is the highest authority in the organisation and approves, disapproves, or makes recommendations concerning the actions and policies of the executive body, the General Council. In fact, the congress only marginally affects decision-making in international affairs and the three main entities in the process are the General Secretary, the International Committee of the General Council, and the International Department of the secretariat.[1]

[1] Information on the informal decision-making processes in this section has been derived from interviews with British trade unionists.

THE GENERAL SECRETARY

The General Secretary of the British TUC is elected by the annual congress. He is, by the constitution, a member of Congress and of the General Council and is charged with conducting the business of both Congress and General Council.[2] He is the chief officer of the secretariat with the power of appointment and dismissal over all other staff members. He need not have been an active trade unionist coming from the rank-and-file and may well be a career staff member of the secretariat. As the person in the highest position in the organisation dealing, on a full-time basis, with the affairs of the national centre, he exercises considerable power. Officially his basic directives come from the General Council and sometimes from the Congress but his personal inclinations towards projects or special sections of the organisational work are invariably manifested in the policy or actions of the organisation.

The latter is especially true of international affairs as they are as an accessory function of the organisation. The personal beliefs of different General Secretaries as to the importance or lack of importance of international affairs have had tangible effects on the historical development of policy in the organisation. During the period 1938–67, the British TUC has had three General Secretaries: Walter Citrine, 1926–46; Vincent Tewson, 1946–60; and George Woodcock, 1960–69. Apart from their views on specific policy issues they have also had differences of opinion on the place of international affairs in the British trade union movement in general.

[2] TUC: *Rules and Standing Orders*, 1962, rule 10, p. 8.

For Citrine, international matters were considered important and he very early took an interest in both trade union as well as state international relations.[3] Tewson responded vigorously to demands made on the British TUC as a member of the ICFTU in which he played a leading role, while Woodcock has expressed his relative disinterest in international matters when compared with the domestic tasks of the organisation.

The interest or lack of interest in international matters of the General Secretary helps determine the importance of other persons and bodies involved in the decision-making process.

THE INTERNATIONAL COMMITTEE OF THE GENERAL COUNCIL

The General Council is elected by Congress in accordance with nominations made from various trade groups into which the affiliate are divided for election purposes. The thirty to forty members of the General Council are usually heads of their own unions and therefore the body represents the most powerful group of trade unionists in Britain. The General Council is required to transact the business of the TUC between the annual congresses and for this purpose meets at least once a month. Rule 8 in the constitution of the TUC precisely spells out, in ten points, the constitutional duties of the General Council; on international matters the Council is directed to "enter into relations with Trade Union and Labour Movements in other countries with a view to securing united action."[4] This directive is immediately

[3] See W. Citrine, *Men and Work*, London, 1964, pp. 88–94.
[4] TUC: *Rules and Standing Orders*, rule 8, para. f, p. 7.

preceded by a clause outlining the duties of the General Council concerning the strengthening of domestic trade unions and promoting common action on wage and work conditions. Thus the international securing of "united action" appears to relate to the preceding and basically domestic objectives.

The Council is also empowered to "make grants to any organisation or person, whether in Great Britain or abroad for such purposes as it seems desirable, . . ." but in doing so it is supposed to regard directions, if any, from Congress.[5] The only other mention of the international work of the Council comes in paragraph "k" which enables a Special Congress of the TUC to be called to decide on "industrial action" so that the "Trade Union Movement may do everything which lies in its power to prevent future wars."[6]

To perform its constitutional duties the Council has formed committees of its members, the most important of which are: Finance and General Purposes; Economic; Education; Organisation; International; Social Insurance and Industrial Welfare and Production. It is generally considered that of these the Finance and General Purposes Committee and the Economic Committee are the most important, although several trade unionists interviewed (selected, however, because of their interest in international affairs) claimed that the International Committee ranked as a third "senior" committee. Membership of either the Finance and General or Economic Committees was considered as important for advancement within the organisation but this was not the case for the International Committee.

The members of the International Committee, as the other committees, are selected by a "committee to select

[5] *Ibid.*, rule 8, para. g.
[6] *Ibid.*, rule 8, para. k.

committees" after the General Council has been elected at the annual congress. A trade unionist of long General Council experience said that the selection for the three senior committees was on a "basis of service" and that at least five years' service on other committees was necessary before a person could easily get on to one of these committees.

To acquire membership of the International Committee an interest in international affairs is expected, as, for example, prior participation in the corresponding International Trade Secretariat (ITS) of the member's union. Many of the trade unionists interviewed said that contact with their respective ITS was the first experience which aroused their interest in the international aspects of the trade union movement. Essentially there are no consistently followed informal criteria concerning the membership of the International Committee although it is usual for the larger unions to be represented.

Trade unionists with a special interest in international matters cannot be considered as a distinct sub-group within the General Council or within the organisation. Resolutions at Congress and lively debates within the International Committee were often attributed to "left-wingers" who, it was generally felt, always showed a greater interest in international affairs. In sum, all that can be said is that members of the International Committee show a willingness to become engaged, and attempt to develop a competence, in matters outside the exclusive domestic functions of their trade unions.

The Committee has varied in size, having approximately ten members up to 1955 and between fourteen and sixteen from that year. The turnover of committee members is not great and in 1959 eight of the thirteen members had been five years or over on the committee.

The procedure is informal, there is no official quorum, and it rarely meets with all members present.

The most important member of the Committee is the Chairman and he emerges as another key person, together with the General Secretary, in the decision-making process on international matters. He is elected by the Committee and there are no recognised qualifications for chairmanship, but an examination of the records of past chairmen shows that, with rare exceptions, they had already served over five years on the Committee before being elected.[7] Political ideology as well as organisational politics sometimes enter into the selection of a Chairman but this is not so common as it is with other committees.

The importance of the Chairman results from his relationship with the General Secretary and the informal nature of the Committee. His main function, as described by a Chairman of the Committee is to "liaise with the General Secretary" with whom "he must nominally accept responsibility for international affairs." The informal nature of the Committee's work has meant that the Chairman has usually assumed final responsibility for the Committee's decisions and has become more than a mere link between the Committee, the General Secretary, and the General Council.

During the period 1938–67, there have been three important Chairmen of the International Committee: Arthur Deakin, 1947–55; Alfred Roberts, 1958–63; and Fred Hayday, 1964–. The level of control or restriction exercised by the Committee over the Chairman depends on the "personalities" on the Committee. This widely used description is most often applied to members who are known to be aggressive, opinionated, or profess a strong

[7] TUC: *Annual Congresses, Report of Proceedings, 1950–1965.*

political ideology but the fluctuation on the Committee of such persons, however, only marginally affects the importance of the Chairman.

THE INTERNATIONAL DEPARTMENT

The International Department evolved from within the TUC secretariat, especially when staff members began to specialise in international affairs in the period 1919–20.[8] When Citrine, as founder of the modern secretariat, formally created the International Department in 1924 the two existing specialists made up the total staff of the Department. In 1964 the functions of the Department were described as "maintains relations with trade union centres and other organisations abroad including the ICFTU and the ILO: deals with questions of international trade union policy and watches the Government's colonial, Commonwealth and foreign policies; advises and assists in the development of trade unions overseas."[9]

The main importance of the Department lies in its control of information on specific matters which is used by the International Committee, its power of recommendation to that Committee, and the access the head of the Department has to the General Secretary.

The matters discussed by the International Committee not only include the well-reported major international events but the specific matters which require a more intimate knowledge of the politics of the country or territory in question. In such cases the Department prepares a report for the Committee and, having time, in-

[8] See Political and Economic Planning: *British Trade Unionism*, London, 1948, pp. 98–101.
[9] TUC: *The ABC of the TUC*, London, 1964, p. 12.

formation and expertise which the Committee does not, the Department's report is usually accepted. In this way, one interviewee claimed, the majority of policy on less sensational matters is made by the Department staff. Whether such a claim is justified or not, it is the practice of the Department to attach to most reports recommendations for action and most of such recommendations are accepted.

The head of Department has, under most administrations, easy access to the General Secretary, which means that the "Department view" is well heard by an important person in the decision-making process. The Department head is also secretary of the International Committee and is therefore in a similar position to the Committee as he is to the General Secretary. The head of the International Department is thus the third key individual in the international policy-making process. During the period 1938–67 there were three different heads of the Department although they did not change in relation to either changes in the General Secretaryship or the Chairmanship of the Committee. One of these started early with the Department and held the position from 1941 to 1953.

THE GENERAL COUNCIL AND CONGRESS

Both of these bodies have a large formal role in policy-making but, at least in international affairs, their actual role is marginal.

The General Council must every year present a report to be discussed at Congress and is collectively responsible for all that is contained therein. Thus it is possible for the General Council to alter or veto policy matters coming from the International Committee.

Debates in Congress on international matters are often extensive. It is generally agreed that Congress exerts less influence on international affairs than on other matters. But its potential as an effective bar to organisational action and as a forum for mobilising trade union and public opinion should not be overlooked.

Development of Policy Towards Less-Developed Countries

During the period of interest there have been several changes in terminology to describe less-developed countries. Starting from "backward countries," "colonies," "underdeveloped," and "poor" it has ended in "developing countries." In general, the term "less-developed country" will be used but "colonies" must also be used when the colonial relationship was of importance.

The British TUC paid little attention to the colonies until after World War I despite the interest shown by the socialists in general and the Labour Party in particular. As a portent of future divisions there was, before World War I, some differences of opinion between trade unionists and the party socialists.[10] The latter were opposed to capitalist imperialism, while the former, especially those involved in the cotton textile industry, condoned such imperialism when it supported British domestic industrial establishments. In 1905, for example, a textile trade unionist in the House of Commons argued

[10] See P. Kellogg and A. Gleason, *British Labour and the War*, New York, 1919, p. 225.

for the development of cotton growing in the Empire to support British production.[11]

After World War I, and before the creation of the International Department, there were two staff members concerned with international affairs, one of whom spent most of his time on colonial matters. Thus at an early stage in the development of general policy the TUC attempted to acquire a specialised staff competence and knowledge of colonial trade unionism.

The direct involvement of the TUC in the colonies, however, started in the mid 1920s, when the first British Commonwealth Labour Conferences were held. One of the first recorded appearances of a TUC representative at a colonial trade union conference was that of F. O. Roberts, MP, at the British Guiana and West Indian Labour Conference in 1925. The reason for such representation, as stated by the 1926 TUC Congress report, was that the Labour Party and the TUC wished to "encourage the natives in the British Dependencies" to organise trade unions and Labour Parties. Further it was felt that "the general opinion seems to be that a constitution on the lines of the British Movement is desirable."[12]

In 1928 the first fact-finding tour of the TUC was completed which was in India. This mission was approved in a *Times* editorial: "The interest which the British TUC has lately taken in Indian labour conditions may be very beneficial, if it leads to the better organisation of Indian labour unions and the expulsion of communist elements."[13]

[11] B. Hennessy, "British Trade Unions and International Affairs 1945–1953," unpublished Ph.D. dissertation, University of Wisconsin, 1955, p. 46.

[12] TUC: *58th Annual Congress, Report of Proceedings, 1926*, pp. 254–55.

[13] D. Davies, "The Politics of the TUC's Colonial Policy," *Political Quarterly*, Vol. 35, No. 1, January–March 1964, p. 23.

TUC AND GOVERNMENT COOPERATION

The *Times* view of the TUC supporting government policy had no organisational manifestations at that time and it was not until the early 1940s that the TUC really became closely associated with government policy. The Passfield Memorandum of 1930, with its proposals for limited promotion of trade unionism in the colonies, to some extent pre-empted any possible TUC direct activity designed to encourage unions.[14] But the TUC under Citrine soon established the principle that colonial policy should not be made by the TUC alone. A Colonial Advisory Committee was established in 1935 to advise the International Committee on colonial matters and from 1937 it reported directly to the General Council. The most interesting aspect of the Advisory Committee was that it was tripartite with representatives from the General Council, corporations, and governments, although all sat in their private capacities. Also, at least since the foundation of the International Affairs Department, TUC staff members have kept close contact with the Foreign Office, a practice which persists to the present day. The TUC staff was thus able to gather information from industrialists with interests in the colonies, their own representatives, and the Colonial Office. The importance of the Advisory Committee is difficult to assess. It met infrequently but continuously until the early 1950s, but its use declined thereafter although it remained in existence and was recently renamed the Overseas Labour Consultative Committee.

There are some indications that the TUC continued to

[14] See Chapter VII.

pursue the policy of encouraging constitutions on British lines mentioned in 1926. In 1938 the secretariat issued *Model Rules, Agendas, and Standing Orders for the Guidance of Colonial Organisations.* But unrest in the late 1930s, especially in the West Indies, brought attention to the fact that the Passfield and subsequent circulars issued to Colonial Governors had not solved the labour problems. A lengthy resolution passed by the 1938 Congress and coming from a member of the General Council indicates that there were persons in the organisation who had realised this fact: "This Congress views with grave concern the persistence in many British Crown Colonies and Dependencies of deplorable conditions of native labour which are entirely incompatible with present day social and industrial standards which have been the main cause of the outbreaks of disorder in various West Indian colonies during the past year. While Congress recognises the new colonial policy outlined in the circular of August 1937, to Colonial Governors, the Government is urged to insist that colonial administrations shall give immediate effect to this policy . . . and . . . Congress instructs the General Council to maintain the closest possible connection with the Trade Union Movements in the Colonies and to assist them to the utmost of its power towards the development of trade union organisations and the realisation of civilised conditions of life and labour."[15]

The mandate contained in this resolution that the TUC should rely less on cooperation with the government and more on direct union-to-union contact was not used before and during World War II. More evidence, however, was forthcoming that the Colonial administrations were reluctant to implement the stated Colonial Office

[15] TUC: *70th Annual Congress, Report of Proceedings, 1938,* p. 433.

policy. Citrine's experience on the West Indian Royal Commission was a case in point and even before the report was completed, *Labour,* the monthly magazine of the TUC, was reporting Citrine had discovered that trade unions were not being encouraged by colonial administrations.[16] There was also some sensitivity within the organisation concerning the image of the British as a nation; commenting on the 1940 Colonial Development and Welfare Act, *Labour* argued that it did not "go far enough toward removing the reproach that British Colonial rule is more concerned with the exploitation of the natives than with their well-being."[17]

It was the belief, as was well illustrated in the West Indian Royal Commission Report, that the age of governmental imperialism was over and as the new governments were humanitarian and liberal it was quite legitimate for the TUC to cooperate fully with the Colonial Office. The Colonial Office hinted in the late 1930s that government promotion of trade unions alone was something to be praised.[18] But the TUC did not become fully involved until the establishment, within the Colonial Office, of a Colonial Labour Advisory Committee, which had four TUC representatives. At a later date the TUC representatives were also included on the Colonial Economic and Development Council but even more important was the appointment of Labour Officers from the TUC for the Labour Departments which had been set up in some colonies since 1937. TUC nominations for Labour Officers began in 1942 but by 1945 only about a dozen such appointments had been made and

[16] *Labour,* Vol. 1, No. 5, January 1939, pp. 12–14.
[17] *Labour,* Vol. 2, No. 7, March 1940, p. 357.
[18] *Colonial Office Press Section:* "Trade Unions in the Colonial Empire: How They Are Being Encouraged to Develop," Press Release, 1941.

there were practically no applicants.[19] By 1950, twenty-two appointments from the TUC nominations had been made.

DIRECT ACTION

During and immediately after World War II, the TUC was unable to take any direct action in the colonies and even modest programmes, such as especially written newsletters, had to be postponed.

The renewed interest in trade union international matters immediately after the war also brought to the fore the problems of less-developed countries. At the 1945 World Labour Conference and the first Congress of the World Federation of Trade Unions (WFTU), Britain was castigated by colonial delegates for the conditions in the colonies. In 1947 the TUC moved to become more directly involved in the colonies by establishing a Colonial Fund to which affiliate members were asked to contribute and to which the General Council gave £500. In the same year, Andrew Dalgleish, a British trade unionist, was sent to Burma to investigate trade unions and he recommended such measures as the furnishing of TUC literature, model agreements, and, in particular, a British trade union adviser, but *not* acting as a government official.[20] Between 1947 and 1950 the Colonial Fund operated with a capital never exceeding £3000 and made grants worth approximately £1500. Out of the remaining fund, seven colonial trade unionists were brought to England for one-year courses, eight on

[19] TUC: *77th Annual Congress, Report of Proceedings, 1945*, p. 145.

[20] TUC: *79th Annual Congress, Report of Proceedings, 1947*, p. 206.

a month's training course, and fifteen correspondence courses were organised.[21]

These activities were supplemented by several TUC missions to various colonies and less-developed countries, including India and Trinidad.

In 1950 far-reaching changes were made in the TUC colonial programme. The TUC had always guarded its independence when dealing with British colonies and Deakin, as Chairman of WFTU and the TUC International Committee, had prevented the colonial section of the WFTU secretariat from obtaining any financial power.[22] With the creation of the ICFTU, the TUC faced the prospect of the new International becoming very active in the colonies. British TUC participation and power could only be ensured by a substantial financial contribution and so affiliation fees to the TUC were raised in order to finance a promised £60,000 to the ICFTU Regional Activities Fund. At the same time, the TUC's independent activities were to be greatly increased. The major colonial policy statement in 1950 argued that although the ICFTU was to be largely responsible for assisting less-developed countries the TUC "must maintain direct contacts."[23] These contacts were to be through assistance to national centres, on-the-spot advice and educational work for which an estimated £40,000 was needed for a three-year programme. Thus in 1950–51, the TUC agreed to commit a total of £100,000 to colonial operations.[24]

Tewson, while General Secretary, was the Chairman

[21] "Colonial Workers Look to Us to Help Their Unions," *Labour*, Vol. 1, No. 1 (Revised Series), September 1950, p. 7.

[22] See D. Davies, "The Politics of the TUC's Colonial Policy," p. 30.

[23] TUC: *82nd Annual Congress, Report of Proceedings*, 1950, p. 561.

[24] Total income for the organisation for 1950 was a little over £100,000.

of the ICFTU Regional Fund Committee and the International Solidarity Fund, which replaced the former in 1956. Thus the British TUC had strong representation in the disbursement of funds through the ICFTU. By 1956 the payments to the ICFTU were reduced and more funds were channeled into direct TUC activity. In 1957 grants on a continuing basis were being awarded, for example, £220 per month was given to the British Guiana Manpower Citizens' Association for a year and £100 per month for six months to the All-Trinidad Union.[25]

Up to 1950, then, the direct participation of the British TUC had been mainly through education and occasional grants within a very limited budget. From 1950 onwards, involvement was more substantial and included education, grants, loans, advisers, and commissions.

GENERAL COLONIAL POLICY

There are no indications that up to the late 1940s the TUC policy-makers had developed any specific ideas concerning the growth, nature, or functions of trade unions in less-developed countries. There was a basic acceptance that organisations in the colonies would naturally follow British structural and functional lines. Citrine had not displayed a great interest in colonial problems[26] but had cemented the Colonial Office/TUC relationship.

[25] TUC: *89th Annual Congress, Report of Proceedings, 1957*, p. 225.

[26] See W. Citrine, "World Wide Growth of Trade Unions," *Labour*, Vol. 1, August 12, 1939, pp. 6–9, where, despite the title, no mention was made of colonial trade union developments.

There had been some early entanglements with the problems of politics and trade unions and in the 1930s imprisonment of Indian trade union leaders had been dismissed as no concern of the TUC because the arrests were "political."[27] In 1948 a trade unionist writing a report for the Colonial Office (he had been recommended by the TUC) spoke disparagingly of political trade union leaders in Trinidad.[28] But the politics of trade unions in the colonies were often centred on the issue of national independence and on this the TUC leaders were traditionally reticent. At the founding congress of the WFTU, Citrine was less than sympathetic to the problems of less-developed countries, opposing a motion to scale fees in accordance with national income and also a motion which suggested that the new International should assist territories in gaining national independence.[29]

The attacks on British colonial policy came from the Communist bloc unions in WFTU as well as from the colonial and American unions in the ICFTU. Deakin, the very active Chairman of the TUC International Committee, sought to answer the first critics by pointing to the danger of communism in less-developed countries and to, what he claimed to be, the irresponsible demands made that conditions in colonies should approximate those in the metropolitan countries. On this issue he argued: "It is only by a progressive approach, by building surely and well, that we shall achieve that."[30] His answer to calls for immediate improvement of condi-

[27] D. Davies "The Politics of the TUC's Colonial Policy," p. 24.
[28] F. Dalley, "Trade Unionism in Trinidad," *Labour*, Vol. 10, No. 5, January 1948, p. 155.
[29] WFTU: *Report of the World Trade Union Conference Congress, 1945*, pp. 33–34.
[30] A. Deakin, "The International Trade Union Movement," *International Affairs*, Vol. XXVI, No. 2, April 1950, p. 171.

tions was that more effort should be put into the United Nations specialised agencies. Tewson countered the attacks on British colonialism by pointing out that the current colonialism was much better than the past colonialism and that the British TUC was for self-government, but only if it meant something to the bulk of the people.[31] In an impassioned and defensive speech at the ICFTU Congress in 1955, Tewson sought to show that the TUC had made efforts in the colonies for many years; referring to the West Indies he recounted: "In the past 25 years–not just the past five–the British trade union movement has been trying to develop organisations, and time after time we have found that we have built an organisation in a locality and have passed on to make an attempt to create an organisation in another territory, and as soon as we have turned our backs the movement has been collared, just as Frank Walcott has said, by, sometimes, a single person who is not concerned with the development of trade unionism but with using the organisation and power of the workers for his own personal petty political ends."[32]

The promotion of British style organisations in the various territories had, however, been criticised from within the TUC and, on paper at least, the organisation moved from a universalist policy to a more relativist position. In this context a relativist policy may be described as the formal acceptance by policy-makers that trade unions would not necessarily appear in identical forms throughout the world and that they would be, in fact, relative to the society and culture in which they were situated. This position was succinctly outlined in the 1950 colonial policy statement; when referring to the possible results of TUC assistance to colonial unions

[31] ICFTU: *Report of Fourth World Congress,* 1955, p. 348.
[32] *Ibid.*

it warned that "structurally they can benefit from the experience in this country but it has to be appreciated that as the movement in this country has developed in the light of our own circumstances the pattern is not indigenous to the Colonies. The industrial, social and, in general, the educational standards there are different."[33] As one important policy-maker of that period told this author, 'we were not there to build little TUC's all over the world.' It should be noted, however, that the relativist position was not adopted in relation to the final results of organisational growth but to the *process of development* of trade unions. The possibility of a different path to trade unionism had been accepted, but the expectation remained that the final result would be an industrial-country model, and in ex-British colonies, more than likely, the British model. The relativist policy did not therefore eclipse all deliberate promotions of the British model—as an indication of the progress of the TUC colonial aid programme, the 1953 Congress Report notes that four hundred and eighty copies of *What the TUC Is Doing* went to thirty-eight colonial trade union centres.[34]

The formal relativist position, however, did permit TUC leaders to be less adamant on the issue of political unionism. Political unionism was seen as only one stage in the development of unions and that the final product would be mature and non-political. As the 1950 policy statement pointed out, "the time is short for the effective development of Trade Unions seeking to protect the industrial interests of their members and to establish

[33] "Colonial Workers Look to Us to Help Their Unions," p. 9; and TUC: *82nd Annual Congress, Report of Proceedings, 1950*, pp. 560–63.
[34] TUC: *85th Annual Congress, Report of Proceedings, 1953*, p. 212.

them as independent organisations determining their own policy and acting as independent bodies."[35]

Such a "maturity" theory was expressed by Assistant General Secretary Woodcock in a speech in Jamaica in 1950. Tewson, however, was more rigid in his belief that unions should both follow the British model and should also be mainly non-political; in 1957, after defining union functions narrowly, he stated that "trade union and political aspirations may focus on the same ultimate goal but we do not regard trade unions as political instruments."[36]

The experience, described by Tewson, of the long attempts to build organisations, the general evolutionary policy outlined by Deakin plus the British colonial policy of incremental preparation for self-government produced an important element in the TUC policy—the "grass roots" approach to trade union development. It was argued from the early 1950s onwards that trade unions could not be built from the "top downwards," that membership support created unions and these unions created national centres. In 1959 the General Council felt that in practice "the first task should be the strengthening of individual unions, with the development of national and regional bodies as and when there is a sound basis for local organisation."[37] This policy also resulted from conflicts with the AFL-CIO in Africa, where it was claimed that "outside organisations often attempt to build African unionism from the top downwards."[38] The grass roots theory of union development was stated in great detail by Woodcock as General Secretary at the

[35] *Ibid.*
[36] V. Tewson, "Trade Unionism in the Colonies," in *The British Labour Party Commonwealth Conference Report,* 1957, p. 30.
[37] TUC: *91st Annual Congress, Report of Proceedings,* 1959, p. 209.
[38] *Ibid.*

1965 ICFTU Congress[39] and was mentioned by all trade unionists interviewed as being the most important element in British TUC policy.

Throughout the development of policy towards less-developed countries, the TUC has concentrated almost exclusively on the problems of organisation building and has shown only passing interest in examining the complexities of economic development. References to economic problems before 1960 were general and showed little appreciation of the difficulties; Deakin, for example, stated that for living standards to be raised in less-developed countries "their resources must be expanded so as to make them more productive and enable them to participate more fully in the developing of wider economic units and the freer exchange of commodities which is necessary."[40] Even when an increased interest in economic development became prevalent in the United Nations Development Decade of the 1960s, the emphasis was still placed on organisational aid to unions. Thus, a composite resolution passed at the 1965 TUC Congress referring to the United Nations Trade and Development Conference held in 1964, instructed the General Council "to make a comprehensive examination of ways in which assistance to trade unions in developing countries can be undertaken . . ."[41] Some resolutions were also passed which indicated an interest in the problem of wealth transfer between industrial and less-developed countries. In general only scant attention was paid to the basic problems of economic development on which a policy of trade union development might be built. No attention was formally given to such policy issues as

[39] ICFTU: *Report of Eighth World Congress, 1965*, pp. 599–600.
[40] ICFTU: *Report of First World Congress, 1949*, p. 37.
[41] TUC: *97th Annual Congress, Report of Proceedings, 1965*, p. 523.

private versus public investment, direct or indirect capital transfer, or objectives of foreign aid and technical assistance.

THE USA LABOUR ORGANISATIONS

The primary interest of this study is the national labour organisation as an independent actor which, in the case of the USA in Jamaica, is the United Steelworkers of America. This union, however, was from 1938 affiliated to two national centres of the USA, the CIO until 1955 and the AFL-CIO thereafter.

The general policy of the United Steelworkers of America (USWA) was thus developed in circumstances in which other national labour organisations to which it was affiliated were engaged in the same task. Such affiliation also altered the means of USWA involvements abroad as it was affiliated to the WFTU through the CIO until 1949 and then to the ICFTU, which the CIO helped to create, in the same year.

In examining the historical development of policy towards less-developed countries in the American labour movement, for several reasons the AF of L must take a predominant place. The CIO was formed in 1938 and between then and 1945 the AF of L prevented it from representing the USA in international labour diplomacy. Independent action by the CIO was also proscribed by the difficulties of organising domestically and the onset of World War II. Furthermore, the AF of L had been involved with USA and labour foreign policy for over fifty years and had developed traditional attitudes towards some policy issues of relevance to less-developed countries. Finally, foreign policy cooperation between the AF of L and CIO began in 1948 and although there had been substantial differences between the leaders of the organisations before that time, they had centred more on the politics of European unionism than on less-developed countries or colonialism.[42]

Thus, although the USWA is a CIO union, the account of the development of policy towards less-developed countries will to a large extent deal with the AF of L and the AFL-CIO.

As already outlined, studies of trade union organisations in the USA have shown that decision-making in general is centralised and tends to be bureaucratic and elitist.[43] In 1955 a thorough investigation was made of decision-making in relation to the international activities of the AF of L. The author found that a small group at the apex of the organisation developed attitudes and made policy.[44] In contrast to the British TUC, however, this study showed that the specialist staff played a less important role in foreign policy-making owing to the hostility between the younger men with professional background on the staff and the older men with union background in the formal policy-making structures.[45] At a later date the International Department of the AFL-CIO acquired greater prominence and the head of the department, J. Lovestone, together with the President, George Meany, and a largely acquiescent

[42] See J. Anderson, "The Power of American Trade Unions Abroad," p. 38.

[43] See W. Galenson and S. Lipset, *Labor and Trade Unionism: An Interdisciplinary Reader*, New York, 1960, p. 217.

[44] See W. Hamilton, *The Development of Foreign Policy Attitudes in Certain American Pressure Groups*, unpublished Ph.D. dissertation, Yale University, 1955, attached abstract (no page no.).

[45] *Ibid.*, pp. 255–56.

Executive Board, has been one of the most important policy-makers for the organisation.[46]

Development of Policy Towards Less-Developed Countries

In a study of the development of the AF of L foreign policy made in 1935, the author states that one of the first stands the AF of L took on a foreign policy issue was to oppose imperialism.[47] The imperialism opposed was that of the USA, which in 1899–1900 was in the process of annexation of Puerto Rico and the Philippines. Also in the early years, the organisation made "academic professions of pacifism" and of humanism which Hardy argues came from an American absorption of the Marxist socialism of the European labour movement. Although the policy of the AF of L was "paternalistic" in relation to Central America it was to make "self-determination" a major and lasting feature of its formally stated policy.[48] At the 1933 Convention, the AF of L passed a resolution that "it must be clearly understood that the American Federation of Labor stands firmly for the principle of self-determination on the part of the people in each country in their choice and support of governmental systems within the borders of their own lands."[49] Self-determination, both of governmental system and of na-

[46] See S. Lens, "Lovestone Diplomacy," *The Nation*, July 5, 1965, pp. 10–16.
[47] M. Hardy, *The Influence of Organized Labor on the Foreign Policy of the United States*, Liège, 1936, p. 246.
[48] *Ibid.*, p. 251.
[49] *Ibid.*, p. 100.

tional independence, was also later to become a major principle of the AFL-CIO foreign policy.

Two aspects of the development of the foreign policy of the AF of L became evident in the early period; first, an interest was taken in external affairs only if they had a direct impact on American labour, and second, a desire to propagate internationally American-style unionism and the American political system.

The first aspect arose out of the conditions in the USA in the early part of the twentieth century; immigration, tariffs, and low wages abroad were all important to the economic and social conditions in the USA at that time.[50] The second aspect has similarities to the British stated universalist doctrine in the 1920s and 1930s. Hardy, in 1935, noted that: "In the same way, but to a lesser extent, the American labor movement parallels the attitude of the nation looking upon itself as a champion of democracy, civil liberties and religious toleration wherever they may be in jeopardy" and that therefore there was a "constant effort to keep Central American labor movements moving in the channels of trade unionism as practised in the United States."[51]

POST WORLD WAR II

These policy lines emerged almost untouched after World War II but the impact of the war intensified the connection between the self-interest orientation and the promotion of a political ideology. Government and unions

[50] See H. Lasswell, "Foreign Influences on American Labor," in J. Hardman and associates, *American Labor Dynamics*, New York, 1928, pp. 360–63.

[51] M. Hardy, *The Influence of Organized Labor on the Foreign Policy of the United States*, p. 251.

joined together after the war when labour advisers were appointed from AF of L and CIO personnel to serve with the Allied European occupation authorities. Such appointments were continued with the European Recovery Program and special provisions made for union participation in government foreign policy operations.

In 1945 the CIO entered WFTU without the AF of L participating; at the first conference Sidney Hillman, a CIO delegate, showed a sensitivity to charges that foreign trade unions could interfere in the domestic affairs of another state—"we shall, of course, require that the important task of the World Federation will be to render assistance—not interference—to struggling Labour Organisations of smaller or economically inferior nations."[52] The CIO was in a position in WFTU to influence the execution of such a policy as a CIO representative, Elmer Cope, was placed in charge of colonial matters for the International. Although the WFTU was to some extent prevented from effective action in the colonies by the British, Cope himself was not considered enthusiastic about his responsibilities and was eventually accused by the Secretary General of WFTU of "deliberately paralyzing" the activities of the colonial department.[53]

The AF of L began extensive involvement in less-developed countries in the mid 1940s and did so more as a result of opposition to WFTU and the CIO than through political developments in the countries concerned or in the USA. Thus, in 1946, the Latin American representative of the AF of L started operations which were instrumental in creating a regional organisation

[52] WFTU: *Report of the World Trade Union Conference Congress, 1945*, p. 42.

[53] See L. Lorwin, *The International Labor Movement*, New York, 1953, p. 233; and CIO: *Proceedings of 10th Constitutional Convention, 1948*, p. 118.

which was to oppose the WFTU regional affiliate.[54] The involvement in Latin America continued an historical association the organisation had had with Latin and Central America. Leading foreign policy decision-makers were, as a result, more exposed to conditions in Latin America than elsewhere but even so there was little substantive consideration of the social and economic conditions of economic underdevelopment or policies which might alleviate them. Serafino Romualdi, the Latin American representative of the AF of L from 1946 to 1965, outlined some rudimentary development policies in 1947. They proceeded by direct analogy from the perceived history of USA economic growth and argued for the creation of a "saving wage," for free trade and for direct foreign investment from USA corporations as the latter paid higher wages and had greatly improved compared with their past behaviour.[55]

In his study of the AF of L foreign policy for the period 1945–50, Hamilton states that the publications of the organisation made no attempt to explain the differences in living standards between industrial and less-developed countries and that articles on such countries "contained little information on conditions in those countries except for warning of the threat of communist infiltration."[56]

It was not really until the founding of the ICFTU in

[54] See *Survey of the Alliance for Progress, Labor Policies and Programs* (a study prepared for the Subcommittee on American Republic Affairs by the staff of the Committee on Foreign Relations, US Senate), Washington, 1968, p. 8.

[55] S. Romualdi, "Labor and Democracy in Latin America," *Foreign Affairs,* Vol. 25, No. 3, April 1947, pp. 477–89.

[56] W. Hamilton, *The Development of Foreign Policy Attitudes in Certain American Pressure Groups,* p. 289; see also AFL-CIO: *Proceedings of 4th Constitutional Convention, 1961* (South American Aid Resolution), Vol. 1, p. 239.

1949 that the AF of L and CIO began to make policy statements on less-developed countries, colonialism, and national independence. The emphasis at the ICFTU Preparatory Conference by the AF of L delegation was that the new International must pay attention to Latin America, Asia, and Africa to prevent communist influence in those regions.[57] Walter Reuther, as CIO delegate, warned against "narrow political nationalism" and sought to prove that the USA unions were not arms of the State Department.[58] The AF of L delegate, Irving Brown, continuing the AF of L traditional policy, noted: ". . . Capital investment, yes, but with no political conditions that take away the rights of free self-determination of the peoples of the east."[59]

Even more mention was made of less-developed countries when two years later, after having withdrawn for a year from the ICFTU in protest of the dominant position of the British in ICFTU affairs in less-developed countries, the AF of L issued a "Bill of Particulars." One point of the Bill was that the ICFTU should act "as the foremost champion of the peoples fighting for their national independence."[60] The twin historical lines of self-determination and self-interest emerge from most of the speeches of the AF of L spokesmen at the ICFTU: George Meany, in one of the few direct references to economic development, pointed out in 1955 that the

[57] L. Lorwin, *The International Labor Movement*, p. 265.

[58] ICFTU: *Report of World Labour Conference and First Congress, 1949*, pp. 96–98.

[59] *Ibid.*, p. 84; see also AFL-CIO: *Report of Proceedings of 5th Constitutional Convention, 1963*, Vol. 11, p. 109.

[60] J. Windmuller, *American Labor and the International Labor Movement, 1940–1953*, Ithaca, N.Y., 1954, p. 243; see also "Statement of AFL-CIO Foreign Policy for Platform Committee," *AFL-CIO International Affairs Bulletin*, Vol. 1, No. 1, September 1956, p. 1.

poor countries "must industrialize because it will benefit not only the peoples of those countries but also the working people in the industrialized nations."[61]

In 1955, at the first Conference of the merged AFL-CIO, the policy towards less-developed countries was spelled out with precision: "Undeveloped and underdeveloped continents and regions where many hundreds of millions nurse their grievances and their hopes constitute a fertile field for Communist operations. In dealing with rudimentary human problems the world over, we must be concerned primarily with two immediate needs—the need for food, health and irrigation in the under-developed countries and the burning desire for independence and equality. By ministering to such fundamental needs we will be on firmer ground as we seek to win new adherents to the free world."[62]

Since that time there have been some variations in stated policy, often resulting from AF of L disagreements with the ICFTU and some leaders of the CIO. The AFL-CIO leaders had conflicts with the ICFTU in Latin America where, it was considered, the area was suitably serviced by ORIT. Also in 1959 Meany warned the ICFTU Conference concerning Africa: "I can tell you quite frankly that we are going to help these people one way or another; we are not going to let the dead hand of bureaucracy, no matter where it may exist, keep us from helping these people."[63] Individual leaders developed more complex ideas on economic development but they rarely appear as considered organisational policy.[64]

[61] ICFTU: *Report of Third World Congress*, 1953, p. 323.
[62] AFL-CIO: *Report of Proceedings of 1st Constitutional Convention*, 1955, p. 102.
[63] ICFTU: *Report of Sixth World Congress*, 1959, p. 373.
[64] See W. Reuther. *First Things First* (an occasional paper on the Free Society), California, 1964, p. 12.

As in the British TUC a more relativist policy began to be developed at the formal level during the 1950s. In 1953 the USA Worker Delegate to the International Labour Conference (at that time from the AF of L) recognised that conditions in less-developed countries might mean trade unions would have strong government connections.[65] In 1960 the AFL-CIO stated "[African unions] are bound to develop forms of organization most suitable to their own specific conditions. Just as economic developments . . . in the underdeveloped countries will not proceed in the tempo of the 19th century, so it is unlikely that the trade union movement . . . will go through the organic, step-by-step development of the European or American labor movements."[66] Nevertheless, the AFL-CIO has retained a reputation, both domestically and internationally, for a universalism in its conceptions of trade unionism. One of the leading experts in trade union foreign policy stated in 1967 that in Latin America, for at least two decades, "the main thrust has been to support the development of a form of trade unionism which corresponds to American labor's own conception of the proper role of trade unions in a free society."[67] Recognising that there have been deviations based on pragmatic political objectives, a USA Senate-commissioned study concludes, "although the U.S. labor movement in recent years has frequently deviated from

[65] ILO: *International Labour Conference, Record of Proceedings, 36th Session*, 1953, p. 299.

[66] As quoted in *AFL-CIO—The Hands That Build America*, Special Supplement, *The New York Times*, Section 11, November 17, 1963, p. 7.

[67] J. Windmuller, "The Foreign Policy Conflict in American Labor," *Political Science Quarterly*, Vol. 82, No. 2, June 1967, p. 214; see also H. Berger, "American Labor Overseas," *The Nation*, January 16, 1967, p. 80.

strict adherence to these principles [of business unionism] it is this philosophy which U.S. labor leadership has attempted to implant abroad. As the U.S. labor movement has grown to its present status, its leadership has interpreted this growth as confirmation of its philosophy—a philosophy unique to the U.S. labor movement, and particularly its craft union element."[68]

These aims have been pursued in a variety of ways and, unlike the British, no guidelines on the way the policy objectives might be achieved have been published. The AFL-CIO has continued to cooperate with government programmes and in 1969 was granted over $1 million for its international activities from the USA government.[69]

The United Steelworkers of America

DECISION-MAKING

Decision-making in international affairs is the prerogative of the headquarters of the union. Like many industrial unions the USWA is organised into districts and locals and the headquarters is referred to as "the international" (reflecting the inclusion of Canadian districts within the union). Studies of the government of the USWA have shown it to be highly centralised with a

[68] *Survey of the Alliance for Progress, Labor Policies and Programs*, p. 6.
[69] See "With $112 Million AID Grant AFL-CIO Hikes World Effort to Form 'Free Trade Unions,'" *International Herald Tribune*, April 24, 1969, p. 2.

minimal rank-and-file participation in major decisions.[70] In particular the bi-annual convention has been described as largely ineffectual as a policy-making or monitoring body.

The International Executive Board and the President and his staff thus represent the most important participants in decision-making. The Executive Board, composed of twenty-nine district directors (originally thirty-nine) was intended to be a "checkrein" on the President but as a result of a complicated voting procedure and some constitutional provisions the President and his staff can normally prevail over the Board.[71]

The President, who is elected by popular vote of union members, thus emerges as the most powerful officer of the union with little possibility of being checked by either the Convention or the Board. He can, however, lose the presidential election, as did President David J. McDonald in 1964.

For international affairs it is clear that decision-making is centred on the President. Whether or not he permits his appointed staff (or elected Vice-President) to play an important role would be a matter of personal inclination. Under President Phillip Murray, much of the international work was delegated to his Secretary-Treasurer, David J. McDonald. When McDonald became President an International Affairs Department was created, and the staff of this department (and especially the Director of International Affairs) has been involved in most of the union's international activity.

[70] See L. Ulman, *The Government of the Steel Workers' Union*, New York, 1962; and the same author's "Influences on the Economic Environment on the Structure of the Steel Workers' Union," *Proceedings of the 14th Annual Industrial Relations Research Association*, New York, 1961, pp. 227–37.
[71] *Ibid.*, pp. 122–23.

DEVELOPMENT OF INTERNATIONAL POLICY

As would be expected in the case of an individual union rather than a national centre, there was no development of policy specifically on less-developed countries. Attitudes and policies on this issue were developed in a framework of interest in general issues of international affairs.

The USWA was created out of the Steel Workers' Organizing Committee (SWOC) which began operations in the mid 1930s. The SWOC continued to be an active organising force until the formal creation of the USWA and Phillip Murray, leader of the SWOC, became President of the CIO in 1940, two years before the first constitutional convention of the USWA.[72]

The first formal interest in international affairs shown by the organisation's leaders reflected the period of the creation of the USWA during World War II. Resolutions at the 1942 convention pledged support to China, Soviet Union, and Great Britain,[73] argued for the creation of a second front against the Axis powers, and called upon the CIO to work towards securing cooperation between American labour and "trade unions of the United Nations, including Latin American nations."[74]

Two years later in the Officers Report to the Convention of 1944, it was recorded that the organisation

[72] See W. Galenson, "The Unionization of the American Steel Industry," *International Review of Social History*, Vol. 1, Part 1, 1956, pp. 9–40.
[73] USWA: *Proceedings of 1st Constitutional Convention, 1942*, p. 190.
[74] *Ibid.*, p. 149.

would work for "defeating reaction" and "establishing a fuller and better life throughout the world."[75] No mention of colonial territories or less-developed countries was made although it was suggested that wartime conditions made it necessary to "get to know the workers in other countries."[76] In December 1942 Secretary-Treasurer McDonald went to Cuba "to pay respects to and to participate in the deliberations of the Cuban Federation of Labour."[77] In the same period the USWA moved into collaboration with the USA Government international services and agencies. In August and September of 1943, McDonald again went to Latin America as a labour representative sent by the "US Office of Coordination of Latin America." In this capacity he visited almost all the countries of "Latin and South America" and spoke with "the labor leaders of thousands of workers in those countries, discussing common problems and securing information for guidance of our own government and our own labor movement."[78] As a CIO delegate, McDonald also attended (as did George Meany of the AF of L) an inter-government conference—the Inter-American Conference—in 1945.[79]

The dual position of Murray as President of the USWA and CIO brought the union into direct contact with the WFTU when the CIO participated in its founding in 1945. The USWA documents from 1945 onwards reveal a greater concern for the broader issues of international affairs. In 1945 Murray wrote a signed editorial in *Steel*

[75] USWA: *Proceedings of 2nd Constitutional Convention, 1944*, p. 84.
[76] *Ibid.*
[77] *Ibid.*
[78] *Ibid.*
[79] McDonald's visits to Latin America and the Caribbean for the CIO were made as a result of his membership of the CIO Latin-Affairs Committee. See CIO: *Proceedings of 12th Constitutional Convention, 1950*, p. 203.

Labor[80] in praise of the allied "big three" talks and for the first time in 1946 the Convention report contained a special section on "International Labor Cooperation." Significantly it expressed support for the work of the United Nations Rehabilitation and Relief Association and claimed that it was "but natural for organized labor to pledge all effort to have the United Nations take proper steps to secure the colonial peoples their just demand for self-determination and self-government."[81] Fourteen locals also submitted a resolution asking for the "destruction of the social and economic aspects of fascism in Germany and Japan" and that "encouragement and assistance be given to the liberated and colonial peoples to exercise the right for self-determination and to build their own democracies."[82]

The association of the CIO with the USSR unions in WFTU did not deter both Murray and McDonald from making anti-communist speeches from 1946 onwards. McDonald "blasted" communists in September 1946[83] and Murray showed that it was not only directed at American communists: "We've got no more use for any damn Communists coming over here meddling in our affairs than you would welcome our meddling in your affairs," he told a political meeting in 1946.[84]

In 1950 a new phase of direct association between the USWA and USA Government programmes began. A long and complex resolution at the 1950 Convention argued that the "Point 4" technical assistance programme should be accompanied by minimum wages, collective bargain-

80 *Steel Labor*, March 1945, p. 54.
81 USWA: *Proceedings of 3rd Constitutional Convention, 1946*, p. 57.
82 *Ibid.*, p. 200.
83 See report, *Steel Labor*, September 1946, p. 3.
84 Speech to Conference of Progressives, as reported in *Steel Labor*, November 1946, p. 2.

ing, joint settlement of grievances which were "know-hows which our country will export to these under-developed areas."[85] The resolution stated that the USWA would work with the USA Government and unionists abroad to ensure human rights and also quoted with approval President Truman, "the old imperialism—exploitation for foreign profit—has no place in our plans—we look for the development of this program on a basis of democratic fair play with good neighbors, only this way can democracy be extended and the inroads of communism and fascism be checked."[86] The Officers Report of 1950 made no mention of international affairs despite the recent split between the WFTU and the American unions in which McDonald was personally involved.

The USWA up to 1952 was still primarily engaged in European activity in association with USA Government agencies. In 1951, two USWA unionists were in Italy with the Economic Cooperation Administration Team (later the Mutual Security Administration). One of these unionists, who left the USA in 1950, and was Italian born, stayed two years as consultant to the ICFTU-affiliated section of the Italian labour movement and was later re-assigned by the USA Government.[87]

Through the CIO and the activities of McDonald, the union had continued with its connections with Latin America. In 1951 McDonald was part of the CIO delegation at the founding of ORIT, which *Steel Labor* described as "dedicated to wiping Communist and Fascist influence from the labor movements of the Western Hemisphere."[88] Subsequent meetings of ORIT were at-

[85] USWA: *Proceedings of 5th Constitutional Convention, 1950*, p. 203.

[86] *Ibid.*

[87] *Steel Labor*, December 1951, p. 1; and May 1952, p. 9.

[88] *Steel Labor*, February 1951, p. 4.

tended by a USWA representative, often Zonarich. In 1952 the USWA began to show greater interest in Latin America and especially in the metals mining industries. In July 1952 a staff representative of the USWA, representing the CIO, visited the Chile copper mining areas.[89]

In late 1952 Phillip Murray died and was succeeded by his Secretary-Treasurer, McDonald, who was at that time a member of the General Council of the ICFTU and the International and Latin Affairs Committee of the CIO. Initially, McDonald did not reflect, in the organisation, his already considerable involvement in international affairs; his first major address at an installation ceremony in March 1953 made only passing reference to international affairs. This was to the opening up of iron ore fields in Venezuela and bauxite mines in Jamaica which, McDonald said, would be subject to a study by the USWA.[90]

At the 1954 Convention, however, McDonald emphasised the anti-communist nature of union foreign relations, "our representatives travel to the four corners of the world to bring this idea of American trade unionism to the people to combat communists in their lair for what they are, men without truth in their being."[91] He also related the forthcoming merger of the AF of L and the CIO to international affairs and the struggle against communism; among the advantages of the merger was that "in addition, you will have the most militant anti-communist trained personnel in the world to give leadership in the international affairs where it is so badly needed. By uniting our strength in a great united labor movement we will be able to help our country, help the poor people of the world, combat communism and

[89] S. Romualdi, *Presidents and Peons*, New York, 1968, p. 327.
[90] *Steel Labor*, April 1953, p. 6.
[91] USWA: *Proceedings of 7th Constitutional Convention, 1954*, p. 12.

be in a position to express the great American ideal of democracy which needs to be resounded throughout the world."[92] From 1954, McDonald continued to express the formal policy of the USWA in terms of anti-communism[93] although his definitions of communism sometimes departed from the conventional, as for example, in an address to businessmen, "we have but to look at what happened to the trade union movement under Mussolini in Italy—there it was called Fascism or in Germany under Hitler, there it was called Nazism but in both cases it was Marxism. The despotic rulers of the Soviet Union call it Communism."[94] McDonald had had dealings with designated communists at both the domestic and international level. He was present, as a member of the USA delegation, at the WFTU meeting at which the British and USA delegates walked out and which marked the end of their affiliation with WFTU and the creation of the ICFTU. He was also, with Zonarich, active in working against the International Union of Mine, Mill and Smelter Workers when that union was charged with being communist dominated.[95]

At the 1954 USWA Convention, a resolution was passed mandating McDonald to continue his efforts to promote international prosperity as "the well-being of our members cannot be separated from the economic

[92] *Steel Labor*, October 1954, p. 2.

[93] For McDonald's general views on communism see G. Kelly and E. Beachler, *Man of Steel: the Story of David J. McDonald*, New York, 1954.

[94] D. McDonald, *Labor's Long Range Objectives, Address Before American Management Association, General Conference, San Francisco, California, January 25, 1956*, published by United Steelworkers of America, Pittsburgh, 1956, p. 5.

[95] V. Jensen, *Nonferrous Metals Industry Unionism 1932–1954*, Ithaca, New York, 1954, pp. 340 and 237.

security of our fellow workers in other lands."[96] McDonald was also told to continue to participate in both "governmental and non-governmental phases of our international activity."[97] In the same year, and for the first time, the Officers Report had a special section on the "International Level" which detailed some of the USWA activities in the Caribbean and which reflected McDonald's establishment of an International Department in 1953.

The International Department's first Director was Elmer Cope, who had been the director in the colonial division of the WFTU secretariat and substitute member for Murray in the ICFTU. The reports of the Department given at the conventions refer mainly to the Caribbean programme, the international aspects of metal trading and relations with the ICFTU and IMF.

The USWA financial statements never made provision for distinguishing expenses incurred in international activities until 1961 and in that year the expenditure was approximately $35,000 on salaries and expenses. Previous to this the expenses of international activities had been included in the Research Department, which had a salary and expense budget ranging from approximately $61,000 in 1953 to over $100,000 in 1958. It was this department that Michael Manley (of the Jamaican NWU) described in 1964 as having "vast resources." The total income of the USWA has ranged from approximately $10.5 million in 1953 to $16.3 million in 1965.[98]

After the merger of the AF of L and CIO in 1955, McDonald continued as a member of the CIO International Affairs Committee, was appointed to the USA

[96] USWA: *Proceedings of 7th Constitutional Convention, 1954,* Resolution No. 4, p. 232.

[97] *Ibid.*

[98] Figures from budget reports in USAW: *Proceedings of Constitutional Conventions,* bi-annual 1953–65.

Government Commission on Foreign Economic Policy and in 1955 was placed on the advisory committee of the USA Government Export-Import Bank. He was also co-head of a department of the International Metalworkers Federation.

The substance of the USWA foreign activities and policy were summarised in 1962 by the Director of International Affairs, Meyer Bernstein, who succeeded Cope in 1958. He said the USWA had one of the most intensive international affairs programmes to be found in the United States and that there were three sections of it, first, "a policy of chasing our employers abroad" by contacting the local union involved to help it negotiate with the corporation, second, cooperation with the ICFTU and the IMF "in order to play our part in the great struggle that is now taking place between the forces of democracy and the forces of communism," and third, "a kind of international diplomatic program of our own in order to extend and increase democracy in other parts of the world."[99]

If the programmes in which the USWA had been directly associated with government agencies had been mentioned, this would have been an adequate review of the formal policy and its means of execution which have been advocated since the early 1950s. The President changed in 1965 and the new President, I. W. Abel, made no mention of international affairs or USWA foreign policy in his inaugural address and there has been no indication of a radical departure from the policy outlined by the Director of International Affairs in 1962.[100]

[99] USWA: *Proceedings of 11th Constitutional Convention, 1962*, p. 373.

[100] In 1968, seven men with USWA connections were working on labour projects in Africa; see "Our Men in Africa," *Steel Labor*, February 1968, p. 9.

Part II

A Specific Case: Jamaica

CHAPTER V

THE ISLAND OF JAMAICA

This chapter supplies brief descriptions of the social, cultural, and economic backgrounds. The cultural background is of particular importance as it determined both the nature of Jamaican unions as well as the form and strength of foreign elements involved.

Geography

Jamaica is an island of approximately 4.5 thousand square miles with a population, in 1967, approaching two million. It is tropical, having a mean annual temperature of 80° F and a mean annual rainfall of 77 inches at Kingston, the capital.[1] The Caribbean islands are geologically the tops of a submerged mountain range and Jamaica is therefore a mountainous island with 45 per cent of its area described as arable or pasture land.

[1] Unless otherwise stated, statistics in this chapter are taken from Jamaican Government publications, in particular, *Annual Abstract of Statistics*, 1952–67.

Jamaica was thought to be poorly endowed with natural resources, for mineral wealth, important to pre-twentieth-century Europe and the USA, was lacking. The area's greatest resource—sunshine—has not been industrially exploited until recently, possibly because the temperate-climate orientation of world technology has not developed efficient energy transformation systems using the sun as a power source. For other reasons the sea also has only recently been considered as an important economic resource.

Jamaica's natural resource position changed abruptly in the early 1940s, when bauxite, the basic ore for the production of aluminium, was discovered and exploited. Jamaican bauxite is a rich and desirable variety, originally known as the terra rosa type but now is often called Jamaican-type ore.[2] By 1965, Jamaica was supplying over 23 per cent of total world demand for bauxite of all types and also had the third highest estimated reserves in the world.[3] Apart from bauxite, there are some deposits of gypsum which have also been exploited.

The soil of Jamaica has been sufficiently productive to support both tropical-product plantations as well as diversified farming.

INTERNATIONAL POSITION

Its size and population places Jamaica among the smallest of states. The history of the Caribbean area has shown, however, that serious international conflicts can

[2] See Alcan Jamaica Limited: *Jamaican Achievement*, no date (1962?), pp. 3 and 4.

[3] US Department of the Interior: *Mineral Yearbook 1965*, Vol. IV, Area Reports-International, p. 126.

arise from political events in states similar in size to Jamaica.

To major world powers, the geographic strategic importance of Jamaica has been derived from its position in relation to Cuba, the USA, the sea route from Cuba to Latin America, the Spanish Caribbean and the Panama Canal.

To Spain, in the sixteenth century, which was the first era of European colonial rule, the island's prime importance was as a supply base for sorties against Cuba and the American mainland. After these were successful its importance declined, being used only as a provisioning stop for treasure ships returning to Spain via Cuba from Cartagena, Colombia.[4]

To the British, at a later date, the island was important as a refuge for the famed privateers, who constantly harassed the Spanish shipping. For the British also, Jamaica was a useful outpost in the Spanish Caribbean, being only eight hundred miles from the nearest major English-speaking island yet it is only ninety miles from Cuba.

The completion of the Panama Canal in 1914 once again renewed the strategic importance of Jamaica. It is the nearest Caribbean island to the Canal and shipping approaching from the Atlantic must use either the Windward Passage between Cuba and Hispaniola and pass within a hundred miles of Jamaica or the Mona Passage between Hispaniola and Puerto Rico and pass within two hundred miles of Jamaica.

In particular, the Canal awakened the strategic interest of the USA, the basis of which was well expressed by Henry L. Stimson in 1927, when he claimed that the USA had a special interest in ". . . those nations whose territory lies adjacent to and in a naval sense

[4] C. V. Black, *History of Jamaica,* Glasgow, 1958, p. 35.

commands the great sea route from our eastern and western states via the Panama Canal. This situation does not arise out of the Monroe Doctrine but out of certain broad principles of self-defense which govern the policy of all nations which are in any way dependent upon the sea."[5]

USA protection of the Canal and the desire for naval bases nearer Latin America were two causes of the 1941 agreement to lease bases from Britain in the British Caribbean. The USA base in Jamaica was closed in 1962 but, despite the increased use of air power, the area has not diminished in general strategic importance; as a military expert noted in 1967: "Naval control of the Windward Passage, the Mona Passage, and the Panama Canal means control of the passage of supplies, troops, munitions and strategic materials to the rest of Latin America, to Europe and Asia and between North and South America."[6] His conclusion was that ". . . it is important that this strategic area remain in the hands of the Free World as North, South and Central America depend so much on it."[7]

The discovery and exploitation of bauxite in Jamaica, Surinam, and Haiti as well as oil in Trinidad has also increased strategic interest in the Caribbean area. The strategic importance of bauxite arises from the important place that aluminium has in wars and war production.[8]

[5] H. Stimson, *American Policy in Nicaragua*, New York, 1927, pp. 104–11, quoted in G. Pendle, *A History of Latin America*, Harmondsworth, 1963, p. 179.

[6] R. Del Mar, "Strategic Characteristics of the Caribbean," in C. Wilgus, ed., *The Caribbean: Its Hemispheric Role*, Gainsville, Florida, 1967, p. 156.

[7] *Ibid.*, p. 160.

[8] See W. Voskuil, "Mineral Resources and Industries of the Caribbean Area" in C. Wilgus, ed., *The Caribbean: Natural Resources*, Gainsville, Florida, 1961, pp. 130–42; and H. Anderson, *Aluminum for Defense and Prosperity*, Washington Public Affairs Institute, Washington, D.C., 1951.

History

The first European landing in Jamaica was made by Columbus in 1494, and as a result it was first colonised by Spain. The Spanish rule was replaced by British rule in 1660, which remained, in various forms, for over three hundred years until formal independence in 1962.

SOCIAL HISTORY

The social history of the island is closely associated with major economic innovations. The general settlement of Jamaica began with the coming of sugar plantations and as white indentured labour, criminal deportees, and kidnapped Europeans became more difficult to procure, slaves, mainly from West Africa, were imported. Thus, even by 1673, the racial composition of the population was said to be 7700 white and 9500 black.[9] The island was never a settler colony and the African slaves always outnumbered the white population.

The plantation became the basic form of economic and social organisation and exists in a reduced form (at least economically) to the present day. The slaves never succumbed completely to their masters and there were several major, and certainly numerous small and unrecorded, slave insurrections. This situation caused the predominant emotion felt by planters and managers to be one of fear.[10]

[9] J. Parry and P. Sherlock, *A Short History of the West Indies*, London, 1957, p. 69.
[10] *Ibid.*, p. 73.

At later dates, Indian and Chinese indentured labourers came to the island, as did Syrian traders, to add to the already existing minority groups of Europeans and Jews. But the African population and the subsequent mulatto population together have remained numerically preponderant.

Other salient factors concerning the social history of Jamaica, especially in the twentieth century, will emerge in the examination and analysis of the trade unions. For the purposes of this study, the social history preceding the twentieth century can almost be viewed as a succession of events which eventually resulted, in the late 1930s, in sufficient numbers of the population being free and prepared to join, or at least associate, with groups and organisations calling themselves trade unions. In this context the most important event was the final and formal emancipation of the slaves in 1838. Although no immediate improvement in living conditions resulted from this emancipation it was a necessary step in the creation of a population which could, exactly one hundred years later, be politically organised.

GOVERNMENT AND POLITICS

From the standpoint of government, the period before the twentieth century saw the establishment of semi-representative government, that is, government to some extent in the hands of Jamaican residents. It should not be concluded, however, that the bulk of the population was thus involved, for semi-representative government meant representation of the planters and the economic elite of the island, in short, representation of the "plantocracy," rather than of workers and peasants.[11]

The conditions in Jamaica and its geographic relationship to the metropolitan state had always allowed local power holders to seize a measure of freedom from colonial rule. But it was not until 1938 that pressures began for the local rulers to share power with other less-powerful sections of the population. In 1938, economic conditions in the West Indies, the world political situation, the weakness of the metropolitan power and the forcefulness of leaders and population of Jamaica started a process of substantial constitutional change.[12] In rapid succession, compared with other governmental reforms, the island acquired, first, the end of the Crown Colony status, second, internal self-government, and, third, complete formal independence.

The Crown Colony period, which had lasted in various forms for over one hundred years, was characterised by a partially elected and partially nominated legislature. This system was brought to an end with the new constitution of November 20, 1944, which provided for two chambers of the legislature—the House of Representatives and the Legislative Council, the former to have thirty-two members elected on a full adult suffrage basis.

The Constitution of 1944, still left the Governor and an appointed Council with considerable administrative and policy power. This situation came to an end with full internal self-government of the island which was officially achieved in 1959 and left Jamaica with absolute domestic control but with foreign affairs still in the hands of the British.

[11] See A. Burns, *History of the British West Indies*, London, 1965, p. 653.
[12] *Ibid.*, p. 715.

Before Jamaica acquired full political independence, the British Government attempted to launch the Federation of the West Indies. Plans for the West Indian federation were discussed during the 1940s and continued until 1958 when the Federal Government was established and located in Trinidad. But the central government structure was the result of many compromises, was weak in power and finance, and, for a variety of reasons, received less than widespread support from the composite territories.[13] In 1961 a referendum on whether Jamaica should stay in the federation was held in Jamaica and the majority of the electorate voted for Sir Alexander Bustamante, who had identified himself with the anti-federation position. As a consequence Jamaica withdrew from the federation and soon after it was dissolved.[14] Jamaica had been the largest unit in the federation and its withdrawal, plus some already existing divisive forces in the East Caribbean, meant that the federal goal could no longer be pursued. The causes of the failure of the federation, however, are much deeper than constitutional and political rivalries and lie to some extent in the economic, cultural, and personality differences of the various units, which the metropolitan powers basically ignored.

The federation, during its short life, did not have an appreciable impact on the administrative aspects of the Jamaican Government. The established ministries or departments remained intact despite the formal centre of power in Trinidad. The collapse of the federation meant that Jamaica and Trinidad and Tobago became individually independent and Jamaica thus came into formal control of domestic and foreign affairs as a fully accredited nation state in August 1962.

[13] P. Sherlock, *West Indies*, London, 1966, pp. 88–89.
[14] See H. Mitchell, *Europe in the Caribbean*, Stanford, 1963, pp. 69–71.

POLITICAL PARTIES

Among the events of 1938 was the founding of the first formally organised and so-named political party in Jamaica, the People's National Party (PNP), which was founded with British Labour Party and left wing support and led by Jamaican barrister Norman Washington Manley. Three years later the Jamaica Labour Party (JLP) was formally established by Alexander Bustamante on the basis of his already existing organisation, the Bustamante Industrial Trade Union.

The initials JLP and PNP, as well as the names Bustamante and Manley, were to become the verbal framework of Jamaican politics from that time to the present. To attempt to describe the parties in European ideological terms would be in error, but it can be said that, at least in the earlier period, the leaders of the PNP expressed an adherence to the principles of British Fabian Socialism.[15] Both parties eventually became closely bound to trade unions.

Since the end of the Crown Colony period, there have been six general elections. In the first two in 1944 and 1949, Bustamante and the JLP were successful but in 1955 and 1959, Manley and the PNP were successful. The last two general elections in 1962 and 1967 were again won by the JLP, although, since 1965, Bustamante had been in semi-retirement owing to ill-health.

These shifts in power of the union-associated parties affected the growth, structure, and policies of trade unions substantially.

[15] See M. Ayearst, *The British West Indies*, New York, 1960, p. 71.

Economy

Jamaica has five identifiable divisions of its economy: first, tropical produce for export; second, smallholdings and farms for production of domestically consumed agricultural produce; third, the more recent manufacturing for import substitution and export; fourth, extraction and processing of bauxite; and fifth, the tourist industry.

While not strictly accurate, the first two divisions may be described as the traditional sector and the remainder as the modern sector.

THE TRADITIONAL SECTOR

The traditional sector of the Jamaican economy is largely associated with sugar plantations and the growing of sugar cane in general. At the end of the nineteenth century, bananas were exported to the USA, and thus sugar and bananas became the two main tropical products for export. The problems these industries face are well known–fluctuating world demand, production and prices,[16] changes in preferential policies,[17] and competi-

[16] See A. McIntyre, "De-Colonisation and Trade Policy in the West Indies," in F. M. Andic and T. G. Mathews, *The Caribbean in Transition*, Institute of Caribbean Studies, Puerto Rico, 1965, pp. 189–212.

[17] See G. Beckford, "The Growth of Major Tropical Export Crop Industries," *Social and Economic Studies*, Vol. 13, No. 4, 1964, pp. 413–30.

tion from countries with mechanised production techniques.

The sugar industry is one of the most important employers on the island and is organised in plantations, commercial and small cane farms. In the mid-1940s, commercial and small cane farmers accounted for 30 per cent of production but this had risen to approximately 50 per cent in 1968. The other 50 per cent is produced by the large estates which also own the mills for processing both the estate and farm cane.[18]

Food production from farms and peasant holdings for domestic consumption is not sufficient for domestic needs and has shown very little growth in the past thirty years.

The traditional sector of the economy, however, still employs and supports most people on the island, even though in 1965 it accounted for only approximately 12 per cent of gross domestic product.

THE MODERN SECTOR

The Jamaican industrial growth since 1950 has been widely publicised. The spectacular nature of this growth, 7.2 per cent increase in gross domestic product per annum 1950–65, has usually been described in words similar to those of Balogh in a report to the Jamaican Prime Minister, Manley, in 1962: "The record of the Jamaican economy over the last ten years, but more especially since 1956, has been remarkable. Apart from Japan and Puerto Rico it is certainly unparalleled in any of the less-developed areas of the world. Not only did per capita income approximately double in the

[18] Financial Times Survey of Jamaica, "New Agreements Brighten Outlook for Sugar," *Financial Times*, January 1, 1969, p. 1.

decade but, and what is most impressive, gross fixed capital investment in terms of the gross national product increased from 9 per cent in 1950 to well over 20 per cent in 1956 . . ."[19] Most general works on Jamaica report this record and make only passing reference to the traditional sector.[20]

Rapid growth, reflected in gross national product figures, has arisen mainly from manufacturing and the bauxite-alumina industry. In 1968 there were 1382 factories in production and during the last sixteen years the Jamaica Industrial Development Corporation brought 178 "new industries to the island."[21] Bauxite mining began in the middle 1940s and alumina production started in 1952. By 1965 they together accounted for nearly 10 per cent of gross domestic product.

Tourism has also shown a rapid increase, especially since the middle 1950s and, although adding some impetus to the construction industry, it is most usually noted as a large earner of foreign exchange.[22] It is rarely pointed out, however, that the tourist industry absorbs approximately 40 per cent of its own foreign exchange earnings to service its almost exclusively luxury trade.[23]

The record of growth in the modern sector of the Jamaican economy appears impressive but it can be shown that over shorter time periods, the growth rate has fluctuated widely and is now definitely showing a

[19] T. Balogh, *The Economics of Poverty*, London, 1966, p. 293.
[20] See, for example, US Department of Labor: *Labor Law and Practice in Jamaica*, Washington, 1967, pp. 3–4; and H. Mitchell, *Caribbean Patterns*, London, 1967, pp. 133–42.
[21] *Financial Times Survey of Jamaica*, p. 15.
[22] See, for example, "IFC Investment in Jamaica," *International Financial News Survey*, International Monetary Fund, Vol. XX, No. 44, November 8, 1968, pp. 379–80.
[23] O. Jefferson, "Some Aspects of the Post-War Economic Development of Jamaica," *New World Quarterly*, Vol. III, No. 3, High Season, 1967, pp. 8–9.

decline.[24] More important, however, is that it has had very little effect on employment.

INTERNATIONAL ECONOMIC ASPECTS

Jamaica's principal exports have traditionally been sugar and associated products and tropical agricultural produce. This pattern was broken in 1957 when bauxite-alumina replaced sugar products as the major export and soon after that bauxite-alumina exports became larger than total agricultural exports. Tourism from North America supplied the impetus to start a tourist industry in the late 1940s and it has grown rapidly, mostly between 1955 and 1962. Since 1963 some manufactured goods have also been exported.

Apart from changes in the composition of Jamaican international trade during the period 1938–67, there has been a substantial change in the direction of trade. The principal trading partner of Jamaica had been Britain and in 1938 Britain took nearly 60 per cent of Jamaican exports, mainly in sugar, rum, and bananas. In 1947 the USA took less than 4 per cent of exports while Britain took 75 per cent, but eight years later exports to the USA began to increase and by 1959 equaled those to Britain. In 1961 the USA, for the first time, took more Jamaican exports than Britain and by 1965 absorbed 31 per cent of total exports, mainly in bauxite, but also in sugar, rum, and other products. Canada doubled its imports of Jamaican produce between 1951 and 1955 (largely attributed to alumina) and by 1965 the USA, Britain, and Canada together took a total of 81 per cent of exports. The USA and Britain also changed places in

[24] *Ibid.*, p. 2.

regards to Jamaica's imports, with the USA becoming Jamaica's major supplier in 1962 and Britain and Canada sharing second and third place, respectively.

Investment has followed a similar pattern to external trade. Direct investment was traditionally from Britain into the sugar industry, transport, and communications. This situation existed until the late 1940s when investments from the USA and Canada started in the mining and utility industries.

From 1950 the USA became a major supplier of capital, particularly to the new mining and tourist industries, but also in light manufacturing and service industries.

POPULATION, LABOUR, AND WORK

Two complete censuses have been taken of the island, one in 1943 and one in 1960, which, together with sample surveys taken in 1957, provide good indicators for the period of interest for this study.

In 1943 the population of Jamaica was 1,237,000; in 1956, 1,579,000; and in 1967 it was approaching two millions. Thus the population has grown almost 40 per cent since 1943.

This was in spite of large-scale emigration. Before World War II, Jamaicans had emigrated generally to the USA, Cuba, and, at an earlier date, Panama but after the war Britain replaced the USA as the principal country to which Jamaicans emigrated. Beginning with approximately 2000 immigrants in 1953, by 1955 this figure had risen to 17,000 per year and reached a peak in 1961 of 39,000 but declined rapidly thereafter owing to legislative action in Britain. During the period 1953–65 over 200,000 Jamaicans left the island for Britain.

Seasonal migration as farm workers to the USA began at the beginning of the century and continued until a peak was reached during World War II, but has since declined.

The population density of Jamaica has, since 1938, always been above 300 persons per square mile, making it among the most densely populated states in the world. The bulk of Jamaican people live in areas which can be described as rural, thus in 1960, 67 per cent lived in in rural areas. In 1938 this proportion would have been higher because the period 1943 to 1960 has shown a marked increase in the numbers of people living in urban areas, especially Kingston and its environs, where the population doubled during the period. This trend continues and the Kingston area now houses over 20 per cent of the total population.

The population of the island is likely to grow even more rapidly now that emigration has basically ceased and the birthrate has risen. In 1964 the birthrate was 3.98 per cent and in 1967 over 40 per cent of the population was under fifteen years of age.

For a study involving analysis of trade unions, labour force, and occupation distribution, statistics are of prime importance. In the case of Jamaica these are even more important because the publicity surrounding the modern sector and high per capita income often hides the fact that the bulk of the people live in sectors of the economy which figure only marginally in gross domestic product and national income statistics.

Labour force statistics are complicated and must always be treated with caution, but various censuses have shown a classifiable labour force (defined as persons over fourteen years old employed or unemployed) of approximately 500,000 in 1943, 600,000 in 1960, and in

1968 unofficially estimated at 700,000.[25] Of this labour force the wage-earning population has been estimated at 266,000 in 1938; 284,000 in 1943; 319,000 in 1950; and 357,000 in 1960.

The occupational distribution of the labour force has created statistical difficulties owing to the changes in the number of women and unpaid family workers working in agriculture.[26] It can be said with some certainty, however, that throughout the period 1938–67 the number of people engaged in agriculture as wage-earners or own-account farmers has ranged from 50 per cent of the labour force in 1938 to 40 per cent in 1967. The important fact emerges that such a high percentage of the labour force in agriculture means that the vast majority of the population is dependent in some form or other on an agricultural income. Wage-earners in agriculture (agricultural labourers and sugar plantation workers) represent approximately 40 to 50 per cent of the total agricultural labour force which, throughout the period, has between 100,000 and 125,000 workers.

In 1943, 12 per cent of the labour force was employed in manufacturing, that is, approximately 59,000 workers, and this rose to only 15 per cent in 1960, or approximately 89,000. Thus during the period of greatest growth of the Jamaican economy, less than 30,000 new jobs were created in the modern sector. The reasons for this are clear. Bauxite mining, for example, is highly mechanised and has never employed more than 5000 workers.

[25] "Growing Number of Unemployed," *Financial Times Survey of Jamaica*, p. 17 (the labour force has not grown at a similar rate to the population owing to migration and changes in age structure).

[26] For a critical examination of government labour force statistics see G. Cumper, "A Comparison of Statistical Data on the Jamaican Labour Force 1953–1961" (article in fact covers 1943–1961), *Social and Economic Studies*, Vol. 13, No. 4, December 1964, pp. 430–39.

It has been calculated that the 149 factories established during fourteen years of government incentive programmes have resulted in approximately 9000 jobs, less than is needed to absorb one year of natural growth of the labour force.[27] When Norman Manley was Prime Minister he noted that it required £2000 of outside capital to create one job.[28]

These problems are reflected in unemployment even though accurate statistics are lacking. The census of 1943 indicated an unemployment ratio of 25 per cent of the labour force; in 1952, between 15 and 20 per cent; in 1960, 13 per cent, and in 1968, approximately 16 per cent but unofficial estimates still put it as high as 25 per cent.[29] These percentages also do not take into account under-employment, which is considerable in the traditional sector.

While it would be wrong to consider unemployment in Jamaica as having the same individual effects as in an industrial European country, it nevertheless still precipitates social and economic disruption and personal hardship.[30]

WAGE AND INCOME DISTRIBUTION

Income and wage rates in Jamaica illustrate in monetary terms the several severe inequalities which characterise the society: inequality between rich and poor, between

[27] O. Jefferson, "Some Aspects of the Post-War Economic Development of Jamaica," p. 4.
[28] C. Rickards and F. Henriques, "The English Speaking West Indies," in C. Veliz, *Latin America and the Caribbean—a Handbook*, London, 1968, p. 33.
[29] US Department of Labor: *Labor Law and Practice in Jamaica*, *op. cit.*, p. 140.
[30] See W. Maunder, *Employment in an Underdeveloped Area: a Sample Survey of Kingston, Jamaica*, New Haven, 1960, p. 163.

agricultural and urban workers, between workers in mining and other industries, and, to some extent, between racial groups.

Jamaican per capita income has risen steadily since 1938 when it was £17 per annum; in 1942 it was £27.1; in 1955, £85.2; and in 1961, £131.4. Thus, it is among the less-developed countries with the highest per capita income. However, the only survey of income distribution in Jamaica of any significance was completed in 1958 and the researchers concluded that: "Measuring the inequality of incomes of households before tax in Jamaica, we found that the index of concentration based on the Lorenz Curve is 53, which ranks the island among the countries with the highest recorded rate of inequality of incomes."[31] The survey found that 50 per cent of households received about 13 per cent of measured income, while the top 5 per cent received 30 per cent of income, and that, on the average, households in the highest group have 120 times as much income as those in the lowest group.[32]

Income inequality is even greater in the rural areas than in the urban areas. Balogh noted in his report to the Jamaican Prime Minister that, "agricultural income distribution is as unequal as in almost all the Caribbean and Latin American countries: 5 per cent of the farmers accounting for 60 per cent of the acreage, while 83 per cent of the farmers account for less than a quarter of the total income."[33]

The discrepancy between rural and urban incomes is also large and the survey found that an urban household received 2.25 times that of a rural household,[34] a

[31] A. Ahiram, "Income Distribution in Jamaica 1958," *Social and Economic Studies,* Vol. 13, No. 3, September 1964, p. 337.
[32] *Ibid.*
[33] T. Balogh, *The Economics of Poverty,* p. 298.
[34] A. Ahiram, "Income Distribution in Jamaica 1958," p. 335.

situation which caused Balogh to comment: "The discrepancy between rural farmers and urban industrial incomes, shocking as it is already, is growing."[35] An economist at the University of the West Indies estimates that per capita income in the agricultural sector is about "one fifth of that prevailing in the rest of the economy."[36]

Apart from the differences between rural and industrial incomes there are also wide differences between different industries. The bauxite-alumina industry is the most noticeable example where wage rates for the same occupations are often two or three times those in other industries.[37]

The history of Jamaican trade unionism and the foreign involvements in it must thus be set in a period of economic turbulence. During the period an industrial sector was created, the USA replaced Britain as the major trading partner and investor, population, urbanisation, and income inequality grew, unemployment remained high, and agricultural income remained low. The changes in the labour movement and foreign involvements were sometimes a function of these changes.

Culture

It has been noted above that to understand the nature and functions of social organisations it is necessary to understand the socio-cultural complex in which they

[35] T. Balogh, *The Economics of Poverty,* p. 298.
[36] O. Jefferson, "Some Aspects of the Post-War Economic Development of Jamaica," p. 2.
[37] See H. Brewster, "Wage, Price and Productivity Relations in Jamaica, 1957–62," *Social and Economic Studies,* Vol. 17, No. 2, June 1968, pp. 107–32.

are found. A knowledge of the cultural patterns which exist in Jamaica is essential to subsequent analysis of trade unions and foreign involvements in them. For this study the most important factor is the plural cultural situation which exists in Jamaica.

Furnival was one of the first scholars to note the phenomena of plural societies which existed in the colonial situation and to relate its importance to economic development. Examining the position in Burma, he noted that "the obvious and outstanding result of contact between East and West has been the evolution of the plural society . . ." which he described as "different sections of the community living side by side but separately, within the same political unit."[38]

Many commentators on Jamaica, observing the apparent dualism of the society, have attempted to describe it in class or elite/mass terms. The Marxist notion of class clearly has some bearing on the Jamaican situation but Marx saw cultural and life-style differences arising exclusively from economic conditions. In Jamaica the divisions have arisen more from a slave and colonial experience[39] and the consequential imitation, by one section of the society, of the metropolitan culture which had been developed in relation to a vastly different environment. So it is, for example, that even the most basic communicative device—language—separates the Jamaicans; thus a West Indian linguistic expert can say: "In Jamaica, the language of uneducated rural peasants

[38] J. Furnival, *Colonial Policy and Practice, op. cit.*, pp. 304 and 305; pluralism is considered as merely a stage in economic growth in M. Harg, "Social and Cultural Pluralism as a Concept in the Social Systems Analysis," *American Journal of Sociology*, Vol. 73, No. 3, November 1967, pp. 294–304.

[39] For the historical development of the two cultures, see O. Patterson, *The Sociology of Slavery: an Analysis of the Origins, Development and Structure of Negro Slave Society in Jamaica*, London, 1967, and especially conclusions on pp. 286–87.

is not mutually intelligible with that of the elite; and the general mass of the urban population can only communicate efficiently with the elite on a very superficial level."[40]

For these reasons it is not sufficient to analyse Jamaican society exclusively in terms of class. An elite-mass division may be better but it can lead to confusing images derived from the notion of industrial society "establishments" which would not be applicable to Jamaica.

The factors which mark off the divisions in Jamaican society are ones which are more usually associated with cultural differences and therefore this analysis will be based on cultures rather than on classes or elites. This does not exclude the divisions created by income or occupation but rather emphasises that the divisions are greater and deeper than these.

The cultural duality of Jamaica is reflected by the general observation of scholars and commentators concerning the "twoness" of Jamaica. The phrases "two faces," "two worlds," "two cultures," and "two nations" appear in almost every published work, academic or otherwise, about Jamaica.[41] West Indian expatriate au-

[40] M. Alleyne, "Communication Between the Elite and the Masses," in *Caribbean Symposium*, pp. 12–19.

[41] See Curtin, Philip C., *Two Jamaicas*, Harvard University Press, Cambridge, Mass., 1955; C. McGlashan, "The Two Jamaicas," *The Observer*, November 23, 1969, p. 25; M. G. Smith, "The Plural Framework of Jamaican Society," *British Journal of Sociology*, Vol. XXII, No. 3, September 1961, pp. 249–92; and R. Glass, "Ashes of Discontent: Jamaica Today," *The Listener*, Vol. 67, No. 1714, February 1, 1962, p. 208; on the Caribbean in general see M. Smith, *The Plural Society in the British West Indies*, Berkeley, 1965; V. Rubin, *Social and Cultural Pluralism in the Caribbean*, New York, 1960; and H. McKenzie, "The Plural Society Debate, Some Comments on Recent Contributions," *Social and Economic Studies*, Vol. 15, No. 1, March 1966, pp. 53–60.

thor Naipaul, although talking mainly in terms of economic class, writes a typical comment: "So always in Jamaica one lived in two unrelated worlds, the world of the middle class—the businessman's Jamaican-grand, pseudo-American talk, the women's chatter about the wages of servants and treachery of servants—and the vaster, frightening world beyond it."[42] In the vast and frightening world beyond live over 80 per cent of Jamaicans, sometimes known as the black masses, and they represent the second culture.

Nomenclature of these cultural divisions is varied. Some authors refer to "primitive" or "cultured" divisions, others refer to "African" and "middle class" or distinguish a "European section" in the society.[43] A more meaningful terminology might be developed from the observation by West Indian intellectuals that one cultural division is characterised by a high degree of mimicry or imitation. The two cultures could then be described as the imitative culture and the evolved culture.[44] The imitative culture is so-called because it imitates behaviour patterns and purports to hold values taken from other cultures with different environments. The evolved culture is the culture which, by necessity, has had to develop a closer, more intimate, relationship with the local environment of Jamaica and conditions of life created by it.[45]

[42] V. Naipaul, *The Middle Passage*, London, 1962, p. 223.
[43] See, for example, L. Despres, "The Implications of Nationalist Politics in British Guiana for the Development of Cultural Theory," *American Anthropologist*, Vol. 66, No. 5, October 1964, pp. 1051–77.
[44] Ogburn has used the phrase "adaptive culture" but it refers to a cultural adaptation to a change in environmental conditions by one section within a culture. See W. Ogburn "The Hypothesis of Cultural Lag," in J. Parsons and associates, eds., *Theories of Society*, Vol. II, New York, 1961, p. 1271.
[45] See F. Henriques, *Family and Colour in Jamaica*, London, 1953, p. 172.

THE IMITATIVE CULTURE

The members of this cultural division represent approximately 20 per cent of the population of the island. Within it are two important sub-divisions which affect intercultural relations.

In the first sub-division the model of proper behaviour is the British one and in it are the people who often staff the most blatant of British-style organisations, the civil service, the university, the school system.[46] Entrants to this sub-division had to adopt "British attributes, such as a very exaggerated Oxford accent, a formal dark suit in the hottest weather, pompous speech and mannerisms and ultra-British names for their children and houses."[47] Here are the greatest examples of dysfunction resulting from cultural imitation; metropolitan events and circumstances are better known than local ones, education, values, life-style, clothes and architecture are temperate-industrial rather than tropical-agricultural.

In the other sub-division the imitative culture is perhaps a little more adjusted to Jamaican circumstances. The fear and violence which has historically been extant in Jamaica, the modern proximity of the USA, Miami, and inputs from Hollywood, have resulted in the highest value being placed on fast cars, guns, model girls, "style," violence, and colour. This is indeed the Jamaica of the creator of James Bond, Ian Fleming, as he makes quite clear in one of his last pieces written from his Jamaican

[46] See B. St. John Hamilton, *Problems of Administration in an Emergent Nation: a Case Study of Jamaica*, New York, 1964, pp. 135–42.

[47] K. Norris, *Jamaica, the Search for an Identity*, London, 1966, p. 10.

home.[48] It was in this sub-division of the Jamaican imitative culture that James Bond was truly born.[49]

THE EVOLVED CULTURE

This culture, in terms of numbers of participants, is the Jamaican culture, for it involves the vast majority of the people.

Many of the cultural products or practices in the evolved culture are African, African-based, or represent a syncretism between pre-slave cultures and the conditions of Jamaica.[50] The conditions of life for the urban members of the evolved culture were well described by Proudfoot in 1954: "In Kingston, Jamaica, for instance, hundreds upon hundreds of families live crowded side by side in minute shacks made of old car bodies, pieces of boarding, sometimes just cardboard. In some of the slum areas where the people are squatters upon private land there is neither water nor light nor roads. The inhabitants live mainly by crime, preying upon the life of the urban area proper."[51] A rural equivalent of these conditions also exists.

[48] M. Cargill, ed., *Ian Fleming Introduces Jamaica*, London, 1967.

[49] Interestingly, and without referring to Bond's creator's connection with Jamaica, American Black Power advocate Eldridge Cleaver sees James Bond as the last desperate attempt of the white man to project a "triumphant image" of himself. See E. Cleaver, *Soul on Ice, Selected Essays*, London, 1968, p. 70.

[50] See M. Smith, "The African Heritage in the Caribbean," and the discussion of that paper by G. Simpson and P. Hammond, both in V. Rubin, ed., *Caribbean Studies: a Symposium*, Seattle, Washington, 1960, pp. 34–53.

[51] M. Proudfoot, *Britain and the United States in the Caribbean*, London, 1954, p. 76; see also W. Maunder, *Employment in an Underdeveloped Area: a Sample Survey of Kingston, Jamaica*, p. 34.

The evolved culture is clearly made up of the poorer people, the unemployed, and the rural people, but they are distinguished from the imitative culture by more than income and locale.

THE CULTURAL DIFFERENCES

The usual distinguishing differences between cultures are language, family structure, religion, cultural practices and products, values, and behaviour patterns, and to these, in Jamaica, we can add the class-oriented divisions of colour, income, and occupation.

The language of the imitative culture is English, often of a formal, dated, and ponderous style when compared with current British and American usage. The language of the evolved culture is creole, a language evolved from African dialects and the necessity to survive in a society ruled by English-speaking people.[52] The dialect verse of Jamaican entertainer Louise Bennett, although sometimes criticised for not being pure, may be used to illustrate the difference between creole and English:

An all dem mawga smaddy weh
Dah-gawn like fat is sin,
All dem deh weh dah-fas' wid me,
Ah lef dem to dumplin![53]

The family structure of the imitative culture is formally nuclear and patriarchal while the evolved culture family

[52] G. Lamming, "The West Indian People," *New World Quarterly*, Croptime 1966, p. 66; on creole, see also F. Cassidy, *Jamaica Talk*, London, 1961, and R. Le Page and D. DeCamp, *Jamaican Creole*, London, 1960.
[53] L. Bennett, *Jamaica Labrish, Kingston*, 1966, p. 121.

structure is extended and matriarchal.[54] Legal marriage is the rule for the imitative culture but not for the evolved, consequently 70 per cent of the children born in Jamaica are "illegitimate" and are brought up by female members of the family in the extended structure.[55]

In religion, the imitative culture will profess to be Anglican but the evolved culture, true to its name, has developed various Christian sects far from their original form. One of these is Pocomania which involves the chanting of hymns, dancing, and behaviour which could not be practised or accepted in the imitative culture. Pocomania and the services of the other churches resemble the revival meetings of the southern black people in the USA.[56]

The imitative culture is largely populated by brown-skinned people who acquired a privileged position early in Jamaican history as a result of the extra attention the white residents gave the offspring of a slave woman and a white man. The evolved culture is solidly black.[57]

The cultural products (music, design, plastic art forms, literature) of the imitative culture are obviously derivative in nature, which does not mean that they are not superior to the same product in the imitated culture. For the evolved culture, cultural products are based on

[54] See W. Davenport, "The Family System in Jamaica," *Social and Economic Studies*, Vol. 10, No. 4, December 1961, pp. 420–54.

[55] See G. Clarke, *My Mother Who Fathered Me*, London, 1957.

[56] For discussion of the African, American, and European origins of religion, see G. Simpson and P. Hammond, "Discussion on M. G. Smith's African Heritage in the Caribbean," pp. 48–51.

[57] Official terminology for the ethnic composition of the Jamaican population is "coloured" and "African." In the context of the cultural background it is more accurate, however, to use the terms "brown" and "black" which are the customary usages in Jamaica and the Caribbean.

the total materials of the Jamaican environment plus a continuing connection with pre-slave cultures. Folk music of Jamaica, for example, has obvious links with the ballad songs of England but the increasing creative possibilities of instrumental groups and records has produced a modern and distinctive musical style. It is sombre, fairly heavy music with a powerful beat, at least in comparison with more well-known calypso music of Trinidad and Tobago.[58]

The final difference between the cultures is income and occupation. The imitative culture is in the highest income bracket and controls the government, business, and foreign relations. To use class and elite notions, it is the educated class and by occupation it is managerial, professional, and semi-professional. The evolved culture is of either rural or urban workers or unemployed whose vastly different life-style has been described. Thus class, colour, and culture combine to make the two Jamaicas.

INTER-CULTURAL RELATIONS—DISTANCE

Despite the demonstratable presence of two cultures which transcend class and colour, the discussion of the distances[59] and antagonisms between the two cultures inevitably involves the use of colour terms. The cause of this is that, within the society, the distance between

[58] Hear, for example, Hopeton Lewis, "Take It Easy," and Derrick Morgan and Prince Buster, "Judge Dread"; and see Peter Black, "Community Violence and Jamaican Pop Music," *Sunday Gleaner*, June 11, 1967, p. 7.

[59] The term "social distance" was used in describing "differential social attraction patterns" between two status groups in a study of a Jamaican rural town. See R. Ellis, "Social Status and Social Distance," *Sociology and Social Research* (Los Angeles), Vol. 40, 1956, p. 241.

cultures is sometimes expressed in colour terms, even though the cultures are clearly nôt totally divided on colour lines.

The imitative culture uses as its model a white society and is populated by the majority of light-skinned people; these two facts have resulted in inter-cultural relations being expressed in terms of the attainment of whiteness and the unspoken reverse—a denial of blackness. These expressions do have some physical manifestations but they are more usually the use of colour terms to describe cultural and psychological phenomena. Thus, for example, a black man wearing a collar and jacket (not the normal attire of the evolved culture) may be mocked in the streets of Kingston as a "whiteman." Whiteness is, then, a description of cultural attributes or life-style and not necessarily of skin pigmentation. It is fashionable to argue that both the physical and psychological manifestations of "white bias" no longer divided the society and that they are merely a "vestigial trade" of what they used to be.[60] Other observers continue to note its prevalence; at the National Workers Union annual meeting in 1966, the Island Supervisor spoke of the continuing colour discrimination in the island and received affirmative applause from the assembled unionists.[61] Regardless of its current potency, it was an important social fact during the major part of the period of interest for this study.

Two basic aspects of inter-cultural relations manifested themselves early in Jamaican history when the brown people of the imitative culture acquired the beginnings of managerial and political power. In discussing the replacement of an elected assembly by a nominated

[60] See comments of R. Nettleford in L. Bennett, *Jamaica Labrish*, p. 211.

[61] National Workers Union 14th Annual Meeting, October 23, 1966, Kingston (author's notes).

legislative council in 1866, an historian records that: "With a few notable exceptions the coloreds and the whites had formed an alliance to keep the blacks in their places and so to prevent the latter from eventually assuming their rightful role as the dominant group in the assembly."[62] After the rebellion of 1865, the *Morning Journal*, a newspaper for the coloured population, recorded that many were "frightened out of their propriety at the wild stories of wide-spread conspiracy and design of universal slaughter [of coloured and whites] circulated for political ends . . ."[63]

The two historical facts illustrated in these passages—alliance with the white planters (many brown people were slave owners before emancipation) and fear of the black man—have persisted in the imitative culture. In more modern times, however, the domestic political alliance with the whites has been replaced by a psychological alliance based on mimicry.

The physical desire for whiteness and its manifestations have been minutely detailed by Henriques in 1953,[64] but if the desire was to be achieved it had to be coupled with a high degree of cultural emulation of the white society. From the standpoint of inter-cultural relations this includes attitudes towards the evolved culture which range from disparagement to a psychological denial of its existence. Naipaul can thus record the remarks of a brown man on a boat going to the West Indies: "A lot of these black fellers in B.G. ain't no fools either."[65] Later the same man averred: "But a lot of

[62] G. Knox, "Political Change in Jamaica (1866–1906) and the Local Reaction to the Policies of the Crown Colony Government" in *The Caribbean in Transition*, p. 141.
[63] *Ibid.*, p. 142.
[64] F. Henriques, *Family and Colour in Jamaica.*
[65] Naipaul, *The Middle Passage*, p. 15.

you English people forget that there is a type of black man—like the Jamaican—who is an animal."[66]

These attitudes are not exclusive to the imitative culture for they are sometimes found in the evolved culture in relation to people considered to be of lower status,[67] but it is only those firmly in the imitative culture who have either the colouration or the necessary access to the white-society accoutrements to make such attitudes either physically or psychologically meaningful. It is thus that the imitative culture seeks to deny the existence of the evolved culture lest it be mistaken in any way as being part of it.

The other predominant and historically developed factor in inter-cultural relations is fear. The conditions of life in the evolved culture have frequently given rise to violence, often on a personal level, but increasingly on a small group level (recently known as "Rudie gangs").[68] The "Riots and Strikes" clipping file in the Institute of Jamaica shows a record of over one hundred years of small-scale riots and disturbances. In recent times states of emergency (1966 and 1968) and special security measures (1967) have been frequent and elections and union activity are often accompanied by violence.

Thus there has developed a widespread fear in the imitative culture of the "black masses," as they are often called, and window bars, guns, guard dogs, and fortified houses are a way of life. One author writes that "nervous people sipping Scotch by the poinsettias on their patios have asked one another how long they will be safe in

[66] *Ibid.*, p. 19.

[67] See R. Ellis, "Color and Class in a Jamaican Market Town," *Sociology and Social Research* (Los Angeles), Vol. 41, 1957, pp. 356–67.

[68] A general and psychological explanation of such violence is found in F. Fanon, *The Wretched of the Earth*, Harmondsworth, 1967, pp. 27–84.

their beds."[69] A scholar who has sought to show that such a fear is in fact unfounded, comments "to many Jamaicans, this popular image of the black masses as hostile would not seem unreasonable or unfounded."[70] The results of this fear are manifested in the treatment of law-breakers and in the massive response to minor disturbances.[71] Such manifestations, as well as the fear itself, clearly impede effective communication between the two cultures.

It is difficult to gauge the attitudes and responses from the evolved culture to these facts. Most studies have been done of a designated elite[72] and the only one relating to the evolved culture cannot be regarded as conclusive, although it showed that hostility was not as high as some observers assessed it and that a large proportion of the sample aspired to the values of the imitative culture.[73]

There have been champions of the black man within the culture, the most notable being the Rastafarian sect, originally founded by black nationalist Marcus Garvey. The sect is a semi-religious group which argues that the world's ills derive from the white man and that Ethopia is the black man's utopia. Although the sect has

[69] M. Hughes, *The Fairest Isle,* London, 1962, p. 12, quoted in J. Mau, "The Threatening Masses: Myth or Reality," in *Caribbean in Transition,* p. 259.

[70] *Ibid.*

[71] See for example, "Gets 40 Years, Lashes for Robbery, Burglary," *Daily Gleaner,* October 21, 1966, p. 1; and response to 1963 "uprising," *Daily Gleaner,* April 13, 1963, p. 1.

[72] See J. Duke, "Egalitarianism and Future Leaders in Jamaica"; and J. Mau, "Images of Jamaica's Future," both in W. Bell, ed., *The Democratic Revolution in the West Indies,* Cambridge, Mass., 1967, pp. 115–40 and 197–224, respectively; also W. Bell, *Jamaican Leaders: Political Attitudes in a New Nation,* Los Angeles, 1964. These studies are based on surveys and are quantitative in approach.

[73] J. Mau, "The Threatening Masses: Myth or Reality" in *Caribbean in Transition,* p. 262.

not made great inroads,[74] significantly, it has been widely feared by the authorities.

Under these circumstances it becomes very clear why the USA Black Power Movement is considered as a threat by the Jamaican authorities. Books by black power advocates, such as Stokely Carmichael and Malcom X, are banned and a black power adherent and lecturer at the university was recently prevented re-entry to the island (he was also said to be a marxist). This latter incident resulted in serious riots.[75]

People interested in the evolved culture are suspect and have been followed by the police or branded as communists.[76] For to champion the black man is not only to champion the "working class" but also to undermine the imitative culture on which power in the society rests.

Clearly communication between the cultures is limited and the barriers to mutual knowledge and communication are great.

INTER-CULTURAL RELATIONS—INTEGRATION

Mention has been made that entrance into the imitative culture is possible and rejection on the basis of colour is not inevitable. This is the phenomena which is at the base of the claims that white bias is declining.[77]

[74] See R. Smith, R. Augier, and R. Nettleford, *The Ras Tafari Movement in Kingston, Jamaica: a Report*, Kingston, 1960.
[75] *Daily Gleaner*, October 16, 1968, p. 1.
[76] See K. Norris, *Jamaica, the Search for an Identity*, *op cit.*, p. 69; and J. Mau, "The Threatening Masses: Myth or Reality" in *Caribbean in Transition*, footnote, p. 260.
[77] See Anon., "The Political Significance of Hugh Shearer–a Blackman," *Rising Star*, Vol. 10, No. 23, 1967, pp. 10–11.

More important, however, is the spread of some values over the two cultures. In particular, the second division in the imitative culture described above often serves as an exemplar of success and manhood for the evolved culture. The imitative culture responds in both divisions by not being true to the model. Thus, for example, a "womaniser" is widely admired in both cultures and even the most proper of dignitaries receive status in both cultures from such activities. In the 1967 elections, politicians appealed to the electorate in value terms of the evolved culture in their advertisements for meetings: "What a Bam Bam—Come in Your Thousands and hear 'Nature Boy'—Candidate for East Central St. Andrew," "JLP' Big Guns Roar Tonight," and "The Train Is Coming Tonight . . . Sounds and Pressure."[78]

Also both cultures, in relative position with some other of the islands, especially Trinidad and Tobago, are noted for a seriousness, purposefulness, and sombreness which has caused Jamaicans to be called the "Teutons of the Caribbean."

The society has changed in recent years and further evidence of integration is arising. The promotion and acceptance, even though in stylised form, of evolved culture modern dance forms by the imitative culture may be cited as one example. Clearly, the social changes required in the industrial sector of the economy, increasing urbanisation and the psychological effects of formal independence and self-government have been disturbing and have caused some change. However, for the main period of interest of this study, it is clear that integration of the cultures was at a minimum.

[78] *Daily Gleaner*, January 21, 1967, p. 3; January 24, 1967, p. 2; February 13, 1967, p. 2.

INTERNATIONAL PROJECTIONS

The internationally projected image of Jamaica is invariably inaccurate. There are three impediments to a reasonably accurate picture of Jamaica being projected outside the island: first, the vast amount of tourist and semi-academic literature depicting the Caribbean as "islands in the sun"; second, the practice of lumping the British West Indies as a cultural and geographic whole; and third, a cultural bias derived from the imitative culture.

For the purposes of this study, the tourist literature cannot be ignored, for this is an important source of information for non-academic persons such as trade unionists and junior colonial administrators. The holiday image of Jamaica existed long before it became a tourist centre and the prevailing sun-worshipping aspect of temperate peoples amplified this geographic attribute of the island beyond all others. It pervades literary, academic, and technical works.[79]

The second impediment is that culturally the British Caribbean has been considered as a whole. Most accounts of Jamaica are found within the framework of works on the British Caribbean and are consequently, for reasons of scope and culture of the writers, often inaccurate, both in fact and interpretation. In popular and even serious accounts, the image of Jamaica is derived from the Caribbean, which in turn derives its imagery almost exclusively from the cultural aspects of Trinidad and Tobago. Calypso, carnival, uninhibited gaiety, all of which

[79] For example, "Industry's New Island in the Sun: Jamaica," *Business Week*, February 12, 1966, p. 66.

come mainly from Trinidad, have no application to Jamaica but, nevertheless, are often ascribed to Jamaica.

The third impediment is that the image of Jamaica is derived, almost exclusively, from the imitative culture. The people of the imitative culture speak the language, figuratively and linguistically, of the reporters. Furthermore the imitative culture precipitates the correct responses to the questions and generally creates an impression of over-all similarity between Jamaica and the developed model of western democracy. Thus, for example, despite the numerous serious disturbances mentioned above, Jamaica is invariably described as "stable" and "democratic."[80] Thus internationally, as well as domestically, the evolved culture tends not to be seen.

[80] For example, A. Bowden, "Jamaica—a Stable Island," *New Commonwealth*, London, No. 8, 1965; and C. Fry, "Jamaica: Democracy Played With a Straight Bat," A Guardian Survey, *The Guardian*, July 28, 1965, p. 9.

CHAPTER VI

JAMAICAN TRADE UNIONS

Although strikes, riots, and demonstrations were common in the British West Indies since the slaves were freed in the middle 1830s, trade unions, or groups calling themselves trade unions, did not begin to appear until the 1890s. They grew in number in the first and second decade of this century but did not become influential until after 1930.[1]

In Jamaica after 1895, several attempts were made to create unions, most of which had disappeared by the early 1920s. The Artisans' Union, with a membership of eighty, was founded in 1898 and functioned until 1901 when extremely depressed economic conditions combined with internal union conflicts caused its collapse.[2] In 1907–8, some printers and tobacco workers organised[3]

[1] Unless otherwise stated, statistics for this section are taken from Labour Department (Jamaica): *Annual Reports 1940–1952* and Ministry of Labour (Jamaica): *Annual Reports, 1953–1961.*

[2] G. Eaton, "Trade Union Development in Jamaica," *Caribbean Quarterly,* Vol. 8, No. 182, 1962, p. 46.

[3] B. Roberts, *Labour in the Tropical Commonwealth,* London, 1964, pp. 10–11.

and in January 1907 the sixty-five members of the printers' union went on strike for higher wages. The strike was eventually broken and the workers defeated when the union treasurer absconded with the funds. One of the strikers was Marcus Garvey, who was later to become a black nationalist leader in the USA and Jamaica; it is claimed that this incident caused him to develop his lifelong antipathy to trade unions.[4]

The Jamaica Trades and Labour Union, a craft union as were its predecessors, also appeared in 1908 but soon became inactive, according to its President, W. G. Hinchcliffe, due to "death and emigration of union members, as well as criticism by union members of the status of the organisation."[5] It was such problems as these, rather than government suppression, which caused the failure of so many unions between the period 1890–1920.

After considerable unrest in Kingston between 1914 and 1917, the administration of Governor Sir Leslie Probyn attempted to improve conditions for the working population to prevent a re-occurrence of civil unrest. One consequent action was the passage of the Trade Union Law and an Employers' Liability Law in 1919. The Trade Union Law made compulsory the official registration of unions and granted the right to strike, although picketing was still illegal and union members still remained liable for loss and damage caused by the strikes.[6]

Before the Trade Union Law, organisation of unions had been on a craft basis and followed the British model but the unions registered immediately after the 1919 Act

[4] A. Edwards, *Marcus Garvey 1887–1940*, London, 1967, p. 5.

[5] G. Eaton, "Trade Union Development in Jamaica," p. 49.

[6] *Summary of Labour Legislation in the British West Indies*, Development and Welfare in the West Indies, Bulletin 28, 1949, p. 86.

organised largely on an industrial basis.[7] Two such unions, the Longshoreman's Union No. 1 (registered 1922) and Longshoreman's Union No. 2 (registered 1926), attempted, according to their constitutions, to develop harmonious relations with employers. But "being the first unions of their kind, they met with opposition from the pseudo-feudal industrial system which was still in existence."[8]

Neither the craft nor industrial based unions aimed at acquiring members from the agricultural occupations. The first union to do so was the Jamaican Workers' and Tradesmen's Union (JWTU), which was organised in 1936 and registered in 1937. Under the leadership of A. G. S. Coombes it sought members from both craft and non-craft occupations and attempted to integrate them into the one union, thus becoming the forerunner of the modern blanket union in Jamaica.[9]

The JWTU and Coombes were later overshadowed by Alexander Bustamante, who became Treasurer of the union in 1937 and a major actor in the events of 1938 which mark the beginning of the modern trade union movement in Jamaica.[10]

[7] Ministry of Labour and National Insurance (Jamaica): *Guide to Industrial Relations in Jamaica*, Kingston, 1966, p. 2. Examples of such industrial unions given include the Builders and Allied Trades Union and the Jamaican Hotel Employees' Association.
[8] Central Board of Statistics (Jamaica): *Trade Unions in Jamaica 1918–1946*, Kingston, 1946, p. 9.
[9] *Ibid.*, p. 10.
[10] G. Eaton, *The Development of Trade Unionism in Jamaica, W.I.* (hereinafter referred to as G. Eaton, *dissertation*), p. 239.

Growth of the Modern Unions

THE BEGINNING, 1938

In 1937 and 1938 there was a wave of riots, strikes, and general unrest throughout the British West Indies.[11] In Jamaica, in December 1937, sugar workers were striking for two shillings per ton for harvesting sugar cane instead of the existing rate which was just under a shilling. The strike coincided with a close-down of part of the government's municipal works programme. As a result, a demonstration of some 1400 workers took place at Serge Island, St. Thomas Parish, where on January 5, 1938, a "volunteer political agitator"[12] addressed a public meeting and, in a position of leadership, succeeded in getting an offer of one shilling from the plantation owner. The meeting rejected the offer and was subsequently broken up by the police and the speakers arrested.

Bustamante's activities then increased in pace and scope with the consequence that on May 24, 1938, he was arrested and held in prison for holding a meeting during a strike of waterfront workers. Norman Manley, founder and leader of the People's National Party and a lawyer of repute, offered to represent the dockers in their dispute and to seek the release of Bustamante. But the strike spread and the Governor announced the appoint-

[11] See A. Lewis, *Labour in the West Indies: the Birth of a Workers' Movement*, London, 1939.

[12] O. Phelps, "Rise of the Labour Movement in Jamaica," *Social and Economic Studies*, Vol. 9, No. 4, December 1960, p. 44.

ment of a board of conciliation. Kenneth Hill, Secretary of the National Reform Association, collected signatures and a small amount of money to assist Bustamante on his release. Hill, with Manley, was also instrumental in creating a Trades Union Committee which had three stated objectives (1) "the formation of the Dockers' Union which had already commenced under the leadership of Mr. Bustamante; (2) an investigation into existing state of Trade Unionism [sic] and an invitation to all existing unions of whatsoever nature, to come in and co-operate with the committee and place all relevant information before them; (3) to form a Central Council of Trade Unions to federate existing unions under an Advisory Body."[13]

With the help of Manley, Bustamante was released from prison on May 27, 1938, and then joined with Manley to present grievances to the government-appointed conciliation board.

BITU, PNP, AND TUAC

Shortly after his release from prison, Bustamante formed the Bustamante Industrial Trade Union (BITU) of which he was to be life president. The BITU was registered under the 1919 Act on January 23, 1939, and claimed a membership of 6000, which consisted mainly of dock and agricultural workers, clerks, and a limited number of factory workers (the two longshoremen's unions were dissolved soon after the BITU was formed).

The BITU was prepared to have members from all

[13] *Daily Gleaner*, May 31, 1938 (no page), as quoted in G. Eaton, *dissertation*, p. 261.

occupations although there is little evidence that the search for members was pursued with much organisation or vigour. The union attempted to settle strikes, achieve minimum wage rates in some sectors, and assist the many small unions which were springing up.

The PNP, which had been founded just before the BITU, tried to gain support from the BITU and other smaller unions but the policies of the PNP leadership did not appeal to the union leaders, and especially to Bustamante. Thus, as an obvious attempt to bring the union into the PNP political fold, Manley founded, as a successor to the Trade Union Committee, the Trades Union Advisory Council (TUAC) in February 1939. The objectives of the TUAC as stated at the founding meeting were "to advise on the organisation, development and practical work of all affiliated trade unions in connection with all matters pertaining thereto . . . to promote the interests of all affiliated organisations and to secure united action on all questions affecting or likely to affect those interests and to develop international contacts and trade union education programmes."[14] From the long term standpoint the TUAC was thus to be a federation of trade unions which would support "other affiliated organisations"—in particular the PNP. But it is clear that the short term objective was to capture and control the BITU, partly for its political power and partly because members of the PNP leadership were not satisfied with the actions of Bustamante in relation to his organisation. The writers of a 1946 report complained that in February 1939 Bustamante had called an all-island strike without "preparation or planning . . . to avenge a personal insult which was quite unconnected with trade union mat-

[14] *Report on the Trades Union Congress of Jamaica to the 30th June, 1946, for presentation on September 21, 1946,* mimeo, Kingston, 1946, p. 2.

ters."[15] Bustamante in fact claimed the general strike was called to celebrate the founding of the BITU, but in any event it only lasted four days, as Governor Richards declared a state of emergency which ended the strike.

TU-COUNCIL VERSUS BITU

In April 1939 the name of the Trade Union Advisory Council was changed to the Trade Union Council (TU-Council) but it was still a federation of unions and not a union within the meaning of the 1919 Trade Union Law and was not therefore registered.

At this time it had seven affiliated unions and although there is doubt whether or not the BITU was formally affiliated, Bustamante was on the executive body. In October 1939 Bustamante left the executive, accused other members of the executive of fraudulent activities, and severed all contact between the BITU and the TU-Council. The BITU had the greatest membership of any trade union on the island and its withdrawal from the TU-Council plus Bustamante's charges of fraud destroyed the TU-Council's ability to function in wage negotiation or industrial disputes in that period.

The events of 1938–39 prompted the British Government to appoint a Labour Adviser to the island in June 1939, who had a mandate to create a Labour Department, attempt to stabilise the trade union movement, set up conciliation boards, and forestall a worsening (at least from the British point of view) labour situation.

[15] *Ibid.*, p. 2. Manley is also reported as stating the TUAC was "to help Bustamante run his unions." *Daily Gleaner*, February 15, 1939, as quoted in O. Phelps, "Rise of the Labour Movement in Jamaica," p. 445.

Following a similar policy, but using different means, the Jamaican Government, which was still not fully Jamaican and still not fully powerful, arrested Bustamante on September 8, 1940, and interned him without charge or trial for seventeen months. During this internment Manley, in the role of adviser, and N. N. Nethersole ran the BITU. PNP supporters were mobilised on Bustamante's behalf and agitated for his release which was eventually secured in 1942, by which time the dues paying members of the BITU had increased from 5200 to 13,741. Bustamante again took his position at the head of the BITU and again split with Manley and the leaders of the TU-Council, dismissed top union officials, and advised BITU members not to become involved with the PNP. A short-lived union, the Jamaica United Workers' Union was created in 1942 by those BITU members who were dissatisfied with Bustamante's policies, but it was dissolved in the same year.

When it was known that the new constitution of Jamaica was going to grant universal adult suffrage and a great increase in power for Jamaicans, both the TU-Council and the BITU took action to prepare for the coming electoral struggle for power. A government publication of 1946 notes "it was at once clear to both groups [BITU and TU-Council] that their existence might be threatened or impaired should they fail to take advantage of the opportunity for independent representation which the party system embodied in the framework of the proposed constitution offered."[16] As the TU-Council favoured the PNP, it was therefore necessary for the BITU, being outside the PNP's trade union wing, to found a political organisation. Consequently in 1943 Bustamante announced the foundation of the Jamaica

[16] Central Board of Statistics (Jamaica): *Trade Unions in Jamaica 1918–1946*, p. 29.

Labour Party (JLP) which was to have both close formal and informal links with the BITU.[17] In March 1943 the BITU claimed a membership of 28,762 (of which 18,498 were dues paying members) representing 88 per cent of organised labour. With this backing the JLP, in the general election of 1944, won 23 of the 32 seats in the new House of Representatives while the PNP took only four. By 1945, seven years after the beginning of the new movement, there were 28 active trade unions in Jamaica, of which 50 per cent had a membership of under 500, which meant that the BITU was the only organisation with any real influence. However, some clerical and administrative unions exercised an influence beyond their numbers, particularly the government workers' unions. Four such unions were the Public Works Employees' Union, the Jamaican Government Railway Employees' Union, the Postal and Telegraph Workers' Union, and the Government and Auxiliary Workers' Union. The total membership of these four unions was 5359 and they were organised by Richard Hart, Kenneth Hill, Frank Hill, and Arthur Henry, all of whom were PNP supporters and were to figure in Jamaican labour and political activities for the coming decade.[18]

TRADES UNION CONGRESS OF JAMAICA

The TU-Council, which had continued to exist after Bustamante's attack and withdrawal in 1942, changed its name in 1945 to Trades Union Congress of Jamaica

[17] C. Bradley, "Mass Parties in Jamaica: Structure and Organisation," *Social and Economic Studies,* Vol. 9, No. 4, December 1960, p. 409.

[18] O. Phelps, "Rise of the Labour Movement in Jamaica," p. 442.

(TUCJ), thus making its name essentially the same as the British national trade union centre. By 1946 it had 21 affiliations, although it was still not registered as a trade union.

The success of a trade union-political party combination in the election of 1944 had not been missed by the PNP and TUCJ leaders and, although the TUCJ was still technically a federation of unions with no formal ties with the PNP, from 1946 onwards preparations were made for its eventual emergence as a blanket union. In 1948 the TUCJ became "one big union by merger"[19] and on July 22, 1949, was registered as a trade union and affiliated to the PNP.[20]

Throughout the 1940s, the TUCJ and the BITU fought battles over worker affiliation and representation with growing bitterness. In 1946, in the course of the Kingston Mental Hospital strike, pitched battles occurred between BITU and TUCJ adherents in which at least nineteen were killed and many wounded.[21] Similar situations occurred in the *Gleaner* strike of 1947 and the bus service strike in 1948.

TUCJ, PNP, AND NWU

The JLP-BITU association was dominated by Bustamante and his appointees and in many respects the two formally distinct organisations could be viewed as one.

[19] Trades Union Congress of Jamaica, Education Department: *Trade Unionism* (*Study Circle Notes, No. 1*), Kingston, mimeo (no date), p. 8.

[20] TUCJ: *Report on the Trades Union Congress of Jamaica . . . 1946, etc.*, p. 7.

[21] *The Masses,* February 23, 1946, p. 1.

The PNP-TUCJ, however, was not such a cohesive combination and in March 1952, an underlying split, particularly in the TUCJ, came to the surface. Four leaders of the TUCJ, Kenneth Hill, Frank Hill, Richard Hart, and Arthur Henry, were accused of communist activities and of disrupting the work of the PNP. They were eventually voted out of the PNP at a special meeting by 128 votes to 75.[22]

Meanwhile, two other TUCJ officials, Thossy A. Kelly and Joseph McPherson, formed a breakaway union, which was in opposition to the TUCJ. However, the PNP leaders obviously felt that a Jamaican political party must have a union base more firmly under its control and so a new union, the National Workers Union, was created. When the new union was registered in October 1952, Kelly, President of the breakaway union, brought over its membership to the new union and was made Vice-President of the NWU.[23]

The NWU was technically a federation of industrial unions but operated as a blanket union. Six months after it was registered it claimed 5025 members but only 1842 were dues paying and the ratio between paying and non-paying members remained low for some time.

The first executive of the NWU was composed entirely of top officials of the PNP, although Norman Manley insisted "the NWU be considered a separate entity from the PNP and trade union leaders should not be in the Party."[24] In the elections of January 1955 the PNP took eighteen seats to the JLP's fourteen.

[22] *New Commonwealth Newsletter*, Jamaica Correspondent, May 1, 1952, p. 428.

[23] In 1953 a union, the Jamaican Federation of Trade Unions, was also founded but remained basically a paper organisation. For details of this organisation and this period of history of Jamaican unions see following chapters.

[24] *Public Opinion*, September 29, 1956, p. 1.

The formation of the NWU in 1952 marked the end of a period of turbulence in the Jamaican trade union movement which had existed from the beginning in 1938. The PNP-NWU joined the JLP-BITU as the second blanket union/political party structure in Jamaica.

Refinements in the union and party structures and organisation were made in the years after 1952 but the JLP, PNP, NWU, and BITU retained their places as the most important unions and parties in Jamaica.

The Trade Union Situation Since 1952

The creation of the NWU started the erosion of the membership of the TUCJ and its position as an effective union in Jamaica. By 1955, three years after its registration, the claimed membership of the NWU was twice that of the TUCJ, and in 1964 the TUCJ became an affiliated union of the NWU. In 1958 the NWU membership roughly equalled the BITU, a situation which has basically remained until the present. Thus, at least from 1954, the BITU and the NWU have been the only two unions of importance.

THE BLANKET UNIONS

The BITU and NWU are both blanket unions. The research department of the NWU describes the NWU as "a blanket union, as distinct from a craft or industrial union. A craft union limits its members to a particular craft. A 'blanket union' covers all crafts, trades, industries, etc. The NWU has within its membership a wide variety of workers in several industries and trade in all parts of the Island. For example, to name a few, there are NWU members in the sugar, banana, bauxite and cement industries, government services and statutory corporations, garment and hotel trade, as well as telecommunications and airline workers."[25]

One of the major differences between the NWU and the BITU is in the workers they claim to represent. As they have no craft or industrial criteria for membership the unions are, in theory, free to compete for members and representational rights in any industry or enterprise. Thus it is possible for one or other of the unions to have almost all the workers in one particular industry or sector of the economy as its members, to the exclusion of the other union. The reasons for one blanket union establishing itself in one particular industry to the exclusion of all others is a combination of politics, union aggressiveness, organisation, personal inclination, and foreign involvement. The BITU, for example, has no members in the bauxite mining and alumina industry, and is weak in the tourist industry. The NWU, on the other hand, has almost exclusive worker membership in these areas.

From 1956 the NWU replaced the TUCJ as major rival of the BITU in the competition for workers in specific industries. Although representation polls were instituted in the 1950s, competition between the unions has been almost as fierce as between the BITU and TUCJ. In 1967 a BITU organiser went to hospital as a result of an attempt to break the total NWU hold at a building project.[26] As work is a scarce commodity it is sometimes

[25] National Workers Union, Research Department: *Fact Sheet on the National Workers Union*, Kingston, May 1967, p. 1.
[26] *Sunday Gleaner*, May 21, 1967, p. 6.

distributed according to party or union affiliation, thus causing more disputes.[27]

From the standpoint of finance, apart from grants coming from external sources, all the unions derive their funds from weekly dues paid by members. There is a provision in law for a voluntary "check off" system by which the worker may, on a prescribed form, authorise his employer to deduct dues from his wages, or by a similar procedure, he can renounce such authorisation. In a society where so many workers are not in continuous employment and are often at very low wage rates the collection of dues has been a major problem. Even though both unions' constitutions make provision for suspension of a member who is not paid-up, this is widely ignored, and union records usually quote both total membership and dues paying membership. In 1959, for example, the BITU is listed as having a total membership of 74,343 of which 54,943 were dues paying; the NWU had 82,723 with 22,140 dues paying.[28] The BITU has consistently had a greater proportion of dues paying members than the NWU which has not always been reflected in their budgets, as the BITU members, mainly sugar workers, pay smaller dues than the more industrial workers of the NWU. Thus in the same year, 1959, the declared receipts of the BITU from dues amounted to £48,267 and the declared receipts of the NWU from dues was £57,564. In that year the NWU spent a total of £58,573 against the BITU's £33,486, retaining a surplus of £27,457.[29]

27 See "Allen questions system of work distribution in bauxite industry, asks Manley: Does 50-50 doctrine apply?" *Daily Gleaner*, August 7, 1967, p. 1.

28 See Ministry of Labour (Jamaica): *Annual Report 1959*, Kingston, 1960.

29 Report filed with Registrar of Trade Unions, Spanish Town, Jamaica, 1959, as quoted in G. Eaton, *dissertation*, p. 416.

ORGANISATIONAL STRUCTURE

The formal structures of the BITU and NWU differ considerably. From its creation the NWU had a "democratic" constitution while the BITU (more recently) converted its established procedures into constitutional form. While the constitutions of unions rarely reflect the true political and governing processes they do, especially in this case, represent the formal and stated principles by which the leaders profess to govern the union. Even more important to this study is that the nature of the constitutions is often given as a determining factor in the granting and withholding of external assistance.

The NWU constitution states that its annual conference is "the supreme authority" of the organisation. It elects all the union officers who make up the governing executive, the General Executive Council.[30] The Council then appoints two major officers, the General Secretary who is the principal administrative officer and an Island Supervisor who is the official responsible for industrial relations on a nation-wide basis.[31] Provision is also made for the election of a Chairman and Vice-Chairman for locals and chartered locals.

The BITU constitution places the President in almost complete control and, by Rule 36, Sir Alexander Bustamante is the President of the union for life unless removed by a two-thirds vote of all union membership.[32]

[30] See NWU: *Constitution and Rules and Regulations of the National Workers Union of Jamaica*, Kingston, 1960.
[31] NWU: *Fact Sheet on the NWU*, p. 2.
[32] BITU: *Rules of the Bustamante Industrial Trade Union*, no date (1962?), p. 14.

The only elected official of the union is the Vice-President, and his election is subject to the nomination of the Managing Executive Committee which is in turn comprised of the President and his appointees. A General Secretary and an Island Supervisor are appointed by the President and have similar functions to those of the NWU. At the branch level a "local sectional council" is elected although the Chairman is appointed by the Managing Executive Council.

In practice, in both unions, the President has emerged as a powerful official while the General Secretaries are less important. The Island Supervisors are also important in the union hierarchy especially as both unions have weak branch and local structures when compared with unions in industrial countries.[33]

UNIONS AND PARTIES

The unions' relationship with the parties differs greatly, although formally more than informally. The JLP was founded after the BITU and Bustamante has remained leader of both organisations. Nevertheless, he has constantly maintained that his prime source of interest and his prime source of support has been the union and that the party was secondary, a reluctant necessity of political life.

This is reflected in the formal links between union and party. The Central Executive of the JLP has a union representation of approximately sixteen, not including officials of the BITU who are also members of the House of Representatives. Likewise, in the JLP Standing Execu-

[33] According to G. Eaton, *dissertation*, pp. 436–37.

tive, a smaller and more powerful body, out of approximately twenty members, three are from the union but the figure would be much higher if the background of other members were examined. While the BITU has rights to name some of the JLP executive, the JLP has no rights to name officials for the BITU. Of particular importance is the permission the union grants to its officials to hold government ministerial posts at the same time retaining their trade union positions. It is this circumstance that in 1967 allowed Hugh Shearer to become Prime Minister and also retain his position as Island Supervisor of the BITU, although without a salary.[34]

The BITU's relationship with the JLP has been fairly constant[35] but the relationship between the TUCJ and NWU and the PNP has undergone several changes. The TUCJ was never as closely integrated with the party as the BITU was with the JLP, although up to 1949 the leadership of the party and the union was almost identical. In 1949 the TUCJ was officially affiliated with the PNP but the split between the TUCJ leaders launched a new party, the National Labour Party, which disintegrated after electoral defeats in 1955. The new union, the NWU, was not formally affiliated to the PNP until 1962 but, before that time, had very close association, the leadership of the two organisations being well integrated.

The formal union-party structure does not grant an important position to the NWU. The NWU's representation at the PNP party conference amounts to fifty delegates out of a potential eight hundred; on the PNP

[34] *Daily Gleaner*, "PM's Name off BITU Payroll," May 25, 1967, p. 1.

[35] The effective retirement of Sir Alexander Bustamante has distorted this constancy. See "Play Stronger Role in Party, Sir Alex Urges BITU Members," *Daily Gleaner*, December 5, 1966, p. 2.

executive the NWU has ten delegates out of an average of one hundred. One important difference between the JLP and PNP is that an officer of the NWU must resign from the union when accepting a cabinet post. The informal links between the NWU and the PNP have been strong; Michael Manley, son of N. W. Manley, founder of the PNP, was for sixteen years Island Supervisor of the union, before being elected as PNP candidate to the House of Representatives and succeeding his father as leader of the party in 1969.

The closeness of the unions to the parties as such is sufficient to make it clear, therefore, that any assistance granted, or opposition mounted, is almost certain to have political impact in the constitutional and formal sense as well as the informal sense. The unions are both committed to operating within the political framework of Jamaica which is at the moment, and has been for some time, a two party system, each party being supported by a blanket union.

INDUSTRIAL RELATIONS SYSTEM

The trade unions, as accepted representatives of workers, operate within an industrial relations structure which has been established by practice and legislation since the beginning of the century. The laws regarding trade unions were, from the beginning, based on those in the United Kingdom, although there were notable exceptions.

The Trade Union Law of 1919 legislated for compulsory registration of unions (not the practice in the United Kingdom) and for the vesting of property in trustees but it did not provide for protection of the union in the case of a suit against it for damages resulting from strike action. Provisions for peaceful picketing and freedom from action in tort were not created until the 1938 amendment of the 1919 Act.

The basic policy of industrial relations pursued in Jamaica is "voluntary collective bargaining," or, as the government has consistently called it for the past twenty years, "self-government in industry." When the Labour Department became the Ministry of Labour in 1955, the Report for that year stated that the Ministry of Labour would continue the policy of encouraging "the policy of self-government in industry whenever possible."[36] In 1966 a Ministry of Labour publication stated "the policy of the government exercised through the Ministry of Labour and National Insurance is to foster self-government in industry as it is felt that the settlement of issues by the parties themselves tend to make these settlements more lasting. Accordingly collective bargaining is encouraged."[37]

Collective agreements so created are not binding at law, thus, the success of such agreements depends on the strength of the unions and companies involved, to enforce them against each other. Agreements are made usually on a plant-to-plant basis although more recently there has been industry-wide negotiation. The latter pattern has been encouraged since the early 1950s by government-assisted Joint Industrial Councils. In well-organised industries where terms and conditions of employment can be readily negotiated, the Ministry of Labour assists in the establishment of joint negotiating bodies on which the workers are represented by the trade unions, and usually the employers by an employers' association. "The function of the council is not merely to

[36] Ministry of Labour (Jamaica): *Annual Report 1953*, Kingston, 1954, p. 10.
[37] Ministry of Labour and National Insurance (Jamaica): *Guide to Industrial Relations in Jamaica*, p. 7.

settle terms and conditions of employment but to secure a large measure of joint action in order to develop the industry as part of the National Life and to improve the conditions of those employed therein."[38]

Thus the Ministry of Labour seeks to establish the Joint Industrial Councils and to keep them in existence as autonomous bodies. The councils established so far involve the Port of Kingston (both dockers and tally clerks), building and construction, wharf and shipping labour in the banana industry, outports of Jamaica, printing industry, plumbing industry, and banana cultivation. It is noteworthy that no Joint Industrial Council exists for the sugar industry, although the unions which win representation at the various estates are required to bargain with the Sugar Manufacturers' Association of Jamaica.

Of particular interest in Jamaican industrial relations is the procedure for solving representational issues. As a consequence of union rivalry it became clear that one of the most disruptive problems in industrial relations occurred when both unions claimed the right to represent the workers at a particular plant, estate, or other economic unit. Since 1950 the Ministry of Labour has evolved a procedure for such cases, although it does not have the force of law.[39] When either a union or an employer feels that the representation aspect of a dispute or a negotiation is not satisfactory they may request the intervention of the Ministry of Labour which then conducts a secret ballot poll among the workers as to their choice of union to represent them. Neither closed shop nor union shop exist as a general rule in Jamaica.

Statutory requirements in industrial relations are few.

[38] *Ibid.*, p. 8.

[39] Jamaica Industrial Development Corporation: *Legislation Affecting Labour,* Kingston, 1961, p. 6.

For certain so-called "essential services" such as water, gas, electricity, health, public passenger transport, hospital, fire brigade, civil aviation, cable and wireless, there exist compulsory arbitration and enquiry procedures, as it has been declared illegal for workers to strike, or employers to lock-out, in these industries. A minimum wage law empowers the Minister of Labour to make proclamations concerning wages when it is considered that unreasonably low wage rates exist in an industry. Minimum wage and proclamation orders have been issued for dry goods, catering, hotel, bread, bakery, laundry, dry cleaning, printing, alcoholic and non-alcoholic beverages, retail petrol, and in the sugar industry. Jamaica has also ratified the two International Labour Organisation Conventions relating to organisational rights. Both Convention 87, concerning freedom of association and protection of the right to organise, and Convention 98, concerning the application of the principles of the right to organise and to bargain collectively, have been ratified by Jamaica and are claimed to be a "recognised feature in the industrial relations field."[40]

This review of the history and current situation of Jamaican trade unions, their party relationships, and the industrial relations structure has been necessary in order to put into context subsequent foreign involvement in Jamaica. Almost every feature of trade unionism and industrial relations has, at one time or another, become the centre point of arguments in which foreign models are used and outside help and support solicited. Thus dues check-off, political affiliations, representational rights, democratic constitutions, plant-by-plant negotiations have all been issues in which foreign elements have been involved.

[40] Ministry of Labour and National Insurance (Jamaica): *Guide to Industrial Relations in Jamaica*, p. 4.

The Unions and Cultural Pluralism

The general division in Jamaican society along the lines of the imitative and evolved cultures has already been described. The trade unions were no exception to this division and the two competing unions were reflections of the general cultural divisions.[41]

THE TUCJ, NWU, AND IMITATIVE CULTURE

To some extent the appeal and operation of the trade unions were epitomised by the two leaders identified with them. In the case of the TU-Council, the TUCJ, and the NWU, it was the background and personality of Manley which predominated. Manley, born in 1893, was the son of a produce dealer and attended Jamaica's exclusive public school, Jamaica College, which was run on British public school lines.[42] Classified as a coloured man, Manley acquired a Rhodes scholarship to Jesus College, Oxford, served in the British army in the 1914–18 war, graduated from Oxford, and was called to the Bar in 1921. From that time he began to play an important role in the political and legal life of Jamaica.

[41] Business and other areas of social life also conform to such dualism. See L. Vroom, "The Social Differentiation of Commerce in Jamaica," *American Sociology Review*, Vol. 19, April 1954, pp. 115–25; and T. Bonaparte, "The Influence of Culture on Business in a Pluralistic Society," *The American Journal of Economics and Sociology*, Vol. 28, No. 3, July 1969, pp. 288–300.
[42] See *Who's Who in Jamaica*, Kingston, 1957, pp. 281–83.

By education, profession, background, and inclination Manley was a leading example of the imitative culture and he never claimed to be a creator of organisations to serve the needs of labourers in the evolved culture. In 1936, when addressing dock workers, Manley told them: "I have not pretended to be a labour leader. I am a lawyer and my work is in the courts where I work for anyone who desires my services to the best of my ability . . . when the time comes that organisations are to be formed by labourers to protect themselves and their rights I do not say that it will be possible for me to form these organisations but I am prepared to give my services free."[43]

This basic philosophy of Manley's was reflected in the conception of the early Trades Union Committee and Trade Union Advisory Council, the main functions of which were to be "advisory" to organisations which were expected to naturally emerge.

Manley himself never became a union leader but his party and his personality attracted leaders of similar background who were prepared to become active trade union leaders. These included such people as N. N. Nethersole, a lawyer; Frank Hill, a journalist who was Jamaica's press representative at the United Nations conference in San Francisco in 1945; Richard Hart, a solicitor and also a graduate of Jamaica College; Arthur Henry, accountant; and Florizel Glasspole, also an accountant. This "middle class" and "intelligentsia" nature of the TUCJ and NWU leadership has been noted by many Jamaican and foreign observers of the Jamaican labour movement.[44]

[43] *Daily Gleaner*, May 27, 1938 (no page no.), as quoted in G. Eaton, *dissertation*, p. 258.

[44] See, for example, A. Hart, *Monthly Comments*, Vol. 4, No. 2, May 1960, p. 1.

The organisations created conformed to the requirements of the imitative culture. The Trades Union Congress of Jamaica, as its name suggested, was organised on British structural lines. The early unions associated with the TUCJ, mostly from the clerical and semi-professional occupations, attempted to establish known and customary procedures of organisation, structures, documentation as found in Britain and elsewhere in the industrialised world. Great emphasis was placed on formal organisation, election of officers, and exercise of control over membership.[45] The TUCJ Conference Report of 1946, for example, is a duplicated document with many errors of abbreviation, spelling, typing, and construction and illustrates the attempt, with minimal resources and skills, to emulate the organisational products associated with Europe and North America.

The TUCJ, with such leaders, thus only had a limited appeal to the evolved cultures and throughout the 1940s always claimed less than 10,000 members compared with the BITU's 20,000 to 60,000 members. In 1949, when it was registered as a union, the TUCJ claimed under 2000 dues paying members.

The NWU inherited the TUCJ's inability to acquire a loyal and consistent following from the evolved culture. Although substantially more successful in terms of membership than the TUCJ, its dues paying membership has always been considerably less than that of the BITU and in 1959, after seven years of organising efforts and large expenditures, it was still only half that of the BITU.

The NWU leadership's orientation towards trade unionism had continued in the TUCJ's tradition with great importance being placed from the very beginning on a written constitution and formal structures and pro-

[45] See G. Eaton, *dissertation*, p. 553.

cedures. The 1966 annual conference of the NWU, at which this writer was present, was complete with conference documents, reports, delegate organisation, and ushers. It differed little from such meetings held in Britain or the USA.

THE BITU AND EVOLVED CULTURE

The Bustamante Industrial Trade Union was built around the personality of Bustamante and made viable by his charismatic appeal to the evolved culture in Jamaica. Bustamante, born in 1884 as Alexander Clarke, was first cousin to Manley but unlike him had no formal education. He left Jamaica when fifteen years old and has given conflicting accounts of his life outside the island, but it is sufficient to say that much of it was spent in Spanish-speaking countries of Central America and the Caribbean (some accounts also mention Spain).[46] It was the Spanish experience which caused him to change his name from Clarke to Bustamante after his return to Jamaica in 1932. Bustamante is a brown man but from the beginning he talked to and of the evolved culture and the black man. His leadership was erratic and effective but it antagonised Jamaican members of the imitative culture and the British authorities. Bustamante knew, either rationally, or instinctively as part of his charisma, the traits inherent in the evolved culture. Thus, for example, while at one time opposing self-government because it would "replace the brown man for the white man on the backs of the black man" he recognised the self-deprecatory element within the cul-

[46] See *Who's Who in Jamaica*, Kingston, 1957, *op. cit.;* and P. Sherlock, *West Indies*, London, 1966, p. 87.

ture which would accept, as an exemplar and leader, a brown man as himself.[47]

Bustamante had by reputation riches outside the island and claimed that he did not have to stay to assist the poor people as he had a "castle in Spain." Such claims were important credentials, for one of the major ambitions within the evolved culture is to be able to leave the island. That a man should forego such an opportunity and such riches to serve the "little man" in Jamaica was presented as conclusive proof of serious intent and personal sacrifice.

One author attributes threats on Bustamante's life by Jamaican planters as being the cause of his taking to wearing six-guns,[48] but whatever the reason they became an important part of his public appearances. In 1947, when Chief Minister in the first elected government, a *Daily Gleaner* report described "The Climax to Protest Parade of Jobless"—"tall, towering, angry, his voice staccato, his actions seemingly nervous, William Alexander Bustamante pulled two guns from his hips, yelled at a crowd that was milling around him and discharge one of the weapons with electrifying suddenness . . . in front of the Kingston and St. Andrews Corporation Office, Church Street . . . An onlooker commented, 'The Chief must be losing his power, he was very slow on the draw.' "[49] In the 1946 mental hospital strike, after a scuffle at the hospital Bustamante is reported as having gone to the docks urging the dockers "to come to the Asylum, there's a war on."[50]

[47] See F. Henriques, *Family and Colour in Jamaica*, London, 1953; and incident recorded in *Spotlight*, May 1940, pp. 28 and 33.
[48] F. Mark, *The History of the Barbados Workers' Union*, Barbados, no date (1967?), p. 83.
[49] *Daily Gleaner*, May 13, 1947.
[50] *The Masses*, February 23, 1946, p. 1.

The same style of treatment was meted out to industrial opponents. In 1957, in reply to a series of advertisements by the Sugar Manufacturers' Association, Bustamante placed a signed statement in the *Daily Gleaner:* "Let me warn the conspirators against the BITU that what is happening now in the sugar industry will only be like a slight vapour for up till now I have not taken any direct action in the matter. If I am forced to I am afraid they will have to put on blue jeans and cut their own canes and load their own sugar. The more the union cooperates with the SMA the more we are stuck in the back, and I am fed up with this knifing."[51] These incidents show the style of Bustamante's leadership and also illustrate the extreme disparity of approach, psychology, and style between trade union leaders from the imitative and evolved cultures.

Bustamante spoke the emotional language of the evolved culture and in return received a massive and loyal following on which base he built his union. The organisation reflected the evolved culture and it could be well argued that it was the beginning of an organisational evolvement, fitting a basically industrial country concept to the conditions of Jamaica. For many years the BITU had little formal structure and all problems were dealt with on a "telegraph Duke Street" basis (the union's headquarters in Kingston).[52] Reflecting the basic Jamaican oral tradition, the BITU had no documents or written constitution. There were no election procedures or observable structures.

When a constitution was eventually written, it described in formal language the structure which had grown up around the President. Article 36 of the Con-

[51] *Daily Gleaner*, February 14, 1957.

[52] W. Knowles, *Trade Union Development and Industrial Relations in the British West Indies*, Berkeley, 1959, p. 71.

stitution states: "Sir Alexander Bustamante shall be the permanent president of the Union, and shall hold office during his lifetime" unless he is declared by a special meeting to have "so conducted himself that he no longer has the interest of the working class at heart."[53]

In 1966 the union's annual conference, at which this writer was present, was not organised on model lines, had no widely distributed programmes, conference documents, posters, banners, or ushers. The speakers referred constantly to the name of Bustamante and received vigorous and positive response from the delegates. It bore little resemblence to a union general meeting in Britain or the USA.

THE UNIONS AND FOREIGN MODELS

Division of unions on these lines meant that the leaders showed entirely different attitudes towards the acceptance of foreign models.

When Bustamante emerged in Jamaica as a mass leader in 1938, he called his organisational vehicle a trade union. As far as is known he had had no contact with British or USA industrial relations or trade unions. In an interview with Eaton in 1960, he stated he had no preconceived notions of a trade union philosophy.[54] A contemporary of his in 1940, interviewed in 1967 by this writer, stated that he called the union "industrial" merely to distinguish it from smaller unions which were extant at that time. An editorial in a Jamaican newspaper in 1938 noted, "most trade unionists in Jamaica have little knowledge of trade union principles. That is inevitable.

[53] BITU: *Rules of the Bustamante Industrial Trade Union*, p. 14.
[54] G. Eaton, *dissertation*, p. 300.

The movement is new and its basis largely emotional."[55] This was certainly true for the BITU.

From the beginning, the BITU fitted no standard trade union model and, furthermore, Bustamante consistently refused to heed those who argued in terms of such models. He insisted on calling the organisation by his own name, a matter which still causes some distress to those who are inclined to make international comparisons: "is there anywhere else in the world a labour organisation named after its leader?" asks a writer in *Public Opinion* in 1966.[56] The BITU was attacked in terms of such models throughout its history but always resisted, at least until the mid 1960s. An exchange between the TUCJ spokesman and the BITU representative at the Board of Enquiry into Labour Disputes Between Trade Unions in 1950 is illustrative of dialogues which took place. The TUCJ spokesman said that "there was no knowledge that anywhere in the world leaders of trade unions were heads of Government."[57] This attack on Bustamante's position at the time was further supported by reference to the British practice of trade union leaders resigning when they went into government. The BITU representatives "acknowledged the fact that abroad ministers of government did not hold executive posts in unions but they felt that (a) political position did not affect a union if an executive officer of a union held a ministerial post. It would strengthen rather than hamper a union; benefit the trade union movement and promote industrial harmony. No attempt should be made to debar anyone from holding both posts. (b) Both posts

[55] "Reform Begins at Home," *Public Opinion*, August 20, 1938.

[56] "The Public Interest," *Public Opinion*, October 21, 1966, p. 2.

[57] Government of Jamaica: *Report of the Board of Enquiry into Labour Disputes Between Trade Unions*, 1950, p. 17.

would not be too much for one man to carry on where he had active and able lieutenants."[58]

While Bustamante rejected foreign examples and models the TU-Council and the TUCJ accepted them from the beginning. Even before any major labour organisations were formed, Manley told workers that "what was necessary . . . was to form a union, draw up a constitution with an executive body—decide on subscriptions and benefit schemes."[59] The emphasis on formal structure before dealing with the sociological reality was symptomatic of the necessity the TU-Council leaders felt to conform to a structural model. One of the original purposes of the Trades Union Advisory Council (TUAC) in 1938 had been to "develop and maintain connections with the labour movement in the United Kingdom, the British West Indies and otherwise internationally."[60] This objective was no doubt inspired by the presence of Walter Citrine, General Secretary of the British TUC in Jamaica in December 1939 and his involvement in the restructuring of the Trade Union Committee.[61] This contact plus the general disposition of the TUCJ leaders meant that they accepted from the first the British model. They organised on the basis of a federation of craft or industrial unions associated, but not integrated with, a party and this pure model was followed until 1949.

According to a trade union leader of the 1930s, the British model was emulated since 'being a colony it was a prudent thing to do.' Another, however, felt that alternatives were precluded by the background and education

[58] *Ibid.;* see also G. Daniel, "Labour and Nationalism in the British Caribbean," *Annals of American Academy of Political Science,* Vol. 310, March 1957, p. 167.

[59] *Daily Gleaner,* May 27, 1938.

[60] TUCJ: *Report on the Trades Union Congress of Jamaica . . . 1946, etc.,* p. 4.

[61] W. Citrine (Lord), *Men and Work,* London, 1964, p. 333.

of the leaders as only Bustamante had the 'good fortune' to escape the British cultural influence.

The attacks on Bustamante for not conforming to an acceptable model continued throughout the 1940s and the "free trade union" issue was raised in Jamaica long before it became the slogan of the ICFTU. Recalling the 1942 split between the BITU and the TU-Council, the 1946 TUCJ Report records, "the die was cast, the TUC went on its own exorable march of developing a free democratic trade union movement of Jamaica . . ." and "progressive and sincere trade unionists from the first were doubtful of the motives of Bustamante in view of his reputation and his anti-democratic determination to be made president for life of the union and to call the union by his own name."[62]

Despite these remonstrations, the TUCJ became a blanket union in 1949 in direct conformity with the pattern established by the BITU. After clinging to the British model for over ten years the unshakable power of the BITU and the prospect of continued PNP electoral losses forced the TUCJ leaders to abandon it, at least in its pure form. In 1944 the TUCJ not only faced a government formed and led by Bustamante but also a trade union which was receiving qualified support from domestic employers. The acceptance of Bustamante and his union by some employers occurred because although his previous political and union activities had affected the British colonial administration and the sugar industry, it had not necessarily substantially or negatively affected town-based industry and commerce. Perhaps even more important was the fact that Bustamante did not profess to hold any consistent anti-business ideology and his dealings with businessmen on behalf of

[62] TUCJ: *Report on the Trades Union Congress of Jamaica . . . 1946, etc.*, pp. 1–2.

his followers tended to be pragmatic. Further, his opposition to the TUCJ-PNP caused him to also specifically oppose its formally accepted ideology of socialism. Caught between the unorthodox but powerful nature of the BITU-JLP and the professed socialism of the TUCJ-PNP many holders of economic power opted for the BITU and Bustamante, at least until the early 1950s.

That the TUCJ was faced by a government-backed and domestic employer-accepted union became quite clear during the disturbances surrounding the hospital strike of 1946. Thus one TUCJ leader at that time states that it had to become a blanket union 'to keep it a going concern,' while another reports that it 'was generally accepted that the TUCJ should be remodelled on the lines of the BITU which had been over-whelmingly politically successful.'

In 1952 the NWU resumed the attack on the BITU with just as much disposition to use foreign models as the leaders of the TUCJ. But the basic battle of the structure was over in 1949 and it marked an end to a period of Jamaican union history when the domestic advocates of models were opposing the structure of the BITU.

STRUCTURE AND FUNCTIONS

It is obvious from the foregoing that in the early period of the development of trade unionism in Jamaica the unions, and in particular the BITU, performed functions which went far beyond those of the modern USA or British models.

Some writers have noted this phenomenon, although usually in the framework of a criticism of the unions for not conforming to the industrial-society models. Eaton points out that the TUC was "well equipped to meet the economic and political needs of its members, but not as equipped to meet the emotional needs."[63] Cumper singles out the emotional needs of the Jamaican worker as the function which could not be fitted into the "view of orthodox unionism."[64] It has been recognised that the charismatic political leaders in the Caribbean, many of whom have been trade union leaders, have satisfied some of the emotional, psychological, and welfare demands of the mass.[65] Concentration on the ritual, demagogic, and flamboyant aspects of such leaders has belied their contribution to building of organisations suitable to the existing economic, social, and cultural conditions.

Bustamante's rapport with the evolved culture, his refusal to consider foreign models, and the general lack of preconceived notions of trade unions or organisations enabled him to build a type of union structure most suited to the circumstances. Furthermore, the organisation performed functions for the unemployed, the rural workers, and generally articulated grievances of non-industrial nature to the authorities. The structure and functions of the organisation, in fact, fitted the special social type in the Caribbean which one scholar has called "neither peasant nor proletarian."[66]

[63] G. Eaton, *dissertation*, p. 353.
[64] G. Cumper, "Labour and Development in the West Indies," *Social and Economic Studies*, Vol. 10, No. 3, September 1961, p. 298.
[65] S. Rottenberg, "Labour Relations in an Underdeveloped Economy," *Economic Development and Cultural Change*, Vol. I, December 1952, pp. 250–60.
[66] R. Frucht, "A Caribbean Social Type–Neither 'Peasant nor Proletarian,'" *Social and Economic Studies*, Vol. 16, No. 3, September 1967, pp. 295–300.

Recognition of the BITU's contribution was made in 1949, when the TUCJ became a blanket union and thereby copied the structure of the BITU. It was after this date that a TUCJ publication stated that "... in Jamaica where there are much fewer workers it would be better for all or most workers to be in one Union. When due to historical conditions, numbers of small unions were first formed, these should *merge* together into one, not merely federate."[67] In other words, create the structure that Bustamante had started with in 1938.

The TUCJ did, in fact, in the early fifties move towards a hybrid form, copying the structure of the BITU, broadening its appeal to the rural worker while at the same time showing a competence in the industrial-country model of collective bargaining. The replacement of the TUCJ as an effective union by the NWU in 1952–54 again altered the direction of development.

The general nature and evolution of the functions of Jamaican unions will become even more obvious as the details of the foreign involvements in them are examined. The objective here has been to illuminate the cultural aspects of them and to take the emphasis off the functional associations that they might appear to have with either the British or the USA model.

[67] TUCJ: *Trade Unionism (Study Circle Notes, No. 1)*, p. 6; for account of structural evolution of TUCJ see WFTU: *Rapport D'Activité, 15 octobre 1945–30 avril 1949*, 1949, pp. 99–101.

CHAPTER VII

FOREIGN ELEMENTS AND GROWTH OF TRADE UNIONS

PERIODS IN JAMAICAN TRADE UNION HISTORY

The history of the Jamaican trade union movement can be divided into two periods, using domestic criteria for the division rather than the changes in the nature of foreign involvements. The beginning of the first period is marked by the riots at Frome in January 1938, when Bustamante became a national leader and soon after formed the BITU; it ends in July 1949, when the TUCJ registered as a union. During this period, the unions grew from an almost non-existent organisational base into two blanket unions closely associated with political parties. The second period, from 1949 to 1967, can be characterised as a period of refinement, consolidation, and political changes.

The important issues in the first period involve the general legitimacy of trade unions and the structural forms the movement might adopt. In the second period, the structures having been determined, the issues were connected with the functions of the unions and their specific policies on social and economic matters. It is the difference in the issues between the two periods, as well as the distinct change in the development of unions in 1949, which makes it convenient to discuss the two periods separately, for the issues which arose in these periods were sometimes caused by the involvement of foreign groups and organisations and almost always involved the use of foreign models.

The growth of trade unionism in British colonies was obviously influenced by British colonial policy, although to a widely varying degree. For this reason some discussion of Colonial Office policy as it was directed towards the British West Indies is necessary.

COLONIAL OFFICE POLICIES

The Basic Policies

The history of the British Colonial Office labour policy, or lack of a policy, has been well documented.[1] It is interesting to note, however, that the West Indies played an important role in two of the three phases of development of the colonial labour policy.

The first phase, during and immediately after World War I, saw several debates in the House of Commons on the bad conditions which existed for West Indian labour.[2] The West Indian islands were used as examples

[1] B. Roberts, *Labour in the Tropical Commonwealth*, London, 1964, pp. 169–200.
[2] I. Davies, *African Trade Unions*, Harmondsworth, 1966, p. 38.

in the course of a general attempt to prompt Colonial Secretaries to take action on labour matters in the colonies. This attempt was assisted by the attention international labour affairs were receiving as a result of the creation of the ILO in 1919.

The second phase began with the coming to power of the second Labour Government in 1929. It was characterised by the establishment of Colonial Office labour policy-making machinery and major labour directives to Colonial Governors. Thus in 1930 the Colonial Office formed a Labour Committee comprised of officials of the Colonial Office and Ministry of Labour which was to prepare policies for the Colonial Office and assist in the implementation of the ILO International Labour Conventions in the colonies.[3]

To provide a basis on which such policies and conventions could rest, the then Secretary of State, Lord Passfield (Sydney Webb), issued a memorandum on trade unions to the Colonial Governors which has become known as the "Passfield Memorandum." In it he recommended, among other policies, that trade unions should be made legal by a process of registration as "without sympathetic supervision and guidance, organisations of labourers without experience of combination for any social and economic progress may fall under the domination of disaffected persons, by which their activities may be diverted to improper and mischievous ends."[4] The action which was proposed was the passing of legislation identical to Sections 2 and 3 of the British act of 1871, which had helped legalise trade unions in Britain.

In 1937 the policy entered a new phase. In addition

[3] I. Davies, *African Trade Unions*, p. 38.
[4] *Labour in the United Kingdom Dependencies* (British Government Publication), London, 1957, p. 8.

to Passfield's policy of encouraging trade unions through legislation, even though they were to be "under supervision," the British Government now argued that colonial governments should assist in improving the conditions of colonial workers. Thus the memorandum of that year noted the improvement in the financial position of many of the colonies and colonial enterprises and argued that "it was only right that a fair share of this benefit should be passed on to the workers in the form of improved social services."[5] To effect this policy it was recommended that the colonial governments provide an adequate inspection system of working conditions and establish separate labour departments. The outbreak of war in 1939 meant, however, that even heavier emphasis was placed on proper supervision.[6]

The response to these policies in the colonies is reflected in a survey and report on labour legislation in thirty-three British territories conducted in 1943.[7] At that time, all the governments of the territories had enacted legislation similar to that proposed by the Passfield Memorandum under which trade unions were required to register. But they had gone no further, which meant that the majority of the territories did not provide for the protection of trade unions being sued as a result of industrial action or for the right of peaceful picketing. The report excused these omissions on the grounds that "in the majority of such cases the Governors concerned have intimated that the present stage of development attained by the unions would render the introduction of such provision [peaceful picketing] premature or even

[5] *Labour Supervision in the Colonial Empire, 1937–1943* (British Government Publication), London, 1943, p. 1.
[6] B. Roberts, *Labour in the Tropical Commonwealth*, p. 211.
[7] *Labour Supervision in the Colonial Empire, 1937–1943*.

dangerous and these opinions have been accepted by the Colonial Office."[8]

By 1951, according to another Colonial Office report, most of these omissions had been rectified and, with some exceptions, legislation in the colonies was basically similar to the British. The 1951 report also noted that provisions against violence found in the British Trade Unions Act, 1927, which had been removed in Britain in 1946, were still retained in many territories but "their retention will be necessary only until such time as the local trade union movement has learned that more is to be gained by democratic methods than by intimidation and violence."[9]

In Jamaica the trade union laws had followed the pattern reflected in the Colonial Office reports. The basic registration law, the Trade Union Law, 1919, was amended in 1938 to provide legal protection of trade unions. Other legislation passed in 1938 and 1939 included the Trade Disputes (Arbitration and Enquiry) Law, 1939, which provided arbitration tribunals for settlement of industrial disputes on a non-compulsory basis; a Workman's Compensation Law, 1938, which, under restricted circumstances, provided for compensation in case of injury of a workman; and a Minimum Wage Law, 1938. Jamaica also passed a law which was unique in the colonies and which allowed the Governor to decree holidays with pay (Holidays With Pay Law, 1947).[10]

The spate of legislation in 1938 and 1939 was possibly a response to the disturbances in the West Indies between

[8] *Ibid.*, p. 12.

[9] *Labour Administration in Colonial Territories, 1944–1950* (British Government Publication), London, 1951, p. 10.

[10] For a review of this legislation see "Summary of Labour Legislation in the BWI," *Development and Welfare in the West Indies*, Bulletin 28, 1949.

1935 and 1938; these disturbances also resulted in two reports on the conditions in the West Indies commissioned by the British Government.

An examination of the content of these reports is important for they were supposed to be policy guides for both the Colonial Office and colonial administrators. The conceptions of trade unionism revealed in these reports are also important, for they illustrated the process of reconciling such conceptions with the conditions in the West Indies, a problem which all colonial administrators and foreign trade unionists had to deal with when in Jamaica.

The First West Indies Report: Orde-Browne

The Colonial Office's first permanent Labour Adviser was Major St. John Orde-Browne, CMG. Almost his first task on appointment in 1938 was to investigate the conditions of labour in the West Indies. The subsequent publication, *Labour Conditions in the West Indies,* was entirely his work, opinion, and findings and consequently is commonly known as the Orde-Browne Report.

Orde-Browne's terms of reference were "To investigate and report on labour conditions in the West Indies, British Guiana, British Honduras, the Bahamas and Bermuda."[11] He left England twenty days after the official appointment of the West India Royal Commission, headed by Lord Moyne, whose terms of reference easily encompassed Orde-Browne's.

[11] *Labour Conditions in the West Indies,* London, 1939, p. 3.

CONCEPTION OF TRADE UNIONS

Orde-Browne was aware that trade unions had developed in the West Indies as a response to social and economic conditions; thus he notes "when people were reasonably provided for, the need for trade unions was scarcely felt. With hard times, however, due to combination of falling prices and plant diseases, employment became increasingly scarce and varying degrees of privation became recurrent with large sections of the population in several of the islands. In an endeavour to mitigate this growing evil a movement towards combination arose and various trade unions were established."[12]

Despite this recognition of the recent growth of unions and the fact that they were a response to general economic conditions, rather than to the process of industrialisation, he nevertheless expected them to perform functions characteristic of trade unions developed over a long period of time under industrial conditions: "Owing to the general absence of leaders with any experience of this sort of organisation or of industrial negotiation the first unions were ill-adapted to serve their ends. Local legislation again was frequently lacking in provisions for the establishment of trade unions on modern lines . . ."[13] But in essence Orde-Browne did not see trade unions in the West Indies as essentially bargaining units in a tripartite industrial relations system. His basic conception of trade unions was that they should be partners in assisting the government to enforce laws

[12] *Ibid.*
[13] *Ibid.*, p. 43.

which had been passed for the workers' benefit. The clearest example of this notion is his comment on the prevailing and unfortunate belief that trade unions should strike for higher wages, thus: "There is also a general tendency to regard a trade union as a weapon for precipitating strikes at the most inconvenient moment with a view to exhortation of higher wages; unfortunately these movements were aimed at an increase of pay rather than the more continuous employment and tended in consequence to make the situation worse rather than better."[14]

His view of the government as the prime mover in the field of social and economic reform permitted him to criticise freely the business group, blaming the "short sighted policy of employers' attitudes" for the formation of "irresponsible and irregular unions under non-representative leadership."[15] He thus made it clear that he thought businessmen would be as opposed to the role he thought trade unions should play as they would be to trade unions in general.

The assumptions that liberal government legislation would provide the impetus for improvement of labour conditions and that trade unions would merely assist in their implementation, were to be subsequently adopted by many other British officials and commentators.

RECOMMENDATIONS

Orde-Browne's recommendations were economically sweeping but organisationally meagre. The bulk of his general recommendations concerned agriculture, land

[14] *Ibid.*
[15] *Ibid.*, p. 50.

settlement, and slum clearance. He suggested renewed emphasis on Labour Departments, a Labour Board or Committee, legislation to assist trade union formation and control, and, in particular, the training of union officials by "sending selected candidates to England to study industrial organisation and relations, just as scholarships are already granted in some West Indies for furtherance of professional studies."[16]

These recommendations established a traditional approach which exists almost to the present day; a heavy emphasis on training of trade union officials to ensure their "responsibility" and their competence in industrial relations processes developed in metropolitan centres and a well-constructed legal framework into which the unions could fit, together with legislation ensuring they were "democratic" and that the leaders were responsible to their members.

Of Jamaica, Orde-Browne recorded that trade unions had only recently appeared and were not firmly established, but "the movement is, however, of such recent origin that time has been insufficient for the emergency [sic] of the necessary staff of trained and experienced officials. A valuable service in building up the unions on sound lines might be rendered by an official experienced in such matters."[17] In an appendix he listed the unions registered in 1939 and, without referring to the Bustamante Industrial Trade Union, which was about to be registered, he noted that "other unions have been organised under the leadership of Mr. Alexander Bustamante."[18]

Other recommendations for Jamaica followed those for the West Indies in general but placed special em-

[16] *Ibid.*, p. 44.
[17] *Ibid.*, p. 88.
[18] *Ibid.*, p. 89.

phasis on the appointment of a "well-qualified officer to undertake the supervision of all questions connected with Labour in Jamaica."[19] This recommendation was to be later effected in 1939, with the establishment of a Labour Department and the appointment of F. A. Norman from the British Ministry of Labour as the first Labour Adviser.

The Second West Indies Report: Moyne Commission

The West Indies Royal Commission, organised in August 1938, had broader terms of reference than Orde-Browne. They were simply to "investigate social and economic conditions in Barbados, British Guiana, British Honduras, Jamaica, the Leeward Islands, Trinidad and Tobago, and the Windward Islands, and matters connected therewith, and to make recommendations."[20]

The Commission was appointed by the Secretary of State for the Colonies, Malcolm MacDonald, and was headed by Lord Moyne, and consequently both the Commission and the Report have borne the latter's name. Also included on the Commission was the eminent trade unionist Walter Citrine. The itinerary of the Commission crossed, on two occasions, with that of Orde-Browne and on one occasion the latter gave evidence to the Commission in Trinidad (March 7, 1939) with the result that the Orde-Browne Report is extensively used in the Moyne Report.

[19] *Ibid.*, p. 98.
[20] *West India Royal Commission Report*, London, 1945, p. 5.

TRADE UNION SITUATION IN THE WEST INDIES

The Commission's views on trade unions in the West Indies were not very optimistic. They noted that legislative obstacles still prevented the growth of trade unions and that removal of these obstacles was prevented by "powerful vested interests which have stood in the way."[21]

They concluded, therefore, that "successive Secretaries of State for the Colonies have spoken publicly of the need for the encouragement of trade unions in the Colonial Empire, and from time to time over the last decade they have made representations to Colonial Governments in the West Indies drawing their attention to the desirability of facilitating the development of trade unions. Despite this and repeated statements of the present Secretary of State that Your Majesty's Government would welcome the establishment of trade unions, we were unable to discover that any real effort has been made until quite recent times to assist their formation and development."[22]

The Commission argued that the "powerful vested interests" had stood in the way of the establishing of certain democratic necessities for healthy trade unions of which the most important were the strike weapon, the principle of combination, and the principle that trade unions must be protected against action for damages. As an example, the Commission noted that "nevertheless, the right [freedom from action for damages], so fully

[21] *Ibid.*, p. 198.
[22] *Ibid.*, p. 198.

safeguarded in English law is rendered completely negatory in several of the West Indies. Up to the time of our appointment trade unions were protected against actions for damages consequent upon strikes in British Guiana alone of the West Indian Colonies. In Jamaica this protection was expressly omitted at the instance of the Government of the Colony from the Trade Union Law of 1919."[23]

The Commissioners noted with approval, therefore, the amendment passed in 1938 to the Jamaican 1919 Law, which did provide for such protection. But they were also aware that the establishment of trade unions was not prevented by law alone, thus they pointed out that: "In evidence every body of employers proclaimed a readiness to welcome responsible trade unions. In practice, however, considerable difficulty attended the recognition of trade unions both in private and public employment."[24]

The general claim of the employers was apparently that the unions had no "responsible" leadership. The Commission attempted to answer this by quoting Orde-Browne to the effect that "the leaders of the work people have mostly proved themselves capable and responsible"[25] and advocating (again echoing Orde-Browne) that trade union leaders should be given scholarships in order to study industrial relations in the United Kingdom.

[23] *Ibid.*
[24] *Ibid.*, p. 200.
[25] *Ibid.*

LABOUR RECOMMENDATIONS AND LABOUR DEPARTMENTS

In general, it is obvious that the Commission believed that the promotion of trade unions would have to come from the various colonial governments. Thus, they recommended that each government make a statement that its basic policy was to encourage trade unionism. The extent of the belief in the possibility of government assistance to trade unions is shown by the suggestion that government should allow "public offices or other premises owned by them to be used whenever possible for holding of meetings of trade unions."[26]

One of the recommendations which the Commission emphasised was the establishment of Labour Departments, as they had found only one official in the West Indies with a knowledge of handling labour problems.[27] Such a department was to be regulatory in nature: "In present circumstances and for some time to come the need must be recognised for Governments to assist by every means in the proper regulation of labour relations. For that reason the establishment of Labour Departments in the different Colonies is a matter of great and immediate importance."[28]

Labour Departments, however, were also seen as an over-all protector of workers' rights as they should be established by law. Thus, it was recommended that all of the principal colonies should have a Labour Department commanded by a Labour Commissioner and assisted by

[26] *Ibid.*, p. 201.
[27] *Ibid.*, p. 200.
[28] *Ibid.*, p. 202.

Labour Officers, that the Labour Commissioner be recruited in Britain and that officers should receive training in Britain. It was not demanded that either the commissioners or the officers should be recruited exclusively from the ranks of the civil service, but that the search for suitable men be pushed into industry, trade unions, and organisations of employers. The Labour Adviser was eventually to be an officer of the Federal West Indian Government charged with overseeing the whole of the West Indian policy.

Within the Commission's conception of functions of the Labour Department can also be seen the trust which was to be placed in the governmental authorities. The duties of the Labour Department were to be the "regulation of wages, conciliation and arbitration, the gathering of statistics, inspection of the protective laws, registration of trade unions and auditing accounts."[29] The Commission singled out the conciliation and arbitration function of the Labour Department as being the most important, and sought to give to the department widespread powers to perform this function, even to the point that: "Officers of the Department should also be available to address gatherings of workers on such matters [advice on work peoples' legal rights] either through trade unions or direct."[30]

Finally the Commission recommended that a Labour Department should be established in the Colonial Office, including a tripartite advisory committee "in order that Colonial developments and labour affairs can be kept in close touch with current practises in the United Kingdom."[31] This department within the Colonial Office would also "stimulate Colonial Governments to progres-

[29] *Ibid.*
[30] *Ibid.*, p. 303.
[31] *Ibid.*

sive policies and to keep constant contact with Labour Departments overseas."[32]

The Commission did not therefore envisage the Labour Department having as one of its functions the encouragement of trade unions and nowhere was this mentioned in relation to Labour Departments. The only mention of encouragement of trade unions is found within recommendations concerning the content of a government policy and legislation.

Labour Department and the British Model

CONCEPTIONS OF LABOUR DEPARTMENTS

Within the Orde-Browne and Moyne Commission reports lie two different conceptions of the functions of Labour Departments. While the Commission saw the departments as being in alliance with unions to administer liberal labour legislation, Orde-Browne saw them in two successive roles. The first was as a quasi-official trade union; thus he notes that "the present position must be recognised as a primitive stage if only owing to the lack of efficient trade unions: since development cannot be hurried, machinery is necessary to deal with the existing situation, but so constructed as to admit of modification as progress on modern lines proceeds."[33] Thus, apart from the traditional functions of the civil service in regard to labour matters, the Labour Department must

[32] *Ibid.*, p. 206.
[33] *Labour Conditions in the West Indies*, p. 46.

perform such functions as the application of minimum wage regulations in anticipation "that these will be eventually superseded by the more flexible method of negotiation by union."[34]

The second role the Labour Department would eventually play, according to Orde-Browne, was that of government informer: "The Labour Officer can further perform a most useful function keeping the Government informed of the general labour situation: he should be aware of any impending trouble so as to be able to report it in time for action to be taken with a view to eliminating actual strikes."[35] He also felt that the Labour Officer should bring to the notice of the employer hardships and grievances which could be remedied.

It is in this role that the sharp difference between the Orde-Browne and the Moyne reports can be seen. Both reports perceived that the Labour Departments should fill gaps which existed in labour procedures and relations in the West Indies, but the Commission also saw the Labour Departments as quite definitely protecting workers' interests against employers, and sometimes governments. Orde-Browne, however, saw the department as assisting the government in the prevention of strikes and general strife and guiding the trade unions into policies which would not conflict with the government.

Both Orde-Browne and Moyne recommended that labour organisation in each colony should be in the hands of a policy-making Labour Board which would be impartial and tripartite. Despite this tripartite notion the reports did not comment on the lack of employer or-

[34] *Ibid.*

[35] *Ibid.*, see also a West Indian Governor's confirmation of this role, in International Labour Office: *Labour Policies in the West Indies*, Geneva, 1952, p. 131.

ganisations, which was especially true in the case of Jamaica.

Neither of the reports envisaged, however, the Labour Departments taking the initiative for the encouragement of trade unions. They were always to be supporters of existing government legislation.

The Jamaican Labour Department

The combination of the Orde-Browne Report, possibly that of the Moyne Commission, the Colonial Secretary's directive of 1937, and in particular the disturbances of 1938 caused the island's administrators to take cognisance of labour problems.

For the first time, in 1937, the Annual General Report of Jamaica had a special chapter headed "Labour." Even then the comment was sparse: "There is no Labour Department in Jamaica and there are no statistics as to the approximate number of persons employed in particular industries or as to the labour supply and demand generally."[36] Two paragraphs noted that there were very few manufacturing workers and that some International Conventions have been made applicable to the island.

By the time the report of 1938 was issued, the labour problems and unrest had grown to such an extent that the government was prompted to take action on several fronts. First, in March 1938, a Commission was appointed to enquire into, and report on, the rates of wages and conditions of employment. Before it met there were such serious disturbances that it was replaced by a Concilia-

[36] *Annual General Report of Jamaica, 1937*, Kingston, 1938, p. 32.

tion Board "which did valuable work in settling strikes."[37] The Conciliation Board also "recommended the establishment of a Labour Department,"[38] but neither the labour movement nor trade unions were mentioned. In the same year, the government opened an Unemployment Registration Bureau in the Corporate Area of Kingston to "ascertain the number of unemployed."[39]

From the reports, the Jamaican colonial government, in these years, appeared to have had less than enthusiastic views on Labour Departments. The mention of a Labour Department in 1937 indicates that it was viewed as a mere source of statistics and it could also be argued that the creation of the Unemployment Bureau in 1938 was an attempt to offset the pressure from Britain for the creation of a Labour Department.[40]

The establishment of the Unemployment Bureau, however, meant that when finally a Labour Adviser was appointed for Jamaica by the Colonial Office he had a base from which to build and a small staff with some experience in labour matters.

DECLINING INTEREST

The first Labour Adviser to the Government of Jamaica was F. A. Norman, who was seconded from the Ministry of Labour in London. He took up his post in June 1939, and began the work of establishing a Labour Depart-

[37] *Annual General Report of Jamaica, 1939*, Kingston, 1940, p. 39.
[38] *Ibid.*
[39] *Ibid.*
[40] Given the difficulty in assessing the numbers of unemployed and its doubtful utility. Also in 1938, work-creating projects were started and the ILO Convention of Minimum Wage passed. See *ibid.*

ment. In a letter, written as he was resigning to become Labour Adviser to the Comptroller of Welfare and Development in the West Indies and which was attached to the Annual Report of the Labour Department for 1940,[41] Norman notes that the Labour Department grew as a result of the "need for cooperation with the US for the Panama Canal Zone,"[42] thus, "the Chairman of the United States Committee of Enquiry into the labour and economic conditions in the British West Indies when visiting Jamaica recently told me that having visited a number of other West Indian Islands this was the first example of a Labour Department which he had encountered, that he was impressed thereby, and was intending to report on it to the President of the United States."[43]

On trade unions, Norman was not so self-assured: "In the encouragement of an ordered trade union development in Jamaica there yet remains a good deal to be done."[44] To prevent overlapping it was necessary to "regulate" the scope of trade unions which, Norman argued, could best be done by the then embryonic national centre, the Trade Union Council, but the power and activities of this organisation were "limited owing to the fact that the Bustamante Industrial Trade Union is not affiliated to the Council. In the interest of the trade union movement as a whole, I express the hope that the Bustamante Union will agree to rejoin the Council at an early date."[45] Norman thus became one of the earliest and most official critics of the policies and actions of the

[41] Labour Department (Jamaica): *Annual Report 1940*, Kingston, 1941, p. 1.

[42] Norman examined the labour conditions in Panama in 1940 for the Labour Department. See *Spotlight*, May 1940, p. 14.

[43] Labour Department (Jamaica): *Annual Report 1940*, p. 1.

[44] *Ibid.*

[45] *Ibid.*

Bustamante Industrial Trade Union although he had previously had disputes with Bustamante concerning the latter's claim to represent the workers on the government relief projects. Norman clashed with Bustamante, holding the position that there was no such entity as a non-dues paying member; he told Bustamante, at the Labour Department Office, they either pay dues and were members or did not pay dues and were not members.[46] No doubt this early experience with the Labour Department was one factor which caused Bustamante to become an outstanding critic of the department for nearly fifteen years.

The trade unions also needed "much educational work" which, according to Norman, would help the workers "to realise the desirability of proceeding wherever possible by way of collective bargaining leaving the strike weapon to the last."[47] He also noted that there were not enough employers' organisations and that employers could assist in "fostering collective bargaining."[48] But the employers were not responsive to these suggestions. Arising out of a dispute over wages of shop assistants he wrote to many of the employers in the distributive trade suggesting the formation of an Employers' Association: "The response to the memorandum was not encouraging as many employers were adverse to the suggestion. A Committee of the Chamber of Commerce was, however, formed to deal with wages questions, etc. . . . it cannot be considered as being entirely satisfactory and the real need for an Employers' Association is still apparent."[49]

Norman's objective was to create a tripartite industrial relations system and he therefore placed the Labour De-

[46] According to an interview respondent.
[47] Labour Department (Jamaica): *Annual Report 1940*, p. 1.
[48] *Ibid.*
[49] *Ibid.*, p. 3.

partment in the forefront of the process of establishing collective bargaining. Thus he left the directive that the department should give advice on "industrial organisation" to both employers and trade unions so that they would understand "the principles of collective bargaining as well as making known the general utility of Employers' and Trade Unions."[50]

The situation in Jamaica, however, apparently prevented Norman from ignoring the surrounding social and economic conditions. A colleague interviewed described him as "tolerant" while a Jamaican news magazine commented that Norman's interest moved from "fields of labour into the homes and recreation centres of labour, he believes in the efficacy of good wages, social services, a better and more practical system of education and the employers class handing out a square deal to workers, workers repaying in kind."[51]

In contrast, subsequent Labour Advisers to Jamaica seemed less clear in their objectives and more inclined to be purely administrators.

The next Labour Adviser was also seconded from the Ministry of Labour and National Service, E. F. Smith. From the reports, Smith reflected his background as a junior factory inspector in Britain by placing a heavy emphasis on factory inspection and its surrounding laws. Under the heading "Labour Organisations" he merely lists seventeen unions and records the creation of a Labour Advisory Board to replace the department's Trade Union Consultative Committee.[52] Smith's approach to his work was said to be that of an 'holiday appoint-

[50] *Ibid.*, p. 3.
[51] *Spotlight*, September 1940, p. 18.
[52] Labour Department (Jamaica): *Annual Report 1942*, Kingston, 1943, p. 3.

ment,'[53] and that his knowledge of Jamaica remained limited.

In 1943, Dr. J. Harris, an Irishman who had been locally employed in education, was appointed Labour Adviser, the first Adviser to be recruited in Jamaica.

Harris was content to base his report on that of his predecessor, confining opinion to a few short paragraphs: "Trade Unionism has made further progress and is receiving universal recognition. Seven new unions were formed and registered during the year bringing the total number of active registered unions to twenty-three."[54] Government also appointed an Industrial Relations Committee to bring "some permanent improvement in the relations between employers and workers."[55] Four new employers' associations were recorded in the year, bringing the total to eight.

Despite the increasingly administrative nature of the department it was still apparently disruptive to Bustamante, as evidenced by one of the resolutions presented to the Jamaica Labour Party conference in 1943 "that no Labour Adviser, Labour Officer or Assistant Labour Adviser can be employed in any other capacity than that of an Arbitration Officer."[56]

The department's declining interest in trade unions and the creation of an industrial relations system, as reflected in the reports, was more marked in 1944, when the report of that year merely recorded statistics dealing with disputes and arbitration. The department's work in connection with migratory labour to the USA continued.

[53] This phrase is often used to describe British administrators who showed little interest or commitment to Jamaica.

[54] Labour Department (Jamaica): *Annual Report 1943*, Kingston, 1944, p. 1.

[55] *Ibid.*

[56] L. Nembhard, *Jamaica, The Awakening*, Kingston, 1943, p. 66.

ADMINISTRATIVE DEPARTMENT, 1945–1950

In 1945 another British civil servant was seconded as Labour Adviser from the Ministry of Labour in London. He was a Scotsman and although, according to a contemporary, he never 'talked the language' he remained at the head of the department for three years. The reports of these years reveal little activity, although, at least in 1945, there were indications of the same enthusiasm for the Trade Union Council that had been expressed earlier by Norman. Thus, it is noted with approval, that twenty-two out of twenty-eight labour organisations were affiliated to the Trade Union Council.[57] No mention is made, however, of the Bustamante Industrial Trade Union, which is surprising as according to the department's own statistics of the same year, that organisation had 29,000 members out of a total of 33,000, which meant that all of the twenty-two Trade Union Council affiliates had less than 4000 members.

By 1946 the nature of the work of the department under Cowan did not even meet the approval of all the affiliates of the Trade Union Council (which had by this time become the Jamaican Trades Union Congress). One of the resolutions at its 1946 conference was from the "Federation of Govt., Mun. and Parl. [sic] Workers . . . whereas it has been proven that the Labour Dept. is ill-equipped to mediate successfully in some disputes due to lack of personnel who possess necessary technical

[57] Labour Department (Jamaica): *Annual Report 1945*, Kingston, 1946, p. 7.

knowledge:—proposes the Federation takes to cause the Labour Dept. to due it duty [sic]."[58]

For the first time, in 1948, a Labour Adviser was appointed from the Jamaican Civil Service. C. H. Scott, who was a Jamaican and had been with the department since its origin as the Employment Bureau, guided the department for nearly nine years, first as Labour Adviser and then as Permanent Secretary to the Minister of Labour.[59] Unlike all his predecessors, except Harris, Scott did not have direct experience with the British unions or industrial relations system. Scott was appointed at a significant period in the history of the Jamaican trade union movement, when it was finally settling into the present two blanket-union structure. But the Labour Department under his leadership showed little concern for these developments, its main concern being firstly industrial peace, and secondly, making the present unions—whatever their structure—fit in the emerging industrial arbitration and conciliation system.

It is not surprising therefore that in Scott's first Annual Report he notes with pride that "for the first time since Trade Unionism became active in 1938 the reaping of the crop [sugar] commenced without any of the usual labour disorders."[60] This he achieved by a complicated agreement between the Sugar Manufacturers' Association and the BITU involving 42,700 workers.

In 1949 he attended a Labour Officers' Training Course sponsored by the British Ministry of Labour and in the

[58] TUCJ: *Report on the Trades Union Congress of Jamaica . . . 1946, etc.*, p. 2. (The construction of this document and the background of its writing would indicate that this resolution met with the approval of the executive of the TUCJ.)

[59] *Spotlight,* June 1956.

[60] Labour Department (Jamaica): *Annual Report 1948*, Kingston, 1949, p. 3.

same year, and for the first time, the duties of the staff of the Labour Department were listed. Among them were:
"(iv) to encourage the establishment of sound industrial relations between employers and workers by promotion of collective bargaining, conciliation, and the arrangement for the settlement of disputes by arbitration, where conciliation has not been effective.
"(v) to encourage sound trade union principles and introduce Works Councils and negotiating machinery."[61]

Despite the emphasis on "sound principles," Scott records without comment in the same report the final emergence of two blanket unions in Jamaica: "the Trades Union Congress of Jamaica is now a registered union and not an Association of trade unions. It is a general workers' union covering most categories of workers, both clerical and manual, and corresponds more nearly to the Bustamante Industrial Trade Union which comprises several categories of workers, both clerical and manual."[62]

Apparently, more important and more disturbing for the policy of smooth industrial relations was not the emergence of blanket unions as such, but the problem of union rivalry. Thus, with concern Scott notes also that "two additional Unions drawing their membership from port workers in Kingston were registered . . . the membership of the workers is now divided amongst three unions."[63]

Scott was known and trusted by local people and, more important, he accepted the existing situation and so was able to maintain a relative peace in labour matters.[64]

The final establishment of the two blanket unions in 1949 and the presence of Scott as Labour Department

[61] Labour Department (Jamaica): *Annual Report 1949*, Kingston, 1950, p. 1.
[62] *Ibid.*, p. 5.
[63] *Ibid.*
[64] According to interview respondents.

head enabled the department to begin work immediately on the problems of refinement of the union and industrial relations structure. The basic nature of Jamaican trade unionism was no longer in doubt.

MIGRATION AND TRADE UNION PRACTICES

The Labour Department's effect on the growth of trade unionism in Jamaica would have come through the leadership of the movement as would be the case with other Jamaican groups and foreign organisations. But the general membership of the unions was open to less formal and more individual foreign influences. Three factors which could affect the general membership directly and could possibly give rise to ideas and attitudes concerning unions were, first, the return to Jamaica of Jamaican immigrants from the USA and their subsequent continuing personal and organisational contact with the USA, second, the presence in the 1940s of American military bases, and, finally, the USA farm labour programme which was established in the early 1940s.

JAMAICANS WITH AMERICAN EXPERIENCE

From the turn of the century, the USA had been a major outlet for emigrants from Jamaica and between 1900 and 1921 at least 100,000 Jamaicans went to the USA.[65] These returning emigrants brought what one author has

[65] R. Hart, *The Origins and Development of the People of Jamaica*, Kingston, 1952.

called the "Harlem" influence to the Jamaican population.[66] It is hard to estimate the impact of ideas and practices imported from the USA by such means, although many writers, without offering evidence, state that it was important.[67] The Moyne Report stated clearly that the idea of unionism did not come from Britain but from emigrants returning from the USA, Cuba, and South America; "many of these immigrants have brought with them some knowledge of working trade unionism in other countries; that knowledge has spread and the attempts which have been made to form trade unions in the West Indies are not surprising."[68]

There are certainly individuals with American experience who played some role in the history of trade unionism or mass movements in Jamaica, of whom Marcus Garvey is the most noted, but there were other, less well-known, activists such as Wilfred Domingo and Ferdinand Smith. Contacts like these, plus direct international trade union contacts, could explain why, for example, the first unions among the Jamaican dock workers called themselves longshoremen's unions rather than use the British term docker.

Some organisations which were active among the evolved culture were organised by people with American experience or received funds from the USA. Richard Hart records that "two American based" organisations, the Trade Union Unity League and the Negro Labour Congress attempted to form a Jamaican Trades and Labour Union in 1929–30 but were unsuccessful. Apparently these two organisations were more concerned with the removal of social and legal disabilities of negroes

[66] See W. Knowles, *Trade Union Development and Industrial Relations in the British West Indies*, Berkeley, 1959, p. 128.
[67] See *ibid.*, pp. 128–29; and G. Eaton, *dissertation*, pp. 632–35.
[68] *West India Royal Commission Report*, pp. 197–98.

in the USA than in trade unionism in Jamaica.[69] The association between the civil rights for negroes movement in the USA and Jamaica has been a constant, if fluctuating, one throughout modern history.

Another organisation active in the period was the Jamaica Progressive League, which was formed in New York in 1935 by "intellectual Harlemites" and which approached Manley to secure his services for those arrested during the disturbances of 1937–39.[70] American based organisations also helped finance the regional labour organisations in the 1940s.

USA MILITARY BASES AND FARM LABOUR PROGRAMME

Even more uncertain has been the effect of the American military bases which were built in the early 1940s and staffed by American personnel until their abandonment in 1962. One author claims that the bases introduced new ideas about industrial relations and trade unionism to the countries in which they were built.[71] There is little evidence that this is the case in Jamaica. The bases did have a demonstration effect in the West Indies in relation to economic development, illustrated by a resolution at the Third British Guiana and West Indian Labour Conference on the development of industrial resources which was defended because "no one in British

[69] R. Hart, *The Origins and Development of the People of Jamaica*, p. 26, as quoted in G. Eaton, *dissertation*, p. 236.

[70] W. Knowles, *Trade Union Development and Industrial Relations in the British West Indies*, p. 129; see also M. Ayearst, *The British West Indies*, New York, 1960, p. 70.

[71] W. Knowles, *Trade Union Development and Industrial Relations in the British West Indies*, pp. 129–31.

Guiana can deny the fact that the introduction of American air bases raised the economic standard of the workers and any development of industries in the colony will raise the economic standard of the workers."[72]

Apart from the informal aspects of the workers returning from the USA after a three-year period of work, the USA Farm Labour Recruitment brought officials of the Jamaican Government into close contact with American practices. Several Labour Department officers were seconded as liaison officers for the administration of the farm labour programme in the USA. In 1944 the British West Indies Central Labour Organisation was launched, which gave more American experience to officials.[73] The establishment of conciliation and arbitration in Jamaica has been attributed to a British official who had worked in Washington, attached to the British Embassy, dealing with labour problems.[74]

Regional and International Trade Union Organisations

Regional trade union organisations in the Caribbean appeared early in the history of trade unionism in the area, largely because of the fusion of the federal idea with the beginnings of a West Indian nationalism.

The idea of a federation of the British West Indies

[72] L. Braithwaite, "Federal Association in Institutions in the West Indies," *Social and Economic Studies*, Vol. 6, No. 2, June 1957, p. 307.
[73] B. Poole, *The Caribbean Commission*, Columbia, 1951, p. 202.
[74] According to an interview respondent.

has historic origins, although it was largely conceived and promoted by the British Government.[75] In the Moyne Report, for example, a federation was proposed although the possibility of complete independence was not discussed. For many West Indian leaders federation was associated with nationalism and independence as they felt that West Indian nationalism could be expressed in the federal idea and independence would come as a natural consequence of federation.

For these reasons, then, the two basic attempts to create a regional trade union organisation in the period under discussion were both heavily oriented towards the creation of an independent federation of the British West Indies.

BRITISH GUIANA AND WEST INDIAN LABOUR CONFERENCE

The first attempt at a regional organisation started with the founding conference of the British Guiana and West Indian Federation of Trade Unions and Labour Parties, 1926. The trade union organisation eventually took the name of the founding conference and became known as the British Guiana and West Indian Labour Conference (BG&WILC).

The Conference was originally convened by the British Guiana Labour Union (BGLU) and met in Georgetown, British Guiana, in 1926. This conference can be seen as either premature or far-sighted, for Jamaica, the second largest British territory in the West Indies, had no unions

[75] See L. Bobb, "The Federal Principle in the British West Indies," *Social and Economic Studies,* Vol. 15, No. 3, September 1966, pp. 239–65.

of importance at that time and the same situation existed in most of the other territories. Nevertheless, the British Labour Party sent a delegate to the conference who also acted as the representative of the British TUC, F. O. Roberts, MP. The Conference Reports, according to one author who has consulted them in recent years,[76] show that the Conference "accepted proposals for federation and passed other resolutions of a regional rather than an insular nature. It urged the development of a private telegraphic code which would allow secret labour communications in case of attempts to break strikes by interterritorial transfer of workers, upkeep of a Labour Commissioner in England, compulsory education for the masses, industrial and social legislation, prison reform and a series of resolutions referring specifically to the situation in British Guiana."[77]

There is, in the absence of the reports, no evidence to suggest that Jamaican delegates were at this conference. From the fact that it was not until 1936 that any organisation approximating the British Guiana Labour Union was established in Jamaica, or even attempted, it could be surmised that the basic function of promoting communication between the various territories was not efficiently performed by the BG&WILC.

The Conference met twice more, in 1938 and 1944. In 1938 it called for reform policies in the Caribbean area, discussed the possibility of federation, and the reports showed expertise concerning labour legislation and organisation.[78] The 1938 Conference showed some American influence in passing a resolution noting, "this Con-

[76] These reports were printed and published but the series in the Institute for Social and Economic Research in Jamaica were removed by a visiting researcher.
[77] L. Braithwaite, "Federal Association in Institutions in the West Indies," p. 298.
[78] *Ibid.*

ference regrets the neglect in the past by governments to provide technical training schools for vocational training and is of the opinion that throughout these colonies institutions similar to the Tuskegee Institute of the USA be established."[79]

Knowledge of both the British and American labour practices and industrial relations legislation is shown by two resolutions advocating "an ordinance to penalise unfair labour practices, similar to the National Labour Relations Act of the USA," and "Trade Union law including the immunities and privileges enjoyed in Great Britain."[80]

At the third and last meeting of the BG&WILC in 1944, the resolutions tended to be nationalist rather than labour oriented and federation was, as in 1926, the main issue. Anti-British feelings were evident in the newer leaders "but Cipriani and the other old leaders held their pro-British and anti-American position."[81] Braithwaite claims that the direction of the Conference moved from the British influenced labour movement of 1926 to that of a "middle-class nationalist movement" with socialist overtones in 1944. If this is the case, it might explain the lack of interest of the Jamaican trade unions, being dominated at this time by Bustamante, a known and vigorous critic of the "middle-class socialist."

The BG&WILC was virtually inactive between the Conferences and therefore failed to perform even the most rudimentary function of a regional organisation, that of communication between the various affiliates. It

[79] A. Lewis, "Summary of the Resolutions Passed by the BG&WILC, November 1938," in *Labour in the West Indies*, mimeo, no date (1939?), p. 48. (The Tuskegee Institute was the first all-Negro institute of higher education in the USA.)

[80] *Ibid.*, p. 47.

[81] L. Braithwaite, "Federal Association in Institutions in the West Indies," p. 298.

should also be noted that the Conference did not engage in the promotion of a particular type of union structure of policy but rather confined itself to the broader social and international issues.

THE CARIBBEAN LABOUR CONGRESS

The inefficiencies of the BG&WILC resulted in suggestions for a re-organised regional association. The International African Service Bureau, a pressure group for West Indian and African independence, circulated an open letter in 1938 urging the formation of unions, self-government, socialist principles, and also specifically advocated the creation of a new regional organisation for the West Indies. A new organisation was not created until 1945, although it was similar to the one proposed in the letter of 1938.[82]

The creation of the Caribbean Labour Congress (CLC) did not stop the continuation of trends and policies which had originated in the BG&WILC, namely an increasing nationalism within the Caribbean, an announced attempt to move away from British influence and models, and a fierce championing of the cause of British West Indian federation. In addition to being associated with self-government, federation was also seen as the base for just social and economic policies.

The founding conference of the CLC was convened by the Barbados Workers' Union in Barbados and Jamaican delegates attended this time, although both of them were from the PNP-TUC side of Jamaican politics. Bustamante had been invited, as is recorded by Hart, "in-

[82] F. Mark, *The History of the Barbados Workers' Union*, Barbados, 1967, p. 83.

vitations to the conference had been sent personally to Alexander Bustamante, President of the BITU and JLP, and to N. W. Manley, MP. Mr. Bustamante did not reply and the PNP interpreted the invitation as an invitation to the party and also for the JTUC. Both organisations accepted and chose Richard Hart as their representative."[83] The Bustamante Industrial Trade Union therefore never became an affiliate of the CLC.

At the conference Manley spoke in both nationalist and political ideological terms when he commented that: "I am satisfied that British Socialism is not for export. I am a realist and I am satisfied that West Indian Socialism is for West Indians to create for West Indies."[84] However, other speakers were less willing to oppose things British: the Hon. T. A. Marryshow who was elected President of the CLC at the conference said in his address that the "British Government is being embarrassed by certain American citizens who desire to take over the West Indies as though we were so many chattels. We as West Indians should become solidly entrenched in the democratic field and would have our government more and more in our own hands—we will give strong assurances to the Britishers that we will always remain British as we have been (cheers) and those American citizens who speak so glibly of transferring the West Indies will have to come to the West Indian Commonwealth and speak to the West Indies and we will tell them just where we stand in the British Commonwealth (more cheers)."[85]

[83] R. Hart, "The History of the Caribbean Labour Congress," as an introduction to *Collection of Papers on the Caribbean Labour Congress Complied by R. Hart and Deposited in Library of the Institute of Jamaica*, March 1967, p. 3.

[84] L. Braithwaite, "Federal Association in Institutions in the West Indies," p. 307.

[85] Caribbean Labour Congress: *Official Report of the Conference Held 17th to 27th September 1945*, Barbados, 1945, p. 7.

At the 1945 conference there was also a discussion on political versus non-political unions. Hart stated that it was no use trying to separate trade unions from political parties and was opposed in this contention by Springer of the Barbados Workers' Union. Hart's position was justified on practical rather than political grounds in that a formal separation of union and party did not prevent union funds from being used for political purposes and that any interdictions against such a practice could easily be circumvented.[86] But no cohesive or consistent view of such issues was taken in the name of the organisation.

Such discussions as these did not, however, characterise the conference in general, the overriding interest displayed being the drive for self-government and federation. Hart, in his account of the history of the CLC, gives the impression that under his influence as Secretary, the organisation was essentially preparing the British West Indies for federation and would therefore be a precursor to regional organisations in other social and political fields. In the second and last conference of the CLC, held at Coke Memorial Hall, Kingston, Jamaica, in 1947, the federation issue was again the one which was given most time and space. The popular edition of the Congress report had a banner headline, "Charter for Caribbean Freedom" and the first resolution quoted is that "this conference declares in favour of the establishment of the federation of the British Caribbean Territories and the immediate initiation of all practical steps must be taken to secure that end."[87] Hart sums up the work of the second Congress as, "Congress finalised the proposals for the creation of the self-

[86] *Ibid.*, p. 16.

[87] Caribbean Labour Congress: *Second Caribbean Labour Congress Report (Popular Edition), Coke Memorial Hall, Kingston, Jamaica, September 2–9, 1947*, Kingston, 1947, p. 1.

governing independent dominion of British Guiana and the West Indian Islands with strong central government and unit responsible government."[88]

One factor which emerged from this Congress was that even at this early stage of such organisations, there was dependence on American financial aid. At the 1947 Congress, Resolution 21 notes, "thanks to all persons in the US who have supported our Congress. This Congress places on record our profound gratitude to our American friends who have by their lively interest in our progress and financial assistance to our cause made possible holding of this successful conference and by their assurances of continued interest will be a mighty aid to our struggle."[89] The "American friends" were the American Committee for West Indian Federation and the Chairman, Mr. Austin, is on record as having, on behalf of the Committee, donated $10,000 to the Congress. Despite this American financial assistance, the report of the secretariat of the CLC to the 1947 Congress was uncompromising in its criticism of American policy: "the USA is clearly engaged in a campaign to smash all preferential systems on principal, because on terms of free trade America will be able to dominate the markets of the world."[90]

The CLC never held another conference because of a combination of the split in the international trade union movement in 1949 and subsequent political events in the Caribbean, and especially Jamaica. When the International Confederation of Free Trade Unions (ICFTU) was created in 1949, the CLC President felt that the CLC should become a regional organisation of the ICFTU but Hart pointed out that as many of the

[88] R. Hart, "The History of the Caribbean Labour Congress," p. 3.
[89] CLC: *Second Caribbean Labour Congress Report . . . etc.*, p. 8.
[90] CLC: *Secretariat Report to the 1947 Congress*, p. 3.

affiliates to the CLC were still affiliated to the World Federation of Trade Unions (WFTU) such an action would split the CLC on the same lines as the international movement.[91] The proposal to disaffiliate from the WFTU was defeated and the CLC remained an affiliate of the WFTU until its dissolution in 1952.[92] Hart claims that the international split and the preference of Adams for the ICFTU was a major factor in the decline of the CLC, but it is clear that there were policy disagreements within the organisation even before the international split. Adams had been elected President in 1947; Hart became General Secretary in the same year and the first indication of the obviously serious division in the organisation came in 1948, when Adams, as a member of the British delegation, told the Trusteeship Council of the United Nations that: "I and my fellows firmly believe that the British Government is deeply anxious to help the peoples of the non-self-governing territories for which it is responsible along the road to self-government. We are convinced of the good faith of Great Britain and have no cause to be otherwise."[93] Hart's response to this is expressed in the headline: "Adams' Speech–A Defense of Imperialism–CLC Secretary Condemns President's Stand."[94]

The final demise of the CLC was the withdrawal of the support of some of its major affiliates, the leaders of which were opposed to the affiliation with the WFTU.[95]

[91] R. Hart, "The History of the Caribbean Labour Congress," p. 6.

[92] Hart, however, attended the 1953 Congress of WFTU as Secretary of the CLC and member of a joint delegation of Trinidad, Guyana, and Jamaica, see WFTU: *3rd World Trade Union Congress, 1953*, p. 291. (All references from WFTU sources are taken from the French editions of its publications.)

[93] CLC: *Monthly Bulletin*, September–October 1948, p. 1.

[94] *Ibid.*

[95] G. Eaton, *dissertation*, p. 81.

Thus from 1948 onwards the CLC drifted into much the same position as the old BG&WILC; according to Hart, "between 1947 and 1951, the CLC with very slender resources and no big staff did useful work in providing exchanges of information on wages and conditions and organised some mutual assistance for strikes in the different territories."[96] In 1951, Hart wrote to Adams explaining the CLC failure, "as you are aware we have been unable to hold our congresses as hoped to in 1949 or indeed 1950 due to lack of funds to organise it on a big scale."[97]

While in fact the CLC did not cease to exist formally until 1952, as an organisation capable of fulfilling even minor functions, it had not been effective since 1948. It was, in the light of subsequent history of regional organisations in the Caribbean, the failure of the CLC which proved its independence. During its short history there is no evidence that it was heavily dependent on politically donated funds nor is there any indication that the leaders uniformly pursued policies or followed models promoted by international or national trade union organisations. At the formal end of the CLC in 1952, for example, a CLC delegation proposed, as a last resort, that the CLC not be affiliated to either of the internationals but remain independent.[98]

THE INTERNATIONALS

Owing to World War II, there was little activity in the International Federation of Trade Unions (IFTU) and

[96] R. Hart, "The History of the Caribbean Labour Congress," p. 5.
[97] Letter from Secretary of CLC, Richard Hart, to President CLC, Grantley Adams, ex R. Hart, *Collection of Papers* . . . etc.
[98] CLC: *Letter to Members, 14th November 1952.*

the conditions of the Jamaican trade movement would not have been conducive to significant involvement.

When a conference was called by the British TUC in 1945 to create a new International, Kenneth Hill, of the Jamaican Trade Union Council, was sent as a representative and he addressed both the preparatory conference in London and the first congress in Paris.[99] It was on this trip that he established contact with the British TUC and other British unions and acquired financial assistance from them.[100]

There is no evidence, as already noted, that financial aid or other assistance was given to Jamaican unions directly by the WFTU before the 1949 split, although the situation changed slightly after 1949.

NATIONAL LABOUR ORGANISATIONS

British Labour Organisations

The first recorded contact between the West Indies and the British TUC was the attendance of F. O. Roberts at the 1926 founding conference of the British Guiana and West Indian Labour Conference. The presence of Roberts was recorded in the British TUC Annual Report of 1926, "as the national committees are very anxious to encourage the natives in the British Dependencies to

[99] See WFTU: *Report of the World Trade Union Conference*, London, February 1945, pp. 106–7 and 116–17; and also G. Padmore, *The Voice of Coloured Labour*, London, 1945, p. 5.

[100] H. Jacobs, "Unions and Parties," *The West Indian Review*, October 1, 1949, p. 17.

organise themselves in Trade Unions and political Labour Parties, they agreed to support the young and hopeful labour movement in the West Indies by sending Mr. F. O. Roberts, M.P., to represent them."[101] This contact could not have been meaningful to Jamaica as there were virtually no trade unions at that time in Jamaica, nor were there any Jamaican delegates to the conference. But the BG&WILC leaders were conscious that the British TUC could be a source of aid and at the 1938 conference a specific request was sent by telegram to the British TUC: "West Indian Labour Conference sends greetings, hopes Congress will offer tangible assistance in organising and building unions in BWI, raising standards of living of colonial workers only guarantees maintenance of improved British standards."[102]

Despite the expressed willingness to "encourage the natives to organise" there is no record of British TUC contact with Jamaican unionists before the end of 1938 when Walter Citrine, General Secretary of the British TUC, visited the island as a member of the government-appointed Moyne Commission. He met several trade unionists including Bustamante, Manley, and Glasspole and claims to have promoted cooperation between the existing unions as he "persuaded them to form a Jamaica Trade Union Advisory Council which would be a centre to keep in contact with the TUC in England."[103] Citrine was impressed with the power of Bustamante although he had to "protect" him against questions by the Chairman on the financial aspects of old-age pensions about which he felt "it was evident that Bustamante had not

[101] TUC: *58th Annual Congress, Report of Proceedings, 1926*, p. 254.

[102] TUC: *70th Annual Congress, Report of Proceedings, 1938*, p. 435.

[103] W. Citrine, *Men and Work*, p. 333.

studied the subject at all."[104] He spent some time "inspecting the administrative set-up" of the BITU and concluded that although it "left a great deal to be desired by British standards, it was reasonably satisfactory."[105] After this visit, however, little contact with Jamaica was maintained during the war.

A specific appeal for assistance to the British TUC from Jamaica was made in April 1940 by Frank Hill, an active trade union organiser among government workers, who wrote a letter published in the British newspaper *Tribune:* "I am afraid that the feeling [disgust] at the present time extends to Britain as a whole since workers are not yet at the stage where they can draw the distinction between Britain's Imperialists and the British Labour Party . . . We in Jamaica pay careful attention to the day by day struggle of the British working class. We see our own salvation as inevitably bound up with yours. We are less equipped than you to protect the fragment of democracy which we possess, so we look to you for assistance—we know that you will not fail us."[106]

But during the war no assistance was forthcoming. After expressing satisfaction at the government's agreement to accept most of Moyne's recommendations in advance, the British TUC Annual Report of 1940 commented that while some progress on a quarterly bulletin for circulation in the Caribbean had been made, its actual realisation had been prevented by the war. Contact was maintained, however, by newsletters "providing a periodical review in outline of TUC activities and

[104] *Ibid.*, p. 332. Although Citrine records that Bustamante was knighted (1955) and became Prime Minister (1962) he fails to mention his seventeen-month-long imprisonment by the British administration which began in 1940.

[105] *Ibid.*

[106] *Worker and Peasant,* Vol. 1, No. 1, April 1940, p. 9.

views."[107] Also in 1943 a number of Jamaican workers were granted training correspondence courses from the National Council of Labour Colleges in Britain.[108]

Although the British TUC did not make contact during the war, the TUCJ report of 1946 records two instances of contact with other British non-governmental organisations. In 1942 a representative of the British Council attended a meeting of the TU-Council and he was told of "the necessity of setting up a library in which Trade Union literature should receive prominent consideration."[109] In 1944 the Council also had a conference with the British Empire Parliamentary Delegation at which the status of the Labour Adviser was discussed.[110]

The contact made in 1939 with Citrine, however, had been maintained with some of the Jamaican trade union leaders. Glasspole notes that advice was sought from Citrine concerning the actions of Governor Richards, who attempted to "outlaw" railway workers and took other repressive measures in the early 1940s. Glasspole eventually obtained a British TUC scholarship to study at Ruskin College from 1946–47, which was the first record of tangible assistance from the British TUC to the Jamaican unions and was, in fact, the first of such scholarships. According to Glasspole, while he was in Britain he paid visits to several offices of British unions but was particularly interested in the Transport and General Workers' Union—a general union—and on his return tried to organise the TUCJ on the same lines as the T&GWU.

The connection with Citrine was again evident in 1946 when Noel N. Nethersole, then President of the

[107] TUC: *72nd Annual Congress, Report of Proceedings, 1940*, p. 159.
[108] TUCJ: *Report of the Trades Union Congress of Jamaica . . . 1946, etc.*, p. 18.
[109] *Ibid.*
[110] *Ibid.*, pp. 13–14.

TUCJ, cabled the Under-Secretary of State for the Colonies as well as Citrine, urging them to assist by pressing the Jamaican Government to negotiate with the TUCJ over the current strike at the Mental Hospital which had resulted in considerable violence. Nethersole actually went to London later to "place the position before the TUC."[111]

These events and the TUCJ leaders' personal contacts with Citrine resulted in the TUCJ receiving the first cash grant from the British TUC Colonial Fund established in 1947. The money was given for education and general organising purposes and largely because, as the General Council report explained, Glasspole at Ruskin reported on "the present financial and other difficulties of the movement in Jamaica."[112]

In 1948 Kenneth Hill, then organiser of a transport union, visited London and saw Citrine and the Colonial Secretary, Creech Jones, in connection with a prolonged bus strike in Jamaica which had resulted in the dismissal of all striking bus drivers. The T&GWU donated £250 to assist the dismissed drivers although the General Council expressed regrets that the local nature of the dispute meant that the British Government could not take effective action because "although the Governor possesses special powers the General Council agree with the view that there must be a minimum interference with the colony's elected legislature. The dispute again brought to notice a number of features in the industrial life of Jamaica which are far from satisfactory."[113]

[111] *Daily Gleaner*, February 20, 1946, as quoted in G. Eaton, *dissertation*, p. 359.

[112] TUC: *79th Annual Congress, Report of Proceedings, 1947*, p. 211.

[113] TUC: *80th Annual Congress, Report of Proceedings, 1948*, p. 20; Hill states, from recollection, that the National Union of Mine-Workers also donated £500 for the bus strike.

Thus, by 1948 the British TUC had established a firm connection with one sector of the divided Jamaican trade union movement. There is no record of similar contact or transactions with the BITU, even though Bustamante and the JLP were elected to power in the newly created legislature in 1945.

The confidence of the British TUC in the TUCJ was once again expressed by a further grant approved in 1948 but made in 1949, of £500 for "extension and reorganisation" of the union.[114] At this point the British TUC had made five allocations out of the Colonial Fund amounting to £1300 of which two allocations amounting to £1000 had been to the TUCJ.

Direct British TUC interest then appears to lapse, although in 1949 a British trade union official assisted in a "Trade Union Training Course" organised by the Colonial Development and Welfare Board. Fred W. Dalley, described as a TUC lecturer and who had made a report on the Trinidad trade union movement in 1947, shared the lecturing with C. W. Burrows, who was the Labour Adviser to the Colonial Development and Welfare Board. The trade union history and legislation of Britain and the West Indies were studied and Burrows reported, "the lively reaction of the students to modern problems is indicative of the present mood of labour opinion in the West Indies and is to be welcomed rather than deprecated. The need for guidance and help which was the purpose of this course is therefore very real, but stability and responsibility are not likely to be achieved overnight."[115] Two Jamaicans attended this course, A. S. Bryan, a TUCJ organiser, and H. L. Shearer, Assistant

[114] TUC: *81st Annual Congress, Report of Proceedings*, 1949, p. 185.

[115] C. Burrows, *Trade Union Training Course, Barbados Report*, no place of publication (Barbados?), 1949, p. 11.

General Secretary of the BITU who became Prime Minister of Jamaica in 1967. This is the first time that personnel of the BITU were brought into educational arrangements through the colonial government and the first record of any BITU contact with the British TUC representatives.

American National Labour Organisations

There are no recorded instances of contact between the Jamaican trade union movement and any American national labour organisations between 1938 and 1949.

Early in the history of the Jamaican movement, however, there had been close contact between some of the small craft unions and the American Federation of Labor (AF of L). In 1907 the Jamaica Trade and Labour Union, a craft union, was affiliated to the AF of L and was, in fact, Local 12575 until 1919 when it became Local 16203. In 1907 and 1908 some printers and cigar makers organised and "made contact with the AF of L."[116] The Secretary of Local 12575 wrote to the Secretary of the AF of L in 1919, expressing his regret that he could not attend the 39th Annual AF of L Congress in Atlantic City.[117] In the same year a letter of sympathy was sent to Samuel Gompers, who had suffered a motor car accident, and a donation was sent to be divided between the striking Cigarmakers' Inter-

[116] According to B. Roberts, *Labour in the Tropical Commonwealth*, London, 1964, p. 11.

[117] *Daily Gleaner*, May 19, 1919, as quoted in G. Eaton, "Trade Union Development in Jamaica," *Caribbean Quarterly*, Vol. 8, No. 2, 1962, p. 50.

national Union and the Iron and Steel Workers' Union in the USA.[118]

These early contacts were not re-established during the 1930s and 1940s although there was some non-union organisational contact with the USA.

[118] *Ibid.*

CHAPTER VIII

CONSOLIDATION AND FOREIGN CONTACTS

Although the basic structure of the Jamaican trade union movement was settled when the Trades Union Congress of Jamaica (TUCJ) became a blanket union in 1949, there was one more important change to occur before the trade union/political party relationships settled into their current form. This was the creation of the National Workers Union (NWU) by the People's National Party (PNP) in 1952. Upon its creation Jamaican politics were placed in an organisational framework which has persisted for over fifteen years.

The NWU is especially important to this study as it eventually replaced the TUCJ as the main union with substantial foreign involvements. The events leading to its establishment as a viable union are also important because of the role played by foreign trade unions in them and because they affected the subsequent development of trade unionism and politics in Jamaica. For these reasons it is necessary to add some detail to the brief account of the formation of the NWU which has already been given. At this point, there will be no attempt to analyse the situation or weigh the importance of ideology, power, or international factors, as it is first necessary to have a complete view of the foreign involvements and the international economic and political aspects.

Creation of The National Workers Union

The leadership of the TUCJ and the PNP had always been closely interlocked; thus between 1949 and 1951, for example, the President of the union, Nethersole, was also first Vice-President of the PNP; Ken Hill, originally Vice-President of the union, was second Vice-President of the party; Glasspole, the union's General Secretary, was a member of the party's executive; and Norman Manley, founder and President of the PNP, was the union's legal adviser from its creation. In such a situation the actions of either the union or non-union wings of the party could affect the destiny of both party and union.

It had been clear for some time that there were political differences between some of the TUCJ-PNP participants. Manley, as leader of the party, had on many occasions confirmed his commitment to socialism but the trade union leadership tended to be more militant in relation to the professed socialism of the party. Nevertheless, union leaders, such as the Hill brothers and Glasspole, had had long associations with Manley, beginning in the mid 1930s, and had worked together closely for the election of 1949 which the PNP, as in 1944, lost to the JLP.

Regardless of the possibility of conflicts arising from foreign involvements, which will be detailed later, there were genuine divisions between the party and the union leaders which became more obvious after the 1949 election. The division was also made more real by another, almost exclusively domestically based development—the increase in power of the TUCJ.

RISE AND FALL OF THE TUCJ

The conversion of the TUCJ into a blanket union had not been successful as a party political manoeuvre to unseat the JLP, but it did have profound effects on the power and effectiveness of the TUCJ.

By December 1951 the union had seventy-eight branches and 29,000 members and was thus well on the way to be able to challenge the BITU.[1] But the factor which was likely to increase the power of the TUCJ substantially, was the possibility of concluding a dues check-off agreement with the Sugar Manufacturers' Association (SMA). Negotiations for such a check-off agreement were in progress and its successful conclusion would have meant an income for the TUCJ of £30,000 per year, making it financially independent of the party.[2]

The growing success of the TUCJ occurred at a time when there were significant changes taking place in the investment pattern in Jamaica. These changes arose mainly from the investment of some Canadian and USA companies in preparation for the exploitation of Jamaican bauxite reserves, then estimated to be among the largest in the world. The first company in Jamaica, a wholly owned subsidiary of Reynolds Aluminium Company of Canada (ALCAN), began work on an alumina plant in

[1] *Daily Gleaner*, December 22, 1951, p. 9.
[2] According to interview respondent.

1949 which was completed in 1952 at an estimated cost of £3.5 million.[3] In 1949 a subsidiary of Reynolds Aluminum Company of USA started work on a bauxite mining site to cost £5 million and which produced the first commercial shipment of bauxite from Jamaica in 1952. In 1950 the largest bauxite mining project was started by the USA Kaiser Aluminum and Chemical Corporation which had a projected capital expenditure of £5.5 million.[4] Between 1949 and 1952, therefore, much of the current investment manifested itself in Jamaica as construction work for bauxite mining and alumina production installations. From 1950 onwards, unions were able to conclude agreements with both the construction contractors as well as the companies themselves and the TUCJ was in the forefront with all of these negotiations.

An agreement was signed in 1950 between Reynolds and the TUCJ, which brought forth the comment in *Public Opinion*, the newspaper of the PNP, that "local trade union history was quietly made in mid-December when for the first time an employer organisation contracted not to attempt to use 'strike-breakers' to break a strike called by a union."[5]

In July of 1951 the TUCJ signed a contract with Sprostons Ltd., the construction company for ALCAN (later to be owned by ALCAN). ALCAN later agreed to accept the basic working and wages conditions in the Sprostons' agreement for its directly employed work-

[3] *Daily Gleaner*, August 24, 1950. (As the names of the Jamaican subsidiaries have changed on several occasions they will be referred to by the abbreviated form of the name of the parent company, viz., ALCAN, Kaiser, Reynolds, ALCOA, etc.)

[4] *Daily Gleaner*, August 2, 1951, and August 23, 1951. (Citations from the *Daily Gleaner* without page numbers indicate that the quote is from the clipping file in the Institute of Jamaica where only the dates are recorded.)

[5] *Public Opinion*, January 27, 1951, p. 3.

ers and also accepted the TUCJ as the bargaining agent for the workers.[6]

The TUCJ and the BITU were also showing signs of cooperation and in August 1951 they made a joint demand for a union shop in the sugar industry and declared that "the unions would not be divided on any political or other grounds" in this matter.[7] In October 1951 the BITU and TUCJ with the Labour Adviser's deputy, C. Greaves-Hill, as Chairman, opened negotiations with Kaiser with regard to union representation.[8]

But the honeymoon period of the TUCJ relations with the bauxite companies was already over. In July 1951, arbitration proceedings had opened between the TUCJ and Reynolds on whether the 1950 contract prevented the union from demanding a cost-of-living bonus before its expiry date in 1952. In December the negotiations between Kaiser, the BITU, and the TUCJ broke down over wage rates and a strike followed immediately.[9]

The TUCJ's and the BITU's attempts for union shop and dues check-off with the Sugar Manufacturers' Association failed in August 1951, when the SMA spokesman claimed that the unions had withdrawn their demands pending settlement of the 1952 sugar prices.[10] It was alleged, however, that leaders of the PNP had requested the SMA to stop negotiations for a union shop because the extra financial power for the TUCJ would "upset the balance of forces in the PNP."[11] This was one of the first signs of the growing political divisions between sections of the party leadership and the union.

[6] G. Eaton, *dissertation*, p. 22. (This author's account of the early negotiations with the bauxite companies is not always consistent with the newspaper accounts.)
[7] *Daily Gleaner*, August 3, 1951, p. 1.
[8] *Ibid.*, October 2, 1951, p. 1.
[9] *Ibid.*, December 1, 1951, p. 1; and December 4, 1951, p. 1.
[10] *Ibid.*, October 29, 1951, p. 1.
[11] *The People*, Vol. 1, No. 1, May 10, 1952, p. 3.

BREAKAWAY UNION AND COMMITTEE OF ENQUIRY

More drastic turbulence became apparent in November 1951, when Thossy A. Kelly, who was then Assistant General Secretary of the TUCJ, and William McPherson, a trustee of the TUCJ, announced the formation of a breakaway union to be known as the National Labour Congress (NLC). It was to be composed of seven unions, the most important being the Union of Sugar Workers, Union of Bauxite and Allied Workers, and unions in transport, light, and power. Kelly made the announcement of his breakaway union at a meeting of Kendal bauxite workers and said that "he was setting up a new bauxite workers' union separate and apart from the TUC."[12] Kelly then resigned from the executive of the TUCJ, claiming that members of the executive had "carried on a campaign to destroy myself and general secretary Florizel Glasspole."[13]

Almost immediately, Kenneth Hill, then President of the TUCJ, accused Kelly of consorting with the managements of the Jamaica Bauxite Co. (ALCAN) and the Jamaica Textile Mills Co. . . . Kelly's reply to these charges was that "ideological differences between Ken Hill, his followers and myself and, in consequence, the administrative policies of the TUC . . . led to the present situation."[14] The PNP, from which executive Kelly was noticeably absent, indicated that unless Kelly and Macpherson abandoned their breakaway union attempt the party would officially hear charges brought against

[12] *Daily Gleaner*, November 27, 1951, p. 1.
[13] *Ibid.*
[14] *Daily Gleaner*, November 29, 1951, p. 1.

them. By this time, however, it was evident that the leaders of the PNP were themselves divided on the issue—a division which was amplified by the new dimension of the claimed "ideological differences."

The PNP eventually named a four-man committee of enquiry to hear the charges against Kelly and Macpherson and other related matters. The committee, which included Norman Manley and N. N. Nethersole, almost immediately dismissed charges against the leaders of the breakaway union, who had offered (before the hearings began) to affiliate the new union to the PNP. Thus the committee began to hear evidence on the alleged "marxist activities and plans"[15] of the TUCJ leaders. Documents were presented which were claimed to be proof that the TUCJ had permitted marxist teaching, had communist connections through WFTU, and was thereby engaged in anti-party (PNP) activity. One document alleged to be used in TUCJ training classes was said to argue that the working class should ally with the PNP until independence and then transfer their allegiance to a Communist Party.[16] A letter from the WFTU secretariat in 1951 was exhibited to show WFTU connections with the TUCJ.[17] The principal persons accused were Kenneth Hill, Frank Hill, Richard Hart, and Arthur Henry, who have since become known in Jamaican political folklore as the "four H's."

The Committee of Enquiry, called in the *Daily Gleaner* "The Marxist Charges Tribunal," found the four H's guilty of permitting marxist doctrines to be taught and of forming a marxist cell within the PNP. The PNP executive asked for their resignations and at a specially

[15] *Ibid.*, December 19, 1951, p. 1.
[16] G. Eaton, *dissertation*, p. 381.
[17] *Daily Gleaner*, March 5, 1952, p. 11.

called party conference the request was repeated with the result that the four H's resigned in May 1952.[18]

THE NWU

The expulsion of the four H's from the PNP still left the power of the TUCJ untouched, although it was now without a party attachment. Thus in September 1952 a new party was created by the TUCJ leaders, the National Labour Party, but it was heavily defeated in the 1955 election and declined in relation to the decline of the TUCJ. The four H's themselves were not in agreement and by 1953 the Hill brothers had expelled Hart and Henry from the TUCJ. Hart started a Peoples' Education Organisation and later a trade union, the Jamaican Federation of Trade Unions (JFTU), in conjunction with Ferdinand Smith, a Jamaican alleged to have been deported from the USA for communist activities.[19] The union was formally created in September 1953 and Smith, as delegate to the WFTU October 1953 Congress, reported efforts to organise the workers in the sugar industry affected by the decline of the TUCJ.[20] The Sugar and Agricultural Workers' Union (SAWU) at that time remained the only operating union associated with the JFTU. In 1954, 1955, and 1956 the SAWU was involved

[18] *Commonwealth Newsletter*, Jamaica Correspondent, May 1, 1952, p. 428.

[19] W. Knowles, *Trade Union Development and Industrial Relations in the British West Indies*, Berkeley, 1959, p. 133.

[20] WFTU: *3rd World Trade Union Congress, 1953*, p. 440. The only information and records of the JFTU are found in the reports of delegates to the WFTU congresses in 1953, 1957, and 1961.

in strikes at various sugar plantations but despite a claim of 25,000 members in 1957, it never became a force to match the BITU or the growing NWU.[21] By 1961 the WFTU delegate reported declining activity of both the SAWU and the JFTU attributed, among other reasons, to the lack of trade union traditions among the workers.[22] The JFTU in that year had only publicity and educational functions of a limited nature and by 1965 neither the JFTU or Jamaica were represented at the WFTU Congress. The JFTU never really established a membership base and from the beginning remained basically a nominal organisation.

Although Kelly had announced, before the expulsion of the four H's, that he was prepared to affiliate his National Labour Congress to the PNP, the party leaders decided in April 1952 to create their own union, the National Workers Union. Kelly brought his NLC membership to the NWU and became first Vice-President, while Nethersole, one of the party judges at the PNP tribunal, became President of the new union.

The BITU, which had been cooperating with the TUCJ, then began raiding the membership of the TUCJ and the NWU almost immediately became the representative union for the bauxite workers throughout the industry, despite the entrenched position of the TUCJ. Thus, from the creation of the NWU, the TUCJ began to decline and within seven years had dropped to third place in power and membership compared with the NWU and BITU.

The NWU became the union in Jamaica which has had the most continuous and intensive connection with foreign and international labour organisations. Its cre-

[21] WFTU: *4th World Trade Union Congress, 1957*, p. 567.
[22] WFTU: *5th World Trade Union Congress, 1961*, p. 823.

ation, therefore, was one of the most important events within the Jamaican trade union movement in relation to foreign involvements.

Foreign National Labour Organisations

The principal foreign national labour organisation involved in the Jamaican trade union movement in the period 1938–49 had been the British TUC. The position changed in the following period (1949–67), for although the British TUC continued its involvement, an American union, the United Steelworkers of America (USWA), also became involved in Jamaica.

The USWA is not, like the British TUC, a national trade union centre, but an industrial union with approximately one million members in 1966, drawn from the metals industry in North America. Like most American unions the USWA has incorporated within it locals and members from Canada as well as the USA. The first recorded presence of a USWA representative in Jamaica was in 1952 and since that time the British TUC and the USWA have been the principal foreign labour organisations in Jamaica, acting both independently and through international and regional labour organisations. In this section, only the direct contacts between foreign national labour organisations and Jamaican unions will be considered.

The United Steelworkers of America

CREATION OF THE NWU AND EARLY INVOLVEMENT

There is no tangible evidence of foreign union involvement in the creation of the NWU between April and October of 1952. However, it is obvious that the break-up of the PNP and TUCJ and the creation of the NWU were centred around the establishment of the bauxite-alumina industry which represented the most heavy investment of foreign capital in Jamaica in modern times. In the previous section it was shown that the first indication of a split in the TUCJ leadership was when Kelly announced to *bauxite* workers that he was setting up a new *bauxite* workers' union even though the union he eventually created, the National Labour Congress, was a blanket union. From the trade union standpoint, the representation of bauxite workers was to become an important source of income, owing to the high wages eventually paid in the industry, but in 1951 and 1952 the wages were almost the same as those prevailing in the rest of the island. The interest in the bauxite-alumina industry would have to be one of future potential rather than immediate gain if the issue was to be considered strictly within the existing framework of unions and industrial relations.

The NWU leadership also showed an overriding interest in the bauxite-alumina industry and by January 1954 the NWU represented all the workers in the bauxite-alumina industry. The establishment of the NWU in the bauxite-alumina industry was assisted by the USWA, which sent a representative, Nicholas Zonarich, to the island in 1952.[23] Zonarich, originally the President of the Aluminum Workers of America which merged with the USWA in 1943, was met in Jamaica by Norman Manley, whose party was at that time in the process of creating the NWU. The arrival of Zonarich in Jamaica marked the beginning of a tripartite relationship, the USWA, the NWU, and the bauxite industry, which has persisted to the present day.

Zonarich addressed workers on a bauxite site and is alleged to have explained that although the current wage rate (about 19 cents per hour) was better than some in the island, the luxuries a worker could obtain from it, such as a bicycle, were nothing compared with American workers who all had cars and that: "A bicycle is a child's toy."[24] This speech, among other factors, caused the JLP-BITU government to protest to the US State Department, and when Zonarich attempted to re-enter the island in March 1953, he was served an order which read: "That you shall not at any time address any group of persons on any topic relating to political and trade union matters, or discuss such matters with any group of persons, or participants in any way in any negotiations arising out of any trade dispute,–21st March 1953."[25]

The USWA then sent a Canadian, Charles H. Millard, the National Director of the Canadian section of the USWA, and, according to the USWA newspaper, "when the authorities realized that Millard, as a Canadian, was also a fellow-citizen of the British Commonwealth the

[23] USWA: *Proceedings of 12th Constitutional Convention, 1964*, p. 177.

[24] This phrase is attributed to a USWA representative in W. Knowles, *Trade Union Development and Industrial Relations in the British West Indies*, p. 137.

[25] From original document in possession of N. Zonarich.

ban was lifted."[26] Meyer Bernstein, International Representative of the USWA in 1954, told a labour conference, however, that the order had been revoked with the aid of the British Labour Party.[27]

What specific occurrence caused the initial interest of the USWA in Jamaica and in the NWU is subject to doubt, as accounts differ. One unionist involved told this writer that a bauxite company in Jamaica requested the USWA to send someone to Jamaica with whom they could negotiate and specified the individual desired. Another ex-USWA executive member said that a person engaged in a United Nations Technical Assistance Programme in Jamaica contacted the USWA, Canada, and advised them to help the NWU. More officially, *Steel Labor*, the weekly newspaper of the USWA, states that "workers" in Jamaica requested aid from the ICFTU, that USWA's Canadian Director, Millard, was on the executive board of the ICFTU and thus through him the USWA became involved.[28]

But regardless of how the USWA became involved in Jamaica, the record of means of involvement from 1952 onwards is well recorded.

ORGANISERS, ADVISERS, AND FINANCE FROM THE USWA

Millard went to Jamaica in April 1953 and addressed striking workers at an ALCAN construction site. On his return to Canada he was reported by Toronto newspapers

[26] "It's Not All Calypso," *Steel Labor*, April 1957, p. 7.
[27] R. Aronson and J. Windmuller, eds., *Labor, Management and Economic Growth*, Conference Proceedings, mimeo, p. 216.
[28] *Steel Labor*, April 1957, p. 7.

as having announced that he would make "available to Jamaican unions the services of the union's [USWA] Canadian Research and Publicity and Education Department."[29] This policy has been followed since that time, although organisers and advisers have not come exclusively from the Canadian Division of the USWA.

At the beginning of 1953, and possibly earlier, the USWA put Kenneth Sterling on its payroll (he was originally an organiser for the PNP) and charged him with organising the bauxite workers on behalf of the NWU. Knowles notes that Sterling did an "outstanding job"[30] in organising the bauxite workers while another USWA executive said that Sterling had been the "real spearhead" of the organising drive and that he had "done more" than any other person in Jamaica for the creation of the NWU. Sterling remained on the payroll until at least the end of 1956, long after the NWU had acquired full bargaining rights for all the bauxite workers in Jamaica, but by this time he was also involved in regional organisations sponsored or assisted by the USWA.[31]

Zonarich and Millard were in Jamaica as advisers and negotiators for various wage claims and arbitrations in the bauxite industry between 1953 and 1956. They had generally sought pay increases for bauxite workers as a normal process of industrial negotiation but had been met by the argument (mostly from Jamaican businessmen) that the wage rates in that industry should not be different from wage rates prevailing in other sectors of the economy. In 1953 an important arbitration report

[29] *Daily Gleaner*, April 22, 1953, p. 2.

[30] W. Knowles, *Trade Union Development and Industrial Relations in the British West Indies*, p. 73.

[31] *National Workers Union 4th Annual Report*, Kingston, 1956, p. 24.

accepted the view that the bauxite industry was a special case and that its wage structure need not correspond with the general wage structure in the island. The NWU case in the arbitration had been made by Cleve Kidd, Research Director of the USWA, Canadian Division, and assisted by USWA-paid Sterling. Kidd kept close contact with Jamaica from that time, so much so that when the PNP-NWU government appointed an official Commission of Enquiry into the causes of sugar industry strikes, they appointed Kidd as a commission member.[32]

Also in 1959, Gower Markle, Director of Education and Welfare for the Canadian Division of USWA, completed a two-month survey of labour education needs in the Caribbean, which was presented at a Conference of Labour Education held under the auspices of the University College of the West Indies.[33] Although the conference was funded by several sources, including the British Government Colonial Development and Welfare Fund (CD&W), whether the cost of Markle's trip and time came from those funds or was paid for by the USWA is not clear and no comment on the financing of the survey, as distinct from the conference, was made. The conference organiser Rawle Farley, Industrial Relations tutor of the University College of the West Indies, claimed that Markle was recommended for the survey by Roby Kidd, Canadian Director of the Adult Education Association, and no mention was made of the, by then, six-year-old close relationship between the USWA and NWU.[34]

In 1958 the NWU appointed as director of its embry-

[32] The CIO claims to have "cooperated" with these missions. See CIO: *Proceedings of 15th Constitutional Convention, 1950*, p. 241.
[33] G. Eaton, *dissertation*, p. 506.
[34] R. Farley, ed., *Labour Education in the British Caribbean*, Georgetown, British Guiana, 1960, pp. 7–8.

onic Research Department, Carl Hall, who had been research assistant to the USWA (Canada), although Hall subsequently acquired a two-year scholarship to Massachusetts Institute of Technology and left the island.[35]

USWA personnel have participated in NWU-sponsored courses for bauxite trainees. Markle, for example, together with Meyer Bernstein, International Affairs Director; Otis Brubaker, Director of the Research Department; and Larry Spitz, Director of Wage Divisions were in Jamaica in 1966 to participate in a seminar for bauxite workers.[36]

In 1967 the NWU requested that the USWA send a "job evaluation and time study expert" to assist the NWU and the Trade Union Education Institute in their work; the USWA responded by sending a person for a year for that purpose.[37] In the same year it is recorded that the NWU requested assistance from the legislative department of the USWA "to prepare a modern and progressive Labour Relations Act, which is to be submitted to Government for implementation. The United Steelworkers of America has agreed to give the assistance, and it is at present preparing such an Act for the NWU's consideration."[38] Two members of the USWA legislative department staff had been in Jamaica the year before. Throughout the period 1963–67, the annual reports of the NWU and the *Daily Gleaner* record visits every year from USWA personnel from almost all of the union's departments, although from the records it was only Michael Manley, Island Supervisor of NWU, who made frequent trips to Canada and the USA to attend USWA meetings.

[35] *National Workers Union 7th Annual Report,* Kingston, 1959, p. 28.

[36] *National Workers Union 14th Annual Report,* Kingston, 1966, p. 41.

[37] *Ibid.,* p. 43.

[38] *Ibid.,* p. 49.

Records of direct financial assistance from the USWA to the NWU are sparse. In 1953, when announcing the intention of the USWA to become involved with Jamaican unions, Millard stated that $3000 had already been paid to the strike fund of the bauxite workers on strike against Alumina Jamaica Ltd. In 1958 the USWA bought the NWU a car for "organising work."[39] The NWU has always had a very low proportion of paying members compared with the claimed figures of the BITU, which has meant that in proportion to the workers it claims to represent its revenue cannot be high.

USWA records specify a gift to the Iron and Steel Workers' Federation of the UK of $10,000 in 1951, but the $3000 gift announced by Millard is not recorded.[40] Until 1960 the USWA did not have a separate International Affairs Department and all expenditures on international affairs came within the research budget. The budget of this department shows no noticeable increase in expenditure upon the involvement of the union in Jamaica and the Caribbean, despite the employment of Sterling and other deployment of USWA personnel.

NWU AND USWA: GENERAL RELATIONS

In 1953 the NWU established close connections with foreign national and international labour organisations but the BITU continued to reject such involvements and the TUCJ rapidly moved out of the previous international contact. The NWU leaders made it clear that they saw international connections as being of prime importance

[39] CADORIT: *Information Bulletin*, December 1957–January 1958, p. 11.

[40] See budget report in USWA: *Proceedings of 7th Constitutional Convention*, 1954.

to the new union; in a special policy statement at the NWU third annual congress in 1953, it was argued that "... the NWU believes that the future strength of the Trade Union Movement lies in the development of International Trade Union ties through and with International Democratic Labour Organisations . . . and now seeks to establish closer relations with other International Trade Union Organisations as well as powerful Industrial Unions": mention was made in the statement of even closer contact with the USWA because "the NWU intends to negotiate terms of affiliation with the United Steelworkers of Canada in the interest of the Bauxite Section."[41]

For several reasons, this latter statement of intention was not realised but it explains, to some extent, changes made in the NWU constitution between 1953 and 1957. Mimeo copies of the two constitutions are deposited in the Library of Congress, USA, and a person unknown has written on the 1953 edition "modeled after the TUC —Revision in process modeled after Amer-Canadian TU's, Chartered Locals instead of unchartered branches," and on the 1957 edition is written "Supersedes 1953 Const., Subject to amendments at the 1957 Conference." The process of remodelling revealed in these documents includes some changes in language and branch structure. In the earlier edition of the constitution, Rule 4, on honorary members, stated: "Persons who are not of the working class on approval of the General Executive Council shall be admitted as Honorary Members." Such a clause is direct reference to the non-working class nature of many of the members of the NWU, including lawyer and President, Nethersole, and accountant, Glasspole. The sensitivity of Jamaican

[41] *National Workers Union 3rd Annual Report,* Statement of Policy, Kingston, 1955, p. 6.

unionists on this issue stems from the early belief that trade unions were "working class" organisations in which educated leaders had a doubtful role. The rewritten constitution states, more sophisticatedly, that "the General Executive council may from time to time admit persons as honorary members."

The only significant changes, however, occurred in relation to "chartered branches." The "remodelling" in fact consisted of insertion of a section which had been written or copied from a North American document. Despite the reference, throughout the 1957 constitution, to "branches," a British term, a special section is on "Chartered Locals" and in this section, and this section only, the North American term "local" is used. Furthermore, the section refers to the General Executive *Board* rather than the correct NWU title, the General Executive Council.[42] The effect of the chartered local section is to give greater autonomy to a chartered local and, in particular, the ability to have its own bank account and negotiate with greater independence. The only chartered local in the history of the NWU has been in the bauxite workers' section. The 1960 edition of the constitution preserves these privileges and refers to locals throughout, although branch is still the word used in Jamaican unionism and by leaders and employees of the NWU.[43]

These inconsistencies indicate that the constitution, especially that section relating to chartered locals, was written by a person with North American experience who had no intimate knowledge of the NWU. It cannot be assumed from such evidence that the USWA staff wrote the constitution although the effect of the chartered locals was definitely a compromise between

[42] Executive Board is the name given to the executive bodies of many USA unions, including the USWA.

[43] NWU: *Constitution and Rules and Regulations of the National Workers Union of Jamaica.*

independence and the stated policy of the USWA (and some leaders of the NWU) to affiliate the bauxite workers directly to the USWA.

The special nature of the bauxite section was again indicated in 1959, when a meeting of bauxite workers was held in Kingston which the NWU claimed was significant because "it represented the first practical attempt on the part of any blanket union in Jamaica to give effect to the principle of closer identity among workers in a particular interest."[44] At the meeting a resolution was passed expressing solidarity with the striking USWA workers in the USA and calling for Jamaican subscriptions to the strike fund.

The NWU leadership apparently was prepared to accept and support both the leaders and the ideology of the USWA. In recounting the USWA ideological influence on the NWU, Knowles records that a NWU union official told him: "I believe in David J. McDonald's brand of 'socialism.'"[45] More formally, the NWU leadership expressed its thanks to the USWA on a scroll which was presented to McDonald, President of the USWA. The scroll read: "to observe the substantial rise in the living standards of our bauxite workers, the great awakening of trade union consciousness in them and to hear them acknowledge with sincerity and due gratitude your fraternal help, would make your heart rejoice and raise in you a special pride and satisfaction. We wish you to know that this spirit awakened in Jamaica is fast spreading throughout the entire Caribbean, ensuring this world for peace and democracy. God Bless you Brother

[44] *National Workers Union 7th Annual Report*, Kingston, 1959, p. 15.

[45] W. Knowles, "The British West Indies," in W. Galenson, ed., *Labor and Economic Development*, New York, 1959, p. 27. (MacDonald was not known as an advocate of socialism of any type in the United States.)

McDonald, and may the United Steelworkers of America live forever."[46]

When Michael Manley addressed the 12th Constitutional Convention of the USWA in 1964, he once again expressed the appreciation of the NWU for the USWA involvement: "Then began in 1953, a collaboration between your organization and ours which has led, I dare to hope, to very considerable results, which I believe has set a pattern of international co-operation which is an example to the entire free world, because throughout these years of our struggle your organization has helped with advice, has put at our disposal all the vast resources of your research department, your experience and has allied to that the moral force of your own purpose."[47]

After the USWA conference Michael Manley went to Europe for a meeting of the International Metalworkers' Federation (IMF), of which he was an executive member, but returned temporarily for the NWU annual conference. The NWU explained publicly, according to the *Daily Gleaner*, that the trip to Europe was at the expense of the IMF while the USWA had paid the return fare for the NWU conference.[48]

Such close relationships between the NWU and USWA have resulted in the USWA personnel being invited to become involved in a wide range of activities in Jamaican unionism, and thereby Jamaican politics. An example came in 1967 when NWU leaders attempted to bring the BITU into a negotiation to create a single national trade union centre for Jamaica, "groups interested in Jamaican unions will be invited including the United Steelworkers of America, the ICFTU, the CCL [the

[46] "It's Not All Calypso," *Steel Labor*, p. 7.

[47] USWA: *Proceedings of 12th Constitutional Convention, 1964*, p. 177.

[48] *Daily Gleaner*, December 3, 1964, p. 1; and December 4, 1964, p. 2.

Canadian Congress of Labor], the British TUC and the AFL-CIO."[49] The attempt to create a national centre failed as the BITU representative did not attend the conference.

The British Trades Union Congress

There was no financial aid from the British TUC to the Jamaican trade unions from 1949 until 1952. Contact was maintained through correspondence and on one occasion a visit was made by the Assistant General Secretary. In 1949 and 1950 there were some exchanges between the TUCJ and the British TUC on the subject of the former's continued affiliation to the WFTU after the split in 1949. In May 1951, Assistant General Secretary of the British TUC, George Woodcock, was in Jamaica and met "business and labour."[50]

A year later the British TUC became the first foreign labour organisation to support the newly created NWU by announcing, even before the union was legally registered, a grant of £500 for organising purposes. The General Council explained that after the PNP had expelled the "Communist sympathisers the NWU was established under the secretaryship of Mr. F. A. Glasspole and gained immediate support from the workers of the Island. During its first months, the NWU gained exclusive bargaining rights in several important firms . . ." and that an investigation of the trade union situation was "carried out on behalf of the TUC by the General Secretary of the Barbados Workers' Union, Mr.

[49] *Daily Gleaner*, November 8, 1966, p. 2.
[50] *Public Opinion*, May 12, 1951, p. 2.

F. L. Walcott."[51] A *Daily Gleaner* editorial commented that the grant had been "interpreted by local circles as a mark of approval by the British TUC for the new union."[52] In 1954 the British TUC made one of the largest grants ever given to a colonial trade union when it gave £1500 to the NWU. The sum was given after another investigation by Walcott but also after Woodcock had called a conference of West Indian trade union leaders to "discuss further the needs of the movement in this region."[53] The financial support of the NWU ceased after 1954 and British TUC interest in Jamaica was manifested only in occasional visits, as that of British trade unionist Dame Anne Goodwin to the independence celebrations in 1962 and in support of educational programmes.

By 1958 the British TUC was stating clearly its withdrawal from Jamaica and the West Indies. A trade unionist from Jamaica returned from Britain and quoted Woodcock as saying the West Indian trade unionists should be trained at home and that "the training of West Indians in trade unionism at home rather than bringing them to England would be a saving. The money spent on one man in England could be used to train about a dozen in the West Indies."[54] It is possible that in accordance with this statement the British TUC leadership supported the large grant by the CD&W of £3500 for a conference on Labour Education in the Caribbean in 1959. The direct British TUC contribution was meagre, as mentioned by Farley, conference organiser: "we are also highly appreciative of the spirit behind

[51] TUC: *85th Annual Congress, Report of Proceedings, 1953*, p. 215.
[52] *Daily Gleaner*, September 28, 1952, p. 1.
[53] TUC: *86th Annual Congress, Report of Proceedings, 1954*, p. 215.
[54] *Daily Gleaner*, July 24, 1958, p. 5.

the British Trades Union Congress which voluntarily sent a cheque for £25 to aid the financing of the conference."[55]

In 1959 Woodcock made broadcasts in the Caribbean on trade unionism and in 1961 a British trade unionist, Ted O'Leary of the Transport and General Workers' Union (T&GWU), was nominated by the unions [Jamaican] as the union member in a Commission of Enquiry concerning the Port of Kingston.[56]

But even these contacts became less frequent. Thus a request by the NWU for a British TUC representative to argue the union's case before an enquiry board on a strike at the Jamaican Broadcasting Corporation was rejected by the General Council of the TUC. They sent a resume of British precedents in such cases but stated firmly that "no useful purpose will be served by sending a representative."[57]

By 1965 it was possible for Fred Hayday, Chairman of the British TUC International Committee, to outline British TUC policy in the following terms: "The West Indian Territories have the most highly developed trade union system in the Commonwealth—outside Britain—and need very little help from us . . . They have developed in a very encouraging way, they are well-established and well-run and though they can occasionally do with a spot of financial help from us it is not often that they need advice . . . We meet with the delegates on a most friendly basis of common expression and their problems are usually ours as well—we learn a lot from each other."[58]

The opening of the Trade Union Education Institute

[55] R. Farley, ed., *Labour Education in the British Caribbean*, p. 7.
[56] *Daily Gleaner*, December 2, 1961, p. 1.
[57] TUC: *96th Annual Congress, Report of Proceedings, 1964*, p. 268.
[58] *Daily Gleaner*, May 27, 1965, p. 3.

(TUEI) in Jamaica permitted the British TUC to renew its contacts with the NWU. When the latter union requested British TUC assistance in drawing up a time and motion study agreement with a new British company, a representative was sent who lectured at the TUEI as well as assisting the NWU in its negotiations.[59]

In 1967 another British TUC-appointed trade unionist lectured at the TUEI. In the same year the NWU, seeking funds for the TUEI, wrote to Woodcock "outlining the origin of the institute, the proposals for future financing and requesting the TUC for financial support."[60] After consultation in London between Woodcock and Nettleford, Director of the TUEI, the British TUC agreed to supply £500 for three years towards the operating costs.

Other Foreign National Labour Organisations

There have been some recorded instances of direct involvement of foreign national labour organisations other than the USWA and the British TUC. The NWU states, for example, that the Cuban Workers' Federation (CTC) supplied "substantial financial assistance" in 1954 for organising purposes.[61]

Direct contacts between Jamaica and the USA national trade union centres have been sparse, although sometimes important. President of the AFL-CIO George

[59] TUC: *98th Annual Congress, Report of Proceedings, 1966,* p. 268.

[60] *Daily Gleaner,* April 12, 1967, p. 27.

[61] *National Workers Union 2nd Annual Report,* Kingston, 1954, as quoted in *Man of Destiny,* PNP publication, Kingston, 1954, p. 72. W. Knowles describes this Cuban union as "The Cuban Sugar Workers' Union," *Trade Union Development and Industrial Relations in the British West Indies,* p. 73.

Meany visited the island in 1962 and conferred with Norman Manley, then Prime Minister, as well as Bustamante, then Opposition Leader, about immigration policy, the sugar quota, and the treatment of Jamaican farm workers in the USA.[62] He had previously consulted in Washington with Jamaican Ministry of Labour officials on these matters. More important for the AFL-CIO was the appointment of William C. Doherty, a Vice-President of the AFL-CIO, as USA ambassador to Jamaica in 1963.

Visits to the NWU from the AFL-CIO, the Canadian Labour Congress, and individual unions have been recorded frequently. In 1961 a group of unionists touring the island from the New York branch of the International Brotherhood of Electrical Workers, AFL-CIO, supplied funds from a collection to support a NWU strike at a metal goods factory.[63]

According to a BITU trade union official interviewed, the union has had some connections with the Utility Workers' Union of America (New York local) which he said had supplied some funds for the building of the BITU headquarters in Kingston. No other record has been found of such connections.

In 1956 an unnamed union of the German Democratic Republic attempted to send a film projector to the Jamaican Federation of Trade Unions (JFTU). The delegate to the WFTU conference in 1957 reported that it was seized by customs and sent back to the donor.[64]

[62] See "Meany and AFL-CIO Officials Visit Jamaica as Guests of Government," *Inter-American Labor Bulletin,* Vol. XIII, No. 4, April 1962, pp. 1 and 4.

[63] *Inter-American Labor Bulletin,* Vol. XII, No. 6, June 1961, p. 3.

[64] WFTU: *Fourth World Trade Union Congress, 1952,* p. 568.

REGIONAL AND INTERNATIONAL TRADE UNION ORGANISATIONS

Before considering the involvement of regional and international trade union organisations in Jamaica some of the history of international and Caribbean organisations must be outlined.

It is not important to examine in detail the international trade union split which occurred in 1949, for its importance in the Caribbean and Jamaica will emerge in the course of discussing the regional and national labour organisations. However, in view of the identification of the British TUC and the USWA as the two principal foreign national labour organisations involved in Jamaica, the relationship of these two organisations with the Internationals is of some importance. The British TUC had been one of the national centres which organised the founding conference and the eventual creation of the WFTU. As part of the CIO, the USWA had also been affiliated to the WFTU and the USWA President, Philip Murray, was also President of the CIO during the period in which it cooperated with the WFTU. The AF of L had not participated in the WFTU, objecting to the membership of unions from communist countries and the CIO. The British TUC also played a major part in the splitting of the International and the creation of the ICFTU in 1949, to which both the AF of L and the CIO became affiliated.

The affiliation of these unions and the split which occurred in 1949 both had a bearing on events and policies in Jamaica. One consequence at the regional level was that in the period 1949 to 1967 three regional organisations in the Caribbean came into existence—the Caribbean Labour Congress (CLC), the Caribbean Area Division of the Inter-American Regional Organization of Workers (CADORIT), and the Caribbean Congress of Labour (CCLab).[65]

In 1950, as has been detailed in the last chapter, the CLC was already in difficulties arising from the withdrawal of many of its member unions (necessary for affiliation to the ICFTU) and the resulting reduction in income. It was unable to perform even the most basic functions of a regional organisation in connection with conferences and exchange of information between affiliates. In June 1952 the CLC was declared "moribund" and replaced by the Caribbean Area Division of ORIT.

The Inter-American Regional Organization of Workers (ORIT) had replaced the Inter-American Confederation of Workers (CIT) which had been created in 1948. Officially a regional organisation of the ICFTU, ORIT maintained, however, a large measure of independence from the International. The Caribbean Area Division when created was closely associated with its parent, ORIT, as the Assistant Secretary for International Relations of ORIT indicates with his claim that: "It was my task to guide CADORIT activities while I remained in charge of ORIT's International Relations."[66]

Following the meeting to create CADORIT, which was called the West Indian Workers' Conference and held in Barbados, Grantley Adams, President of the CLC, sent a letter to the affiliates of the CLC suggesting a meeting to

[65] The abbreviation CCLab is used rather than the more standard usage of CCL in order to distinguish more clearly the CCLab from the earlier CLC.

[66] S. Romualdi, *Presidents and Peons*, New York, 1968, p. 343.

disband the organisation as the "establishment of a division of ORIT, the inevitability of a final cleavage in the Caribbean area between the unions affiliated to the ICFTU and the WFTU . . ."[67] raised doubts as to the future of the CLC. A delegation of CLC affiliates visited Adams and suggested that there should be a Caribbean Federation of Trade Unions "which would embrace all trade unions in the area regardless of international affiliations and which would control its own affairs . . ."[68] Also suggested was an approach to both the Internationals to tell them that if they "were really concerned with the welfare of the workers in the Caribbean they should be prepared to assist the local affiliates in equal proportion, without attaching obligations to the assistance . . ."[69]

Adams rejected these suggestions and officers of CADORIT tried to explain the "fundamental differences that exist between the ICFTU and WFTU."[70] The affiliates to CLC subsequently withdrew their support, joined ORIT and thereby CADORIT, which resulted in the decline and formal dissolution of the CLC.

CADORIT remained the only regional organisation for the Caribbean until 1960 when a new organisation was formed—the Caribbean Congress of Labour (CCLab). At the founding conference of the CCLab, CADORIT was described as "a hybrid organisation" and an "extra-territorial Caribbean body affiliated to the ICFTU" which should be replaced by a fully Caribbean organisation.[71]

At the time of the founding of the CCLab, the Fed-

[67] Quoted in letter to CLC members from the Secretary General, dated 14 November 1952.
[68] CADORIT: *Second Conference Report, 1955*, Trinidad, p. 5.
[69] *Ibid.*
[70] *Ibid.*, p. 6.
[71] *Report of the Founding Conference of the Caribbean Congress of Labour*, Grenada, September 14 and 15, 1960, pp. 9 and 20.

eration of the West Indies was in existence and the Minister of Labour for the Federation pointed out that there was no "national" (i.e., West Indian national) trade union centre. The CCLab must then be seen as part of the reshaping of organisations in preparation for the formal independence of the West Indian Federation.

The CCLab has remained in existence since that time, despite the failure of the federation, and continues to be the regional organisation for the Caribbean.

INTERNATIONAL TRADE UNION ORGANISATIONS AND JAMAICA

The TUCJ was affiliated to the WFTU in 1945 and the TUCJ leader, Kenneth Hill, attended the founding conferences in Paris and London. There is no evidence before 1951 to indicate that the TUCJ received funds or other assistance from the organisation. In 1952, however, a letter alleged to be from the WFTU secretariat was produced at the PNP committee hearing charges against TUCJ leaders. Among other matters the letter, dated November 1951, stated, "no doubt you have received the contribution, in the sum of five hundred pounds made by the secretariat of WFTU to the TUC fund in aid of workers who have been victims of the recent hurricane in your country . . . we would like to discuss with you the question of our participation in the projected conference of the Caribbean Labour Congress."[72]

The letter was offered as part of the proof that the TUCJ was connected with a communist organisation, al-

[72] *Daily Gleaner,* March 5, 1952, p. 11.

though by the time it was made public the TUCJ had already applied for affiliation to the ICFTU.

When the split occurred in the international trade union movement the British TUC withdrew from the WFTU and helped create the ICFTU. The TUCJ leaders were invited to do likewise but at first they refused. Grantley Adams, of the Barbados Workers' Union and President of the CLC, went to Jamaica in October 1949 in an attempt to persuade a Jamaican representative to attend the founding conference of the ICFTU. Although the TUCJ was not mentioned by name, Adams explained to the conference that a Jamaican "representative . . . specifically said he was not coming because he was afraid that racial discrimination in American unions was still in existence and Russia had no racial discrimination."[73] Sympathising with and seeking to explain this view, Adams reminded the delegates: "If you push the inhabitants of non-self governing territories into the hands of the Russians it will be because they will say no racial discrimination by Russia. At any rate Russia has made promises and has not broken any of them. She has not had a chance to show whether she would break them or not."[74]

The TUCJ eventually withdrew from the WFTU but temporarily refused to affiliate with the ICFTU. It finally made an application for affiliation in 1951.

The only important indication of WFTU involvement in Jamaica came in 1953 with the formal creation of the Jamaican Federation of Trade Unions (JFTU) which

[73] ICFTU: *Report of Free World Labour Conference and of the First Congress of the ICFTU*, 1949, p. 120. One hundred and thirty-four organisations were invited to the conference and only one refused. The refusing organisation was not named. See *ibid.*, p. 18.

[74] *Ibid.*, p. 120.

was a WFTU affiliate until 1961. Apart from Richard Hart, the leading figure in the JFTU was Ferdinand Smith, the signer of the 1951 letter from the WFTU secretariat. For many years active in the National Maritime Movement in the USA, Smith came to Jamaica in 1953 and Hart, in a speech to the 1953 WFTU Congress, thanked the secretariat of WFTU "for having facilitated the return of our comrade to his country."[75] Smith, at the same Congress, reported the creation of the JFTU and sketched plans for its future.

The financial conditions of Jamaican trade unions in general plus the nature of the JFTU might indicate, in the absence of substantial evidence, that financial assistance for the JFTU and its leaders came from the WFTU. Certainly the fares and expenses of the delegates to the 1953, 1957, and 1961 WFTU congresses were no doubt paid by the WFTU secretariat.

The 1953 report of the ICFTU records that the NWU, the TUCJ, and the breakaway union, the National Labour Congress (NLC), had all applied for affiliation. The NWU was accepted and became an affiliate in December 1952 but the other applications were held pending an investigation, the results of which prevented their affiliation.[76]

There is no record of application of the BITU for affiliation to the ICFTU until 1967 when, in October of that year, the Executive Board accepted the union into affiliation.[77]

The NWU thus became for fifteen years the exclusively

[75] WFTU: *Third World Trade Union Congress, 1953*, p. 294.
[76] ICFTU: *Report of Third World Congress, 1953*, pp. 17–19.
[77] ICFTU: *Report on Activities 1965–1969*, Brussels, 1969, p. 138. (This report was issued prior to the Ninth World Congress, July 1969.)

ICFTU-ORIT recognised union in Jamaica; in 1954 it received a £250 grant from the ICFTU "to assist in acquiring transport for organisational work."[78] The TUCJ eventually affiliated to CLASC and remained an affiliate of that organisation until it became an affiliate of the NWU in 1963.

The affiliation of the NWU to the ICFTU also enabled the various international trade secretariats to become involved in Jamaica. The various sections of the NWU were affiliated to a number of trade secretariats, notably the International Metalworkers' Federation (IMF), the International Federation of Plantation and Agricultural Workers (IFPAAW), and the International Transport Federation (ITF).

The closest association the NWU has held has been with the IMF, of which Michael Manley has been an executive member and, together with other NWU personnel, has attended IMF meetings in Europe. Manley has also attended IFPAAW conferences in Europe.

The publications of the various international trade secretariats frequently claim that assistance rendered the NWU has been decisive. Thus the ITF claimed an "intervention" in a bus strike of 1963 which resulted in a satisfactory conclusion of an agreement.[79] Likewise, the IMF provided "advisory services" to the NWU in an attempt to get two broadcasting workers re-instated at the Radio Corporation of Jamaica with a successful outcome.[80]

Although such incidents reveal contact between the

[78] *National Workers Union 3rd Annual Report*, Kingston, 1955, p. 6.
[79] *Inter-American Labor Bulletin*, Vol. XV, Nos. 1–2, January–February 1964, p. 5.
[80] *Metal*, Vol. VI, No. 1, December 1965–January–February 1966, p. 7.

international trade secretariats and the NWU, the importance and impact of such assistance is difficult to assess.

REGIONAL TRADE UNION ORGANISATIONS AND JAMAICA

When CADORIT was founded in June 1952, both the TUCJ and the BITU applied for affiliation but were refused on the grounds that only one national trade union from each country could be accepted.[81] A few months later the NWU became the affiliated union from Jamaica to both ORIT and CADORIT and Romualdi states "one of the CADORIT's first tasks was to assist in the development of the Jamaican NWU."[82] In this connection he visited Jamaica and attended the first two annual conferences of the NWU in 1952 and 1953.

CADORIT was generally accepted in the Caribbean, and especially in Jamaica, as an anti-communist organisation, specifically designed to combat the CLC, which was widely considered as a communist organisation (an important trade unionist interviewed in 1967 was still of this opinion).[83] The belief in the anti-communist nature of CADORIT was sustained by speeches of the first Chairman, Frank Walcott, who, while referring to British Guiana in 1954, said: "I am convinced from all my ex-

[81] CADORIT: *Second Conference Report, 1955*, p. 37.
[82] S. Romualdi, *Presidents and Peons*, p. 354.
[83] Knowles notes that unions admitted to ORIT-ICFTU "are given the stamp of legitimacy as democratic, noncommunist unions, seeking traditional objectives." "The British West Indies" in W. Galenson, ed., *Labor and Economic Development*, New York, 1959, pp. 273.

perience that there is a well-planned movement coming right through South and Central America to spread communist doctrine and the trade unions are being used as a means to do this."[84]

From the standpoint of Jamaica, the involvement of ORIT and CADORIT came through the NWU, and officials of that union moved into positions within the regional organisations. Kelly, President of the NWU, became a member of the CADORIT Administrative Committee while Glasspole became a substitute member of ORIT's executive board.

Further, Sterling, while still on the USWA payroll, became Executive Secretary to CADORIT early in 1956, bringing another Jamaican with him as organiser, Osmond Dyce, then of the TUCJ.

In 1956 a Caribbean regional organisation came into existence to deal exclusively with workers of one industry; the Caribbean Aluminium and Allied Workers' Federation (CAAWF) was created "mainly through the assistance" of the USWA, the International Metalworkers' Federation, and CADORIT, with the NWU being the "moving spirit."[85] The Federation embraced the entire bauxite production workers of the Caribbean Islands, with the exception of Haiti, and Zonarich and Millard, who were at the founding conference, assured the Federation of the support of the USWA.[86] In 1958 the USWA, through CADORIT, gave the CAAWF $11,000 to be used for the purchase of a motor boat and to pay a full-time organiser for one year.[87]

[84] *ICFTU Information Bulletin*, April 15, 1954, p. 55.
[85] *National Workers' Union 4th Annual Report*, 1956, pp. 13–14.
[86] *Daily Gleaner*, July 9, 1956.
[87] *AFL-CIO International Affairs Bulletin*, Vol. 2, No. 1, September–October 1957, p. 5.

The NWU was important as a founding member and when the organisation was renamed the Caribbean Bauxite and Mine Workers' Federation (CBMWF) in 1961, Michael Manley of the NWU became President. The reorganisation conference was held in Jamaica and called by Cleve Kidd of the USWA "at the request of the bauxite unions in the various Territories."[88] Soon after the establishment of CBMWF, Kidd attempted to create a research and coordination centre for Caribbean trade union activities.[89]

Such a centre was not established, but in 1964 the USWA appointed a Caribbean Representative, G. Funk, who had become Research and Education Director of the CBMWF when it transferred to offices close to the NWU in 1967. The CBMWF has held many seminars and meetings for bauxite workers in the Caribbean since 1961.

When the CCLab was created in 1963 the NWU moved into closer relationship with it than with the CADORIT and ORIT. As affiliation to the CCLab was only open to "democratic" unions the nature of the BITU prevented its entry to the organisation and so the four Jamaican delegates to the CCLab founding conference were all from the NWU. Kelly was made Second Vice-President of the new regional organisation and Dyce became General Secretary, a position which he held until 1967 when he returned to Jamaica to take up a position in the NWU. The Jamaican delegate on the General Council was M. Manley. In 1966 Sterling was appointed to replace Dyce when the latter finished his term.

[88] *National Workers Union 9th Annual Report*, 1961, p. 8.
[89] *International Federation of Plantation, Agricultural and Allied Workers SNIPS* (IFPAAW SNIPS), No. 6/62, June 1962, p. 2.

AIFLD

The American Institute for Free Labor Development (AIFLD) has to be treated separately as it is neither a regional organisation nor an international trade union organisation. The stated purpose of the AIFLD, which was created at the suggestion of the AFL-CIO executive in 1962, was to oppose communism and other totalitarian forms of government in Latin America and to assist the growth of "democratic trade unions," principally through trade union educational activities and assistance to trade unionists in raising their standard of living.[90] The AIFLD is backed by the AFL-CIO, business organisations with interests in Latin America and the Caribbean, and the USA Government. In 1962, for example, the AFL-CIO contributed $200,500; business groups between $150,000 and $160,000; and the USA Government $3 million.[91] The AIFLD is directed by William Doherty, Jr., and at its creation, Sam Haddad, a local union officer of the USWA became Education Director.[92]

The organisation has been involved in Jamaica in three ways. Firstly, the year after the TUCJ became affiliated to the NWU and ICFTU instead of to CLASC, Hopeton Caven, a long-time TUCJ leader, was granted a scholarship to an AIFLD residential course in the USA.[93] These ten-week courses in trade union subjects are followed by an international tour (in Caven's case, to Israel, Britain, Italy, the Federal Republic of Germany, Belgium,

[90] See M. Riche, "The American Institute for Free Labor Development," *Monthly Labor Review*, Vol. 88, No. 9, September 1965.
[91] *Business Week*, August 27, 1966, p. 48.
[92] *Inter-American Labor Bulletin*, September–October 1962, p. 2.
[93] *Daily Gleaner*, November 24, 1964, p. 19.

Switzerland, and France) and nine months on the AIFLD payroll as "interns" in their own unions.

Secondly, the AIFLD administered a grant for the foundation and operation of the Trade Union Education Institute (TUEI) at the University of the West Indies, which is charged with the basic operation of the Institute. The TUEI has residential courses and seminars for trade unionists in the Caribbean and is described in the *Inter-American Labor Bulletin* as "AIFLD's center at the University of the West Indies."[94] The TUEI has trained Jamaican unionists from all unions, and representatives from the BITU and TUCJ are on its advisory board.

The third involvement in Jamaica by the AIFLD was the creation in 1963 of a "Jamaican Democratic Trade Union Alliance for Housing and Social Development." The project, which resulted in two AIFLD Social Projects Department Officers being permanently assigned to the island, is connected with the building of low-cost housing for trade unionists. A constitution for the Alliance was prepared by the AIFLD's Social Projects Department's technicians.[95]

The AIFLD was the only foreign or international labour organisation which up to 1967 brought together the BITU and the NWU and it is the only organisation which (until 1968) accepted the BITU as a trade union in Jamaica.

[94] *Inter-American Labor Bulletin*, Vol. XVI, No. 9, September 1965, p. 4.
[95] *Inter-American Labor Bulletin*, Vol. XIV, No. 12, December 1963, p. 6.

Foreign National Unions and Regional Trade Union Organisations

The extent to which an international or regional organisation can be used as an instrument of policy for an individual national labour organisation is dependent on the power which the individual organisation can wield in the larger grouping. Such power would vary according to inclination and issue but three reliable indicators of individual affiliate power are the funds it contributes, the involvement of its personnel, and the degree of conformity between organisation and affiliate policies. The first two of these will be examined here in relation to ORIT, which was the regional organisation most important in Jamaica and the Caribbean in the period 1949–67. The policy aspects will be discussed in a following chapter.

ORIT AND USA UNIONS

In 1946 the AF of L started to promote a Latin American trade union organisation to oppose the WFTU regional organisation, the Latin American Confederation of Labour (CTAL).[96] As a result of these activities the AF of L was instrumental in creating the Inter-American

[96] L. Lorwin, *The International Labor Movement*, New York, 1953, p. 297.

Confederation of Workers (CIT).[97] The AF of L also attempted to launch an overtly political organisation when it sponsored a conference in 1950 to create the Inter-American Association for Freedom and Democracy.[98] The proposed executive board of this organisation had both representatives of the AF of L and the CIO but there were no Latin American delegates to the conference and the organisation never became important.

With the organisation of the ICFTU it was decided to transform the CIT into a regional organisation of the ICFTU and at a conference in January 1951 the CIT officially became ORIT and affiliated to the ICFTU. Its position in relation to the ICFTU was ambiguous, however, as it was an already existing autonomous body and it, therefore, retained its basic independence despite its association with the International. One important factor in the evolution of this arrangement was the position of the AF of L in ORIT and the ICFTU. As sponsor and major financial contributor of ORIT the AF of L leaders were not prepared to see the organisation controlled by the ICFTU headquarters. Furthermore, the AF of L officially disassociated itself from the ICFTU Regional Fund programmes which were designed to give aid to unions in less-developed countries.

S. Romualdi, who since 1946 had been the AF of L International Representative in Latin America and who had assisted in the organisation of the CIT, records that the decision to create ORIT was taken by American unionists in April 1950 and that it was agreed at the

[97] See J. Barbash, "International Labor Confederations (CIT) (CTAL) (WFTU) in Latin America," *Monthly Labor Review*, Vol. 66, May 1948, pp. 449–503; and Vol. 67, August 1948, pp. 147–51.

[98] S. Romualdi, "For Freedom and Democracy," *American Federationist*, Vol. 57, No. 6, June 1950, p. 24.

meeting that the AF of L and CIO would furnish one Assistant Secretary each.[99] At the ORIT conference this was effected and two of the members of the earlier North American meeting were made Assistant Secretaries, Ernst Schwartz of the CIO and Romualdi of the AF of L; both retained their CIO and AF of L positions and were authorised to work from their respective AF of L and CIO offices.[100]

The budget of ORIT is not made public nor are details of the ICFTU contributions readily available. An author of a major work on ORIT, however, has assembled from various documents some basic facts concerning the financing of ORIT: officially, on the basis of membership of affiliates, the income of ORIT in 1961 should have been approximately $87,000, of which the official contribution of the AFL-CIO would be between $70,000 and $80,000. In addition, the AFL-CIO makes a supplementary contribution in the region of $30,000 which, with other donations, made the total budget in 1961 in the region of $100,000 to $120,000.[101]

The ICFTU recorded that it provided a "substantial loan" to ORIT to help it with its programme in 1953 but it was clear that with the heavy North American financial backing ORIT was not dependent upon the ICFTU.[102] Thus, Romualdi notes, that "until 1954 the ICFTU Secretariat in Brussels left ORIT pretty much alone."[103] It is also clear that Romualdi never accepted that ORIT was a dependent regional organisation of the ICFTU, describing a member of the ORIT Executive Board as

[99] S. Romualdi, *Presidents and Peons*, p. 119.
[100] *Ibid.*
[101] P. Reiser, *L'Organisation Régionale Interaméricaine des Travailleurs (O.R.I.T.) de la Confédération Internationale des Syndicats Libres (C.I.S.L.) 1951–1961*, Geneva, 1962, pp. 156–57.
[102] ICFTU: *Report of Third World Congress, 1955*, p. 31.
[103] S. Romualdi, *Presidents and Peons*, p. 128.

a "stooge for the ICFTU Secretariat" and violently opposing activities of ICFTU personnel, particularly those of the Director of Organisations (Millard, originally of the USWA, Canada) in Latin America.[104] The efforts of AFL-CIO President Meany and others prevented, according to Romualdi, the ICFTU from being powerful in its regional organisation and in 1960 "ORIT was finally left in peace."[105]

Personnel of the AF of L, CIO, and AFL-CIO continued to move into many key ORIT positions, as, for example, the appointment of Daniel Benedict of the AFL-CIO Department of International Affairs as Education Director to ORIT in 1955.

ORIT AND REGIONAL ORGANISATIONS

The two trade union organisations with independent involvement in Jamaica also had connections with ORIT and CADORIT. McDonald of the USWA was part of the CIO delegation at the founding conference of ORIT and Tewson of the British TUC was present as President of the ICFTU.

The USWA was also active in CADORIT. At its second conference in 1956, both Zonarich and Millard attended although the latter was now attached to the ICFTU. Zonarich spoke of the necessity for the Caribbean to extract a good price for its natural resources from North American companies while Millard stressed the importance of a single national centre for the various countries and territories.[106]

104 *Ibid.*, p. 131.
105 *Ibid.*, p. 133.
106 CADORIT: *Second Conference Report, 1955*, pp. 64 and 66.

The possibility of direct American union participation in the West Indies was emphasised in 1955 when Romualdi said at a press conference in Barbados that "if requests are made to the American labour movement and satisfactory arrangements can be worked out between Britain and the United States, the movement in the United States can give some help to these parts."[107] He added that requests for assistance from the USA labour organisations would have to be made through ORIT.

The position of independence of ORIT from the ICFTU and the close personal and financial relations with the AFL-CIO is reflected in the Caribbean regional organisations. This situation makes it difficult to discover the exact financial basis of these organisations as CADORIT operational costs were shared between ORIT and the ICFTU Regional Activities Fund. In spite of the apparent desire of the West Indian speakers at the first meeting of the CCLab to dissolve CADORIT because it was an "extra territorial" organisation, the CCLab became as financially dependent on ORIT as CADORIT had been. In the 1961–62 financial year over 50 per cent of the CCLab's total budget of $84,736 came from "ORIT-ICFTU grants."[108]

One of the first appointments made after the founding of the CCLab in 1960 was that of Cleve Kidd, Research Director of USWA (Canada), which was said to be in response to "an appeal from the recently established CCLab."[109] Kidd, on a one- or two-year assignment, was to serve as a coordinator of activities and services of the affiliated unions. Kidd recommended a former USWA

[107] *ICFTU Information Bulletin,* February 15, 1955, p. 27.
[108] See CCLab: *Secretaries' Report, 1961–1962.*
[109] *Inter-American Labor Bulletin,* Vol. XIII, No. 12, December 1961, p. 1.

research assistant, Carl Hall. George Eaton[110] was also recommended by Kidd.

The close association between ORIT and its sub-regional organisations in the Caribbean was a question of some sensitivity and Romualdi claimed in 1958 that up to that year the North Americans had not assumed a large share of the administration of ORIT.[111] But such protestations did not dispel the belief that ORIT was a creature of North American unions, especially when its policies as well as finances and personnel were examined.[112] At the second conference of CCLab, held in Jamaica, the *Sunday Gleaner* published an editorial on the opening day: "The CCL is the latest regional organisation which has been formed to serve the West Indies along the trade union front. It is the foster-child of ORIT the Latin American arm of the ICFTU and as such it has a political purpose as well as a trade union identity . . . its major support is the ICFTU and this organisation is now becoming suspect in many countries across the world as not being a genuine trade union movement so much as it is an arm of the United States' State Department. Internationally and regionally the Caribbean Congress of Labour is considered by those competent to know to be a political organisation rather than a workers' organisation."[113] President Kelly of the NWU, as the host union, apologised for this editorial to the USA personnel at the conference, among whom were Harry Pollack of the AFL-CIO and Benedict of ORIT.

[110] Minutes of the meeting of the CCLab Administration Committee, January 15–16, 1962, p. 3.
[111] S. Romualdi, "ORIT at the Crossroads," *American Federationist*, May 1958, p. 23.
[112] See P. Summerfield, "Regional Organisations of Trade Unions in the Caribbean," *New World Quarterly*, Vol. 4, No. 4, 1968, pp. 3–6.
[113] *Sunday Gleaner*, September 8, 1963, p. 8; as quoted, *ibid.*, p. 5.

Regardless of any association between ORIT and the USA State Department, the evidence of finance and personnel alone indicates that ORIT relied on the AF of L, CIO, and AFL-CIO for its power and direction.[114] ORIT with its Caribbean associates must therefore be considered as an important instrument of North American trade union organisations rather than an entity pursuing its independent policies.

[114] Windmuller notes that the "powerful position" of North American unions in ORIT has often brought resentment against the organisation. See J. Windmuller, *Labor Internationals,* New York, 1969, p. 30.

CHAPTER IX

MODELS, ISSUES, AND ADVOCATES

In the period before 1949 the British model of industrial relations and trade unionism had been the only one of importance. The coming of the American model in the early 1950s created a dual model situation, intensified the debate about political unionism, and brought new organisations and individuals as advocates of foreign models.

THE ARRIVAL OF THE AMERICAN MODEL

The American model of trade unionism became a point of discussion in Jamaica as a result of American investment and the following involvement of American unions.

The first recorded incident in which American industrial relations and union procedures were given a substantial and public hearing was at the Board of Enquiry into Labour Disputes Between Unions in 1950. John Kilpatrick, legal representative of Reynolds Aluminum Company of North America, outlined in detail American practices in relation to representational disputes. Kilpatrick advocated the adoption of USA-style representational polls unless Jamaica wanted to lose foreign investment, and although he had only been in Jamaica "a couple of weeks" it can be assumed that other American investors and companies were taking such positions. Glasspole also confirmed that in the early 1950s the growing number of employers in Jamaica from the USA expressed a desire for the trade union practices current in their own country. As Minister of Labour, at a later date, he recalled dealing with some American companies which would only yield under government pressure to conform to some of the remnants of the British industrial relations system. Eaton, referring exclusively to the bauxite companies, notes that they made a valuable "contribution towards the establishment of stable unionism along conventional lines."[1]

The employers, however, were supported in some of their demands concerning industrial relations practices by the new union, the NWU, and to a lesser extent by the declining TUCJ. Knowles says of Kenneth Sterling, then Acting Secretary of the NWU and a USWA employee, that through: "Advocating the philosophy of the United Steelworkers he has demonstrated that strong unions can be built in the West Indies by stressing dues payments, local organisation, shop steward system, attention to grievances, and emphasis on collective bargaining."[2]

The NWU has used North American practices as example of what should be done in Jamaica in much the same way as the TUCJ used British examples in the previous period. Kelly, for example, wrote to the Minister

[1] G. Eaton, "Trade Union Development in Jamaica," *Caribbean Quarterly,* Vol. 8, No. 182, 1962, p. 621. This author is consistently laudatory concerning the policies, effects, and contributions of the bauxite companies in Jamaica. See *ibid.,* pp. 715–29.
[2] W. Knowles, *Trade Union Development and Industrial Relations in the British West Indies,* Berkeley, 1959, p. 136.

of Labour (Glasspole) in 1957 asking that the trade union laws be amended to prevent the formation of company unions: "the time for this is undoubtedly now and it should be borne in mind that if this is not done it will not be creating a precedent since the formation of company unions is prohibited by law in countries like Canada and the United States of America."[3]

In a more academic manner, Michael Manley, Island Supervisor of the NWU, in arguing for more rules to control employer-union bargaining, which is more associated with the American model, stated: "I might add that these seven ground rules are accepted in virtually every civilised community which has recognised the worker and his institutions as full, equal, integral and responsible parts of the socio-economic complex."[4]

The NWU, unlike the TUCJ and BITU, has also used the ILO conventions for the promotion of its labour and political policies, especially in arguing with the government, which has since 1962 been the BITU-based Jamaican Labour Party.

NEW COMPARISONS

It had been pointed out very early in the history of the Jamaican trade union movement that the causes attributed to the rise of unionism in Britain were not all to be found at the beginning of the Jamaican movement. In 1938 a writer in Jamaica argued that, "it was no good talking of revolt against capital . . ." in the disturbances of 1938 as the real causes were simply those of lack of

[3] *Daily Gleaner*, August 30, 1957.
[4] *Daily Gleaner*, April 10, 1964, p. 12.

work, high taxes, and general poverty.[5] As already noted, the different historical circumstances between British and colonial trade union movements were often used when debating the advisability of passing legislation in the colonies identical to that of Britain.

In 1951, a writer, in an article on Jamaican unions entitled "It's Very Different," stated that the trade union conditions in Jamaica "are not only different from those in England but very different."[6] Considering the obvious and vast economic and social differences that exist between the two countries, such an argument is testimony to the unreal extent to which Jamaican conditions were compared with those of the metropolitan power.

Perhaps even less similarity existed between Jamaica and the USA, but as with the British model, the coming of the American model had to be supported by social and historical comparisons between the two countries. Typical of such comparisons was the statement made by William C. Doherty, Vice-President of the AFL-CIO and later USA Ambassador to Jamaica. It is reported that on the occasion of the Jamaican formal independence celebration he linked Jamaica's multi-racial development and its slogan "Out of Many–One People" to the "history and principles of the USA trade union movement . . ."[7] More directly a Canadian trade unionist conducting a labour education survey of the Caribbean in 1954 pointed out that "in Great Britain there is a relatively homogeneous population, about two hundred years of background and tradition in trade union affairs–and besides everyone there plays cricket. But it seems to me that in the Carib-

[5] H. Jacobs, "Mass Movements in Jamaica," *Public Opinion,* October 1, 1938.

[6] Percy Miller, "It's Very Different," *Daily Gleaner,* August 31, 1951.

[7] *Inter-American Labor Bulletin,* September–October 1962, p. 3.

bean the climate and milieu for industrial relations have much more in common with North America and Canada than with Great Britain. We have a heterogeneous population, many with little or no understanding or experience in trade unionism or industrial relations, rapidly developing and unstable economies, and a federal political system."[8] Almost the identical sentiments were expressed to this writer in 1967, in an interview with a trade unionist who said he had realised, after 1950, that the British model was inapplicable to Jamaica and that the short history and rapid rise of American unions made them more similar to Jamaican unions. But the British model had not been totally abandoned, as evidenced by a West Indian trade unionist who flatly contradicted the Canadian quoted above at the same conference in 1959: "as we read the history of the Trade Union movement in Britain we are struck by a number of similarities in the circumstances attending the origins of that movement and those of our own."[9]

PROBLEMS OF TWO MODELS

The problems associated with the currency of two models of industrial relations in Jamaica, the necessity to distinguish conditions and find similarities to support the desired model, are classically illustrated in a *Joint Statement for Public Information* published by the Jamaica Employers' Federation and the Jamaica Chamber of Commerce in 1961.

[8] G. Markle, "Report of the Labour Education Survey," in R. Farley, ed., *Labour Education in the British Caribbean*, p. 71.
[9] H. Springer, "Education for Trade Unionists," in R. Farley, ed., *Labour Education in the British Caribbean, ibid.*, p. 15.

The statement was made after speeches by the Minister of Labour and Prime Minister in the second PNP-NWU government, which, the leaders of the employers believed, seemed to propose legislation to compel employers to hold polls to decide bargaining rights between two competing unions. They felt that there was little difference between compulsory poll-taking and compulsory recognition of unions. In arguing against such legislation, the employers stated that although they were agreed to the right to organise they were "in favour of the British Labour practices which keep legislation and compulsion to the minimum," but that if the government was moving towards "the American or Canadian Labour laws the matter of recognition cannot be dealt with in isolation but only in the context of comprehensive laws covering every phase of industrial relations."[10] Having proposed the British model and opposed the American, they now had to distinguished the conditions between Jamaica and North America and then show why the British model was more apposite. Thus they claimed, in contrast to Jamaica, in the USA and Canada there was a "real trade union membership" (a reference to the non-dues paying membership of Jamaican unions), that the unions were "non-political," that recognition of unions was part of a complex industrial relations system and administrative procedures which ensured that "malpractices . . . are the subject of big investigations from time to time. Where guilt is established the unions are accordantly punished."[11] This latter reminder was a veiled threat to a union-based government that American procedures would mean legal investigation of their trade union affairs and

[10] "A Joint Statement for Public Information by the Jamaica Employers' Federation and Jamaica Chamber of Commerce," *Daily Gleaner*, January 18, 1961.
[11] *Ibid.*

therefore the government too would find advantages in retaining the British model. But, in striking contrast to the earlier period, the British model could not be advocated merely because it was British, or because similarities between Britain and Jamaica were deemed to exist. Being one year before independence, the respectability of the British model had declined and it was now necessary to find a substantial and observable reason for pursuing it, other than the fact that the employers did not wish to be compelled to hold representational polls. The reason found was that the West Indian federal system, started in 1958, was composed of several units which, as a result of colonial policy, had followed the British pattern of industrial relations and that for Jamaica to depart from it now would create "an invidious position . . . if there is a differing pattern of trade union procedures legislated for in the various unit territories."[12]

Discussions such as these characterised the early 1950s but were not always confined to a specific issue in industrial relations. More often such arguments arose over the merits and demerits of political unionism.

The Issue of Political Unionism

Close formal or informal links between trade unions and political parties had been the rule rather than the exception in the Jamaican trade union movement since its beginning. When the JLP-BITU combination formed the first Jamaican Government in 1944 and the TUCJ became a blanket union allied with the PNP in 1949, the issue

[12] *Ibid.*

would seem to have been settled in favour of political unions, at least for the foreseeable future.

In the early 1950s, however, several factors combined to bring the issue to the fore and make it important for the rest of the decade and beyond. The first of these was the arrival of the American model, and the second, the foreign and domestic employer demands for settlement of the turbulence caused by political trade unions which followed the second victory of the JLP-BITU in 1949. Finally, the creation of the NWU by the PNP caused the NWU to justify this unusual process by foreign standards (i.e., party creating a union) by constantly claiming to be less political than the BITU. Thus many foreign and domestic groups and organisations became embroiled in the arguments concerning the legitimacy of an integrated union-party system.

REPRESENTATIONAL ISSUE AND THE AMERICAN MODEL

The Labour Department, still with Scott as the Labour Adviser, recorded the problems created by the 1949 elections in the Annual Report for 1950. Scott showed that the number of labour disputes in 1950 had risen in comparison with other years and that there was a marked deterioration in industrial relations during the year. One of the causes, he argued, was that owing to the outcome of the election in which one party had only a small majority over the other, the trade union of the minority party (TUCJ) tried to increase membership "by making claims on employers which had hitherto negotiated with the other union, and using the strike weapon as a means of proving that they had the preponderance of membership."[13]

To solve this problem Scott initiated a Board to discuss the representational issue in public. The Board met between April and August 1950 and published a report for consideration by the government. Evidence was taken from interested parties, including the trade unions, employers' associations, Norman Manley (President of the PNP) and Kilpatrick, the attorney and legal representative of Reynolds Mines Ltd. (a company which, according to Appendix II of the report, had not been involved with unions on representational issues). The latter gave an account of contemporary trade union practices in the USA which occupied just under half of the total evidence which was printed in the report and presented to the Board.

No other representative was asked to give an account of trade union practices of other countries, although the Board had on hand relevant legislation or literature on the British, American, Canadian, and Australian acts relative to labour relations procedure and, in a separate category, the USA Labor Management Relations Act, 1947.[14] Kilpatrick's report is the first recorded instance in which the American models of industrial relations and union procedures were given a substantial hearing in an official and public body. During his submission, Kilpatrick was asked by the members of the Board what the effect of representational disputes in Jamaica would have on the introduction of capital from the outside. He replied: "Capital will be reluctant to venture into certain areas of the States where the labour conditions are tur-

[13] Labour Department (Jamaica): *Annual Report 1950*, p. 4.

[14] Government of Jamaica: *Report of the Board of Enquiry into Labour Disputes Between Unions*, 1950, p. 8.

bulent and it is even more true in foreign countries, especially where there is no legislation to stabilise the situation. *American capital is not afraid of bargaining with unions: we are used to that.* We do that every day. They are not afraid of sitting down and applying the economic principles of supply and demand with the union to determine the rates of pay the workers should receive but they are very much afraid of situations in which the employer is unable to help himself, in which he is caught between conflicting union forces and the employer can do nothing about it. That is true in the States, is true all over the world and it will be true here."[15] The desire to settle the representational issue thus resulted in the introduction of a model of industrial relations in which a practice had been established for solving such disputes. But as the Board's questions to Kilpatrick made clear, it was not only the provision for representational polls in the USA that created discussion of the American model but also the relationship between industrial relations in Jamaica and the current and future investment from the USA.

GOVERNMENT ATTEMPTS TO SETTLE THE ISSUE

Scott was Labour Adviser and then Permanent Secretary to the Ministry of Labour (as the Labour Department became in 1954) during the first four years after 1949. As has been seen, Scott argued that the existing conditions in Jamaican unionism should always be accepted as a starting point. His position was well recorded by the 1950 Board of Enquiry: "strong criticisms were directed against the principle of the affiliation or association of

[15] *Ibid.*, p. 21.

trade unions with political parties . . . [but] . . . In any case no practical aim will be achieved by an academical [sic] consideration of the political or ethical implications of trade unions and political parties in close association and collaboration. This situation, desirable or undesirable, is now a *fait accompli* and must be accepted."[16] Scott also pointed out that while causes of industrial unrest were most often attributed to "the existing union-political set-up" of equal significance was the economic situation which made workers find "it more difficult to make two ends meet."[17]

Such a balanced view as Scott's did not prevail among other groups and organisations involved in Jamaica which continued to oppose political unionism. Thus, when the first politically appointed Minister of Labour, J. A. McPherson, from the JLP-BITU took charge of the Labour Department, political unions were described, without qualification, as a permanent feature of Jamaican society. The Ministry of Labour Annual Report for that year states, "in the local trade union movement a trade union is not only concerned with the workers in industry but also takes an active part in the political and economic life of the country . . ." and ". . . all are affiliated to political parties."[18] The policy of the Ministry changed to some extent when the PNP-NWU took office in 1955 and Glasspole became Minister of Labour with Greaves Hill as Permanent Secretary, the latter being a noted opponent of political unionism.[19] When the JLP-BITU again took office in 1962, the political unionism issue was not as current and important as in the early 1950s.

[16] Government of Jamaica: *Report of Board of Enquiry into Labour Disputes Between Trade Unions*, 1950, p. 2.
[17] *Ibid.*, p. 2.
[18] Kingston Ministry of Labour and Labour Department (Jamaica): *Annual Report*, 1953, *op. cit.*, p. 11.
[19] See "Voices of the Employers," *Newday*, September 1958, p. 3.

EMPLOYER OPPONENTS TO POLITICAL UNIONISM

The first record of foreign comment and opposition to political unionism came in the report of Kilpatrick, the American representative of Reynolds, who argued that the Jamaican union situation should be "stabilized" because wage rates were "not so frightening" in countries "where the labour situation is unstable."[20] Kilpatrick did not equate stability with the absence of political unionism but his remarks were made in the context of an official board discussing such problems.

Two years later, a mission sponsored by an international agency rather than a company lawyer again used the word "stability," only in this case it was clear that "stabilisation" was equated with the eradication of political unionism. The seven-man mission organised by the International Bank for Reconstruction and Development (IBRD) described the Jamaican union situation and, unlike the Jamaican Labour Adviser, attributed it almost exclusively to the political situation. After recording that "the Labour Adviser has required extraordinary ingenuity and patience to resolve the complicated situation which has arisen" (as a result of politics in unions), the mission recommended that the Labour Adviser should be able to assist in "settling disputes before they erupt into strikes," and should "have more listening posts throughout the Island."[21] Echoing Kilpatrick, the IBRD mission finally warned that: "Progress toward higher levels of produc-

[20] Government of Jamaica: *Report of Board of Enquiry into Labour Disputes etc.*, p. 20.
[21] IBRD: *The Economic Development of Jamaica*, p. 80.

tion must be arrested as little as possible by prolonged interruption through strikes. The private foreign capital which is so indispensable to development will be attracted only if Jamaica can establish a reputation for orderly settlement of Labour disputes."[22]

Jamaican employers used the political union issue for a variety of reasons. In 1956, for example, the Gleaner Company argued, in a printed statement in its newspaper, that a proposed union of journalists should not be allowed as it would be affiliated to a party and would, therefore, jeopardise the "political independence" of the newspaper. The journalists' reply used the British model for support, pointing out that their proposed constitution was "closely modelled on that of the National Union of Journalists in Great Britain" which was allied to the British TUC and through it to the Labour Party, and no newspaper had found this inconsistent with freedom of the press.[23]

There was also a generalised opposition to union-political association from employers. When Greaves Hill left his position as Permanent Secretary at the Ministry of Labour he joined the Sugar Manufacturers' Association as chief industrial relations officer. In this position he vigorously opposed, in a speech reported in a Jamaican magazine, the political union arrangement drawing on quotes from Beatrice Webb and the current Chairman of the British TUC to support his argument.[24] The Jamaican employers' statement of 1961 showed, however, that the presence of political unionism could also be used as a positive fact to argue against imported legislation unpalatable to the employers.

[22] *Ibid.*, p. 82.
[23] *Daily Gleaner*, August 30, 1956, p. 1.
[24] "Voices of Employers," *Newday*.

The opposition of North American employers to political unionism is not well recorded, although events surrounding the bauxite companies' establishment and the final solution achieved would be evidence of their position. One example occurred in 1964 when the Canadian Chairman of the Caribbean Cement Company in Jamaica criticised the union rivalry because he claimed it discouraged foreign investment. Sir Alexander Bustamante, as Prime Minister, immediately replied, stating the Chairman's claim was "unfortunate" and that there had been union rivalry in the USA where "it had caused no slump in confidence on the part of investors."[25]

The employers were supported, but not completely, by a number of foreign trade unionists and dignitaries who visited Jamaica and the Caribbean and commented publicly on the trade union political situation.

OTHER OPPONENTS OF POLITICAL UNIONISM

F. W. Dalley of the British TUC, who wrote a report of trade unionism in Trinidad and lectured in Colonial Development and Welfare Fund (CD&W) courses in the 1940s, wrote in retrospect that political contacts in the early years of Caribbean trade unions could not be avoided and were almost essential to the growth of the movement.[26] British trade unionists and politicians accepted political unionism at the foundation of the movement but argued that "maturity" would enable unions to see the difference in political and labour matters. This

[25] *Daily Gleaner*, January 24, 1964, p. 2.
[26] F. Dalley, "The Labour Position: the Trade Unions and Political Parties" (Survey of the British Caribbean), *The Statist*, September 1956, p. 31.

view was well stated by George Woodcock, General Secretary to the British TUC, when he visited Jamaica in 1951: "the political nature of Jamaican trade unions could be an important factor in their development. The fact that the unions are closely related to political parties does not distress me. I hope that with the growing respect for the trade unions they will find it possible to distinguish between political and labour interests."[27]

Other British visitors were sometimes more adamant about trade unions being free from politics.[28] A British writer for the Fabian Society commented that trade unions in the colonies (specifically including Jamaica) had "been in varying degrees split or wrecked by political activity irrelevant to trade union issues . . ."[29]

Statements of American trade unionists in Jamaica, or outside, on the political issue have been rare. Eaton claims (without examples) that the "North American associates of the NWU [the United Steelworkers of America] have, whenever the occasions have arisen, spoken strongly in favour of business unionism pointing out that political involvement of the Jamaican trade unions have led to a dissipation of energies on their part."[30] Yet the only recorded statement of a USWA unionist or staff member, possibly seeking to reconcile the support of his union for the NWU with the "non-political" American model, adopted a similar position to the British: "a labour union has no choice but to be concerned and in politics . . . The critical point here for the labour union is that it

[27] *Public Opinion*, May 12, 1951, p. 2.

[28] See "Unions Should Be Free of Politics," report of speech by Edwin Leather, British MP, *Daily Gleaner*, March 26, 1956; and *Text of Broadcast by Rt. Hon. Hilary Marquand, Radio Demerara*, Georgetown, British Guiana, mimeo, 1954.

[29] W. Bowen, *Colonial Trade Unions*, p. 7.

[30] G. Eaton, *dissertation*, p. 631.

must distinguish clearly between its function as a labour union and the political party."[31]

The ability to distinguish between party and union function and to have a party-union relationship similar to the British model were exactly the attributes claimed by its leaders for the NWU and emphasised as lacking in the BITU.

It is widely accepted that such organisations as ORIT promoted business style unionism in their areas of operation.[32] The exclusive support of the NWU by ORIT and CADORIT could be viewed as one manifestation of this policy but there were also many other more practical reasons for support of the NWU.

CADORIT is claimed to have made "outspoken declarations" that political and trade union leadership should be separated.[33] Knowles notes that unions admitted to the ICFTU via CADORIT were only those which were "seeking traditional trade union objectives."[34] No doubt the belief that CADORIT actively promoted business unionism was enhanced by the fact that officials of CADORIT worked closely with the NWU and that NWU's Sterling was CADORIT Secretary and was well known to favour a pragmatic approach to unionism.[35]

The AIFLD, as we have seen, showed no hesitation in dealing with both Jamaican unions despite their political associations, although a business union philosophy could have been pursued through the AIFLD connections with the Trade Union Education Institute.

[31] R. Farley, ed., *Labour Education in the British Caribbean,* p. 60.

[32] See S. Lens, "Labor Between Bread and Revolution," *Nation,* September 19, 1966, p. 250.

[33] R. Farley, "Caribbean Labour Comes of Age," *Free Labour World,* No. 94, April 1958, p. 33.

[34] W. Knowles, "The British West Indies," p. 273.

[35] G. Eaton, *dissertation,* p. 389.

The belief that international support of non-political unions was generally forthcoming, however, made the degree of political association a yardstick of respectability on which the NWU claimed to be in a better position than the BITU.

THE NWU AND BITU—A QUESTION OF DEGREE

The standard accusation against Bustamante and the BITU was that by its constitution he was made life-President and was also President of the JLP. This situation, it was argued, was not compatible with a free, democratic trade union. Furthermore, Bustamante refused to relinquish his union position when he became Chief Minister upon the assumption of power by the JLP. BITU officers who became ministers likewise kept their union positions.

This practice was opposed by the TUCJ at the 1950 Board of Enquiry, the official finding of which stated "with one notable exception it was agreed that this practice [trade union leader as government cabinet member] should be discountenanced."[36] The notable exception was the BITU, whose leader was at that time Chief Minister of the government.

Bustamante did not yield to such protests and consequently, as the Jamaica correspondent for the *Commonwealth Newsletter* put it, "the situation can and indeed does arise in which he finds himself dealing with himself in trade disputes."[37]

[36] Government of Jamaica: *Report of Board of Enquiry into Labour Disputes etc.*, p. 2.

[37] *Commonwealth Newsletter*, Jamaica Correspondent, February 1, 1954, p. 144.

This opposition to the party-union relationship of the JLP-BITU has persisted; in 1967, in an interview with this writer, Kelly, President of the NWU, explained that the NWU had opposed the BITU joining the ICFTU for many reasons, one being that the BITU leaders and the government leaders were the same people. This was not the case with the NWU, he said, and that as a trade union negotiator, when he talked with the present Prime Minister (Shearer from the BITU) the situation was difficult as it was not known "whether he was wearing his trade union or Prime Minister's hat."

Thus the claim by the NWU that it is more respectable is a question of degree rather than substance, namely that it is less politically dominated than the BITU. But despite both unions being politically affiliated and highly integrated with political parties, the attacks on political unionism have basically been directed at the BITU.

Models, Concepts, and Trade Union Education

One obvious area in which models of trade unionism and industrial relations could be promoted is within the framework of a trade union education programme. Since the early colonial reports, foreign persons and organisations had been urging Jamaican unionists to be "responsible" and usually coupled this demand with a plea for more union education in industrial relations procedures. At the beginning of the 1950s, there were several pressures from different sources for beginning trade union education.

The IBRD-sponsored mission recommended that trade union leaders in Jamaica should be educated because "for the labor unions the development of good leadership, particularly at the local and regional level, is all-important. Lack of experience and poor education make many trade union officials poorly qualified for their jobs."[38] Earlier, the report of the Board of Enquiry into Labour Disputes Between Unions noted that while there was a "general wish for peace and better Labour relations . . . there was evidence also from certain quarters of a lack of comprehension of trade union practices."[39] The *Daily Gleaner,* in an editorial devoted to trade union education in 1952, recorded that the British Council had donated four study boxes of books and leaflets for use by the Labour Department and labour leaders "to disseminate principles and practices among rank and file membership," but, the editorial continued, only one trade union had a study group and that it was "alarming to view the disregard shown by BITU and TUC towards the efforts of the Labour Department and the British Council to interest them in courses of study in the fundamentals of trade union principles and practices."[40]

COLONIAL AND JAMAICAN GOVERNMENT PROGRAMMES

The support for trade union education was thus well secured. The British Government had first started courses for trade unionists in 1948, funded by the Colonial De-

[38] IBRD: *The Economic Development of Jamaica,* p. 82.
[39] Government of Jamaica: *Report of the Board of Enquiry into Labour Disputes etc.,* p. 9.
[40] *Daily Gleaner,* March 20, 1952, p. 6.

velopment and Welfare Fund (CD&W), and in 1952 a similar course of three months duration was given in Barbados. The Jamaican Government (JLP-BITU), however, did not make the necessary recommendations for trade unionists to attend the course, claiming that "all suitable candidates are too occupied with union affairs in Jamaica."[41] In 1954, another CD&W course, in collaboration with the University College of the West Indies and Caribbean governments, was more successful with the BITU since two officials from that union attended as well as one from the TUCJ and one from the NWU. Even though the course was sponsored by the British Government (through CD&W) and organised by a university professor from Britain, one of the lecturers appointed was Professor G. Blumer of the University of California and courses were given in labour-management relations and the structure of West Indian, British, and American societies.[42] The inclusion, for the first time, of the latter subject and of an American lecturer in the course is evidence that the British authorities anticipated, agreed, or conceded that the role of the USA industrial relations model in Jamaican society would become increasingly more important. The basic orientation of these courses in the early 1950s is not clear, although the earlier CD&W courses, possibly under the influence of Dalley, had adopted a broad approach coupled with some specific instruction in trade unionism and industrial relations as practised in Britain.

The first Jamaican government activity occurred in the first year of office of the PNP-NWU in 1955, when it organised what was to become an annual Trade Union Training Course under auspices to the Ministry of Labour.

[41] *Ibid.*, March 20, 1952, p. 1.

[42] Reports in *Daily Gleaner*, January 28, 1954, and February 1, 1954.

A press release from the Ministry concerning this first course said the objective was to provide a short course for trade unionists who would be the "future participants in the field of industrial relations in Jamaica."[43] But the Ministry had no more success in attracting the BITU than did the earlier efforts of the CD&W, for although nominations for the course were sought from all unions "the Bustamante Industrial Trade Union, in spite of our greatest efforts, have not nominated anyone to attend."[44]

The basic objective of the courses was stated in the opening speech of Glasspole, as Minister of Labour: "Someone may very well ask, why all this trouble? The answer is quite simple. In the teething period of trade unionism as a mass movement from 1937 onwards, the problems were different and the approach was then necessarily different. A belligerent attitude, fire and brimstone approach by trade union leaders of all levels was then quite in order, it was taken for granted. But the pattern has changed over the years; today men who are charged with the responsibility of representing workers can no longer rely on pure militancy to represent the case for the workers. Leaders must have facts to answer the case."[45] At the closing of the course, Norman Manley, then Chief Minister, also noted the need for a new unionism, explaining that "there was a time when trade unionism was a rumbustious sort of thing but the trade union movement was growing up."[46]

To achieve these basic objectives the Ministry of Labour argued that the courses should be for lower level secretaries and branch secretaries, especially as other courses and organisations were concerned with the training of the

[43] *Daily Gleaner*, December 13, 1955.
[44] *Ibid.*
[45] *Ibid.*
[46] *Ibid.*, December 21, 1955.

higher level leaders.[47] In fact, this policy was not adhered to and by 1957 the two-week course had one hundred and sixty-two participants from all levels of trade union administration. In that year the Extra-Mural Department of the University College of the West Indies became involved with some aspects of the Ministry course, dealing with the higher level leaders. Subsequently, this division became accepted and the Ministry course was reduced to twelve days and restricted to branch organisers, secretaries, and shop stewards, in accordance with the government's policy "to promote an enlightened approach to industrial relations."[48]

The Ministry courses were less inclined than the CD&W to employ lecturers foreign to the Caribbean. The first one in 1955, for example, had as lecturers: Eric Williams, later to become Prime Minister of Trinidad and Tobago; Robert Lightbourne, who was to become Minister of Trade and Industry for Jamaica; and Hugh Shearer, subsequently Prime Minister of Jamaica.

When the course was partly taken over by the University College of the West Indies, the foreign tutors and specialists once again entered the trade union education field.

UNIVERSITY OF THE WEST INDIES, AIFLD, AND USA GOVERNMENT

The Extra-Mural Department of the University College had established some courses in industrial relations three year after its foundation in 1948. In 1952, for example,

[47] *Ibid.*, December 14, 1955.
[48] Ministry of Labour (Jamaica): *Annual Report 1955*, 1956, p. 9.

an American professor, Simon Rottenburg, Director of the Labour Relations Institute, University of Puerto Rico, visited to lecture on personnel management and industrial relations.[49] At this time any courses in industrial relations were in the hands of the Staff Tutor of Training for the Department of Extra-Mural Studies, who were successively: Eric James from Columbia University, USA; David Matthews from Glasgow University, Scotland; and in 1954, Rawle Farley from British Guiana.

The basic organising initiative came in 1953, however, from Philip Sherlock, later to be Vice-Chancellor of the University of the West Indies, in his capacity as Director of Extra-Mural Studies. He recorded in a memorandum on trade union education in 1953 that "labour emerged after 1937–38 in the West Indies as an important industrial and political force. Education was therefore essential to help labour to exercise its legitimate functions with maturity and responsibility at a critical time in West Indian history."[50]

Thus in 1954 Sherlock appointed the first full-time tutor in industrial relations to establish a complete and continuous programme. The new tutor, Rawle Farley, was able, before assuming his duties, to take special courses at the University of Glasgow, Oxford University, and the British Ministry of Labour, funded by an ILO fellowship and a CD&W grant. He was also able to make a study of industrial relations in North America as a result of an award of a USA International Education Exchange Foreign Leaders Grant "(with the further help of the United States Department of Labour)," while the Canadian Labor

[49] *Daily Gleaner*, January 4, 1952.

[50] R. Farley, A *Report on the University College of the West Indies Extra-Mural Studies Industrial Relations Programme, June 1956–September* 1958, Kingston, 1958, p. 1.

Congress provided an expense paid tour of Canada.[51]

In 1959, preparatory to another shift in the provision of trade union education, Farley arranged a Conference on Labour Education in the Caribbean, which was, as a foretaste of future events in the field, supported by a variety of foreign sources. He stated that the conference would not have been possible without the interest of Frank McCallister, Director of Labor Education Division, Roosevelt University, and the aid of the Federal Government of the West Indies, and the Caribbean unit governments, universities, Ford Foundation, British TUC, the Canadian Labour Congress, ORIT, CADORIT, West Indian trade unions, and the British Colonial office, which made available a CD&W grant of £3700.[52]

The final resolution of the conference was that an "Institute of Industrial Relations should be established as rapidly as possible at the University College of the West Indies."[53]

This recommendation came to fruition four years later, in May 1964, when the Trade Union Education Institute (TUEI) of the University of the West Indies was opened. The TUEI was a gift of the USA and a grant of £65,000 for three years' operation was given by the USA Government through its Agency for International Development (AID), to be administered by the American Institute for Free Labor Development (AIFLD). Thus representatives of the AIFLD are on the TUEI advisory board; other members are from the NWU, BITU, TUCJ, and the University of the West Indies.[54] In preparation for the

[51] R. Farley, ed., *Labour Education in the British Caribbean*, Georgetown, British Guiana, 1960, p. 6.

[52] *Ibid.*, p. 7.

[53] *Ibid.*, p. 114.

[54] Trade Union Education Institute: *Annual Report 1965–1966*, Kingston, 1966, p. 33.

expiry of the USA grant in 1967, Jamaican unions started a fund-raising drive which resulted in the British TUC promising £500 per year for a three-year period.[55]

The Institute has been directed by Rex Nettleford, a Jamaican, and lecturers, apart from the staff of the University of the West Indies, have come from Britain, Denmark, Canada, and the USA, and included George Eaton, then of York University, Canada.

Because of these provisions within Jamaica and the lack of internationally sponsored programmes, Jamaican trade unionists participating in educational programmes abroad were limited during the 1950s. Sterling (NWU) and Shearer (BITU) both attended a conference in 1956 in England on Human Problems of Industrial Communities. More opportunities have been available since 1960; B. Edwards, Assistant Secretary of the NWU, went to the International Institute for Labour Studies in 1964 in Geneva; in 1964 T. Forrest (BITU) spent a year at Harvard studying Industrial Relations and Economics; Hopeton Caven of the TUCJ attended an AIFLD course in the USA in the same year; I. Davis, NWU publicity officer, went on a State Department sponsored study tour of the USA in 1966 and in 1967; four NWU officers participated in a three-month training programme sponsored by a foundation in the Federal Republic of Germany.[56]

The educational programmes within Jamaica involved a substantial number of foreign individuals, organisations, and national labour organisations. The general orientation of the concepts and models advocated from within the educational framework can be discovered by examining some of the arguments of the major participants in the programmes.

[55] *Daily Gleaner*, April 12, 1967, p. 27.
[56] *National Workers Union 14th Annual Report*, Kingston, 1966, p. 42.

Sherlock, as director of the University College of the West Indies Extra-Mural Department, may have been certain of what was meant by education to help labour to exercise its "legitimate functions with maturity and responsibility" but the Industrial Relations Tutors had to be more specific and define labour's "legitimate function." Farley, the first West Indian Tutor in Industrial Relations, felt that trade unions should acquire a "philosophic approach which is consistent with the good of the organisations and the good of the nation which these organisations serve."[57] Thus education was needed so that unionists could resolve, in the interest of the community, "the most tremendous question of the twentieth century—the problem of the use of power."[58]

The concept of a trade union serving the society, nation, or community, rather than narrow pressure group interests, was shared by several West Indians involved in the programmes. Hugh W. Springer, a lawyer, Oxford graduate, and one-time General Secretary of the Barbados Workers' Union, argued in 1959 that trade unions "while protecting and promoting the interests of their members will see their function in the context of their country's whole economy."[59]

These conceptions were not shared by some of the

[57] R. Farley, *Report of UCWI Extra-Mural Studies Industrial Relations Programme*, p. 14.

[58] R. Farley, ed., *Labour Education in the British Caribbean*, p. 5.

[59] H. Springer, "Education for Trade Unionists," in R. Farley, ed., *Labour Education in the British Caribbean*, p. 18.

foreign visitors invited to give advice. The Conference on Labour Education in the British Caribbean, mentioned above, was based on a *Labour Education Survey* conducted in June and July 1959 by Gower Markle, Director of Education and Welfare for the United Steelworkers of America, Canadian Division.

Markle began his report by defining a trade union as "a free and voluntary association of workers for the purpose of promoting and protecting their interests and the total welfare of themselves and their families."[60] This definition contrasted sharply with the conceptions of both the organiser of the conference, Farley, and of Springer, whose address to the conference was also attached to Markle's survey.

Other speeches at the conference showed differences in conception of trade unions in society and especially in relation to the type of education needed in the Caribbean. Markle viewed trade union education as basically technical, but of two kinds, first, that which is necessary for the "development of a mature, democratic, and stable labour movement," and second, that which is necessary for collective bargaining.[61] Although he felt both were needed, most of his findings related to the second kind. In relation to the first, however, Markle warned of the dangers of workers "maturing" while lacking the necessary ingredients for integration, "if a society ignores the education and development of its workers while they are maturing, it should not be surprised if they arrive at maturity and take their places as workers in an economy with only resentment instead of understanding and respect for tradition."[62]

[60] G. Markle, "Report of Labour Education Survey," in R. Farley, ed., *Labour Education in the British Caribbean*, p. 58.
[61] *Ibid.*, p. 57.
[62] *Ibid.*, p. 62.

The British participants at the conference described British efforts in labour education which had placed emphasis on the broader aspects of education. The British experts, Hilary Marquand and Allan Flanders, considered "trade union education" to be education of trade unionists, although Flanders agreed that technical education in trade union matters was also necessary.[63] The American participants, Frank McCallister and Lois Gray, stated the American experience and the former averred that "where [labour education] has been successful and effective in our country it has been geared to the practical needs of the membership for strengthening the organisation."[64] Daniel Benedict, as the representative of the regional organisation, ORIT, presented three operational programmes for education to suit three different types of country but the content of the teaching was to place emphasis upon "techniques of organization training and shop-level representation . . ."[65]

The different conceptions of trade union education were never solved as, in general, the narrow view prevailed in the programmes later established. The conflict between the conception of a trade union serving the nation, as held by some West Indians, and the foreign concept of it functioning as a sectional interest group was not so easy to resolve.

It was made less apparent and disruptive by gaining acceptance of the notion that management and labour, within a collective bargaining relationship, worked together for the good of the whole, even though they

[63] A. Flanders, "Trade Union Education in Great Britain," in R. Farley, ed., *Labour Education in the British Caribbean*, pp. 26–27.
[64] F. McCallister, "Labour Education in the United States," in R. Farley, ed., *Labour Education in the British Caribbean*, p. 38.
[65] D. Benedict, "Trade Union Education and Organisation—The International Content," in R. Farley, ed., *Labour Education in the British Caribbean*, p. 53.

were pursuing their own specific aims. This idea was raised at the conference in a paper, which was not completely in context with the nature of the conference, entitled "Some Reflections on Collective Bargaining." The author, Neil Chamberlain, noted that management and labour "commonly resolved their differences without open conflict . . ."[66]

Two years after the conference, the Industrial Relations Tutor who had succeeded Farley, Zin Henry, made the same point, "the society of industry is probably unique in one respect. Its two conflicting interest groups are permanently joined in wedlock."[67] In 1967, Nettleford, Director of the Trade Union Institute at the University of the West Indies, stated in an address marking the closing of a course that he felt "it was unfortunate that some of the relationships in West Indian society was [sic] still thought of in terms of those who were bosses and those who were labourers . . . But over the past 30 or 40 years, good sense had prevailed and they had managed to develop a rational system of bargaining based on the recognition of mutual rights and respect."[68] Thus the problems of reconciling a technical education programme with the requirements that unions should serve the broad national interest have, on the level of formal rationality, been solved.

As befits the nature of education and the academic leanings of the instructors, most of the actors referred to above treated the advocacy of a specific national trade union model with reserve. Many of them were aware

[66] N. Chamberlain, "Some Reflections on Collective Bargaining," in R. Farley, ed., *Labour Education in the British Caribbean*, p. 49.

[67] Z. Henry, *Background Lectures on Industrial Relations in the Caribbean*, Georgetown, British Guiana, 1960, p. 11.

[68] *Daily Gleaner*, May 22, 1967, p. 10.

of the political necessity and practical desirability to give recognition to the possibility of indigenous forms of unionism. Springer, at the Labour Education Conference, cited with approval an ICFTU report which warned against "blindly copying the pattern and structure of the movement in other countries."[69] Henry argued in 1961 that: "There are no model trade unions today which can be transplanted into or applied to any other society with a certainty of success. The trade union movement of a country exists within the socio-economic, legal, and political environment of that country, not to mention other factors . . ."[70]

It can be assumed, with the possible exception of the early CD&W courses, that most of the foreign instructors in the educational programme accepted the stated sentiments of the experts at the Labour Education Conference that they were not instructing Jamaican or West Indians how to run their societies and that generalisations about West Indian trade unionism could not be made.[71] But the nature of their subject, the underlying conceptions of trade unions, and the current political and social objectives invariably brought them back to making comparisons and generalisations which were based on the particular model that they knew or had adopted.

[69] H. Springer, "Education for Trade Unionists," in R. Farley, ed., *Labour Education in the British Caribbean,* p. 15.
[70] Z. Henry, *Background Lectures on Industrial Relations in the Caribbean,* p. 12.
[71] See, for example, McCallister and Markle, in R. Farley, ed., *Labour Education in the British Caribbean.*

Part III

Analysis and Conclusions

CHAPTER X

FOREIGN UNION OBJECTIVES IN JAMAICA

In Chapter II it was suggested that there were several categories of incentives for trade union involvement in international affairs. These were listed as: performing basic functions in international society; increasing or maintaining domestic power; serving the nation; supporting ideologies; and finally, satisfying leadership needs.

It is now possible to examine these incentives in relation to the Jamaican involvement, assess their importance, and investigate the general objectives of foreign trade unions in Jamaica.

Basic International Functions

THE USWA

When McDonald became President of the USWA his inaugural speech outlined some new plans for the USWA international activities: "You have all been reading about the development of iron ore mines in Venezuela and Guatemala and the development of bauxite mines, which as you know, we use for the manufacture of aluminum, in Jamaica.

"We must have concern for the working conditions of the iron ore miners in the United States and Canada. We must protect their standards. I don't know how you mean you can protect their standards if thousands of virtually enslaved men who go down into the mines of Venezuela, Guatemala, and Jamaica for a standard wage of a dollar a day . . . Great rich fields of ore, owned by American corporations, are being developed by American corporations to be worked by the natives of those countries at miserable wages. I propose we look into this problem . . . I am going to have a study made of these situations, because we must protect the standards of our people here at home, and as a result of this study the International Executive Board shall make determinations as to what we, the International Steelworkers of America, shall do."[1]

This speech was made on March 11, 1953, and the first recorded presence of a USWA representative in Jamaica had been a few months previously. Since that date to the present any mention of Jamaica in the records of the USWA or by leaders of the organisation has been in association with the raw material of bauxite. In 1954 and 1956 the Officers Reports record the continued assistance to the Jamaican bauxite workers which was given partly because of "the union's bargaining position with the same companies in the United States and Canada where it represents workers from bauxite to finished pots and pans, from Arkansas in the South to Kitimat in the Canadian Northwest."[2]

[1] V. Sweeny, *The United Steelworkers of America, Twenty Years Later 1936–1956*, Pittsburgh, pp. 141–42.
[2] "It's Not All Calypso," *Steel Labor*, April 1957, p. 6.

The USWA activities in Jamaica have invariably been explained as necessary for the protection of labour standards in the USA. The USWA became involved in Jamaica in the year that the first of the continuous and massive shipments of bauxite and alumina to the plants of North America were made. The basic contact in Jamaica for the USWA had always been with the National Workers Union and particularly the bauxite mining autonomous branch.

A section of the USWA membership had direct technical and trade links with workers in Jamaica; thus the USWA had primary functions to perform in Jamaica relating to those workers. This connection supplied the initial and sustaining incentive for involvement of the USWA in Jamaica.

THE BRITISH TUC

There is no evidence that the British TUC membership had any direct technical or trade connections which required the organisation to serve its interests in Jamaica. Until 1957 Britain was Jamaica's main trading partner but trading connections were diffuse and were small relative to Britain's total trading volume. Alumina from the Jamaican plants supplied British smelting plants and at one time Britain was dependent on aluminium from ALCAN, which derived large supplies of alumina from Jamaica.[3] But these connections were tenuous and were never mentioned in policy statements concerned with Jamaica.

The pattern of the British TUC involvement does not

[3] H. Huggins, *Aluminium in Changing Communities*, London, 1968, p. 58.

reveal any special interest in economic connections and it can be concluded that the British TUC leaders did not conceive of any primary functions of the organisation which had to be performed in Jamaica.

Serving the Nation[4]

THE USWA

Three aspects of the USWA policy and organisational connections intensified the incentives to bring the union to the service of the nation in international affairs. First, the early association of the union with government foreign policy agencies; second, the strategic nature of bauxite; and third, the desire to promote a nationally associated political ideology. The first and second of these will be considered in this section and the third in a section dealing with ideology as an incentive.

The USWA's known connection with USA Government agencies have mainly concerned the union's activities in Latin America. McDonald, soon after the USWA was founded, had been associated with government agencies with operations in Latin America. As a partial consequence the union has been active in organisations in the Caribbean and Latin America, especially the regional organisations, ORIT for Latin America and CCLab for the Caribbean. The involvement of the USWA in Jamaica does not appear to have arisen from the involvement of the union top leadership with government agencies. McDonald made it clear, however, that

[4] This subject is further discussed in greater detail in the following chapter.

he was prepared to assist the government if it was necessary: "leaders of your organization do not hesitate to talk to anyone from the national administration if we can be of assistance, not only to the United Steelworkers of America but to our world economy."[5]

The incentive of serving the nation was more important in relation to the bauxite-alumina industry in Jamaica. Bauxite is the basic ore from which aluminium is produced and in Jamaica in the late 1940s there were two corporations mining bauxite and one preparing for the manufacture of alumina (the intermediate stage between bauxite and aluminium) for shipment to Canada and Europe. The USA Government's interest in bauxite and aluminium was indicated in the early 1940s by the £2.5 million loan to ALCAN for its alumina plant, the loan to be repaid by shipments of alumina to the USA. In this way the USA became the owner of the alumina produced in the first years of ALCAN production in the early 1950s. The strategic importance of aluminium began to be stressed with renewed vigour in the late 1940s with the commencement of the Korean War and the acceptance that the communist bloc was expansionist. After noting that wars required the creation and destruction of large quantities of aluminium, a writer for a public affairs organisation argued that "our main concern with aluminum right now and for the next several years is that we have enough of it available to the free nations to build up an adequate defense . . . Action must be taken now to provide reliable and expanding sources of aluminum supply to defend ourselves and our allies and to carry any war that must be thrust upon us to a successful and earliest possible conclusion."[6]

[5] USWA: *Proceedings of 7th Constitutional Convention, 1954,* p. 11.

[6] H. Anderson, *Aluminum for Defense and Prosperity,* pp. 5 and 9.

Such pressures as these resulted in President Truman establishing a Materials Policy Commission, the final report of which—*Resources for Freedom*—was published in 1952 and showed the USA using up its strategic materials at a rapid rate.[7] The recommendations of this report were taken up by President Eisenhower in his inaugural address on January 20, 1953: "No free people can for long cling to any privilege or enjoy any safety in economic solitude. For all our own material might, even we need markets in the world for the surpluses of our farms and our factories. Equally we need for these same farms and factories vital materials and products of distant lands. This basic law of interdependence, so manifest in the commerce of peace, applies with a thousandfold intensity in the event of war."[8]

The bauxite stock-piling programme was thus made permanent and Jamaica became the major USA supplier, while domestic bauxite production was reduced on a planned and continuing basis.

In 1952 the first major shipments of bauxite and alumina from Jamaica to the USA were made and the USWA involvement in Jamaican unions began. Four years later the USWA Department reported to the bi-annual Convention that "to protect our miners in non-ferrous metals industries and at the same time to provide for adequate stocks of strategic materials for defense security, your union has been active in promoting sound governmental policies relating to these commodities . . . At the same time policies enunciated by our union encouraged foreign production in order to supplement our limited supplies without injuring the workers at home."[9]

[7] See *Resources for Freedom*, a report by the President's Materials Policy Commission, Washington, D.C., 1952, Vol. II, pp. 65–73.
[8] *Keesing's Contemporary Archives*, Vol. IX, 1952–54, p. 12701A.
[9] USWA: *Proceedings of 8th Constitutional Convention, 1956*, p. 98.

This combination of stated union self-interest and of national security arising from strategic materials was placed in a prime position by USWA personnel acting in Jamaica. One executive interviewed noted that when he met with some opposition from the Jamaican Government, he explained to its members that he should be able to continue his activities as 'we had an economic interest down there.' Thus serving the nation through involvement in the supply process of strategic material was an important incentive for USWA involvement in Jamaica.

THE BRITISH TUC

The British TUC moved into close association with the British Government from the very beginning of its interest in the colonies. The creation of the tripartite Colonial Advisory Committee, the presence of the TUC members on Colonial Office committees, Citrine's involvement in a Royal Commission on colonial problems, and finally the joint government/TUC programme for the appointment of trade unionists as government officers advising trade unions in colonial territories establish that cooperation with the government was a consistent policy.

Furthermore, the record of TUC involvement in Jamaica shows that it never deviated from British government policy as laid down in the Passfield Memorandum in 1930, that democratic unions should be encouraged and the movement protected from "disaffected persons." The twenty-year support of organisations opposing Bustamante and the BITU reveal this policy in the specific, while Tewson's admission that "as soon as we turn our backs the movement has been collared . . .

by, sometimes, a single person . . ." confirms it on the general level.[10]

In practice, then, the British TUC did not deviate from government policy and in this sense served the nation in Jamaica. To argue, however, that this was the major incentive for involvement would be to ignore some political factors in the British domestic situation. The most important of these was that trade unionists conceived of the British Government in general as supporting the labour movement ideology in the colonies and opposing reluctant and illiberal local colonial administrations.[11] Deakin, one of the leading figures of the TUC in international matters in the period, said of the charges made of union/government association in 1949: "It is said that we are closely associated with our own government. Well I ask you, is that a crime? Is it wrong that we are doing things in cooperation with our own colleagues, our own government?"[12]

Unlike McDonald, the British TUC leaders did not talk of assisting the nation in its policy but rather of the government and nation assisting the TUC in execution of its own policy. For this reason the incentive for involvement in Jamaica came more from movement ideology than from the idea of national duty. However, the question is to some extent concerned with the perception of the various policy-makers and although the policy towards colonies may have been believed to come from the labour movement, the incentive to cooperate

[10] ICFTU: *Report of Fourth World Congress, 1955*, p. 348.

[11] This was especially true during the Labour Government of 1945–52, but see also speech of British Worker Delegate, ILO: *International Labour Conference, Record of Proceedings, 24th Session, 1938*, p. 302.

[12] TUC: *81st Annual Congress, Report of Proceedings, 1949*, p. 323.

with the government in effecting it was a powerful one and led to the long history of government/TUC collaboration.

Supporting Ideologies

Three types of ideology supported by trade unions at the international level were identified in an earlier chapter as political ideology, movement ideology, and group ideology.

POLITICAL IDEOLOGY

The USWA involvement in international affairs was, from its beginning, explained in terms of opposing communism and promoting democracy. The principal USWA officer, President McDonald, had, throughout his career and in many different forums, spoken on foreign policy issues in terms of anti-communism. North American unionists and economists have also stated that Caribbean bauxite was a prime target for communists.[13]

Despite these events, the USWA leaders never referred to the involvement in Jamaica in terms of being an anti-communist programme. The support of the NWU against the TUCJ could have been perceived as an anti-communist policy but USWA reports and accounts of the Jamaican programme never refer to the TUCJ as

[13] See, for example, D. Gage, "Aluminum Links the Pacific Coast with Jamaica," *Oregon Business Review*, No. 24, January 1965, p. 6.

a communist organisation or to any of its leaders in similar fashion. Likewise, there are virtually no references to the BITU. For the USWA it does not appear that the ideology of liberal democracy, or its negative statement of anti-communism or anti-fascism, was an important incentive. Reference here is made only to the USWA direct involvement, for there were other organisations in which the USWA had some power, in particular ORIT, which did not hold the same position.

The British TUC support of the TUCJ against the BITU, which was designated anti-democratic by the TUCJ leaders, could also be construed as promoting a democratic ideology. But, as with the USWA, there is little evidence that the Jamaican involvement was seen in these terms and, for example, the PNP purge of TUCJ leaders accused of being communists was recorded by the TUC without comment[14] although support was switched to the new NWU, for which there are other explanations than one of supporting political ideology. Some emphasis was placed on the importance of the liberal democratic nature of self-government for the colonies and Tewson was prepared to associate the creating of unions on British lines as being instrumental in achieving ultimate democratic regimes. In this sense promotion of liberal democracy can only be seen as a weak incentive for the British TUC.

MOVEMENT IDEOLOGY

USWA statements have stressed the union-to-union aspect of its foreign policy programme, and that the as-

[14] TUC: *85th Annual Congress, Report of Proceedings, 1953*, p. 215.

sistance rendered the NWU has been successful in assisting the workers of Jamaica. The emphasis has been specific and pragmatic and rarely linked to a generalised notion of the benefits to be derived from trade unionism which is an essential element in movement ideology as previously defined. Movement ideology as an incentive has not been important for the USWA.

The British TUC has been in a different position. The first contacts the British TUC made in Jamaica were made in the belief that unions in Jamaica were necessary to alleviate the general conditions of poverty found in the West Indies. The belief that unions were necessary, not for national independence, but for social reasons, was expressed by Citrine through the West Indies Royal Commission Report and by Tewson at the ICFTU.[15]

The policy change made by the British TUC in 1952 was a function of an attempt to cement Anglo-American labour relations at the international level—also part of the belief of the importance of an international trade union movement. Supporting a movement ideology was thus an important incentive for the British TUC leaders regarding their actions in Jamaica.

GROUP IDEOLOGY

Both the USWA and the British TUC promoted, by various means, their respective group ideologies of nationally associated unionism. The importance of group ideologies as incentives differs between the two organisations, largely because of the difference in their respective state relations with Jamaica.

[15] See ICFTU: *Report of Fourth World Congress, 1955*, p. 348.

The Caribbean, and some other areas in which the USWA was active, had had long exposure to trade union models from Europe and was often still in the process of adopting or adapting such models. Thus, the USWA model-promotion was competitive, as it was an attempt to replace the existing model by the USA model. The USWA leaders believed that there were general "know-hows" of American unionism which were worthy of export to less-developed countries. Specifically listed were minimum wages, grievance procedures, and collective bargaining, namely, those facets of industrial relations most commonly associated with the USA trade union group ideology of business unionism. The USWA references to activities in the Caribbean uniformly refer to the success of the union in spreading these practices. However, group ideology was not an important incentive in itself but rather an operational tactic resulting from a presence inspired by other incentives.

For the British TUC, group ideology was a more important incentive. Coupled with the movement ideology, the belief that unions in the colonies should follow British lines was strong, especially in the early period. The absence of over-riding incentives meant that this was able to be expressed in action unmitigated by other considerations. Even after the organisation formally adopted a relativist policy, the idea that the British model was the most effective remained among officers engaged in international affairs; 'a trade union in a less-developed country should be what it is in my own country,' stated an important TUC representative interviewed in 1964. The belief that the trade unions in Jamaica should evolve in conformity with British union group ideology was of some importance as an incentive for the British TUC.

This importance was lessened, however, by the circumstances in which promotion of the British group ideology was not competitive with any other group ideology. Such competition in Jamaica did not occur until after 1952 and by that time the British TUC was cooperating with the USWA and did not seriously oppose business unionism.

Increasing or Maintaining Domestic Power

There is no direct evidence that the British TUC used its Jamaican (or Caribbean) involvement to increase its power in relation to the government, other unions, or corporations. It is unlikely, therefore, that the possible use of the involvement in this manner would supply an incentive. This is not to ignore the fact that the expenditure in Jamaica and interest given after World War II were the first proofs to the government that the British TUC was prepared to play an active role in the colonies.

There are some indications, in the case of the USWA, that the Jamaican involvement was useful in demonstrating the efficiency and power of the union to corporations which operated in both Jamaica and the USA.[16] It has been clearly stated that one of the policies of the USWA was to follow USA companies abroad, and in this sense to increase its power vis-à-vis corporations would be an incentive for activities in Jamaica.

[16] See "It's Not All Calypso," *Steel Labor*, and USWA: *Proceedings of 11th Constitutional Convention, 1962*, p. 373.

Leadership Needs

The incentive to involve the organisation in international affairs and in Jamaica for personal reasons of the leadership is relevant to both the USWA and the British TUC, although more so in the former case.

The career of McDonald as President of the USWA shows that he was very interested in becoming integrated in government politics. He was a champion of cooperation between management and labour and he served on important government commissions. When he lost the election in 1965, he was described as being "more respected in Washington than in our own union."[17] His vigorous championing of a foreign policy for American labour can be seen as a facet of this personal desire for national political acceptance and one unionist interviewed described him as over-responding to the praise of Washington diplomats. That the USWA, despite its association with the CIO, IMF, ORIT, and ICFTU, developed its "own program of diplomacy" during the McDonald administration was also an expression of McDonald's personal interest in foreign affairs. The desire for a specific and personal programme in international affairs by an important leader can thus be seen as an incentive for the USWA. It should also be mentioned that the frequency of visits of USWA personnel to the Caribbean, from sometimes only marginally involved departments, may also serve a personal as well as union function and may well contribute to organisational enthusiasm for the continuation of the programme.

[17] B. Farrell, "Labor Leaders, Tough, Remote—or Feuding," *Life*, Vol. 61, No. 9, August 26, 1966, p. 35.

Although both Citrine and Tewson reveal a personal interest in international affairs and no doubt acquired prestige from their vigorous participation in them, the TUC colonial programme in Jamaica cannot be seen as a function of their personal inclinations.

General Objectives in Jamaica: an Assessment

It has been noted that the categories of incentives for foreign union involvement are divisions of convenience and more of a heuristic device than a reflection of reality. The foregoing examination has shown that most of the categories of incentives were overlapping and therefore all relevant, although varying widely in importance to each organisation. In summary, it is useful to designate some of the incentives as of primary importance and others of secondary, or supportive, importance only.

For the USWA the most important incentive for involvement in Jamaica was the economic connection between bauxite mining and a section of the membership which the organisation served in the USA. This primary incentive was strengthened or supported by the possibility of serving the nation in matters of strategic concern, of promoting a political ideology and, to some extent, of satisfying personal leadership needs.

For the British TUC the situation is more complex in that the most important incentive, that of promoting movement ideology, was coupled with a national foreign policy and both were perceived as pursuing the same ends. Promoting movement ideology and serving the nation could thus be viewed as primary incentives and given equal weight while others were secondary, and that of internationally performing a basic function for membership was non-existent. From these incentives the general policy objectives in Jamaica were derived.

GENERAL OBJECTIVES—BRITISH TUC

In the case of the British TUC, the policy described as universalistic plus the incentive of movement ideology made the general objective in Jamaica the creation of an organisation approximating the British TUC committed to general worker welfare. At the same time, Jamaican trade unions were not to become instruments of "disaffected persons" disturbing the perceived national policy of reform in the colonies and evolutionary self-government.

The general objectives in Jamaica changed, however, during the period 1949–52. There is evidence to suggest that the reason for this change was that the Jamaican involvement became a function of objectives at the international level, especially within the ICFTU.

In the first place, the British unions were active in the split of the International and were ardent promoters of the new ICFTU. Jamaica was still a colony and while the TUCJ had been an affiliate of the WFTU it refused originally to affiliate to the ICFTU; the BITU was unacceptable which meant Jamaica was not represented in the ICFTU. The assistance in the creation of a new union which would be affiliated to the ICFTU was thus an interesting proposition to the TUC leaders.

More important, however, were the attempts by Deakin and Tewson to cement Anglo-American trade union relations. Significantly, in 1949, the British TUC had faced charges that it was dominated by the American unions. Deakin replied to this charge in public debate by admitting that the TUC leadership was close to the Americans because "those people hold the same views that we hold."[18] A TUC staff member interviewed recounted, in relation to colonial policy, that until 1950 the British TUC had been in full control of its own policy but after that it became more difficult because Tewson and Deakin would do nothing to upset the Americans.[19]

Thus the British TUC policy in Jamaica was designed in the later period to ensure cooperation and cohesion between British and American unions in other spheres of international trade union activity.[20] Further evidence of this interpretation is found in the operational aspects of the TUC involvement in the period 1952–59, which will be discussed in the next chapter.

GENERAL OBJECTIVES—USWA

The case of the USWA requires more attention because here organisation spokesmen, unlike the TUC, have

[18] TUC: *81st Annual Congress, Report of Proceedings, 1949,* p. 323; see also E. Windrich, "British Labour's Foreign Policy," *World Affairs Interpretation*, Vol. 21, July 1950, pp. 169–75.

[19] For TUC activities to create a "rapprochement" between AF of L and ICFTU see also J. Windmuller, *American Labor and International Labor Movement, 1940 to 1953*, New York, 1954, pp. 203–7.

[20] It should be noted that inter-governmental cooperation which involved unionists was also extant at the time. For one which had economic connections with Jamaican bauxite see Anglo-American Council on Productivity: *Non-Ferrous Metals (wrought), report of a visit to the USA in 1950 of a productivity team representing wrought non-ferrous metals industry*, London, 1951.

made statements specifically concerning the general objectives in Jamaica. These have been that the object of the organisation was to protect the labour standards of workers represented by the USWA in the USA. Such statements have been coupled with reports on the success of the union in raising wages for bauxite workers in Jamaica, with the implication that workers in similar occupations in the USWA are thus protected by this action. In 1954 a USWA staff member is reported as having pointed out that USWA workers were under a "competitive handicap" and that "wage rates in the ore mining industry in the United States exceeded $2.25 per hour while employees in the new mines in under-developed countries were receiving on the average only $1.50 or $2.00 per day. At the same time the latter were ordinarily in possession of machinery more modern than the machinery used in the United States. Consequently when a new bauxite mine was recently opened in Jamaica, the USWA decided to send an international representative to that country to help Jamaican workers strengthen their organization."[21] As a result of such statements as these it has been accepted by academic commentators that the basic objective of the USWA in Jamaica was the raising of wages to offset low-wage threats from Jamaica.[22] This interpretation is not, however, consistent with either the economics of the aluminium industry nor with the actions of the USWA in Jamaica.

[21] M. Bernstein in R. Aronson and J. Windmuller, *Labor Management and Economic Growth.*

[22] G. Eaton, *dissertation*, p. 389; W. Knowles, *Trade Union Development and Industrial Relations in the British West Indies, op. cit.*, p. 136; and J. Windmuller, "External Influences on Labor Organizations in Underdeveloped Countries," *Industrial and Labor Relations Review*, Vol. 16, No. 4, July 1963, fn., p. 569.

Bauxite is the raw material which is at the base of an industry employing workers in alumina production and aluminium smelting and fabricating. Alumina production is a chemical process and can be located basically anywhere while aluminium smelting, up to the present, requires large amounts of electricity and is therefore usually located close to such a power source. Bauxite is an ore which is the result of a natural leaching process requiring heavy rainfall and is consequently nearly always found in tropical or semi-tropical areas. It is thus outside the industrialised countries of Europe and North America. The basic pattern is for the ore to be imported to industrial countries from less-developed countries to be transformed into alumina, aluminium, and fabricated products.

Bauxite comes in various qualities and its value is judged by its alumina content and its accessibility. On these criteria bauxite found in the USA is undesirable, being both poor in quality and not always easily accessible. In 1949 the USA started a stockpiling programme and its own production declined rapidly; the 1949–54 average bauxite production in the USA was approximately 1.5 million tons per annum and from 1955 it remained steady at approximately 2 million tons.[23] In 1955 Jamaica produced 2.5 million tons and from the beginning of production the entire bauxite shipments were to the USA. One company, ALCAN, converts the bauxite into alumina before shipping the bulk of its production to the company's smelters in Canada. Jamaica has, since the early 1950s, supplied over 50 per cent of the bauxite needs for the USA aluminium industry and in 1965 the domestic supply of bauxite in the USA

[23] Commonwealth Economic Committee: *Non-Ferrous Metals,* London, 1963, p. 38.

was only 13 per cent. While the production of bauxite in the USA dropped, production of aluminium increased at 11.4 per cent per annum between 1947 and 1957.[24]

BAUXITE, THE USWA, AND JAMAICA

The bulk of USA domestic bauxite is mined in Arkansas in Saline County, which has contributed over 75 per cent of the total USA production since the late 1940s. In 1964 the area accounted for 98 per cent of total domestic USA production.[25] According to a USA government statistical publication, *Growth Patterns in Employment by County, 1940–1950 and 1950–1960*, employment in mining in Saline County was, in 1940, 590; in 1950, 957; and in 1960, 575.[26] This reflects the usual open-cast mining of bauxite, which is a capital intensive process.

The conclusion is that if the USWA represented all of the workers employed in bauxite mining they would never have amounted to more than one thousand workers compared with USWA total membership of over a million.[27] These are the members of the USWA who, it is claimed, would be directly threatened by the low

[24] US Department of Labor: "The Aluminum Industry," *Technological Trends in Major American Industries*, Washington, D.C., 1966, p. 85.

[25] US Department of the Interior: *Minerals Yearbook, Vol. III, Domestic*, Washington, D.C., 1964, p. 149.

[26] US Department of Commerce: *Growth Patterns in Employment by County 1940–1950 and 1950–1960*, Washington, D.C., Table 7(36)63, p. 7–352.

[27] This was confirmed in an interview with a USWA executive when bauxite miner membership was described as a "few hundred."

wages of the bauxite workers in Jamaica. However, in the above quoted statement concerning this issue, the inference was that the Jamaican rates were a threat to all mining rates in the USA. It is difficult to see how this could be the case, except as a psychological international degrading of wages for miners, for the connections between Jamaican bauxite workers and, for example, USA iron ore miners would be tenuous. If such an argument could be accepted, it would not withstand the further difficulty associated with the notion that USA workers were placed under a "competitive handicap" by a new mine in Jamaica.

Firstly, there could be no question of a competitive ore derived from low wages in Jamaica, which would be the traditional low-wage unionist argument against competitive international trade. Not only was Jamaican ore naturally superior to that found in the USA but it was government and corporate policy, supported by the USWA itself, to deliberately reduce domestic production in favour of foreign sources. Secondly, the USWA argued in Jamaica that low wages were not an important factor for the corporations mining bauxite in Jamaica. In the 1955 arbitration between the NWU and Reynolds, the NWU case was presented by Kidd of the USWA. Kidd argued that the corporations were not in Jamaica to take advantage of low wages and that they could not logically use this factor to prevent the bauxite rate rising above the general island level. This was known as the "ability-to-pay" doctrine. The arbitrator agreed with Kidd and declared that the corporations "have come to Jamaica not because of any economic means of low wages of their operation, but because of the situation in this Island of an extremely valuable mineral source."[28]

[28] *National Workers Union 3rd Annual Report*, 1955, p. 4.

In effect the argument was that the bauxite mining wage rate did not make an appreciable difference to the cost of bauxite or of aluminium. This was a true statement of economic fact as, for example, the bauxite mining labour costs were less than one-hundredth the market value of aluminium in 1958. From this it is clear that the only "competitive handicap" to which the USWA workers could be subjected was if foreign miners could be employed in the USA at foreign rates. As immigration and other laws prevent such an event, a direct economic threat from the Jamaican miners to USA workers was not possible.

More relevant to the general objectives of the USWA in Jamaica is the fact that the USWA represents large numbers of workers in the aluminium industry engaged in primary production and fabricating. This arose from the merger with the USWA, in 1944, of the Aluminum Workers of America (AWA) which had been founded in 1936 and led from that time by Zonarich. At the time of the merger the AWA had over 30,000 workers organised.[29] Between 1947 and 1964 workers in primary production and fabrication rose from 36,000 to 76,000. In Canada, where 65 per cent of the alumina production of Jamaica is shipped, aluminium workers make up an important section of the 125,000 Canadian members of the USWA.

These workers in North America were, barring bauxite stockpile releases, dependent upon the two thousand Jamaican workers in the bauxite mining and alumina producing facilities. In the only statements concerning the connection between these workers and the USWA involvement, CADORIT, answering an attack on foreign union

[29] See USWA: *Proceedings of 2nd Constitutional Convention, 1944*, p. 223; but Ulman, *The Government of the Steel Workers Union*, New York, 1962, states this figure as 70,000, p. 90.

aid, pointed out: "From the United States [sic] Steelworkers quite naturally and quite rightly has come technical and financial assistance for workers in the bauxite industry, producing the raw material processed in the USA and Canada by workers in that union."[30] It was for these latter workers that the USWA was involved in Jamaica and the general objective was to ensure the uninterrupted supply of bauxite and alumina to the plants of the USA, thus preventing work disruption among members and at the same time fulfilling a national strategic policy.

GOVERNMENTS, CORPORATIONS, AND UNIONS

The objectives of the unions were shared and, as we have seen, sometimes precipitated by other entities interested in Jamaica. Obviously the corporations shared with the USWA a concern over the attitudes and organisation of the bauxite workers. On several occasions the attitudes and motivations of the bauxite workers were tested and investigated by social and behavioural scientists working for the corporations. Eaton records that in 1959 an attitude survey was carried out by an American professor at an unnamed American bauxite company as part of a study on the impact of industrialisation on agriculture. This survey showed that attitudes of the employees towards the company were 60 per cent indifferent, 20 per cent loyal, and 20 per cent hostile.[31] Stud-

[30] CADORIT: *Information Bulletin,* Nos. 5 and 6, May–June, 1956, p. 4.

[31] G. Eaton, *dissertation,* pp. 714–15. Neither the study nor the data appear to have been subsequently published.

ies were again made in 1961[32] and 1964, the latter being undertaken by the American consultant company, the Psychological Corporation, in the course of setting up training schemes at the ALCAN plant.[33]

From the standpoint of international politics, the British and USA government interest was centred on the strategic situation of the island, and, more specifically, the strategic importance of bauxite. Some of the notions of "presence" or hegemony inherent in the historical positions of the governments were also to be found in the attitudes of the national corporations and business groups.[34] For example, the change of policy the British TUC effected in 1952 caused the Secretary of the British Employers' Federation to complain that the British unions had not been active enough in the Caribbean; "because of the negligence of the British TUC . . . Caribbean workers have been driven into American trade unions . . . but it is probably better for us to submit to American infiltration rather than Communist . . . I would rather see the British TUC there."[35]

More direct tripartite association concerning Jamaican objectives is noticeable in the case of the USA corporations, Government, and unions. The direct association between the USA Government and the bauxite mining companies did not continue after the liquidation of the government loan to ALCAN. Corporate management,

[32] R. Aronson, "Labour Commitment among Jamaican Bauxite Workers: a Case Study," *Social and Economic Studies,* Vol. 10, No. 2, June 1961, pp. 156–62.

[33] G. Gill, "Setting up Training Schemes in a Jamaica Mining Company," in J. Lauwerys and D. Scanlon, eds., *Education Within Industry,* 1968, pp. 347–48.

[34] For an attempt to distinguish the union interest from state and corporation, see E. Davies, "Anglo-American Trade Union Cooperation," *Political Quarterly,* Vol. 14, No. 1, January 1943, p. 69.

[35] CADORIT: *Information Bulletin,* Nos. 5 and 6, May–June 1956, p. 2.

however, was equally prepared to proclaim the strategic importance of bauxite. This is permanently inscribed on an aluminium plaque unveiled in Jamaica in 1952 by Walter L. Rice, President of Reynolds Jamaica Mines Ltd.: "on this property in 1942 the Hon. Alfred H. D'Costa in the hope of improving the agricultural productivity of the sterile soil took the sample which on analysis proved to be aluminium ore, thus bringing the people of Jamaica a new industry and to the peoples of the free world a new resource against aggression. This plaque is cut from the first aluminium made from Jamaican ore and erected by Reynolds Jamaica Mines Ltd., 1952."[36] Thus although the immediate and pressing reasons were different in each case, all parties expressed the interest in the strategic nature of the material and in cold war terms.

An economist writing on the economics of the bauxite-alumina industry points out that although bauxite reserves ". . . are found largely outside the industrial centers, they are in areas to which non-Communist industrial countries should continue to have access."[37] At the state level, and within the formally accepted law of national sovereignty, continued "access" could only be legitimately secured by the pursuance of friendly relations and diplomatic bargaining with the access-granting state. The internal political and social conditions conducive to continued access cannot be easily detailed at the state level without infringing the formally accepted notion of "non-intervention."

The requirements of corporations in relation to direct investment—that is, access to the market and materials—are not, however, subject to such sensitive considerations

[36] Reynolds Jamaican Mines Ltd., *pamphlet commemorating the event*, Kingston, no title, no date (1953?).

[37] S. Brubaker, *Trends in World Aluminum Industry*, Baltimore, 1967, p. 149.

of diplomacy and international law. The desired political, economic, and social conditions are often detailed within a description of a "favourable investment climate."[38] The investment climate indicates the total conditions in a country affecting the safety of direct investment, return on capital invested, and continued access to materials. The objective is to minimise the risks involved in "investment exposure" resulting from foreign locations.

In discussing the investment climate necessary for establishing alumina plants or aluminium smelting complexes, the above-quoted author remarks that: "A favorable juxtaposition of bauxite and cheap power, *along with political conditions* conducive to investment, could provide a basis for production of alumina outside the present centers . . ."[39] Further, the location of alumina plants near bauxite sources in less-developed countries had to be offset against ". . . increased investment exposure and somewhat higher costs of other materials in the process."[40] It is argued then that location of alumina rather than smelting complexes kept investment exposure to one-quarter of what a whole complex would cost and although there is not an economic case for locating alumina plants, given a "secure investment climate" such a location might have advantages.[41] The author's conclusion is that it is the investment climate which is the important variable and illustrates the point with reference to major company policies in 1967: "Jamaica offers a good investment climate and convenient shipping point to numerous markets for alumina. Alcoa favors its supplier, Surinam,

[38] See W. Clarke, *Private Enterprise in Developing Countries*, London, 1966; and H. Robinson, *The Motivation and Flow of Private Foreign Investment*, Stanford, 1961.

[39] S. Brubaker, *Trends in World Aluminum Industry*, p. 149. (this writer's italics)

[40] *Ibid.*, p. 151.

[41] *Ibid.*, p. 153.

with an alumina plant, ALCAN does the same thing, perhaps with more trepidation, in Guyana."[42]

The securing of a safe investment climate was thus in the interest of the corporations and the governments concerned. With this situation as a background the USWA and the British TUC commenced their respective operations in Jamaica.

[42] *Ibid.*

CHAPTER XI

OPERATIONS IN JAMAICA

The achievement of the general objectives of foreign unions in Jamaica could be assisted or hindered by the various other foreign elements present. An assessment of the roles and achievements of the latter is necessary in order to acquire a balanced picture of the importance of the role of foreign unions.

At base, the success in achieving the desired objectives in Jamaica rested on the ability of the representatives to deal with the operational environment. The economic, social, and cultural aspects, analysed in previous chapters, comprise the general operational environment. However, as the unionist's involvement rested on the accepted legitimacy of cross-national group contact the most important factor was the structure and nature of the existing trade union movement. In the case of the Jamaican dual union situation the first, and most fundamental, decision to be taken was which of the two unions should be supported. It was this question which presented the first of the many cross-cultural problems faced by the foreign union representatives.

Cross-Cultural Problems of Foreign Actors

For foreign actors, the nature and structure of the Jamaican trade union movement, and particularly the BITU, presented problems of perception and adjustment. The personal and cultural dimensions of the operational aspects of foreign policy have already been discussed.[1] Here it is necessary to consider the degree of the reaction to these problems and the results they produced.

The foreign actors in Jamaica were all from Britain or the USA and there were, therefore, some similarities, at least at the imitative level, between the domestic and the operational environment. The situation was complicated by the presence of the two cultures in Jamaica which also had important repercussions in operational decisions. As individuals none of the actors were trained or experienced in cross-cultural operations, with the possible exception of Romualdi of ORIT. They came, however, with considerable power from the metropolitan government—in the case of the staff of the Labour Department—and financial and status-derived power in the case of the unionists.

In general, the actors showed a marked inability to deal with the operational conditions. Many of them showed the characteristics of cultural shock in resorting to inaccurate analogies between the domestic and operational environment, documented in the last chapter.[2] Others remained culturally absolute, showing no signs of recogni-

[1] See Chapter I.
[2] See Chapter IX under "New Comparisons."

tion that conditions were not identical with their home culture. Examples of this latter phenomena can be illustrated from most of the recorded speeches; the statement of an American trade unionist in 1952 that "a bicycle is a child's toy" is a classic example, for a bicycle is a child's toy in the USA, but had a much different position within the social and economic framework of Jamaica.[3]

Cross-cultural projections were likewise manifested by most actors. Often such transpositions took the form of suggestions and proposals of an unrealistic nature in the context of the conditions and culture of the area but valid in the proposer's own environment.[4] Romualdi also noted this phenomena when describing a unionist who had extensive connections with Jamaica in the early 1950s; "As far as Latin America was concerned he remained obdurate in his belief that the area's geography, culture, history, ethnic makeup, economic development, and labor movement were really no different from Canada's."[5]

In the case of Jamaica, cross-cultural operations were complicated and the cultural shock was exacerbated by the presence of the two cultures. While principal foreign actors were primarily absorbed into the imitative culture the points of familiar reference this supplied were not fulfilled in reality either in the imitative culture, where the imitation was not perfect, or in any attempted transposition to the evolved culture. Thus, for example, and as will be shown in a following section, the British officials of the Labour Department were never able to reconcile their expectations with the operational conditions of Jamaica.

Similar reactions on the part of foreign trade unionists

[3] There are also some British-American differences here, for in Britain, likewise, a bicycle at that time was a serious means of personal transport.

[4] For examples see R. Farley, ed., *Labour Education in the British Caribbean,* Georgetown, British Guiana, 1960.

[5] S. Romualdi, *Presidents and Peons,* New York, 1968, p. 130.

in Jamaica resulted in some constants within the foreign involvements which persisted throughout the history of the trade union movement.

The history of foreign involvement in Jamaican unionism reveals a constant—that all foreign elements were involved either with the TUCJ or the NWU and never with the BITU. It is possible that explanations of this constant can be sought in the attitudes of the leaders and, in particular, those of Bustamante. He was not inclined to allow foreigners to be involved in his union but, at the same time, he was rejected by foreigners, even, for example, when he made official attempts to enter regional organisations such as CADORIT. The rejection of the most powerful union in Jamaican history eventually reached a point where internationally its existence was denied. The explanation for this can be sought as much in the problems of cross-cultural operations by foreign actors as in the individual personality and inclination of Jamaican leaders.

The BITU bore little functional similarity and almost no structural similarity to any trade unions from the foreign actors' domestic environment of an industrial society. To reconcile the activities of the BITU, its leadership-style or structure with pre-existing models drawn from the actor's culture would be almost impossible. The organisation could only be effectively understood in relation to its own social ecology of Jamaica and particularly that of the evolved culture.

Under these circumstances, foreign actors made recourse to those organisations which showed structural similarity with the model from their domestic culture and whose leaders confirmed, at least verbally, the validity of the model and agreed to its application in Jamaica. The British officials of the Labour Department thus favoured and dealt with the TU-Council, the TUCJ, and their leaders from the imitative culture. This rendered the Labour Department ineffectual for many years as the most important union could not be sufficiently accepted to commence accommodation, negotiation, or development of an industrial relations system.

The British officials, as temporary residents and charged with dealing with the operational conditions in Jamaica, could not, however, ignore the power of the BITU except by removing themselves completely. In this respect the visiting trade unionists, who made policy for their various organisations, were more fortunate, for they could opt for a policy of ignoring the BITU and leave their chosen agents in Jamaica with the operational problem of dealing with its power.

Citrine was the first unionist to establish relations with the trade unions and leaders of the imitative culture, even though he claimed to be impressed by the BITU. At that time to support Bustamante would have been difficult as he was considered dangerous by both the Jamaican and British governments.

Later foreign union involvements were less encumbered with metropolitan-colonial relations and illustrate more clearly the unacceptability of the BITU. When the USWA became involved in 1952–53, there were three unions competing for representation of bauxite workers; the immensely powerful BITU, the increasingly successful TUCJ, and the virtually non-existent NWU. By this time the BITU had acquired some elements of structure and technical competence in industrial-country industrial relations. Furthermore, Bustamante had become a dedicated anti-communist, often referring to Norman Manley and his associates as being "Communists or whatever."[6] In 1953 he directed the Labour Department to have no dealings with communist organisations and unions and

[6] M. Ayearst, *The British West Indies*, New York, 1960, p. 211.

ordered police raids on Hart's Peoples' Educational Organisation.[7] The TUCJ leaders claimed to be socialist and the NWU, apart from its small membership was created by, and associated with, a professedly socialist political party.

Of these three, however, the USWA chose the NWU to be its main contact. This choice contrasted with both the general policy of the USWA and the stated policy of the USA labour movement. Questioned as to the reasons for this choice one USWA executive said that the relationship between the PNP and the NWU was 'the counterpart of the British Labour Party—and I could recognise that.' Another person involved in Jamaica at the time said he was met on his first visit by Norman Manley who impressed him as being a charming man.

All British and USA trade unionists interviewed, and all documents relating to the Jamaican situation, show that the actors had only the vaguest notions concerning the BITU and, with one exception, had no conception of the political or social functions of the organisation. The exception was one British TUC staff member who recognised that 'Bustamante's power rested on the large mass of poor workers and he tended to regard their interests.' Citrine had also been impressed by Bustamante and his organisation but nevertheless maintained all contact with the TUCJ leaders.

In entering the new culture, foreign trade unionists were looking for familiar points of reference and easy accommodation with their perceptions and objectives. The imitative culture supplied both, cushioning the cross-cultural operational difficulties and cultural shock which would have been encountered with the evolved culture. In rejecting the BITU the British and USA unionists rejected power in favour of familiarity.

[7] *New Commonwealth Newsletter*, February 1, 1954, p. 144.

ESTABLISHED PATTERN

Thus a three-part pattern was established; first, contact was made with the unions and leaders of the imitative culture; second, the BITU and evolved culture were ignored; and third, foreign models were promoted through the contacts established. All foreign contacts have therefore been through the TUCJ or NWU and internationally the BITU has been ignored. In all the journals and publications there is only rarely reference to the BITU, and even then usually in disparaging terms. The USWA publications and bi-annual conference reports make no mention of the BITU or any other union except the NWU in Jamaica. Reference to the NWU is made as if it were the only union in Jamaica, and that, in giving aid to it, the USWA was assisting in organising the total Jamaican labour force for which there were no pre-existing organisations.[8] In the British TUC General Council reports between 1946 and 1949, there were several comments on the conditions in Jamaica and the awards to the TUCJ. There was no mention of the BITU, nor was it mentioned that dual unionism existed in Jamaica and that the British TUC's contact was with the smallest union. An International Trade Secretariat, despite a functional relationship with the workers represented by the BITU, referred to it in 1956 as "another industrial trade union" in competition with the NWU.[9]

The explanation that this pattern was started by the

[8] See, for example, "It's Not All Calypso," *Steel Labor*, April 1957, and USWA: *Proceedings of 2nd Constitutional Convention, 1956*, p. 101.

[9] International Union of Food and Drink Workers: *News Bulletin*, *1956* (bound edition), p. 113.

personal cross-cultural difficulties of the foreign actors is not intended to be a single cause explanation. There were obviously many other factors involved but the problems of dealing with an organisation so different from all the previous experience of the foreign actor must be considered as among the most important, if not the most important.

Models as Foreign Elements

GENERAL USE OF MODELS

The use of foreign models of trade unions by various groups in Jamaica seeking their various specific objectives has been shown to be extensive. Such a widespread use of foreign models is evidence in itself that they are more than mere rhetorical tools.

Within the imitative culture the charge that behaviour or structure was not consistent with a foreign model could be a powerful psychological pressure towards establishment of the desired model. By its very nature the imitative culture is one in which the criteria of social, economic, and organisational viability is drawn from external sources and usually from the metropolitan power. Legitimacy, security, and self-esteem are thus sought by reference to a foreign model; an apposite example of this trait is found in a statement made by the Mayor of Kingston concerning the Artisans' Union which was extant in the 1890s: "One cannot fail to be struck with the utter absence from Jamaica of any of these associations for the protection of crafts which abound in Europe and the

United States. The organisation in which you are engaged must therefore be regarded as one of the evidences of the advancement among our people."[10]

For these reasons the use of foreign models by the domestic groups was an important element in the growth of the trade unions. Foreign actors were able thereby to find willing domestic proponents of their particular models and attached policies. The actual effect of the use of such models is difficult to discern; in some cases it is clear, such as the TUCJ adherence to the British model, but in other cases the use of models was one factor in a general effort to acquire specific goals. For example, the Jamaican Chamber of Commerce promotion of the British rather than the North American industrial relations system has been basically successful but this outcome was obviously not solely the result of the use of foreign models.

Up to 1949 the continuing connections with Britain meant that the model promoted was the British one and the greatest emphasis was placed on the structure of unions. After 1950, when the American model became more current, the functions of unions became more of an issue and the concept of a union as a specialised pressure group became more prevalent.

As already noted the power and political nature of the BITU polarised model promotion around the issue of political and non-political unionism, the advocates of business unionism thus using it as a means to attack the BITU rather than any belief in its suitability for Jamaica. Likewise, one of the most important mediums for the narrower concept of trade unionism and, at least in the early stages, for an attack on the BITU was the various trade union education programmes.

[10] As quoted in G. Eaton, *dissertation*, "Trade Union Development in Jamaica," *Caribbean Quarterly*, Vol. 8, No. 182, 1962, p. 206.

TRADE UNION EDUCATION

Specific references to national models of trade unionism were characteristic only of the early CD&W courses in which the history and operation of British trade unionism was a standard subject. The courses did not attempt to be locally relevant and were often broad in the range of subjects offered.

In the mid 1950s sensitivity developed on the question as to whether the British or American model should be advocated as vigorously as in the past. In the government courses started in 1956, foreign models as teaching devices as used in the CD&W courses were dropped.

But the attempts to make the BITU more manageable via education resulted in most of the courses adopting the narrowest interpretation of trade unions and therefore of education. At the opening of the government courses, the Chief Minister (Norman Manley) and the Minister of Labour (Glasspole) claimed respectively that trade union education would lessen the need for trade unionism to be a ". . . rumbustious sort of thing" and would also diminish the ". . . belligerent attitude, the fire and brimstone approach."[11] Such obvious references to the BITU were not customary in the records of the later educational conferences but they were equally committed to the narrow view of unionism. Trade union education involved nearly all foreign labour organisations which have been associated with Jamaica—the British TUC, the USWA, AFL-CIO, ORIT, and CADORIT.

Under this impact the education programmes became

[11] *Daily Gleaner,* December 13, 1955, and December 21, 1955.

and remained technical training in industrial-country trade union skills and, with the retirement of Bustamante, the BITU personnel began to participate in the programmes and to accept the narrow or non-political view of unionism. The evolution can be observed in the following three statements: in May 1955 Shearer of the BITU told some business executives that education of trade unionists acquired through lectures and seminars had to be supplemented by political activity so that they could have a "direct impact on political activities in the country"[12]; in 1959 Markle of the USWA, in his preface to a report on education needs in the Caribbean, told the assembled experts that a union would not be free "if it becomes merely a dupe or tool for a politician or a political party"[13]; at the end of the first course at the TUEI (of which Markle's report was the precursor), the Minister of Labour in the BITU-JLP government opined, "I think it is primarily the duty of trade unionists to see that politics does not enter into their trade union practices . . . If you introduce politics in your trade union activities you are using the workers as pawns."[14]

The impact of the narrow interpretation of unionism in education has been an important factor in increasing the distance between the party and union in the case of the BITU, a fact which was concerning Bustamante as late as 1966. As this was the expressed objective of the foreign and domestic opponents of the BITU it can be seen that education was an important element as a means to change the nature of the trade union movement and as a vehicle for foreign models and organisations.

[12] *Daily Gleaner*, May 7, 1955.
[13] R. Farley, ed., *Labour Education in the British Caribbean*, p. 60.
[14] *Daily Gleaner*, March 9, 1964, p. 15.

FOREIGN ELEMENTS 1938–1949: AN ASSESSMENT

In the following sections as assessment will be made of the role of the foreign elements identified in achieving general and specific objectives in Jamaica. The greatest changes in foreign involvements in Jamaica took place in 1952. However, from the end of 1949 to the beginning of 1952, overt foreign involvement was minimal and therefore the previous period divisions, based on domestic criteria, still remain convenient.

Foreign National Labour Organisations —The British TUC

In this period, the British TUC was the only national labour organisation directly involved in Jamaica and its general objective, as has been shown, was to create trade unions approximating the British model.

When Citrine visited the island with the West Indies Royal Commission in 1938, Bustamante was in the process of establishing the BITU and had a large following, estimated by Citrine to be in the region of 50,000, all of whom "owed allegiance to him."[15] But from Webb onwards the Colonial Office and the TUC had feared the dominance of trade unions "either by 'wizards' or by un-

[15] W. Citrine, *Men and Work*, London, 1964, p. 332.

scrupulous politicians."[16] Bustamante at this time would have fitted perfectly Webb's earlier description of "disaffected persons" and in fact the Colonial Office in 1941 specifically singled out the BITU from all the unions in the empire as being both political and "notorious."[17] Finally, the general cross-cultural problems that British unionists had in understanding and dealing with the BITU were always present. Thus for national political as well as trade union objectives the BITU could not be supported. But the general objective to see a British-style trade union movement gave rise to a specific objective—that of opposing the BITU.

Both opposition to the BITU and creation of a British model union were pursued through the TUCJ. This organisation received, among other assistance, over £1250 during four years, from the British TUC and associated unions, which was a considerable sum as the TUCJ never claimed more than 5000 dues-paying members in the period. The British TUC involvement was heavier than most writers credit, the standard reference being to the Glasspole scholarship in 1946.[18]

These efforts were, however, unsuccessful and in this period the British TUC failed to acquire either its general or specific objective. The British TUC and its contacts in Jamaica were unable to prevent the BITU from becoming more dominant or, conversely, to increase the power of the TUCJ. Furthermore, although the TUCJ followed the British model throughout the 1940s, it eventually had to adopt the BITU structure in 1949 and direct structural

[16] I. Davies, "The Politics of the TUC's Colonial Policy," p. 28.
[17] Colonial Office Press Section: "Trade Unions in the Colonial Empire: How They Are Being Encouraged to Develop," mimeo, no page nos.
[18] See M. Proudfoot, *Britain and the United States in the Caribbean*, London, 1954, p. 233.

resemblance between the Jamaican trade union movement and the British ceased.

International and Regional Trade Union Organisations

Despite the TUCJ's affiliation to the WFTU, Kenneth Hill's attendance at the founding conferences and the prominent position of the British TUC in the organisation, the WFTU played no significant role in Jamaica before 1949. The veto on the colonial activities by the British TUC and the general inefficiency of the colonial section of the secretariat were contributing factors but the WFTU in any case did not make less-developed countries as important an issue as did the ICFTU. Even if there had been such an interest, the size of Jamaica and its industrial potential at that time would probably not have made it an important country for any funds which were available. The Jamaican unions did not respond to solidarity pleas from the WFTU and both the BITU and an independent union, the United Port Workers' Union, refused to comply with a solidarity strike of dockworkers even after the British dockers had responded positively.[19]

Regional trade union organisations in the Caribbean before 1949 had no noticeable effect on the growth of the Jamaican trade union movement.

The original organisation in the Caribbean—the BG&WILC—had no recorded contacts with Jamaica, largely because the period of its greatest activity came before the establishment of powerful unions in Jamaica. How-

[19] See *Daily Gleaner*, July 5, 1949, p. 8.

ever, the principal leader, Critchlow, was instrumental in bringing the West Indies and general colonial problems to the attention of the British TUC. At a Commonwealth Labour Conference in 1926 he vigorously answered the criticism that West Indians were taking jobs from the English by referring to the reverse case of Englishmen coming to the West Indies about which he claimed to have heard little mention.[20] The BG&WILC illustrated the possibility, if not the need, for regional organisations and at the same time developed the organisational objective of anti-imperialism which was later to be accepted by the successor organisation—the CLC.

The CLC impact on Jamaica was slight and indirect. The leaders of the organisation did not attempt to develop a "West Indian" view concerning the development of trade unions, although at conferences there were some discussions on which was the most pertinent structure to adopt in the West Indies. The existing documents of the organisations do not reveal that it followed any political or ideological line. It was internally divided and short of funds. Its financial difficulties are an indication of its independence, as none of the unions in the Caribbean were wealthy, with the possible exception of the BITU, and it was not a CLC member.

Like the British Guiana and West Indian Labour Conference, the CLC was primarily involved in geo-political issues. Its leading members, also like the BG&WILC, tended to be nationalist, independent, socialist, or Marxist. But its lack of involvement in the substantive and detailed problems of trade unionism in the region plus the general lack of funds meant that the regional organisations were not important to Jamaican unions in the pre-1949 period. The involvement of leading members of

[20] TUC: *Report of the Commonwealth Labour Conference, 1926*, mimeo, no page nos.

the TUCJ, particularly Hart and Hill, in regional organisations was later to be duplicated by the NWU.

The Colonial Policies and the Labour Department

Colonial Office policy in regard to labour in the colonies could be effected through two basic policy instruments, legislation passed by colonial administrations (in Jamaica the Governor and the Legislative Council) and through the Labour Departments.

COLONIAL POLICY, MOYNE AND ORDE-BROWNE

The Colonial Office policy on labour movements in the colonies was one of basically attempting to duplicate the British pattern of trade unions and industrial relations. It should be noted, however, that three important policy considerations prevented the advocacy of the pure British model. First, there was little consideration that the colonies would soon become formally independent; second, the Colonial Office was willing to accept colonial governors' advice or excuses for not following British lines when it was considered too dangerous; and third, an underlying acceptance that trade unions in the colonies would not be identical to those in Britain and therefore would need "supervision," "control," or "guidance."

It was these considerations which made the basic Colonial Office policy expansive and restrictive at the same time—expansive in encouraging trade unions by enabling legislation and restrictive in attempting to ensure by supervision that trade union demands would not be too unpalatable to colonial administrations and business groups.

These underlying considerations, as well as basic Colonial Office policy, are to be found in the Moyne and Orde-Browne Reports as well as the legislative policies followed by the Jamaican Government.

Jamaica passed the standard compulsory registration law in 1919 which, as in other colonies, was itself not consistent with the British model.[21] The Governor of Jamaica at that time, Sir Leslie Probyn, was also permitted by specific request, as Moyne pointed out, to make a greater departure from the model of British legislation by not providing for peaceful picketing and protection against action in tort. The amending legislation in 1938 brought the trade union laws of the colony into line with the British (with the exception of the compulsory registration clause).

It was argued, however, that such a legal framework was a distorting influence on the growth of "responsible unions" on the lines of the British model. In Jamaica, an official with long experience in labour matters felt that the whole policy 'was quite wrong as the British workers had fought for 250 years to be recognised, whereas in Jamaica a model statute was handed to people with no knowledge of trade union procedures.'[22] He maintained that there should have been stricter legislation, eased as the unions showed 'responsibility.'

The Colonial Office, in accordance with the tradition of British administrative procedures, could not have been expected to supply specific and detailed policy direc-

[21] See A. Couzens, "Colonial Trade Unions," *Corona*, Vol. II, No. 7, July 1950, p. 259.

[22] The same argument was made by A. Couzens, Commissioner of Labour, Nigeria, in 1948; see *ibid.*, p. 260.

tives.[23] The colonial administrators were left to implement freely the basic policy of encouraging and supervising the growth of trade unions on the lines of the suitably tempered British model.

The West Indies, however, were subjected to special attention arising from the British government-sponsored reports of the Moyne Commission and Orde-Browne, both of which were given the opportunity to make specific recommendations concerning the labour movement.

The underlying conceptions of the framers of the two reports were, with the exception of the different views of the function of the Labour Department already outlined, basically similar. Differences arose in degree rather than on fundamentals.

First, both reports operate on the conception of trade unionism as it existed in Britain at that time. Orde-Browne was prepared to give passing recognition to the difference in conditions between the West Indies and Britain but nevertheless did not expect that significantly different forms of unionism would therefore evolve. If any new forms did evolve they were to be supervised to ensure that they followed responsible paths, especially as he recognised the politically disruptive nature of trade unions. Moyne, perhaps because Citrine was on the Commission, was not so prepared to accept that unions were potential dangers to colonial administrations.

Second, both operated with a tripartite conception of an economic system. Orde-Browne, however, noted that colonial governments would have a role to play in preventing strikes and economic disturbances and was therefore aware of the possibility of business-government alliances. The Moyne Commission, in contrast, never recognised that there could be an identity of interests be-

[23] A. Creech-Jones, "The Colonial Office," *The Political Quarterly*, Vol. XIV, No. 1, January–March 1943, pp. 19–32.

tween government and business or that they could join in even a fragile coalition against unions, even though it was critical of both employers and governments individually.

Third, both reports were essentially Keynesian in that they expected government to solve the problems of unemployment and bad working conditions. As representatives of the British Government it would be logical to advocate government action for the solution of problems for it was only through the colonial governments that any recommendations would be put into force. Yet the conception of government action was more than that of passing basic legislation. The government was to be in the forefront of the drive for social and economic betterment and the unions were merely to assist this drive.

Fourth, despite the heavy orientation towards a tripartite notion of the economic system, neither of the reports commented on the lack of business organisations, a fact which was to disturb the first Labour Adviser in Jamaica.

Finally, the reports did not take note of the already existing unions in the West Indies which were not following the British model and were acting contrary to the basic conception of the framers of the reports as outlined above. Thus they did not consider specific issues, such as structure or political association, which colonial administrators were eventually going to encounter. They either did not see, or chose to ignore, the existing trade union movement's political content, as either a nationalist/independence movement or groups pressuring for a change in the personnel, if not the system, of government. Unions were not, in fact, considered as political entities at all, which contrasted sharply with the reality in Barbados, British Guiana, and, more immediately (at the time of the reports), in Jamaica.

The result of the assumptions and failures was that the Colonial Office, Moyne, or Orde-Browne never formulated identifiable policies which could give guidance in any of the specifics which the proposed Labour Commissioners or advisers could follow. The directives mostly revolved around vague phrases connected with control such as "sympathetic supervision and guidance" (Passfield), "building unions on sound lines" (Orde-Browne), and "responsible leadership" (Moyne). With such a background the Labour Department was established in Jamaica.

LABOUR DEPARTMENT AND THE BRITISH MODEL

With such weak directives from the Colonial Office, Moyne, and Orde-Browne, the policies of the Jamaican Labour Department tended to vary widely with the personality and experience of the Labour Adviser.

It was only the first Labour Adviser, F. A. Norman, who could be cast in the role of a champion of the British model. "The history of British Trade Unionism is long and instructive and it should be read in the West Indies as a general guide and as an example to be followed . . . with proper development of trade unions the position of the worker should be improved and the employers should profit by the increased sense of discipline and the responsibility on the part of the worker,"[24] he opined when introducing a series of lectures on British trade unionism for the Caribbean Service of the British Broadcasting Corporation. He also pursued the tripartite model by attempting to found employer organisations.

[24] In V. Feather, "Broadcast to the West Indies on British Trade Unionism," *Development and Welfare Bulletin*, No. 3, 1941, p. 2.

Despite his being enamoured with the British model, Norman was broad enough to be prepared to accept Bustamante as a trade union leader and attempt to integrate the BITU within the framework he was building.

The next Labour Adviser arrived in 1941, when Bustamante was interned and the TU-Council was the most important union body in the island. This latter group's stated policy to adopt the British model plus Bustamante's internment supplied a good opportunity for the Labour Adviser to promote trade unions and the creation of a British-style national centre. But, according to a Jamaican contemporary, he had a 'holiday approach to the job' and, moreover, found it 'difficult to reconcile his experience with UK unions with what he saw in Jamaica.' He thus concentrated on such matters as factory inspection, reflecting his experience as such an inspector in Britain. This inability to accept and deal with the Jamaican trade union situation characterised the subsequent Labour Advisers until the appointment of a Jamaican to the position in 1946. The basic power of the clearly un-British BITU could not be challenged, especially when Bustamante became Chief Minister of Jamaica in 1944. Thus any directives the Labour Advisers might have had from the Colonial Office in terms of the British model became meaningless and the department, frustrated in its basic purpose, became inert in relation to the trade unions and industrial relations system.

It is significant, in view of the problems encountered by foreign actors in dealing with Jamaican environment, that Scott, the first Jamaican Labour Adviser, was the most successful and had the greatest impact on the evolution of the industrial relations system. Known by local people and integrated with Jamaican life, he did not have the problem of reconciling a model derived from another society and experience with the Jamaican situation. He was thus able to concentrate on refinements within the already existing system, construct negotiating machinery to get the BITU and TUCJ to cooperate, arrange agreements regulating sugar plantation workers, and, in 1950, make a major contribution to settling the disruptive representational issue. Scott consistently pointed out in his reports that the issues which arose from a resort to foreign models were "academic" inasmuch as they had little bearing on the Jamaican situation as it existed or was likely to evolve.

Thus from 1939 to 1949, the department had a very brief period in which it was used as a promoter of the British model, a five-year period of basic retirement and subsequently concentration on refining accepted structure. The Labour Department was thus ineffectual in altering or directing the structural aspects of Jamaican unionism and played only a minor role in the growth of the movement.

FOREIGN ELEMENTS 1949–1967: AN ASSESSMENT

Foreign and International Labour Organisations

In the previous period foreign national and international labour organisations could be treated separately. In the period 1949–67 the centre point of the involvement of all foreign and international labour organisations was the creation of the NWU. Thus their policies and specific impact were to a large degree interlocked and will have to be considered in like manner.

FOREIGN INVOLVEMENTS IN THE NWU

It has been shown that there is no evidence of USWA involvement in Jamaica before the end of 1952 and that neither regional nor international labour organisations paid much attention to the Jamaican situation. The first indication that the Jamaican movement was of international interest was the visit of an ORIT official in March 1952 to confer with TUCJ leaders on the TUCJ's application.[25] This application made it clear that by this time the TUCJ leaders were willing to affiliate with the ICFTU, their connection with WFTU having been dissolved.

The ICFTU, in July 1953, stated that the applications of the TUCJ and the National Labour Congress of Jamaica were pending "investigation by ORIT."[26] But in December 1952 the NWU became the Jamaican affiliate to the ICFTU with a claimed membership of 5000 in ICFTU records, and 1873 dues-paying members in Jamaican official records. Thus two months after it was a registered union and seven months after it was formally created, the NWU was the accepted affiliate. The TUCJ at that time had 26,560 members of which 10,628 were claimed as dues-paying. The reason given by the ICFTU for the refusal to affiliate the TUCJ in its report of 1955 was that it was in "opposition to the present ICFTU affiliate, the National Workers Union."[27]

The report neglected to point out that the TUCJ had apparently applied for affiliation before the NWU was

[25] *Daily Gleaner*, March 1, 1952, p. 1.
[26] ICFTU: *Report of Third World Congress*, 1953, p. 19.
[27] ICFTU: *Report of Fourth World Congress*, 1955, p. 15.

even created or in existence. It would therefore appear that the TUCJ was unacceptable to ORIT-ICFTU and that the pending "investigation" meant pending changes in the Jamaican trade union movement which might precipitate an applicant more acceptable to foreign national and international trade union organisations.

The main lines of this policy were revealed by Romualdi, Assistant Secretary of ORIT in April 1953: "In Jamaica the picture is different. The labour movement there is now divided into three groups. One, the Bustamante Industrial Union, with strength in the sugar fields, is a personal instrument of Mr. William Alexander Bustamante himself, now majority leader of the Jamaican Legislative Council. His popularity is fast decreasing. Another group is the Jamaica Trade Union Congress, led by Ken Hill, which is following the policy of the Communist-ruled World Federation of Trade Unions and is, to all intents and purposes, the trade union arm of the Communist Party. Until fairly recently Hill and his associates were members of the People's National Party of Jamaica and were collaborating with the local Social Democrats, headed by Norman Manley. An investigation revealed Hill and a number of his supporters as agents of the Communist Party and they were therefore expelled from the People's National Party. This led to a split in the trade union movement, with the anti-Communists taking the initiative of organising the National Workers Union last year. This organization has made strong progress in a very short time. It now has the workers of the two bauxite companies (Reynolds and Kaiser) which are operating in the island, in addition to strong support in sugar, transportation, manufacturing, and the port workers."[28]

[28] S. Romualdi, "Labor in the Caribbean," p. 14.

This interpretation is revealing because it was anticipatory of future events rather than a statement of current facts. If the known facts are considered in relation to those stated, the pattern becomes clear: "Bustamante's popularity is fast decreasing"—the BITU in that year represented 70 per cent of the organised labour force; "The TUCJ is following the policy of WFTU"—the TUCJ had disaffiliated with WFTU and applied to ORIT (Romualdi's own organisation) at least a year before the article was written; "the NWU has made strong showing in a short time"—the NWU membership was well under 2000 and confined mainly to bauxite workers.

This article is also the only one which openly refers to connections between communists and trade unionism in the bauxite industry. This statement plus those referring to the TUCJ as an agent of the Communist Party express a duality between communism and bauxite which marked the birth of the NWU—it resulted from a claimed communist purge of the PNP and its first objective was organising in the bauxite-alumina industry.

NWU, "COMMUNISM," AND BAUXITE-ALUMINA INDUSTRY

According to a PNP party publication of 1961, the TUCJ leaders had been expelled because they were "in breach of Party Policy and of solemn declarations publicly given, by forming a Communist cell within the Party and giving active support to Communist teachings and the spreading of Communist doctrines."[29] Newspaper reports at the time of the tribunal, however, only referred to

[29] People's National Party: *Man of Destiny*, Kingston, 1954, p. 63.

"Marxist cells." There was never any charge in Jamaica at that time, contrary to the ORIT report, that the expelled four H's were members of a Communist Party or had international communist connections.

There can be no question that the TUCJ leaders involved were socialists, as might be expected in a party which claimed to be socialist. Hart and Henry were more radical than the Hill brothers and a document used by Henry in educational classes (as reported by Eaton) echoed the Soviet policy of that time, that the Communist Party should cooperate with the bourgeois nationalists until after independence and then move into opposition in order to acquire control of the new and independent state.[30] Hart was outspokenly anti-imperialist and was involved in the organisation of the Jamaican union affiliated to the WFTU after 1952. In 1953 he attended the WFTU Congress as General Secretary of the CLC and member of a joint Trinidad, Jamaican, and British Guiana delegation and in his speech to the congress analysed the colonial situation in Jamaica in Marxist terms.[31] In 1962 he wrote in laudatory terms of the political and economic system of the Soviet Union[32] and in 1963 was employed by Prime Minister Jagan of British Guiana to edit the People's Progressive Party newspaper.[33] However, Hart's approach to CADORIT in 1952, suggesting that the CLC should not be affiliated to either of the trade union internationals, would seem to indicate that his association with WFTU was not predetermined and that, as characterised most of his speeches, the issues

[30] See I. Spector, *The First Russian Revolution: Its Impact on Asia*, Englewood Cliffs, N.J., 1962, pp. 110–13.
[31] WFTU: *3rd World Trade Union Congress, 1953*, pp. 291–95.
[32] See R. Hart, *What Is Socialism*, Socialist Party of Jamaica, 1962, pp. 2–4.
[33] British Guiana Trades Union Council: *The Communist Martyr Makers*, Georgetown, no date (1965?), p. 26.

of West Indian federation and independence were of paramount concern.

To describe the Hill brothers as communists requires a much greater recklessness in the use of the evidence available. Apart from an interest in a religious organisation, Moral Rearmament, not likely to be mistaken for a communist organisation, they had disaffiliated the TUCJ from the WFTU, applied to ORIT-ICFTU, and expelled Hart and Henry. Hill at the preparatory conference and congress of the WFTU in 1945 spoke on behalf of colonial territories in support of self-government and against imperialism, argued for greater social legislation in the colonies, and several times mentioned the necessity to destroy racial discrimination.[34] There was no discussion in these speeches of the causes of imperialism and no attacks against capitalism or the capitalist countries; for five years after this visit and appearances at the WFTU conference the British TUC financially supported the TUCJ.

After the expulsion from the PNP a newspaper, published by "Friends of the Nation" who were "appalled at the unjust accusations" levelled against the four H's, records that Norman Manley was confronted publicly and asked, "Do you believe Ken Hill is a communist?" to which Manley would not reply; on March 6, 1952, the TUCJ executive issued a statement which denied "any connection whatever with any communist organisation or movement anywhere."[35]

[34] WFTU: *Report of the World Trade Union Conference, 1945*, pp. 116–17; and WFTU: *Report of the World Trade Union Conference–Congress, 1945*, pp. 26, 80, and 217–18.

[35] *Workers Voice*, March 1952, p. 1. This denial and the general background to it has not caused any subsequent writers to qualify their accounts of the events of 1952 (which are, in any case, frequently factually or chronologically inaccurate), *viz.*: "expelled for communist activities" (Knowles, *op. cit.*); "Communist group

Romualdi, after having specifically described Hill and the TUCJ leaders as "agents of the Communist Party" in 1953, in his memoirs in 1967 came to the conclusion that Ken Hill was not a "full-fledged Communist" but was "surely a fellow-traveller."[36] Romualdi's re-interpretation of the communist issue is a further indication of its original doubtful base.

What is more clear, however, is that the TUCJ leaders, from their writing and statements, were nationalists, anti-imperialists, socialists, aggressive in industrial negotiation, and believed in (together with Bustamante) political unionism. In addition, Ken Hill, at least, was sensitive to racial discrimination and aware of the condition of black people in the USA.

Such a group in control of one major union and Bustamante in control of the other, represented the twin operational problems preventing the extensive cooperation necessary for securing effective control of the workers in the bauxite-alumina industry.

It has been previously briefly recounted that the NWU was associated with the bauxite-alumina industry since its creation. The reason for this was the failure of Kelly's breakaway union, the National Labour Congress (NLC), to organise the bauxite-alumina workers in the first few months of 1952. The NLC had its prime objective in organising the bauxite workers and acquiring representation of workers at bauxite construction sites. In this

---

of trade union leaders" (Roberts, *op. cit.*); "expelled the Communists" (Kirkpatrick, *op. cit.*); "agents of the Communist Party" (Romualdi, "Labor in the Caribbean"); "Communist group" (Ayearst, *op. cit.*). Ayearst also refers to "two former Hill henchmen" who made the charges and formed a breakaway union. One of these was Kelly, soon to become long-term and revered President of the NWU; see M. Ayearst, *The British West Indies*, p. 211.

[36] S. Romualdi, *Presidents and Peons*, p. 354.

venture it had support of some members of the PNP executive. For example, quite contrary to party policy of support for the TUCJ, Ivan Lloyd, a member of the party executive and PNP member of the House of Representatives, wrote to his constituents in February 1952 that the East St. Ann PNP constituency committee had decided to "give the NLC full and vigorous support. Under the circumstances I am directed to request that you leave no stone unturned to get all Bauxite workers to work for the NLC on Friday next, the day of the poll [at Reynolds]."[37]

The NLC was not successful at this poll and on April 2, 1952, the NWU came into being. Official reports, as a point of pride, recount the fact that the early activities of the NWU were primarily directed at wresting the representation of the bauxite workers from the TUCJ. The TUCJ leaders charged that the funding of both the NLC and the NWU was by businessmen who were approached for contributions on the basis that it would help fight communism in Jamaica.[38] Within three months the NWU represented bauxite construction workers at the Kaiser site, by December 1953 it represented the workers at ALCAN and Kaiser, "the majority of the bauxite industry,"[39] and in January 1954 finally acquired the rights at Reynolds after a twelve-day strike and a Labour Department poll. Thus, within two years, the NWU had acquired representation of all the workers in the industry and within a year the majority of such workers. The membership figures for the first years of the NWU show the narrow base and correspond with the numbers of workers in the bauxite industry—in 1953,

[37] *The PEOPLE*, Vol. 1, No. 3, June 7, 1952, p. 1.
[38] *Ibid.*, p. 3.
[39] *National Workers Union 1st Annual Report, 1953*, as quoted in *Man of Destiny*, Kingston, 1954, p. 71.

1842 members and in 1954, 2658. From January 1954 no other union has represented any workers in the bauxite-alumina industry or any work contracted by the companies, a fact which has caused considerable unrest.

Internationally the NWU is often referred to in official publications as the "Jamaican Bauxite Union"[40] and the bauxite section of the union, despite its small numbers, is given great prominence; one author described it in 1959 as "the backbone of the union."[41]

The expulsion of the four H's, the breakaway of the NLC, and the creation of the NWU has been classified by most actors and writers as elements in a domestic power struggle precipitated by the left-right political division in the PNP and the growth in power of the TUCJ. That these were important factors is obvious but they cannot be accepted as full explanation for two reasons, first, the polarisation of opposition to the left and to the TUCJ around the bauxite-alumina industry when first supplies were beginning to leave for the USA and, second, the obvious foreign interest in the destruction of the TUCJ and the creation of the NWU. The latter was an internationally supported operation; the ICFTU, the British TUC, the USWA, and the Cuban Workers' Federation were among the known financial donors at the early stages and they were later joined by the AIFLD and the IMF. The individual roles and success in achieving basic objectives for the British TUC and the USWA can now be examined.

[40] US Department of the Interior: *Mineral Yearbook 1965*, Vol. IV, Area Reports–International, p. 127.

[41] W. Knowles, *Trade Union Development and Industrial Relations in the British West Indies*, Berkeley, 1959, p. 73.

THE BRITISH TUC

Until 1949 the British TUC had supported the TUCJ and Ken Hill had been well received on his visits to London. It was thus an abrupt change of policy for the British TUC to become the first international supporter of the NWU in September 1952, when, moreover, the latter was an unregistered group only active in the bauxite-alumina industry.

The explanation for this change has been given that the objectives changed in the 1952–59 period from one of directly promoting the British model of trade unions in accordance with national policy in colonies, to using Jamaican involvement as support for an attempt to cement Anglo-American trade union relations at the international level.

The operational aspects of the British TUC involvement lend support to this view of the change in objectives. It has been noted that ORIT and CADORIT were involved in the creation of the NWU and that both these organisations had strong connections with the AF of L and CIO finance and personnel. CADORIT was created with the aid of the AF of L and CIO to counter the influence of the CLC and the first Chairman of the CADORIT executive committee was Frank Walcott, under whose chairmanship the body rejected both the BITU and the TUCJ. In 1953 the British TUC announced, without reference to the previous support of the TUCJ, that its grant in 1952 to the NWU had been as a result of an "investigation of the trade union situation carried out on behalf of the TUC by the General Secretary of the BWU [Barbados Workers' Union],

Mr. F. L. Walcott . . ."[42] No mention of Walcott's connection with the CADORIT was made. Walcott made another report in 1954 upon which grounds the TUC claimed to have advanced the unusually large grant of £1500.

Thus it would appear that the British TUC accepted a policy for Jamaica which was based largely on information and interpretations supplied by USA unions or West Indian unionists who were assisted by and cooperated with USA unions. Further, the policy pursued was one of heavy support for a union, the creation and development of which had been effected with heavy involvement by USA trade unions.

In assessing the British TUC successes in achieving its objectives in Jamaica since 1949, it is therefore necessary to consider the impact outside of Jamaica.

Inasmuch as a strong union was eventually created which was an active participant in the ICFTU and ORIT, the objectives were fulfilled. Likewise, as the USA and British unions cooperated in the ICFTU, and Tewson was able to keep his key position as Chairman of the Regional Fund, the objectives could also be said to be fulfilled, but in this case the role of the Jamaican policy is merely one factor among many.

THE USWA

The USWA, as has been seen from the foregoing, obtained its basic objective of effective control of the bauxite-alumina workers. The close contact between the leaders of the NWU and officials of the USWA has

[42] TUC: *90th Annual Congress, Report of Proceedings*, 1953, p. 215.

been detailed. The NWU leaders have been content to allow USWA officials to negotiate on their behalf with the bauxite-alumina corporations and received substantial financial and technical aid. Also in the Jamaican context the representation of the bauxite-alumina workers has meant a higher-than-average income from their membership dues. On the basis of a payment of 1/6 (21¢) per week, specified in the 1957 constitution, for every member earning £1 to £10, the 3000 workers in bauxite-alumina would yield over £11,000 per annum on a continuing basis. Assuming that this sum would be the same in 1959 (and it would probably be much larger) when the union had an income of £57,504 from dues it would mean that one-fifth of the NWU total income would come from one-seventh of its workers represented.

One of the earliest and most open attempts to acquire control of the bauxite-alumina workers was the suggestion that the bauxite workers section should become directly affiliated with the USWA. This idea was extant in 1955, and was considered as a possibility for at least two years.[43] Its failure to materialise came from opposition in Jamaica and from within the USWA itself. The Minister of Labour of the PNP government recalled the suggestion and stated that he was opposed to it on the grounds that the Federation of the West Indies was to become an independent nation and therefore unions should be independent. In the USWA the idea was opposed from Canada because "it would mean the Jamaicans would eventually come under Pittsburgh," the USA headquarters of the union.[44]

The result was that the attempt failed but a later change in the constitution to permit greater autonomy

[43] See *National Workers Union Annual Reports*, 1955 and 1956.
[44] Interview with an ex-USWA executive.

to "charter locals," of which the bauxite section was the only one, was a compromise solution.

The most important gain for the USWA in its search for effective control, for the NWU in finance, and for bauxite workers in increased wages was the achievement of special status for the bauxite-alumina industry in 1955. This permitted wage rates in the bauxite-alumina industry to rise two or three times above the general rate. In 1957 comparative rates for the same occupation in the three industries of bauxite-alumina, construction, and agriculture were: carpenters—5/8 per hour in bauxite-alumina, 2/2 in construction, and 1/6 in agriculture; drivers—5/9 in bauxite-alumina, 2/2 in construction, and 1/7 in agriculture; unskilled labour—3/1 in bauxite-alumina, 1/6 in construction, and 9d in agriculture.[45] In each case the bauxite-alumina rate is between three and four times that of the agricultural rate, and agriculture employs the most workers on the island. Workers receiving such rates are placed in a wage-earning elite which has no equal in Jamaica. A carpenter at the above rate for a 40-hour week would be among the top 3.7 per cent of households in Jamaica with such an income.[46] Workers with these advantages, and being serviced by wage increases from collective bargaining, are less likely to be a disruptive force in the industry, to wish to change unions, or otherwise disturb the steady flow of bauxite and alumina to North America. Since the turbulence of the early 1950s when the NWU was created, there have been no strikes in the bauxite-alu-

[45] Department of Statistics (Jamaica): *Digest of Statistics*, No. 17, December 1957, Table 7.03, p. 44. Quoted in shillings/pence, 20s= $2.80.

[46] Calculated weekly wage as applied to income distribution data in A. Ahiram, *Income Distribution in Jamaica, 1958, Social and Economic Studies*, Vol. 13, No. 3, September 1964, p. 338.

mina industry. Thus the USWA primary objective in Jamaica was achieved.

THE INTERNATIONALS

The involvement of WFTU in Jamaica supports the thesis that between 1949 and Stalin's death, the organisation showed little interest in the colonial territories and that the activity in 1952–53 was as much a response to the ICFTU as it was from indigenous objectives.[47] Thus WFTU became involved only after the ICFTU regional organisations and USA unions showed interest in Jamaica. The only possible objective at that time was to keep alive a WFTU affiliate and this project was never substantially successful and had completely collapsed by the late 1950s, if not before.

The TUCJ had affiliated to CLASC but the latter's interest in Latin America rather than the Caribbean and the decline in the power of the TUCJ prevented any serious involvement in Jamaica.

The ICFTU supported the NWU but, apart from the direct £250 grant in 1954, most of the contact was made through its regional associate, ORIT. ORIT was the principal organisation in the Caribbean and most of the activities of its Caribbean Division (CADORIT) as well as the direct activities of the ICFTU were subject to its approval. It was, for example, ORIT which was permitted to judge for the ICFTU the acceptability of the TUCJ, NLC, or NWU for affiliation.

[47] G. Lichtblau, "The Communist Labor Offensive in Former Colonial Countries," *Industrial and Labor Relations Review*, Vol. 15, No. 3, April 1962, p. 377.

ORIT's main connection in Jamaica followed the standard pattern and was with the NWU. Note has already been made of ORIT's anti-WFTU and anti-communist basis, and the most obvious target in the Caribbean was the CLC. This organisation was already in difficulty in 1951 when ORIT was founded, but the presence of Hart as its Secretary plus the affiliation of other radical trade union leaders in the Caribbean made it a potential counter to ORIT.

The creation of CADORIT by ORIT in June 1952 was thus designed to replace the CLC by an organisation under ORIT-ICFTU auspices. The collapse of the CLC was already far advanced and CADORIT quickly became accepted as the Caribbean Regional Organisation. Affiliation record of Jamaican unions to CADORIT was identical to that of the ICFTU, with the NWU being accepted, even though it was only two months old, and the other applications rejected.

The new organisation came under some pressure to supply tangible assistance to the Caribbean area and in 1955 the Secretary explained in a report that the ICFTU had heavy commitments to finance in South East Asia as there "were several organisations in the territories [S.E. Asia] which constituted a large proportion of the population of the world and which were linked with the WFTU" and that funds had to be concentrated "in those areas to keep truly democratic unions in being."[48]

Nevertheless, CADORIT was active in some of the smaller islands and sponsored Caribbean-wide conferences. In St. Lucia, in 1957, the Executive-Secretary of CADORIT and Harry H. Pollak, AFL-CIO Inter-Ameri-

[48] CADORIT: *Report of the Second Conference, 1955*, Trinidad, p. 41.

can Representative, were present during a sugar strike and assisted in a settlement.[49]

In Jamaica, however, CADORIT was not important as it was NWU personnel who were involved in the CADORIT rather than the reverse and this situation continued with the creation of CCLab in 1960.

NWU AND REGIONAL ORGANISATIONS

The NWU, from the founding of CADORIT, became one of the most important unions in the Caribbean regional organisations. The interchange of high-level officers between the NWU, CBMWF, and CCLab has been detailed. It began with Sterling as Executive Secretary of CADORIT while still on the USWA payroll and ended with Michael Manley as President of the CBMWF and Osmond Dyce as Secretary of the CCLab.

The NWU position of dominance is illustrated by the income of the CCLab in 1962. Of a total income in 1961–62 of $84,736 over 50 per cent came from ORIT-ICFTU grants and less than one-sixteenth from affiliation fees. Of the affiliation fees, the NWU with payments of $1927 in 1961 and $2460 in 1962 gave twice as much as the next largest fee-paying union member.[50]

In this position it is not surprising that the NWU leaders have been seconded to the CCLab for various specific purposes. Michael Manley went, as a CCLab representative, to British Guiana in 1961 "to assist the Labour Movement in their struggles against the attempt of the PPP to dominate or crush the trade union move-

[49] AFL-CIO: *International Affairs Bulletin*, Vol. 1, No. 8, April–May–June 1957, p. 3.

[50] Caribbean Congress of Labour: *Secretary's Report, 1961–1962.*

ment. The ICFTU were asked and agreed to fund his expenses."[51] In both CADORIT and the CCLab, the USWA and ORIT officials were active.[52]

In conclusion, the main Jamaican operations of the regional organisations came between 1952 and 1955 and inasmuch as a formally democratic and strong union associated with the ICFTU was created they were successful. After 1955 the activities lessened as the NWU continued to be the important affiliate of the regional and international organisations.

Foreign Corporations

In Chapter V, foreign corporations were identified largely as promoters of industrial relations practices associated with the domiciliary base and with the anti-political unionism campaign.

It is impossible to segregate the foreign corporation, of which the main ones are the bauxite-alumina companies, from the labour organisation involvements in the period 1949–67. In one sense it was the presence of bauxite and the arrival of the corporations which started the chain of union involvements which began in 1952. The corporations had specific objectives in industrial relations for they encountered very early the disruptive nature of dual unionism. The first priority was, therefore, to prevent labour disturbances caused through competing unions, and the establishment of a representation poll system in 1950 helped solve these difficulties. Other

[51] Caribbean Congress of Labour: *Minutes of Meeting of Administrative Committee, January 15, 1962.*

[52] See Caribbean Congress of Labour: *Secretary's Report, April–September 1961.*

objectives included efficient grievance procedures and collective bargaining.[53] All these came as a result of the creation of the NWU and the emphasis and autonomy which was given to its bauxite-alumina section.

The acceptance of the corporations of the "ability-to-pay doctrine" in 1955, as analysed earlier, was one of the most important factors in acquiring industrial peace in the industry. Bauxite rates were in any case higher than those in agriculture and the resistance to the "ability-to-pay doctrine" came more from local businessmen than from the corporations.[54]

From the corporations' standpoint the issue was marginal. This is because the labour costs of bauxite extraction in relation to the total cost of aluminium are negligible. In 1958–59, for example, disbursements of wages and salaries in Jamaica per ton of bauxite were 7·5 per cent of value.[55] In 1962 the total wages and salaries of workers in the bauxite-alumina industry, including administration, mining, prospecting, construction, processing, and farm workers, were £4,094,000 and the bauxite output was 7,519,000 tons, which means the labour cost was approximately 10s 6d per ton.[56] In general, taking the price of unwrought aluminium as £200 per ton and a 4:1 bauxite/aluminium reduction ratio, the labour cost of bauxite mining would be less

[53] See G. Eaton, *dissertation*, p. 661; and W. Knowles, *Trade Union Development and Industrial Relations in the British West Indies, op. cit.*, p. 75

[54] See H. Mitchell, *Caribbean Patterns*, London 1967, p. 314.

[55] See N. Girvan, *The Caribbean Bauxite Industry*, Studies in Regional Economic Integration, Vol. 2, No. 4, Institute of Social and Economic Research, University of the West Indies, Kingston, 1967, Table A, p. 3.

[56] Calculated from figures in Jamaican Government: *Economic Survey 1965*, pp. 72–73; and H. Huggins, *Aluminium in Changing Communities*, London, 1968, p. 124.

than 1/100th of value per ton of aluminium.[57] The bauxite-alumina corporations, therefore, had little economic reason to strongly resist the ability-to-pay doctrine.

In addition to the high wages, in some cases the corporations have extensive housing projects and the workers therefore enjoy a high standard of living. The high pay and perquisites of working for a bauxite-alumina company, the well-established industrial relations procedures and the technically efficient union have resulted in over ten years of industrial peace. In these circumstances the unions assume functions for the corporations which have been likened to a recruiting and screening process resulting in a supply of skilled and stable workers.[58] One author, after interviewing corporate executives, noted that their opinion was that the union (NWU) was accepted in Jamaica "as a useful social institution serving a police function which is of value to the company."[59] The corporations thus were able to achieve the desired conditions in Jamaica.

[57] As a lower than 4:1 reduction ratio is possible the bauxite labour cost could be well below this 1 per cent.

[58] R. Aronson, "Labour Commitment among Jamaican Bauxite Workers," p. 164.

[59] G. Eaton, *dissertation*, p. 624.

CHAPTER XII

CONCLUSIONS

The specific findings of the case study concerning the making, execution, role, and impact of trade union independent foreign policy can now be summarised. These findings can also be set against some theories, or generally held notions, concerning the role of trade unions and non-governmental organisations in international relations.

Trade Union Foreign Policy

PARTICIPATION IN POLICY-MAKING

This study confirms the general finding that there is little rank-and-file control over trade union international activities. Although the British TUC had more foreign policy discussions at the conference level than the USWA, in both cases any discussions were of a very general nature and did not deal with specific cases. In the USWA there was one occasion when Jamaica was mentioned in debate and that was from a delegate seeking to endorse, rather than examine or criticise, the USWA policy in Jamaica. Jamaica was never specifically mentioned in the discussions at any of the British TUC congresses.

In both organisations there was little attempt to supply full information concerning the Jamaican operations. The USWA Officers' Reports to the bi-annual conferences detail the stated objectives and some of the actions taken by the USWA representatives in Jamaica. Likewise, the General Council Reports to the British TUC annual congress state the size of the grants and the administrative procedures by which they were awarded. In the latter case there were occasional mentions of the "industrial relations" conditions which existed in Jamaica but in both organisations no mention was made of the dual union situation, or the political nature of the unions. Yet these were the most important facts which would determine the effectiveness of any expenditures, regardless of the objectives. The information as supplied would not be sufficient for even a rudimentary understanding of the situation or for an assessment of the wisdom of the specific actions or policies taken in the name of the organisation.

At the level of the general membership, information was even more sparse. Neither *Steel Labor*, nor *Labour*, the monthly journals circulated to members, detailed on a continuing basis the level, results, or conditions of the organisational involvement in Jamaica. Further, at the general membership level both organisations show a sensitivity concerning the financial grants, loans, or other expenditures involved in the Jamaican operations, neither organisation revealing any of such financial aspects in their journals.

The assumptions and conclusions of the studies made

of union rank-and-file interest in international affairs are that without direct connection there is little interest in the matter. This may be generally true but this case study shows that the rank-and-file and even lower-level leadership was either not informed or only partially informed of the organisations' activities. The effect of publicly detailing the background of the involvement and particularly the partisan support of one union, the number and cost of trips to the area by union personnel and the number and purpose of financial grants and loans, can only be speculated. Certainly it would seem unlikely to lead to a decrease in interest and participation by the rank-and-file. It might well lead to an increase in suggestions, comments, criticisms, or protests articulated by leaders not normally associated with the international aspect of their organisation's activities. It is presumably such occurrences which appeared undesirable to the leadership involved and why complete accounts of the organisations' activities in Jamaica were not made available.

POLICY-MAKING AND ORGANISATIONAL ECOLOGY

It was suggested earlier that the organisational ecology of the policy-maker and in-field actor might be an important determinant of general policy and operational action.

An assessment of the place of values, norms, and experiences derived from the domestic environment is not the basic objective of this study. To satisfy even the most rudimentary requirements of scientific investigation a programme of attitude testing and structured interviews would have to be made. The following observations, derived as they were from documents, informal and unstructured interviews, can only be suggestive and sometimes speculative.

In formulating general policy on less-developed countries and on Jamaica the direct impact of organisational experience of actors appears to have been dampened by two factors: first, the absorption of the trade union foreign policy decision-makers into a foreign policy-making elite at the national level and, second, the establishment and continuing presence of a body of experts in the organisations' staff.

This first factor is illustrated, in the case of the British TUC, by the close association between the trade union foreign policy-makers in the national policy-making structures. It was not difficult for the general secretaries, two of whom had spent the major part of their careers as officials of the TUC and had had virtually no trade union leadership experience, to move into the policy-making elite, as was also the case with the International Department personnel. This phenomena can be observed during both Labour and Conservative governments, although during the Labour Government of 1945–52 the trade unionists were more inclined to conceive of themselves as ex-officio members of government.

The political system thus demanded of British trade unionists that they did *not* act as unionists but rather as quasi-government policy-makers with an area of special competence and interest in trade unions. The correlation between organisational background and the general foreign policy is therefore not strong. Explanations of such policy are more likely to be found in the policy-makers' contacts with government departments and foreign trade unionists.

The same conclusion applies to the USWA, although

the process of acceptance into the national policy-making elite was somewhat different. Perhaps reflecting the general position of trade unions in American society, leaders of the USWA had to make continuous and strenuous attempts to become and remain part of the policy-making elite while, in the British case, the process was more automatic.

The second factor dampening the impact of the domestic environment on general policy—the presence of international experts—was one of the reasons why, at least on paper, it was possible to develop a relativist policy towards foreign trade union development. In the British TUC it was the experts in the International Department who advocated a relativist policy and brought continuity of policy to the organisation. Although the USWA did not develop such a relativist policy the establishment of an International Department likewise brought continuity of policy and expertise to the organisation. The two departments, staffed by officials usually without trade union experience, and both having considerable power, thus formulated policy more on general and non-union experience and knowledge.

OPERATIONS AND ORGANISATIONAL ECOLOGY

As has been shown, the direct projection of the organisational ecology at the operational level was more pronounced.

To put into practice the relativist policy developed by the British TUC and AFL-CIO, the in-field actors would have to be mentally equipped to deal with cross-cultural situations—to be culture bound would be fatal to a relativist policy.

The foreign unionists involved in Jamaica, however,

for the most part had no special training or expertise with cross-cultural operations and furthermore were not required to consider the Jamaican situation in any way other than as an obstacle to be overcome. Apart from the inability of dealing with the BITU, for reasons enumerated, it resulted in the insistence that structures and functions of the organisations should follow exactly the lines of domestic models.

Differences perceived in Jamaica and the Jamaican unions were easily absorbed in the general notion of backwardness of the society and in the rationale of the unionists' presence, namely that of assisting organisations which were less efficient than their own. The specific objectives, however, sometimes forced the unionists to accept structures not essentially similar to their own—the blanket union and its political connections, for example, would not correspond to the USWA officials' experience. In such cases the differences were absorbed if the Jamaican actors were cooperative, although, as has been shown, even then there were strenuous efforts to bring the organisation into conformity with the domestic model.

Thus any claims to relativity at the general policy level failed in action and the actual policies pursued in Jamaica were usually in accordance with the actors' national universalistic notions of trade unions.

STATED VERSUS OPERATIONAL POLICY

The major objectives and incentives for the Jamaican involvement have already been discussed and in neither organisation was movement ideology, the only incentive which could be characterised as quasi-altruistic, very prominent. This fact, coupled with the projection of the domestic ecology by in-field actors, meant that conditions in Jamaica were never fully understood and feedback was negligible.

Neither of the organisations' policies therefore showed that the possible impact and results in Jamaica had been considered. There are no indications that policy-making criteria were based on a cost-benefit analysis concerning Jamaican society, economic welfare, or general improvement of working conditions. It is only necessary to recount this situation because of the many trade union statements, usually aimed at the general membership and public, which declare the contrary.

Under these conditions the disparity between stated policy and the policy-in-action was great, especially in the case of the British TUC, which, in supporting the NWU, contravened its stated policies of non-interference in self-governing colonies and preference for establishing a strong local base to national unions. For the USWA the disparity was not so great, except that explanations of the Jamaican involvement as necessary for the protection of labour standards did not conform with the fundamental objective of protecting supplies of bauxite.

In both cases the Jamaican experience shows that, except for the nationally identified political ideology of democracy or anti-communism, there was no policy-in-action conformity to stated movement or group ideology.

TRADE UNIONS AND NATIONAL HEGEMONY

The record of involvement in Jamaica has shown that a wide variety of means was used in an attempt to secure the general union objectives in Jamaica and to play a role in international relations. Direct means included personal contacts, written advice, in-field advisers and representatives, financial grants and loans, gifts of capital equipment and direct employment of local organisers. Indirect involvement came through international, regional, and functional trade union organisations, government commissions, variously sponsored educational programmes, and Jamaican non-governmental organisations other than unions.

With these means, the unions became an important factor in determining the political environment in which state diplomacy takes place. While this may be true in all cases of non-governmental organisation involvement in foreign societies, it was particularly true of foreign trade unions in Jamaica. This was because involvement in Jamaican trade unions also meant involvement in the political parties of which the trade unions were the base and therefore raised the possibility that the power of political elites and the policies which they followed could be changed. Further, as a result of the blanket structure of the Jamaican unions, the USWA attempt to control labour in one sector of the economy had important economic and labour relations effects in all the other sectors in which the blanket union was active.

The ability of the foreign unions to be legitimately involved in such a manner was contributive to one of the most striking facts which has emerged from the case study, namely, the cooperation between foreign unions and their nationally associated corporations or business organisations. Political opponents of foreign trade union activities have usually dwelt on the alleged government-union association while the antagonism between corporations and unions at the domestic level has created a disposition to ignore the possibility of their cooperating internationally. The projection of patterns of domestic relations into international relations is theoretically erroneous and the Jamaican case study empirically demonstrates why this is the case. The entirely different conditions experienced in acting internationally and acting domestically produce different patterns of behaviour and precipitate different goals. Thus both international actions and goals of the unions and corporations may reduce antagonism and produce a high level of cooperation.

Such common goals may well vary with different industries and the extractive industries, such as bauxite mining, may be especially prone to such cooperation because foreign labour costs are minimal. But, at least in the British TUC, it has been shown that aspects of cooperation were general in nature and not confined to a special industry with special economic structures.

The involvement of the foreign unions was a means by which the investment climate in a country might be improved. In Jamaica a good investment climate would include a stable union situation, the absence of socialists advocating nationalisation, the absence of nationalists interested in absolute local control of local resources, and the presence of a cooperative government committed to development via direct investment. Each of these latter is characteristic of Jamaica and in the establishment of each of these British and American unions played an important role.

Such conditions were also important to foreign policy and activities at the national state level, for the requirements of a good investment climate are similar to those for national hegemonic power.

While there is no direct evidence that the unions were instruments of state policy, the Jamaican case study shows that there was in fact no deviation from general state policy. In the British case, all of the actions of the TUC were completely in accord with the colonial policy laid down in the 1930s, as well as the later policies pursued by the British in the Caribbean. The USWA policy was cast in cold war terms and the defeat of persons designated communist resulted in new Jamaican political actors more generally prepared to cooperate with all USA organisations.

Jamaica had been under direct British control for three centuries and from the British standpoint the control had been stable and effective. The demands of the post-1930s, intensified after World War II, that the direct colonial relationship should cease was eventually recognised and acceded to in Jamaica between 1945 and 1962. The ceasing of direct control over Jamaica by Britain was also a function of the British economic and military weakness after World War II and thus the release of direct control was also accompanied by a general decline in the strength of hegemonic factors, such as corporate investment, trade, and other non-state contacts. In the period 1945 to 1962 the important British hegemonic contacts were superseded and replaced by those from North America.

In this process of orderly transfer of hegemonic power the foreign trade unions played a considerable role. The replacement of the involvement of British unions by American unions in the period 1949–53 is illustrative of the transfers which were taking place in trade, investment, and other areas. However, the USA non-governmental organisations, and especially the USWA, assumed a role much larger than that of the British during the colonial period. In some cases the USA unions' activities approximated those previously undertaken by the British Government colonial administrators, as for example conducting three-month education surveys, sitting on Jamaican Government commissions, and preparing model legislation to be presented to the Jamaican Government.

In this way the unions played an important part in creating a suitable investment climate for corporations and assisted in the orderly transfer of hegemonic power as between their respective nation states.

Impact on Jamaica

Two cautionary considerations are relevant to any discussion of the impact of foreign trade unions on Jamaican unions and society. First, the political, social, and economic events in which the foreign trade unions were involved were not necessarily initiated or controlled by them and the role they played varied considerably according to time period and current objectives. Second, it is somewhat dangerous to speculate on a course of events which might have occurred without the involvement of the foreign trade unions. It would, in fact, be a comparison of a current "is" with an historical "might-have-been" and as such is open to highly individual perceptions and value judgements. This is the standard problem faced in any historical study which seeks to consider possible results by adding or removing one particular variable.

It is important, then, to bear in mind these considerations in the following discussion of the possible effects of the foreign trade unions in Jamaica, especially the longer-term effects.

The immediate effects of the foreign unions can be stated with some certainty. First, a group of highly paid workers was created; second, the industrial labour force was unionised with a stable union situation and industrial relations system; and finally, important changes were made in the leadership, nature, and function of the existing unions.

An assessment of the long-term effects of these, however, presents more difficulty and is subject to conflicting views. The creation of a small group of highly paid workers in the bauxite-alumina industry, for example, is considered by one author to have acted as a wage reference group for other workers, thereby encouraging the latter to agitate for, and receive, a greater share of the growing gross domestic product.[1] On the other hand, the demonstration effect of such unusually high wages earned by a group of industrial workers has added to the traditional low status of, and exodus from, the rural life and occupations.[2] This has occurred in the context of expensive government programmes designed to discourage the drift from rural to urban areas in search of usually unobtainable industrial work.[3] Further, the acquisition of bauxite rates or mining work have become a major political issue, creating turbulence, strife, and possibly corruption at several levels in the political system.[4]

The stable union situation and the industrial relations procedures established in the early 1950s may well have

[1] H. Huggins, *Aluminium in Changing Communities*, London, 1968, p. 121.

[2] See N. Adams, "Internal Migration in Jamaica: an Economic Analysis," *Social and Economic Studies*, Vol. 18, No. 2, June 1969, p. 151.

[3] See M. Smith, "Education and Occupational Choice in Rural Jamaica," *Social and Economic Studies*, Vol. 9, No. 3, September 1960, pp. 332–54.

[4] An affidavit filed during a court case, brought to set aside an Arbitrator's decision concerning the award of bauxite rates, alleges that the Arbitrator stated that he would award such rates as he supported a political party and "that the award of bauxite rates would be a tremendous help to his party." See *Daily Gleaner*, April 20, 1967, p. 3.

contributed to the island's phenomenal growth in the industrial sector. As a major determinant for a favourable investment climate it certainly assisted in the attraction of foreign capital to the island, which has been a major objective of the government's industrial development programme. However, such stability and the attractiveness of Jamaica for foreign investors was a direct function of changes which took place within the Jamaican trade union movement, the effects of which must also be considered.

The foreign unions brought a number of techniques and structures which Jamaican unions, for the most part, have adopted. They are both well versed in collective bargaining and have staff conversant with the contemporary techniques of economic and manpower planning. In the case of the NWU its organisational proficiency in this respect has caused it to be internationally described as a "model" union in a less-developed country. In this way the foreign unions were instrumental in the creation of efficiently functioning unions on the British-North American model.

While these conditions, as a current "is," are observable and verifiable the side effects are more difficult to discern. The original union movement in Jamaica was created by Bustamante through the BITU and as such this organisation performed more than the accepted functions of unions in industrial countries. As has been noted, both structure and function tended to be developed in relation to the Jamaican social ecology; the blanket union, for example, was clearly a structural form very suited to Jamaican conditions. It was the BITU which created this structure with no foreign contacts while, in contrast, the TUCJ with the heavy foreign involvement sought to establish a structure which was to prove unsuitable in the Jamaican context. It took the leaders of the TUCJ nearly ten years before they admitted that attempts at duplication of the foreign model were neither industrially nor politically effective.

In this early period, then, the effect of the foreign involvement was to resist creative organisational growth and prevent, in some parts of the movement, adaptation of structure and function to the social ecology.[5] Although it is even more difficult to detail the effects of later involvement there is no reason to believe that the prevention of organisational adaptation to the social ecology has ceased and there is, in fact, some evidence that it has increased. What is certain is that the unions have shed some of their original functions. General welfare aspects have become less evident in union leadership statements and agitation on behalf of the unemployed, so much part of the early scene, has ceased. In particular, the emphasis on acquiring industrial-country union skills has made the voice of the rural worker, originally so strong in the BITU, much less evident.

Thus, to some extent the current unions have become dysfunctional to their social ecology. The process of becoming more functionally specific required that the unions be de-politicised and that radical leaders be eliminated from trade union activity. Both of these events had profound effects on the political history of Jamaica, especially as the change in the nature of the unions was not accompanied by the growth of other organisations capable of taking their place. The political parties have so far proven to be poor substitutes and, as compared with the early unions, lack close social rapport with the poorest—and majority of the population.

[5] For the contrary view that foreign involvements strengthen unions and contribute to international integration see H. Jacobson, "Ventures in Polity Shaping: External Assistance to Labour Movements in Developing Countries," in R. Cox, ed., *International Organisation: World Politics*, London, 1969, pp. 195–205.

The elimination of the radical leaders from trade union activity, and thereby from the political scene, in the early 1950s can be seen as a process of selection for the Jamaican political elite over which the foreign unions had considerable influence. Their attempt to ensure that the leading political actors would pursue policies most suited to their objectives was successful. That these objectives in Jamaica, as has been shown from the policy analysis of the unions, were functions of larger over-all objectives extraneous to Jamaica means that it would only be a question of fortuitous chance if such a process of political selection would be beneficial to the development of Jamaican society.

The social and political effects of such involvements could be extended almost endlessly. Two more obvious examples are the retardation of integration between the two cultures and the continuing poor distribution of income. Integration between the two societies or cultures requires political leaders with the ability to converse in both the languages, to be, in effect, a broker between the two sections of society. Inasmuch as such leaders, having a rapport with the evolved culture, would be neither understandable nor acceptable to the foreign actors, they would be removed in any process of political selection in which the foreigners had power.[6] In the case of income distribution, economists have argued that, social justice considerations aside, one of the impediments to continued growth in the Jamaican economy is the extreme nature of the pattern of income distribution. Indeed, a recent study by a United Nations research

[6] For an examination of this process in relation to universities see L. Scherz-Garcia, "Some Dysfunctional Aspects of International Assistance and the Role of the University in Social Change in Latin America," *International Social Science*, Vol. 19, No. 3, June 1967, pp. 387–403.

institute points out that the Jamaican socio-economic profile had less social emphasis in 1960 than in 1950, by which is meant that some indicators of the social situation, such as life expectancy, infant mortality, schooling, etc., have shown a relative decline compared with economic indicators and other developing nations. The study concludes "that present inequalities may, as elsewhere, solidify through the fusion of economic and social factors, and thereby impede integrated development in the future."[7]

The arrestation of organisational adaptation, the depoliticisation of the unions, and the elimination of radical leadership can be seen at least as some reasons why the Jamaican society has not moved towards a more economically and socially healthy distribution of income.

Some General Considerations

It is generally agreed within the discipline of development economics as well as within national and international agencies for economic development that transfers of capital are necessary for development. While this may be true as an abstract economic requirement, this case study would indicate that direct investment sets up a train of foreign involvements which have a profound effect on the politics, economics, and society.

The cross-national vested interests acquired through the investment results in a large range of foreign groups and individuals anxious to change or preserve the political, social, and economic configurations which may well be for the sake of the investment concerned rather

[7] N. Baster and W. Scott, *Levels of Living and Economic Growth: a Comparative Study of Six Countries, 1950–1965*, United Nations Research Institute for Social Development, Geneva, 1969, p. 47.

than for development at large. While this could not necessarily be anticipated, nor its effects predicted, it serves as a warning that consideration of capital transfer must always go beyond the economic.

It is clear that any consideration of the process and possibility of organisation building in countries such as Jamaica must give considerable weight to the cross-national involvements. It is likely that such involvements will impede or even destroy effective and lasting social organisation building unless there is a revolution in education and understanding of cross-cultural management and involvement. If, for example, Max Weber's contention is correct that the creative element in organisation building is the charismatic leader it is difficult to see the possibility of accommodation between foreign actors and such leaders. On the contrary, foreign actors would normally seek those leaders who "speak the same language," and in fact the history of international activities of industrial country trade unions indicates a general policy orientation to oppose and attempt to destroy such charismatic leaders. Any theory or model or organisation building based on the notion of a closed society able to develop its organisations and institutions in accordance with the inherent dictates of that society, would not be relevant to most of the non-industrialised states.

Within the Functional theory of international integration, as well as within the liberal economic theory of a world economy, is the idea that integration will result from the creation of a network of contacts between non-governmental organisations. One of the fundamental criticisms of the validity of this idea has been that the non-governmental group acting internationally will have the same nationalist orientation as its own government. This case study, to some extent, confirms this criticism but indicates that it may be even more valid when relations between industrial and less-developed countries are considered.

One factor which has not hitherto been considered in such theories is the participant nature of such non-governmental interstate contacts. Contacts at the state government level rarely involve actors participating in either the long-term or day-to-day management of organisations or projects. Non-governmental contacts, especially those between industrial countries and less-developed countries, almost invariably involve participation. Such participatory contacts are becoming more prevalent owing to increases in technical assistance and the general activities of international organisations.

If such contacts are to be beneficial it would appear essential to investigate more thoroughly the impact of cross-cultural experience and problems of these programmes. The colonial and missionary experience is relevant here and the large number of instances where there have been disastrous effects (regardless of motives) owing to the inability to see the consequences of actions in a different culture, indicate the potential dangers of such participatory involvement.

In any programme or theory of international integration the participatory dimension would have to be the crucial factor. This case study suggests that unless more attention is paid to the nature of such participation the results are more likely to lead to more autarchic policies rather than to more accommodation as the theories suggest. This is not to suggest that if current patterns in relations between industrial and less-developed countries persist an autarchic policy might not be necessary and beneficial, at least as a starting base.

SCHEMA FOR THE STUDY OF INTER-SOCIETAL PENETRATION BETWEEN SOCIETIES OF WIDELY DIFFERING LEVELS OF ECONOMIC DEVELOPMENT BY NON-GOVERNMENTAL ACTORS

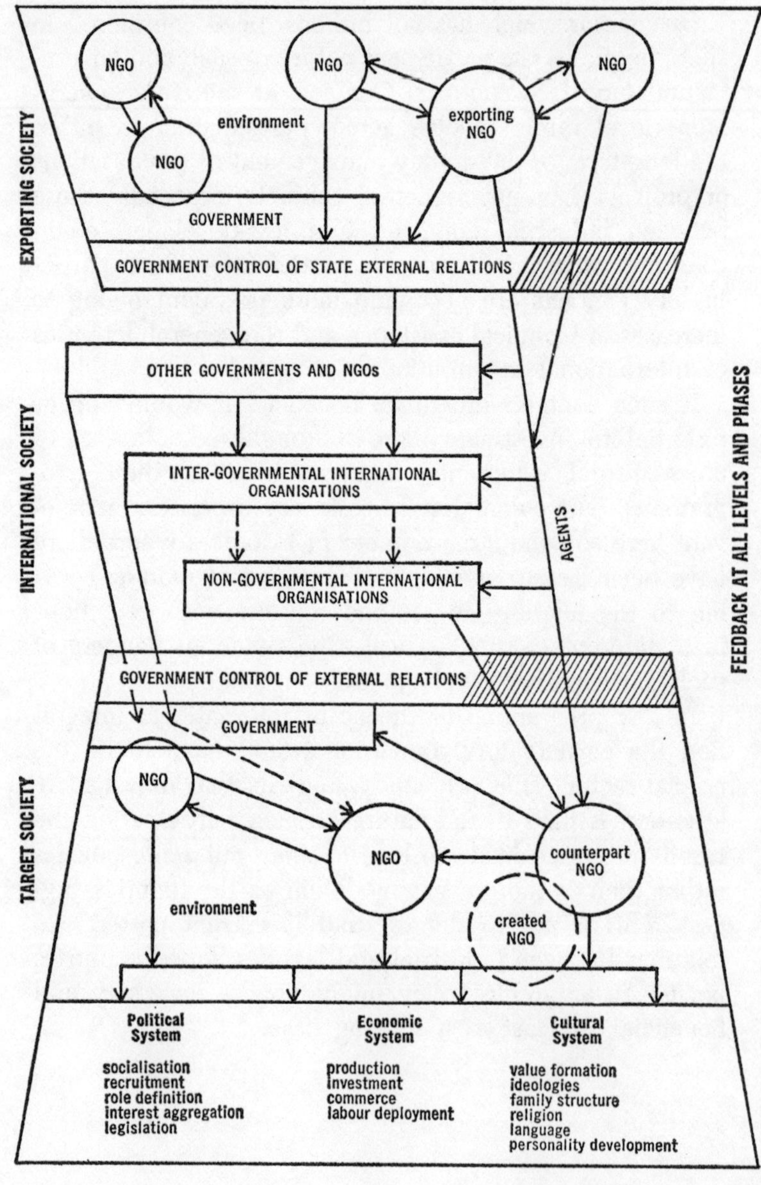

ESSENTIAL AREAS OF STUDY

Exporting Society and Its NGOs

—political, social, cultural and economic aspects
—structure, function and ideology and social ecology of NGO
—decision-making of NGO for foreign involvements
—stated and underlying incentives and objectives for foreign involvements
—general foreign objective

International Society and Means of Action

means of action: role of other states, NGOs and inter- and non-governmental international organisations
—nature of financial grants, education activities and advisory programmes
behaviour of agents: personality, perception, technical competence

Target Society and Impact

—political, social, cultural and economic aspects
—nature of existing or created counterpart NGO
—NGO social ecology
—nature and role of NGO leadership
—specific actions, alliances and objectives of foreign NGO
—intended and unintended consequences of activities of foreign NGOs

BIBLIOGRAPHY*

Bibliography Page Number

* Includes references which are made in the text and also background works not referred to in the text.

JAMAICA: General and Trade Unionism*

SOURCES

General

Jamaican Government:

Five Year Independence Plan, 1963–1968; a Long-term Development Plan for Jamaica, 1964. 240 pp.

Annual General Report, 1938–61.

Legislature: *Report of Proceedings of House of Representatives*, 1950–66.

Registrar General's Department: *Annual Report*, 1947–62.

Department of Agriculture: *Annual Report*, 1942–59.

Jamaica Industrial Development Corporation: *Review of Industry in Jamaica*, 1965.

Central Planning Unit: *Economic Survey*, Jamaica, 1960–68.

Department of Statistics:

Digest of Statistics, 1940–1960.

Annual Abstract of Statistics, 1961–1968.

Census of Jamaica, 1960.

Wage Rates, 1963, 1964.

British Government:

Central Office of Information: *Jamaica*, Fact Sheets of the Commonwealth, 1962, (R 5500). 8 pp.

Financial Times Survey of Jamaica, London, The Financial Times, January 1, 1969, pp. 15–22.

Neita, Clifton, *Who's Who in Jamaica, British West Indies, 1954*, Kingston, 1954. 561 pp.

Newspapers and News Journals:

Daily Gleaner, 1940–67.

Sunday Gleaner, 1940–67.

Public Opinion, –1967.

Spotlight, 1939–67.

Monthly Comments by Ansell Hart, 1960.

* Titles in this section which refer to the Caribbean or West Indies have information of importance relating specifically to Jamaica.

Trade Unionism

Jamaican Government:

Report of the Board of Enquiry into Labour Disputes Between Trade Unions, 1950. 22 pp.

Annual Report on the Work of the Labour Department, 1940–50 and 1951–52 (one volume).

Ministry of Labour and Labour Department: *Annual Report,* 1953–54.

Ministry of Labour: *Annual Report,* 1955–61.

Labour Department: *Report on the Achievements of the Labour Department for the Years 1945–1954,* 1954.

Ministry of Labour and National Insurance:

Report on Manpower Situation in Jamaica, 1959.

Report of the Board of Enquiry into the Dispute Between the Jamaica Broadcasting Corporation and the National Workers Union, June 15, 1965, mimeo. 31 pp.

Guide to Industrial Relations in Jamaica, 1966. 59 pp.

Central Bureau of Statistics: *Trade Unionism in Jamaica, 1918–1946,* 1946.

Department of Statistics:

Employment and Earnings in Large Establishments, 1957 and 1962–65.

Wage Rates and Hours in Selected Industries and Occupations, 1959, 1962.

Labour Force Bulletin, No. 1, October 1946.

Jamaica Industrial Development Corporation: *Legislation Affecting Labour,* 1961.

British Government:

Colonial Office: *Labour Conditions in the West Indies,* Orde-Browne, Major Granville, London, HMSO, 1939.

Conference of British Caribbean Labour Officers: Report, Bridgetown, Barbados, 1950.

Trade Union Training Course: Report, Burrows, C. W., Barbados, 1949, (no publisher).

West India Royal Commission: Report, 1938–1939, London, HMSO, 1945, CMD 6607. 480 pp.

Comptroller for Development and Welfare in the West Indies: *Summary of Labour and Legislation in the British West Indies*, Barbados, Advocate Co. Ltd., 1949. 139 pp.

British Broadcasting Corporation:

Feather, Victor, *British Trade Unionism*, Broadcast to the West Indies, 1941.

Marquand, The Rt. Hon. Hilary, *Industrial Relations and Trade Unions*, two broadcasts on Radio Demerara, Georgetown, British Guiana, September 23 and 30, 1954.

United States Government:

Bureau of Labor Statistics: Kirkpatrick, E. K., *Labor Law and Practice in Jamaica*, Washington, D.C., 1967. 57 pp.

International Labour Office:

Labour Policies in the West Indies, Geneva, Studies and Reports, New Series No. 29, 1952. 337 pp.

Murray, C., *Report to the Government of Jamaica on a Proposed Social Security Scheme*, 1965. 28 pp.

Bustamante Industrial Trade Union:

Rules of the Bustamante Industrial Trade Union, Kingston, no date (1962?). 30 pp.

Labour Day Annual, 1954–58, 1965, and 1966.

Trades Union Congress of Jamaica:

Trade Unionism, Kingston, Trades Union Congress Education Department, no date, mimeo. 35 pp.

Report of the Trades Union Congress of Jamaica for June 30, 1946, for Presentation to Conference, September 21, 1946, 1946. 18 pp.

History of Busmen's Strike (issued jointly by the TUC and the Tramway, Transport and General Workers' Union), Kingston, 1948. 131 pp.

Jamaican National Songs, compiled by Frank Gordon for Trades Union Congress Education Department, 1949. 18 pp.

Newsletter, Nos. 1 and 2, February–April–May 1961.

National Workers Union of Jamaica:

Annual Report, 1955–56, 1959–61, 1963–67.

Constitution, Rules and Regulations, 1960 (?).

The Unionist (official monthly publication of NWU), 1963–64.

Employers' Federation: *Freedom of Association*, Kingston, 1963. 12 pp.

People's National Party: *Man of Destiny*, Kingston, 1954. 83 pp.

University of the West Indies: *Annual Report of Trade Union Education Institute*, 1964–65 and 1965–66.

Farley, Rawle, *A Report on the University College of the West Indies Department of Extra Mural Studies Industrial Relations Programme, June 1956–September 1958*, Kingston, 1958.

———, ed., *Labour Education in the British Caribbean, the Report of a Labour Education Survey Conducted June–July 1959, and of the Conference Held at the University College of the West Indies, Mona, Jamaica, August 4/9, 1959*, Demerara, British Guiana, Daily Chronicle Ltd., University College of the West Indies, Department of Extra Mural Studies, 1960. 119 pp.

Newspapers and Journals:

Worker and Peasant, Vol. 1, No. 1, Kingston, April 1940.

Jamaica Arise, Kingston, (official monthly publication of the People's National Party), March–October 1949.

The People, Kingston, published by Frank Hill, May 10, June 7 and 21, 1952.

Rising Star, Kingston, (student journal of University of the West Indies, Kingston), 1967.

Newspaper clipping files at the Jamaica Institute, Kingston: Agricultural Labour, Jamaica and West Indies; Bauxite, Jamaica; Colonial Development and Welfare; Ministry of Labour; Riots and Strikes; Labour-West Indies and Jamaica; Trade Unions–Jamaica; Trade Unions–West Indies; Industrial and Labour Relations; International Organisations and Conferences; Jamaica Association of Local Government Officers; Labour Disputes.

BOOKS

Abrahams, Peter, *Jamaica, an Island Mosaic*, London, HMSO, 1957. 284 pp.

Ayearst, Morley, *The British West Indies: the Search for Self-Government*, New York, New York University Press, 1960. 258 pp.

Balogh, Thomas, *The Economics of Poverty*, London, Weidenfeld and Nicholson, 1966. 381 pp.

Baster, N., and Scott, W., *Levels of Living and Economic Growth–a Comparative Study of Six Countries, 1950–1965*, Geneva, United Nations Research Institute for Social Development, 1969. 153 pp.

Bell, Wendell, ed., *The Democratic Revolution in the West Indies. Studies in Nationalism, Leadership and the Belief in Progress*, Cambridge, Mass., Schenkman Publishing, 1967. 232 pp.

———, *Jamaican Leaders: Political Attitudes in a New Nation*, Berkeley, University of California Press, 1964. 229 pp.

Bennett, Louise, *Jamaica Labrish*, Kingston, Sangster's Book Stores, Jamaica, 1966. 224 pp.

Black, Clinton V., *History of Jamaica*, London, Collins, 1958. 250 pp.

Burns, A., *The History of the British West Indies*, London, Allen and Unwin, rev. ed., 1965. 848 pp.

Cargill, Morris, ed., *Ian Fleming Introduces Jamaica*, London, Andre Deutsch, 1965. 240 pp.

Carley, Mary Manning, *Jamaica, the Old and New*, London, Allen and Unwin, 1963. 212 pp.

Cassidy, F., *Jamaican Talk*, London, Macmillan, 1961. 468 pp.

Clarke, Edith, *My Mother Who Fathered Me*, London, G. Allen, 1957. 216 pp.

Curtin, Philip D., *Two Jamaicas: the Role of Ideas in a Tropical Colony, 1830–1865*, Cambridge, Mass., Harvard University Press, 1955. 270 pp.

Eaton, George, *The Development of Trade Unionism in Jamaica*, unpublished dissertation, McGill University, Montreal, 1961.

Eisner, Gisela, *Jamaica 1830–1930, a Study in Economic Growth*, Manchester, Manchester University Press, 1961. 399 pp.

Francis, O. C., *The People of Jamaica*, Kingston, Jamaica Department of Statistics, 1963. 154 pp.

Hart, Richard, *The Origins and Development of the People of Jamaica*, Kingston, 1952. 239 pp.

Hall, D., *Free Jamaica 1838–1865, an Economic History*, London, Oxford University Press, 1960. 290 pp.

Henriques, Fernando, *Family and Colour in Jamaica*, London, Eyre and Spottiswoode, 1953. 196 pp.

Hughes, Marjorie, *The Fairest Island*, London, Gollancz, 1962. 160 pp.

Kerr, Madeline, *Personality and Conflict in Jamaica*, London, Collins, 1963. 220 pp.

Knowles, William H., *Trade Union Development and Industrial Relations in the British West Indies*, Berkeley and Los Angeles, University of California Press, 1959. 214 pp.

Le Page, R. B., and De Camp, David, *Jamaican Creole*, London, Macmillan, 1960. 182 pp.

Macmillan, Mona, *The Land of Look Behind: a Study of Jamaica*, London, Faber and Faber, 1957. 224 pp.

Marier, Roger, *Social Welfare Work in Jamaica, a Study of the Jamaica Social Welfare Commission*, Paris, UNESCO, 1953. 166 pp.

Mau, James A., *Social Change and Images of the Future: a Study of the Pursuit of Progress in Jamaica*, Cambridge, Mass., Schenkman Publishing, 1968. 145 pp.

Maunder, W. F., *Employment in an Underdeveloped Area: a Sample Survey of Kingston, Jamaica*, New Haven, Yale University Press, 1960. 215 pp.

Mitchell, Harold, *Caribbean Patterns, a Political and Economic Study of the Contemporary Caribbean*, London, Chambers, 1967. 520 pp.

———, *Europe in the Caribbean: the Policies of Great Brit-*

ain, France and the Netherlands Towards Their West Indian Territories, Thesis 142, Institut Universitaire de Hautes Études Internationales, University of Geneva, 1963. 211 pp.

Naipaul, V. S., *The Middle Passage,* London, Andre Deutsch, 1962. 232 pp.

Nembhard, Len S., *Jamaica the Awakening . . . ,* Kingston, The Jamaica Times Ltd., 1943.

Norris, Katrin, *Jamaica, The Search for an Identity,* London, Institute of Race Relations, Oxford University Press, 1962. 103 pp.

Oliver, Lord, *Jamaica, The Blessed Island,* London, Faber and Faber, 1936. 466 pp.

Palmer, R. W., *The Jamaican Economy,* New York, Praeger, 1969. 185 pp.

Parry, J. H., and Sherlock, P. M., *A Short History of the West Indies,* London, Macmillan, 1957. 315 pp.

Patterson, Orlando, *The Sociology of Slavery: an Analysis of the Origins, Development and Structure of Negro Slave Society in Jamaica,* London, MacGibbon and Kee, 1967. 310 pp.

Pendle, George, *History of Latin America,* Harmondsworth, Penguin Books, 1963. 249 pp.

Proudfoot, Mary, *Britain and the United States in the Caribbean,* London, Faber and Faber, 1954. 434 pp.

Roberts, G. W., *The Population of Jamaica,* London, Cambridge University Press, 1957. 356 pp.

Rubin, Vera, *Social and Cultural Pluralism in the Caribbean,* New York Academy of Science, (*The Annals,* Vol. 83, art. 5, pp. 761–916), New York, 1960.

———, ed., *Caribbean Studies: a Symposium,* Seattle, University of Washington Press, 1960. 124 pp.

Sherlock, P. M., *West Indies,* London, Thames and Hudson, 1966. 215 pp.

Simey, T. S., *Welfare and Planning in the West Indies,* Oxford, Clarendon Press, 1946. 267 pp.

Smith, M. G., *The Plural Society in the British West Indies,* Berkeley, University of California Press, 1965. 359 pp.

St. John Hamilton, B. L., *Problems of Administration in an*

Emergent Nation: a Case Study of Jamaica, New York, Praeger, 1964. 218 pp.

Veliz, C., *Latin America and the Caribbean–a Handbook,* London, Anthony Blond, 1968. 840 pp.

Wilgus, A. Curtis, ed., *The Caribbean: Its Hemispheric Role,* Gainsville, Florida, University of Florida Press, 1967. 202 pp.

Williams, Eric, *Capitalism and Slavery,* Chapel Hill, University of North Carolina Press, 1944. 285 pp.

ARTICLES AND PAMPHLETS

Adams, Nassau A., "Internal Migration in Jamaica: an Economic Analysis," *Social and Economic Studies,* Vol. 18, No. 2, June 1969, pp. 137–51.

Ahiram, A., "Income Distribution in Jamaica 1958," *Social and Economic Studies,* Vol. 13, No. 3, September 1964, pp. 333–70.

Alleyne, Mervin C., "Communication Between the Elite and the Masses," in Andic, F. M., and Mathews, T. C., *The Caribbean in Transition,* Puerto Rico, University of Puerto Rico, 1965, pp. 12–19.

Andic, F. M., and Mathews, T. C., eds., *The Caribbean in Transition,* (Papers on Social, Political and Economic Development, Second Caribbean Scholars' Conference, Mona, Jamaica, April 14–19, 1964), Puerto Rico, Institute of Caribbean Studies, University of Puerto Rico, 1965. 353 pp.

Anonymous, "Labour Conditions in the West Indies," *International Labour Review,* Vol. 44, December 1941, pp. 695–99.

———, "Labour Problems in the West Indies," *International Labour Review,* Vol. 37, April 1938, pp. 492–502.

———, "The Political Significance of Hugh Shearer–a Black Man," *Rising Star,* Vol. 10, No. 23, 1967, pp. 10–11.

———, "It's Not All Calypso," *Steel Labour,* April 1957, pp. 6–7.

———, New World Pamphlet, Kingston, Jamaica, New World Ltd., no date. 16 pp.

Ayearst, Morley, "A Note on Some Characteristics of West Indian Political Parties," *Social and Economic Studies,* Vol. 3, No. 2, September 1954, pp. 188–96.

Balogh, Thomas, "New Deal in Jamaica," *Venture,* June 1957, pp. 5–6.

Beckford, G. L. F., "The Growth of Major Tropical Export-Crop Industries," *Social and Economic Studies,* Vol. 13, No. 4, December 1964, pp. 413–30.

———, "Agricultural Development in 'Traditional' and 'Peasant' Economies," *Social and Economic Studies,* Vol. 18, No. 2, June 1966, pp. 151–61.

Black, Peter, "Community Violence and Jamaican Pop Music," *Sunday Gleaner,* June 11, 1967, p. 7.

Bobb, L., "The Federal Principle in the British West Indies," *Social and Economic Studies,* Vol. 15, No. 3, September 1966, pp. 239–65.

Bonaparte, Tony H., "The Influence of Culture on Business in a Pluralistic Society," *The American Journal of Economics and Sociology,* Vol. 28, No. 3, July 1969, pp. 285–600.

Boulding, K., "Social Dynamics in West Indian Society," *Social and Economic Studies,* Vol. 10, No. 1, March 1961, pp. 25–34.

Bowden, Alan, "Jamaica—a Stable Island," *New Commonwealth,* Vol. 43, August 1965, pp. 397–99.

Bradley, C. Paul, "Mass Parties in Jamaica: Structure and Organisation," *Social and Economic Studies,* Vol. 9, No. 4, December 1960, pp. 375–416.

Brewster, Havelock, "Wage, Price and Productivity Relations in Jamaica 1957–62," *Social and Economic Studies,* Vol. 17, No. 2, June 1968, pp. 107–32.

British Guiana Trades Union Council, *The Communist Martyr Makers,* Georgetown, Guyana, no date (1966?). 45 pp.

Cumper, G. E., "The Social Structure of Jamaica, BWI,"

Extra Mural Department, University of the West Indies, (Carribbean Affairs Service), 1948. 90 pp.

——, "A Comparison of Statistical Data on the Jamaican Labour Force, 1943–1961," *Social and Economic Studies,* Vol. 13, No. 4, December 1961, pp. 430–39.

——, ed., *Report of the Conference on Social Development in Jamaica,* (held at University College of the West Indies, July 1961), Jamaica Standing Committee on Social Services, Kingston, 1961. 181 pp.

——, "Labour and Development in the West Indies," *Social and Economic Studies,* Vol. 10, No. 3, September 1961, pp. 297–305; and Vol. 11, No. 1, March 1962, pp. 31–47.

Dalgleish, A., "Trade Unionism in the Caribbean," *Venture,* April 1957, pp. 4–5.

Dalley, F. W., "The Labour Position: the Trade Unions and Political Parties, Survey of the British Caribbean," *The Statist,* December 1956, pp. 31–32.

Daniel, George T., "Labor and Nationalism in the British Caribbean," *Annals of the American Academy of Political Science,* Vol. 310, March 1957, pp. 162–71.

Davenport, W., "The Family System of Jamaica," *Social and Economic Studies,* Vol. 10, No. 4, December 1961, pp. 420–54.

del Mar, Roland H., "Strategic Characteristics of the Caribbean," in Wilgus, A. Curtis, *The Caribbean: Its Hemispheric Role,* Gainsville, Florida, University of Florida Press, 1967, pp. 155–60.

Despres, Leo, "The Implications of Nationalist Politics in British Guiana for the Development of Cultural Theory," *American Anthropologist,* Vol. 66, No. 5, October 1964, pp. 1051–71.

Doge, Peter, "Comparative Racial Systems in the Greater Caribbean," *Social and Economic Studies,* Vol. 16, No. 3, September 1967, pp. 249–61.

Duke, James T., "Egalitarianism and Future Leaders in Jamaica," in Bell, Wendell, ed., *Democratic Revolution in the West Indies,* Cambridge, Mass., Schenkman Publishing, 1967, pp. 115–40.

Dyce, Osmond, "The Check-Off System in the Caribbean," *Free Labour World*, April 1962, pp. 130–31.

———, "Labour in the Caribbean," *Free Labour World*, December 1962, pp. 472–74.

Eaton, George, "Trade Union Development in Jamaica," *Caribbean Quarterly*, Vol. 8, No. 182, 1962, pp. 43–52.

Edwards, Adolph, "Social Status and Social Distance," *Sociology and Social Research*, (Los Angeles), Vol. 40, 1956, pp. 240–46.

———, "Color and Class in a Jamaican Market Town," *Sociology and Social Research*, (Los Angeles), Vol. 41, 1957, pp. 354–60.

Farley, Rawle, "Caribbean Industrial Relations," *Venture* 10, May 1958, pp. 3–4.

Faber, M., "A 'Swing' Analysis of the Jamaican Election of 1962," *Social and Economic Studies*, Vol. 13, No. 2, June 1964, pp. 302–10.

Feather, Victor, "Broadcast to the West Indies on British Trade Unionism," *Development and Welfare Bulletin*, No. 3, 1941, pp. 16–23.

Frucht, R., "A Caribbean Social Type: Neither 'Peasant' Nor 'Proletarian,'" *Social and Economic Studies*, Vol. 16, No. 3, September 1967, pp. 295–300.

Fry, Gerrard, "Jamaica: Democracy Planed with a Straight Bat," A Guardian Survey, *The Guardian*, July 28, 1965, p. 9.

Glass, Ruth, "Ashes of Discontent: Jamaica Today," *The Listener*, 67, February 1, 1962, pp. 209–11.

Gordon, William E., "Jamaica from Colony to State," *Contemporary Review*, Vol. 203, April 1963, pp. 187–91.

Hadley, C. V. D., "Personality Patterns, Social Class, and Aggression in the British West Indies," *Human Relations*, Vol. 2, No. 4, October 1949, pp. 349–62.

Hall, Marshall, "An Analysis of the Determinants of Money Wage Changes in Jamaica, 1958–1964," *Social and Economic Studies*, Vol. 17, No. 2, June 1968, pp. 133–46.

Hart, Richard, *What Is Socialism*, Socialist Party of Jamaica, Kingston (?), 1962. 24 pp.

Henry, Zin, *Background Lectures on Industrial Relations in the Caribbean*, Georgetown, British Guiana, Daily Chronicle Ltd., 1960. 43 pp.

Hirsch, G. P., "Jamaica–a Regional Approach," *Regional Studies*, Vol. 1, 1967, pp. 47–63.

Hoyt, Elizabeth E., "Voluntary Unemployment and Unemployability in Jamaica, with Special Reference to Standard of Living," *British Journal of Sociology* 11, June 1960, pp. 129–36.

Jacobs, H., "Unions and Parties," *The West Indian Review*, October 1, 1949, pp. 15–23.

Jefferson, Owen, "Some Aspects of the Post-War Economic Development of Jamaica," *New World Quarterly*, High Season, Vol. 3, No. 3, 1967, pp. 1–12.

Katzin, Margaret, "The Business of Higglering in Jamaica," *Social and Economic Studies*, Vol. 9, No. 3, September 1960, pp. 297–331.

Knowles, William H., "Supervision in the BWI–Source of Labor Unrest," *Industrial and Labor Relations Review*, Vol. 8, July 1955, pp. 572–80.

———, "Social Consequences of Economic Change in Jamaica," *The Annals of the American Political Science Association* 305, 1956, pp. 134–44.

———, "The British West Indies," in Galenson, Walter, ed., *Labor and Economic Development*, New York, Wiley and Sons, 1959, pp. 260–300.

Knox, Graham, "Political Change in Jamaica (1866–1906) and the Local Reaction to the Policies of the Crown Colony Government," in Andic, F. M., and Mathews, T. C., eds., *The Caribbean in Transition*, Puerto Rico, University of Puerto Rico, 1965, pp. 141–62.

Lamming, George, "The West Indian People," *New World Quarterly*, Croptime, Vol. 2, No. 2, pp. 63–74.

Lewis, W. Arthur, *Labour in the West Indies: the Birth of a Workers' Movement*, Fabian Publications, Research Series No. 44, London, Gollanz, 1939. 44 pp.

Markle, Gower, "Report of Labour Education Survey," in Farley, Rawle, ed., *Labour Education in the British Carib-*

bean, Demerara, British Guiana, Daily Chronicle Ltd., 1960, pp. 58–74.

Marquand, Hilary, *Text of Two Broadcasts Over Radio Demerara, Georgetown, British Guiana, September 23 and 30, 1954, on Industrial Relations,* mimeo, 1954.

Mau, James A., "The Threatening Masses: Myth or Reality," in Andic, F. M., and Mathews, T. C., eds., *The Caribbean in Transition,* Puerto Rico, University of Puerto Rico, 1965, pp. 258–70.

———, "Images of Jamaica's Future," in Bell, Wendell, *Democratic Revolution in the West Indies,* Cambridge, Mass., Schenkman Publishing, 1967, pp. 197–224.

McGlashan, C., "The Two Jamaicas," *The Observer,* November 23, 1965, p. 25.

McKenzie, H. I., "The Plural Society Debate, Some Comments on a Recent Contribution," *Social and Economic Studies,* Vol. 15, No. 1, March 1966, pp. 53–60.

Nettleford, Rex, "National Identity and Attitudes to Race in Jamaica," *Race,* July 1965, pp. 59–72.

Palmer, R. W., "Financing Corporate Investment in Jamaica," *Social and Economic Studies,* Vol. 16, No. 3, September 1967, pp. 301–7.

Patterson, Orlando H., "Outside History–Jamaica Today," *New Left Review,* May–June 1965, pp. 35–43.

Phelps, O. W., "Rise of the Labour Movement in Jamaica," *Social and Economic Studies,* Vol. 9, No. 4, December 1960, pp. 418–72.

Rickards, Colin, and Henriques, Fernando, "The English Speaking Caribbean," in Veliz, G., *Latin America and the Caribbean–a Handbook,* Anthony Blond, 1968, pp. 324–51.

Sherlock, P. M., "The Constitution of Jamaica," in Institut International des Civilisations Différentes: *The Constitutions and Administrative Institutions of the New States,* Paris, 1965, pp. 497–506.

Singer, Philip, and Aranetta, Enrique, "Hinduization and Creolization in Guyana: the Plural Society and Basic Personality," *Social and Economic Studies,* Vol. 16, No. 3, September 1967, pp. 221–36.

Smith, M. G., "Educational and Occupational Choice in Rural Jamaica," *Social and Economic Studies,* Vol. 9, No. 3, September 1960, pp. 332–54.

Smith, R. T., "Review of Social and Cultural Pluralism in the Caribbean," *American Anthropologist,* Vol. 63, No. 1, February 1961, pp. 143–58.

Springer, Hugh, "Education for Trade Unionists," in Farley, Rawle, ed., *Labour Education in the British Caribbean,* Demerara, British Guiana, Daily Chronicle Ltd., 1961, pp. 13–18.

Thorne, Alfred P., "Size, Structure and Growth of the Economy of Jamaica," Supplement to *Social and Economic Studies,* Vol. 4, No. 4, December 1955. 112 pp.

Tidrick, Gene, "Some Aspects of Jamaican Emigration to the United Kingdom, 1953–1962," *Social and Economic Studies,* Vol. 15, No. 1, March 1966, pp. 22–39.

Tomney, Frank, "Labour Unity in the West Indies," *New Commonwealth,* October 1960, pp. 634–36.

Voskuil, W. H., "Mineral Resources and Industries of the Caribbean Area," in Wilgus, Curtis, *The Caribbean: Natural Resources,* Gainsville, Florida, University of Florida Press, 1961. 315 pp.

Vroom, Leonard, "The Social Differentation of Commerce in Jamaica," *American Sociology Review,* Vol. 19, April 1954, pp. 115–25.

Wilson, D. G., "Bi-Lingualism," *Caribbean Quarterly,* Vol. 15, No. 1, March 1969, pp. 45–48.

BRITISH AND USA TRADE UNIONS AND INTERNATIONAL AFFAIRS

SOURCES

British

Trades Union Congress:

Annual Congress: *Report of Proceedings,* 1926–67.

Trade Unionists Stand Firm for Peace, London, 1950. 23 pp.

Russia 1952: the Complete Report of Twelve British Trade Unionists in the USSR, London, 1952. 23 pp.

The TUC and Communism, London, 1955. 11 pp.

Rules and Standing Orders of Trades Union Congress, London, 1962. 15 pp.

The ABC of the TUC, London, 1964. 24 pp.

Labour (official monthly journal), 1938–67.

Tewson, Vincent, "Trade Unionism in the Colonies," Statement at the British Labour Party Commonwealth Conference, 1957, mimeo. 57 pp.

International Labour Office: *The Trade Union Situation in the United Kingdom, Report of a Mission from the International Labour Office,* Geneva, International Labour Office, 1961. 123 pp.

Gallup Poll: *Trades Unions and the Public in 1964,* London, The Gallup Poll, 1964. 20 pp.

Conservative Party Political Centre: *Trades Unions and International Activities,* London, 1963. 16 pp.

United States

American Federation of Labor: Executive Council, *Toward a Reappraisal of American Foreign Policy and Program of Action,* Washington, D.C., 1954. 80 pp.

Congress of Industrial Organizations: *Final Proceedings of the Constitutional Convention of the CIO,* (annual), 1938–55.

American Federation of Labor and Congress of Industrial Organizations:

Proceedings of the Constitutional Convention, (bi-annual), 1955–67.

For World Peace and Freedom, New York, AFL-CIO World Conference, 1960.

Union Political Activity Spans 230 Years of US History, Washington, D.C., AFL-CIO Publication No. 106, July 1960, n.p.

Meany, George, *Power for What?*, Washington, D.C., AFL-CIO Publication No. 97, 1962. 16 pp.

Why Unions?, Washington, D.C., AFL-CIO Publication No. 41, 1962. 14 pp.

AFL-CIO—The Hands That Build America, The New York Times, Special Supplement, Section 11, November 17, 1963. 43 pp.

American Federationist, (monthly), 1950–66.

Free Trade Union News, (monthly), 1958–68.

International Affairs Bulletin, 1955, 1956.

United Steelworks of America:

Proceedings of the Constitutional Convention, (bi-annual), 1942–68.

Steel Labor, (official monthly journal), 1939–67.

McDonald, David J., *Labor's Long-Range Objectives,* an address before American Management Association, General Conference, San Francisco, Calif., January 25, 1956, Pittsburgh, 1956. 10 pp.

International Labour Office: *The Trade Union Situation in the United States, Report of a Mission from the International Labour Office,* Geneva, International Labour Office, 1960. 148 pp.

United States Government:

Commission on Foreign Economic Policy, report to the President and Congress, Washington, D.C., 1954. 65 pp.

Survey of the Alliance for Progress, Labor Policies and Programs, (a study prepared at the request of the Subcommittee on American Republics Affairs by the

Staff of the Committee on Foreign Relations United States Senate together with a report of the Comptroller General), Washington, D.C., 90th Congress, 2nd Session, US Government Printing Office, July 15, 1968. 86 pp.

American Institute for Free Labor Development: *The Workers of America in a Pioneering Effort of Human Progress*, Washington, D.C., 1965, n.p.

American Institute of Public Opinion: *Public Opinion News Service*, Princeton, (irregular), 1963–64.

BOOKS

Allen, V. L., *Trade Unions Leadership, Based on a Study of Arthur Deakin*, London, Longmans, Green and Co., 1957. 336 pp.

———, *Trade Unions and the Government*, London, Longmans, Green and Co., 1960. 326 pp.

Citrine, W. (Lord), *Men and Work, an Autobiography*, London, Hutchinson, 1964. 384 pp.

Davies, Ernest, *American Labour, the Story of the American Labour Movement*, London, Allen and Unwin, 1943. 100 pp.

Hamilton, William C., *The Development of Foreign Policy Attitudes in Certain American Pressure Groups*, unpublished Ph.D. dissertation, Yale University, 1955.

Hardman, J. B. S., ed., *American Labor Dynamics in the Light of Post War Developments*, New York, Harcourt Brace, 1928. 431 pp.

Hardy, Margaret, *The Influence of Organized Labor on the Foreign Policy of the United States*, Liège, doctoral thesis presented at Graduate Institute of International Studies, Geneva, 1936. 258 pp.

Hennessy, Bernard C., *British Trade Unions and International Affairs, 1945–1953*, unpublished dissertation, University of Wisconsin, 1955.

Kellog, Paul V., and Gleason, Arthur, *British Labor and the War*, New York, Boni and Leveright, 1919. 504 pp.

Kelly, George, and Beachler, Edwin, *Man of Steel, the Story of David J. McDonald*, Pittsburgh, North American Book Co., 1954. 181 pp.

Lester, Richard, *As Unions Mature: an Analysis of the Evolution of American Unionism*, Princeton, N.J., 1958. 171 pp.

Mackenzie, Robert, *British Political Parties: the Distribution of Power Within the Conservative and Labour Parties*, 2nd ed., London, Heinemann, 1963. 694 pp.

Morris, George, *CIA and American Labor: the Subversion of the AFL-CIO Foreign Policy*, New York, International Publishers, 1967. 159 pp.

Pelling, H., *A History of British Trade Unionism*, Harmondsworth, Penguin Books, 1963. 286 pp.

Perlman, Selig, *A Theory of the Labor Movement*, New York, A. M. Kelly, 1949. 321 pp.

Peterson, Florence, *American Labor Unions*, rev. ed., New York, Harper, 1952. 270 pp.

Political and Economic Planning, *British Trade Unionism*, London, 1948. 194 pp.

Roberts, Bryn, *American Labour Split and Allied Unity*, London, Lawrence and Wishart Ltd., 1943. 198 pp.

Sampson, Anthony, *Anatomy of Britain*, London, Hodder and Stoughton, 1962. 662 pp.

Sweeney, Vincent D., *United Steelworkers of America, Twenty Years Later, 1936–56*, Pittsburgh, 1956. 239 pp.

Ulman, Lloyd, *The Government of the Steel Workers' Union*, New York, John Wiley, 1962. 200 pp.

Webb, Sidney and Beatrice, *The History of Trade Unionism*, rev. ed., London, Longmans, Green and Co., 1920. 784 pp.

Wigham, Eric, *What's Wrong with the Unions*, Harmondsworth, Penguin Books, 1961. 233 pp.

Windmuller, John P., *American Labor and the International Labor Movement, 1940–1953*, Ithaca, N.Y., Cornell University Press. 243 pp.

ARTICLES AND PAMPHLETS

Anderson, J. R. L., "The Power of American Trade Unions Abroad," *World Review*, November 1948, pp. 37–41.

Berger, Henry, "American Labor Overseas," *The Nation*, January 16, 1967, pp. 80–84.

Brown, G. T., "Why Should We Be Interested in International Affairs," *American Federationist*, Vol. 64, March 1967, pp. 12–15.

Carlton, F. T., "Labor Policies for the Struggle with Soviet Communism," *American Journal of Economics*, Vol. 16, April 1959, pp. 277–84.

Citrine, W. (Sir), "World Wide Growth of Trade Unions," *Labour*, Vol. 1, August 12, 1939, pp. 6–9.

Cole, John, "The Non-Philosophy of the Unions," *New Society*, August 29, 1963, pp. 20–22.

Davies, D. I., "The Politics of the TUC's Colonial Policy," *Political Quarterly*, Vol. 35, No. 1, January–March 1964, pp. 23–34.

Davies, Ernest, "Anglo-American Trade Union Cooperation," *Political Quarterly*, Vol. 14, No. 1, January 1943, pp. 60–70.

Deakin, Arthur, "The International Trade Union Movement," *International Affairs*, Vol. XXVI, No. 2, April 1950, pp. 167–71.

Edelstein, J. David, "Democracy in a National Union: The British AEU," *Industrial Relations*, Vol. 4, No. 3, May 1965, pp. 105–25.

Farrel, Barry, "Labor Leaders, Tough, Remote—or Feuding," *Life*, Vol. 61, No. 9, August 26, 1966, pp. 30–36.

Flanders, Allan, "Trade Union Education in Great Britain," in Farley, Rawle, *Labour Education in the British Caribbean*, Demerara, British Guiana, Daily Chronicle Ltd., 1960, pp. 23–29.

Galenson, Walter, "The Unionization of the American Steel Industry," *International Review of Social History*, Vol. 1, Part 1, 1956, pp. 9–40.

Heaps, D., "Union Participation in Foreign Aid Programs," *Industrial and Labor Relations Review,* Vol. 9, No. 1, October 1955, pp. 100–8.

Hennessy, Bernard, "Internationalism in British Labor and Socialist Movements, 1864–1945," unpublished seminar paper on International Relations, University of Wisconsin, 1952.

Henser, P., "Labor and Foreign Affairs," *American Federationist,* Vol. 68, April 1961, pp. 20–23.

Hutchinson, J., "Labour and Politics in America," *Political Quarterly,* 33, April 1962, pp. 138–49.

Kerr, Clark, *Unions and Union Leaders of Their Own Choosing,* Santa Barbara, Center for the Study of Democratic Institutions, 1957. 23 pp.

Kurzman, Dan, "Lovestone's Cold War," *New Republic,* June 25, 1966, pp. 17–22.

La Polombora, J. G., "Pressure, Propaganda and Political Action in the Elections of 1950—Techniques Used by Labor," *Journal of Political Science,* Vol. 14, May 1952, pp. 313–21.

Lasswell, Harold, "Foreign Influences on American Labor," in Hardman, J. B. S. and associates, *American Labor Dynamics,* Harcourt Brace, New York, 1928, pp. 360–66.

Lens, Sydney, "American Labor Abroad," *The Nation,* July 5, 1965, pp. 10–16.

———, "Labor Between Bread and Revolution," *The Nation,* September 19, 1966, pp. 241–52.

McCallister, Frank, "Labour Education in the United States," in Farley, Rawle, ed., *Labour Education in the British Caribbean,* Demerara, British Guiana, Daily Chronicle Ltd., pp. 30–38.

Meany, George, "What America Must Do," *American Federationist,* Vol. 61, No. 9, September 1954, pp. 17–19.

Murray, Philip, "Labor in International Relations," *World Affairs,* Vol. 106, June 1943, pp. 95–97.

Randolph, A. Philip, "Labor's Stake in an Emerging New Africa," *American Federationist,* Vol. 64, No. 10, October 1957, pp. 20–21.

Reuther, Walter, "First Things First," Center for the Study of Democratic Institutions, Santa Barbara, 1964. 12 pp.

Riche, Martha F., "The American Institute for Free Labor Development," *Monthly Labor Review*, Vol. 88, No. 9, September 1965, pp. 1049–55.

Tewson, Vincent, "Trade Unions and the Colonies," *New Commonwealth*, 27, April 1, 1954, pp. 317–18.

Ulman, Lloyd, "Influences of the Economic Environment on the Structure of the Steel Workers' Union," *Proceedings of the 14th Annual Industrial Relations Research Association*, New York, 1961, pp. 227–37.

Windmuller, John P., "Foreign Affairs and the AFL-CIO," *Industrial and Labor Relations Review*, 9, April 1956, pp. 419–32.

———, "Labor: a Partner in American Foreign Policy," *Annals of the American Academy of Political Science*, Vol. 350, November 1963, pp. 104–14.

———, "The Foreign Policy Conflict in American Labor," *Political Science Quarterly*, Vol. 82, No. 2, June 1967, pp. 205–34.

Windrich, Elaine, "British Labour's Foreign Policy," *World Affairs Interpreter*, 21, July 1950. 169 pp.

Woddis, Jack, "The Mask Is Off," London, Thames Publications, 1954. 48 pp.

SOURCES

British Government:

Colonial Office:

Labour Supervision in the Colonial Empire, 1937–1943, London, Colonial Office Pamphlet No. 185, 1943.

Labour Administration in Colonial Territories, 1944–1950, London, 1951.

Central Office of Information:

Labour in the United Kingdom Dependencies, London, Reference Division, (RFP 3317), 1956.

Labour News, Background to News from the Colonies, London, No. XXX, December 31, 1943.

United States Government:

Bureau of Labor Statistics: *Directory of National and International Labour Unions,* Washington, D.C., 1961.

Office of International Labor Affairs:

Directory of Labor Organizations, Washington, D.C., 1956–59, (looseleaf).

Public Services International: an international Labor Study, Washington, D.C., 1962. 246 pp.

The International Metalworkers' Federation, Washington, D.C., 1959. 192 pp.

International Labour Office:

Yearbook of Labour Statistics, Geneva, (annual), 1949–68.

International Labour Conference: Record of Proceedings, (annual), Geneva, 1938–1967.

International Confederation of Free Trade Unions:

Annual Report of Activities and Proceedings of Congress, 1951, 1953, 1955, 1957, 1959, 1962, 1965, 1969.

Economic and Social Bulletin, (bi-monthly), Brussels, 1958–68.

Information Bulletin, 1955.

Free Labour World, (monthly), Brussels, 1958–68.

Glossary of Trade Union Terms, Brussels, 1964. 156 pp.

Inter-American Regional Organisation of the ICFTU (ORIT): *Inter-American Labor Bulletin*, (monthly), Mexico City, 1960–66.

World Federation of Trade Unions:

Report of the World Congress of Trade Unions, 1945, London, 1945.

Report of the Conference-Congress, 1945, Paris, 1945.

Report of Activities, 1945–1949, 1949.

Proceedings and Report of Activities, 1953, 1957, 1961, 1965.

International Metalworkers' Federation:

Metal, (monthly), Mexico City, 1964–68.

Documents of the IMF Regional Conference on Metalworkers' Problems in Latin America and the Caribbean, Los Caracas, Venezuela, 1967.

International Union of Food, Drink and Tobacco Workers' Associations:

News Letter, 1935–39.

News Bulletin, (monthly), Geneva, 1950–68.

International Federation of Plantation and Agricultural Workers:

Snips, (monthly news bulletin), Geneva, 1961–69.

Caribbean Labour Congress:

Official Report of Barbados Conference, September 17–27, 1945, Barbados, Advocate Co. Ltd., 1945. 66 pp.

Second Caribbean Labour Congress Report, September 2–9, 1947, Kingston, 1947, (no page no.).

Caribbean Labour Congress: Unpublished Documents in Hart, Richard, ed., *Collection of Documents on the History of the Caribbean Labour Congress*, deposited March 1967, Institute of Jamaica, Kingston.

Secretariat Report to 1947 Congress, 1947, (no page no.).

Letter to Members, November 14, 1952.

Caribbean Area Division of the Inter-American Regional Organisation of the ICFTU, (CADORIT):

Report of the Second Conference, Port of Spain, Trinidad, April 6–8, 1955.

Information Bulletin, 1954–56, December 1957–January 1958.

Caribbean Congress of Labour:

Report of the Founding Conference of the Caribbean Congress of Labour, St. Georges, Grenada, West Indies, September 14 and 15, 1960, Barbados, November, 1960, mimeo. 38 pp.

Reports of the Conferences of Caribbean Congress of Labour, (tri-annual), 1963 and 1966.

Minutes of Meeting of Caribbean Congress of Labour Administrative Committee, January 15–16, 1962, (no page nos.), unpublished.

Caribbean Labour, (bi-monthly, monthly), Port of Spain, Trinidad, 1960–68.

Newsletter, (fortnightly), October 1963–.

Caribbean Commission: Williams, Eric, ed., and Deputy Chairman of Research Council, *Digest of Industrial Legislation in the Caribbean,* Port of Spain, Trinidad, The Caribbean Commission 1952, mimeo. 83 pp.

North Atlantic Treaty Organisation: *The Trade Unions and NATO,* Paris, NATO, Information Division, 1957. 41 pp.

British Guiana Trades Union Council: *The Communist Martyr Makers,* Georgetown, British Guiana, no date (1965?). 45 pp.

BOOKS

Alexander, R. J., *Organized Labor in Latin America,* New York, The Free Press, 1965. 274 pp.

Aronson, Robert L., and Windmuller, John P., *Labor, Management and Economic Growth,* (Proceedings of a Conference on Human Resources and Labor Relations in Underdeveloped Countries), Ithaca, N.Y., The Institute of International Industrial and Labor Relations, Cornell University, mimeo. 251 pp.

Barkin, Soloman, and others, eds., *International Labor,* New York, Harper and Row, 1967. 278 pp.

Beever, Colin R., *European Unity and the Trade Union Movements,* Leyden, A. W. Sijthoff, 1960. 304 pp.

Costo, Ronald D., *The Role of the Trade Union in Developing Countries: a Study on India, Pakistan and Ceylon,* Havana, Nivello, 1963. 182 pp.

Davies, Joan, *African Trade Unions,* Harmondsworth, Penguin African Library, Penguin Books Ltd., 1966. 255 pp.

Foster, W. Z., *History of the Three Internationals,* New York, International Publishers, 1955. 580 pp.

Galenson, Walter, ed., *Comparative Labor Movements,* New York, Prentice Hall, 1952. 599 pp.

———, *Labor and Economic Development,* New York, Wiley and Sons, 1959. 304 pp.

Galenson, Walter, and Lipset, Seymour Martin, eds., *Labor and Trade Unionism: an Interdisciplinary Reader,* New York, Wiley and Sons, 1960. 379 pp.

Ghosh, Subratesh, *Trade Unionism in the Underdeveloped Countries,* Calcutta, Bookland, 1960. 410 pp.

Kassalow, Everett M., ed., *National Labor Movements in the Postwar World,* Chicago, Northwestern University Press, 1963. 256 pp.

Lodge, George Cabot, *Spearheads of Democracy: Labor in the Developing Countries,* Harper and Row, 1962. 249 pp.

Lorwin, Lewis L., *Labor and Internationalism,* New York, Macmillan, 1929. 682 pp.

———, *The International Labor Movement,* New York, Harper and Row, 1953. 361 pp.

Mark, Francis, *The History of the Barbados Workers' Union,* Barbados, The Barbados Workers' Union, no date (1962?). 168 pp.

Millen, Bruce H., *The Political Role of Labor in Developing Countries,* Washington, Brookings Institute, 1963. 148 pp.

Price, J., *The International Labour Movement,* London, Oxford University Press, 1945. 237 pp.

Reiser, Pedro, *L'Organisation Régionale Interaméricaine des Travailleurs (ORIT) de la Confédération Internationale des Syndicates Libres (CISL),* Droz, doctoral thesis presented at Graduate Institute of International Studies, Geneva, 1962. 268 pp.

Roberts, B. C., *Trade Unions in a Free Society*, (2nd ed.), London, Hutchinson, 1962. 206 pp.

———, *Labour in the Tropical Commonwealth*, London, G. Bell, 1964. 426 pp.

Romualdi, Serafino, *Presidents and Peons: Recollections of a Labor Ambassador in Latin America*, New York, Funk and Wagnalls, 1968. 524 pp.

Sturmthal, Adolf, *The Tragedy of European Labour—1918–1939*, London, Gollancz, 1944. 288 pp.

Sufrin, Sidney C., *Unions in Emerging Societies—Frustration and Politics*, Ithaca, N.Y., Syracuse University Press, 1964. 124 pp.

Zack, Arnold, *Labor Training in Developing Countries: a Challenge in Responsible Democracy*, New York, Praeger, 1964. 189 pp.

ARTICLES AND PAMPHLETS

Alexander, R. J., "Labor and Inter-American Relations," *Annals of the American Academy of Political Science*, Vol. 334, March 1961, pp. 41–53.

Allen, V. L., "The Study of African Trade Unionism," *The Journal of Modern African Studies*, Vol. 7, No. 2, July 1969, pp. 289–307.

Anonymous, "Multinational Corporations and Labour Relations," *ICFTU Economic and Social Bulletin*, Vol. XVII, March–April 1969, pp. 2–8.

Barbash, Jack, "International Labor Confederations (CIT, CTAL, WFTU) in Latin America," *Monthly Labor Review*, 66, May 1948, pp. 499–503; and 67, August 1948, pp. 147–51.

Benedict, Daniel, "Trade Union Education and Organisation—the International Content," in Farley, Rawle, ed., *Labour Education in the British Caribbean*, Demerara, British Guiana, Daily Chronicle Ltd., 1960. pp. 51–55.

Bowen, Walter, *Colonial Trade Unions*, Fabian Research Series No. 167, London, Fabian Publications Ltd., 1954. 25 pp.

Braithwaite, Lloyd, "Federal Association in Institutions in the West Indies," *Social and Economic Studies,* Vol. 6, No. 2, June 1957, pp. 286–312.

Braunthal, A., "Economic and Social Aspects of International Trade Union Work," *Annals of the American Academy of Political Science,* Vol. X. March 1957, pp. 21–30.

Collins, H., "Karl Marx—the International and the British Trade Union Movement," *Science and Society,* Vol. 26, Fall 1962, pp. 400–21.

Couzens, A. H., "Colonial Trade Unions," *Corona,* Vol. II, No. 7, July 1950, pp. 259–61.

Chamberlain, Neil, "Some Reflections on Collective Bargaining," in Farley, Rawle, ed., *Labour Education in the British Caribbean,* Demerara, British Guiana, Daily Chronicle Ltd., 1960, pp. 48–50.

Doherty, William C., Jr., "AIFLD and Latin Labor Building a Modern Society." *AFL-CIO Free Trade Unions News,* Vol. 21, July 31, 1966.

Farley, Rawle, "Caribbean Labour Comes of Age," *Free Labour World,* No. 94, April 1958, pp. 29–34.

Fischer, Georges, "Syndicalisme et décolonisation," *Présence Africaine,* Vol. 6–7, Nos. 34–35, octobre 1960–janvier 1961, pp. 17–61.

Friedland, William H., *Unions and Industrial Relations in Underdeveloped Countries,* Ithaca, N.Y., Cornell University Press, State School of Industrial and Labor Relations Bulletin 47, January 1963. 59 pp.

Hart, Richard, "Introduction to the History of Caribbean Labour Congress," in *Collection of Documents on the History of the Caribbean Labour Congress,* deposited March 1967, Institute of Jamaica, Kingston.

Hawkins, Carrol, "The ORIT and the CLASC; a Case of Conflicting Perspectives," *Inter-American Economic Affairs,* Vol. 20, No. 3, Winter 1966, pp. 39–53.

Kwavnick, David, "Pressure Group Demands and the Struggle for Organizational Status: the Case of Organized Labor in Canada," *Canadian Journal of Political Science,* Vol. 3, No. 1, March 1970, pp. 54–72.

Jacobson, Harold K., "Labor, the UN and the Cold War," *International Organization*, Vol. 11, Winter 1957, pp. 55–87.

———, "Ventures in Polity Shaping: External Assistance to Labour Movements in Developing Countries," in Cox, R. W., ed., *International Organisation: World Politics Studies in Economic and Social Agencies*, London, Macmillan, 1959, pp. 195–205.

Kassalow, Everett M., ed., "Trade Unionism in the Development Process in the New Nations: a Comparative View," *International Labor*, New York, Harper and Row, 1967, pp. 62–80.

Langley, David, "The Colonization of the International Trade Union Movement," *New Politics*, 5, Winter 1966, pp. 52–56.

Lichtblau, G. E., "The Communist Labor Offensive in Former Colonial Countries," *Industrial and Labor Relations Review*, Vol. 15, No. 3, April 1961, pp. 376–401.

Lipset, Seymour Martin, and Trow, Martin, "Reference Group Theory and Trade Union Wage Policy," in M. Komarovsky, ed., *Common Frontiers of Social Science*, Glencoe, The Free Press, 1957, pp. 391–411.

Lipset, Seymour Martin, "The Political Process in Trade Unions," in Galenson, Walter, and Lipset, Seymour Martin, eds., *Labor and Trade Unionism: an Interdisciplinary Reader*, New York, Wiley and Sons, 1960, pp. 217–42.

———, "Trade Unions and Social Structure: I and II," Part I, *Industrial Relations*, (University of California), Vol. 1, No. 1, October 1961, pp. 75–89; Part II, Vol. 1, No. 2, February 1962, pp. 89–110.

Lodge, George Cabot, "Labor's Role in Newly Developing Countries," *Foreign Affairs*, 37, No. 4, July 1959, pp. 660–71.

Mehta, Askaka, "The Mediating Role of the Trade Unions in Underdeveloped Countries," *Economic Development and Cultural Change*, Vol. VI, No. 1, October 1957, pp. 16–23.

Neufeld, Maurice, *The Inevitability of Political Unionism in Underdeveloped Countries: Italy the Exemplar*, Ithaca, N.Y., Cornell University, New York State School of Industrial Relations Reprint Series No. 90, pp. 363–86.

Padmore, George, *The Voice of Coloured Labour,* (reports of colonial delegates to World Trade Union Conference, 1945), Manchester, Pan African Service Ltd. 55 pp.

Roberts, B. C., "Labour Relations in (Commonwealth) Overseas Territories," *Political Quarterly,* Vol. 28, No. 4, October–December 1957, pp. 390–404.

Romualdi, Serafino, "Labor and Democracy in Latin America," *Foreign Affairs,* Vol. 25, April 1947, pp. 477–89.

———, "For Freedom and Democracy," *American Federationist,* Vol. 57, No. 6, June 1950, pp. 24–26.

———, "ORIT at the Crossroads," *American Federationist,* Vol. 65, No. 5, May 1958, pp. 22–23.

Rottenberg, Simon, "Labour Relations in an Underdeveloped Economy," *Economic Development and Cultural Change,* Vol. 1, No. 1, December 1952, pp. 250–60.

———, "Income and Leisure in an Underdeveloped Economy," *Journal of Political Economy,* (University of Chicago), Vol. LX, No. 2, April 1952, pp. 3–24.

Sturmthal, Adolf, "International Labor Problems," *World Politics,* Vol. 8, April 1956, pp. 441–53.

———, "Unions and Economic Development," *Economic Development and Cultural Change,* Vol. VIII, No. 2, January 1960, pp. 199–205.

Summerfield, P., "Regional Organisations of Trade Unions in the Caribbean," *New World Quarterly,* Vol. 4, No. 4, Cropover, 1968, pp. 3–6.

Windmuller, John P., "Leadership and Administration in the ICFTU," *British Journal of Industrial Relations,* Vol. 1, No. 2, June 1963, pp. 147–69.

———, "External Influences on Labor Organizations in Underdeveloped Countries," *Industrial and Labor Relations Review,* Vol. 16, No. 4, July 1963, pp. 559–73.

———, *Labor Internationals,* Ithaca, N.Y., State School of Industrial and Labor Relations 1969. 70 pp.

———, "International Trade Union Organizations: Structure, Functions, Limitations," in Barkin, Solomon, ed., *International Labor,* New York, Harper and Row, 1967, pp. 81–105.

GENERAL AND THEORETICAL

BOOKS

Aitken, Thomas, Jr., *A Foreign Policy for American Business*, New York, Harper and Row, 1962. 159 pp.

Almond, Gabriel A., and Coleman, J. S., eds., *The Politics of Developing Areas*, Princeton, Princeton University Press, 1960. 519 pp.

Apter, David E., *The Politics of Modernization*, Chicago, University of Chicago Press, 1965. 481 pp.

Benedict, Ruth, *Patterns of Culture*, Boston-New York, Houghton Mifflin, 1934, (reprinted 1961). 290 pp.

Blau, Peter, and Scott, William R., *Formal Organizations: a Comparative Approach*, London, Routledge and Kegan Paul, 1963. 312 pp.

Borkenau, France, *Socialism, National or International*, G. Routledge, 1942. 172 pp.

Brannen, T. R., and Hodgson, F. X., *Overseas Management*, New York, McGraw Hill, 1965. 238 pp.

Burns, A., *The Colonial Civil Servant*, London, George Allen and Unwin, 1949. 339 pp.

Carr, E. H., *Nationalism and After*, London, Macmillan, 1945. 74 pp.

Cleaver, Eldridge, *Soul on Ice*, selected essays, London, Jonathan Cape, 1968. 164 pp.

Cosen, Lewis, and Rosenberg, Bernard, eds., *Sociological Theory*, New York, Macmillan, 1957. 574 pp.

Cox, R. W., *International Organisation: World Politics, Studies in Economic and Social Agencies*, London, Macmillan, 1969. 319 pp.

Directory of Non-Governmental European Organisations Offering Assistance in the Developing Countries, Centre for Labour and Social Studies, Rome, 1964. 202 pp.

Duverger, M., *Méthodes des Sciences Sociales*, Paris, Presses Universitaire de France, 1961. 478 pp.

Easton, David, *The Political System*, New York, Alfred A. Knopf, 1953. 320 pp.

Erikson, Erik H., *Young Man Luther, a Study in Psychoanalysis and History*, London, Faber and Faber, 1958. 279 pp.

Eisenstadt, S. N., ed., *Max Weber: On Charisma and Institution Building–Selected Papers*, Chicago, University of Chicago Press, 1968. 313 pp.

Fagerberg, Elliot P., *The "Anciens Combattants" and French Foreign Policy*, Geneva, (no publisher), doctoral thesis for the Graduate Institute of International Studies, 1966. 353 pp.

Fanon, Frantz, *The Wretched of the Earth*, Harmondsworth, Penguin Books, 1967. 255 pp.

Fayerweather, John, *The Executive Overseas, Administrative Attitudes and Relationships in a Foreign Culture*, Ithaca, N.Y., Syracuse University Press, 1959. 194 pp.

Frankel, Joseph, *The Making of Foreign Policy*, London, Oxford University Press, 1963. 231 pp.

———, *International Relations*, London, Oxford University Press, 1964. 227 pp.

Furnivall, J. S., *Colonial Policy and Practice, a Comparative Study of Burma and Netherlands India*, Cambridge, Cambridge University Press, 1948. 568 pp.

Galbraith, J. K., *The New Industrial State*, London, Hamish Hamilton, 1967. 427 pp.

Haas, Ernst B., *The Uniting of Europe*, London, Stevens, 1958. 552 pp.

———, *Beyond the Nation-State, Functionalism and International Organization*, Stanford, Stanford University Press, 1964. 595 pp.

Haas, Ernst B., and Whiting, Allen S., *Dynamics of International Relations*, New York, McGraw Hill, 1956. 557 pp.

Hall, Edward T., *The Silent Language*, New York, Doubleday, 1959. 240 pp.

Herskovits, Melville, *Man and His Works: the Science of Cultural Anthropology*, New York, Knopf, 1948. 678 pp.

———, *The Human Factor in Changing Africa*, London, Routledge and Kegan Paul, 1962. 500 pp.

Hoggart, Richard, *The Uses of Literacy*, Harmondsworth, Penguin Books, 1958. 384 pp.

Kapp, K. William, *Toward a Science of Man in Society*, The Hague, Martinus Nijhoff, 1961. 211 pp.

Katz, Daniel, and Kahn, Robert, *The Social Psychology of Organizations*, New York, Wiley and Sons, 1966. 498 pp.

Kelman, Herbert C., ed., *International Behaviour*, New York, Holt, Rinehart, 1966. 619 pp.

Kerr, Clark, and others, *Industrialism and Industrial Man*, Cambridge, Mass., Harvard University Press, 1960. 331 pp.

Krech, D., and Crutchfield, R. S., *Theory and Problems of Social Psychology*, New York, McGraw Hill, 1948. 639 pp.

Lador-Lederer, J., *International Non-Governmental Organisations and Economic Entities*, Leyden, A. W. Sythoff, 1963. 403 pp.

Lasswell, Harold D., *World Politics Faces Economics*, New York, McGraw Hill, 1945. 108 pp.

Lévi-Strauss, Claude, *Anthropologie Structurale*, Paris, Plon, 1958. 447 pp.

Likert, Rensis, and Hayes, Samuel P., eds., *Some Applications of Behavioural Research*, Paris, UNESCO, 1951. 333 pp.

Meyer, Adolph, *Commonsense Psychiatry: Fifty-two Selected Papers Edited by Alfred Lief*, New York, McGraw Hill, 1948. 577 pp.

Meynaud, Jean, *Les groupes de pression internationaux*, Lausanne, (no publisher), 1961. 560 pp.

Morgenthau, Hans, *Politics Among Nations*, 3rd ed., New York, Knopf, 1961. 630 pp.

Morgenstern, Oskar, *On Accuracy of Economic Observations*, 2nd ed., Princeton, N.J., Princeton University Press, 1963. 322 pp.

Northrop, Filmer S. C., and Livingston, Helen H., eds., *Cross-Cultural Understanding: Epistemology in Anthropology*, 1964. 396 pp.

Olivier, Sydney H., *White Capital and Coloured Labour*, edited, rewritten, and revised by Woolf, L., and London, V., 1929. 348 pp.

Ortega y Gasset, José, *Man and Crises*, London, Allen and Unwin, 1959. 217 pp.

Pickard, Bertram, *The Greater United Nations: an Essay Concerning the Place and Significance of International Nongovernmental Organizations*, New York, Carnegie Endowment for International Peace, N.Y., 1966. 86 pp.

Pye, Lucian, *Politics, Personality and National Building: Burma's Search for Identity*, New Haven, Conn., Yale University Press, 1962. 307 pp.

Robinson, H. J., *The Motivation and Flow of Private Foreign Investment*, Stanford, Calif., Stanford Research Institute, 1961. 60 pp.

Schwarzenberger, Georg, *Power Politics*, 3rd ed., London, Stevens, 1964. 614 pp.

Sewell, J. P., *Functionalism and World Politics*, Princeton, N.J., Princeton University Press, 1966. 359 pp.

Shannon, Lyle W., *Underdeveloped Areas*, New York, Harper and Row, 1957. 496 pp.

Sharp, Walter R., *Field Administration in the United Nations System*, New York, Praeger, 1962. 570 pp.

Spector, Ivar, *The First Russian Revolution: Its Impact on Asia*, Englewood Cliffs, N.J., Prentice-Hall, 1962. 180 pp.

Sprout, Harold and Margaret, *The Ecological Perspective on Human Affairs*, Princeton, N.J., Princeton University Press, 1965. 236 pp.

Tannenbaum, Frank, *The True Society*, London, Jonathan Cape, 1964. 199 pp.

Walter, Paul A. F., *Race and Cultural Relations*, New York, McGraw Hill, 1952. 482 pp.

White, Lyman, *International Non-Government Organizations*, New Brunswick, N.J., Rutgers University Press, 1951. 325 pp.

ARTICLES AND PAMPHLETS

Adeney, Martin, "Hatred in Camera," *The Guardian*, December 20, 1969, p. 9.

Balfour, Nancy, "America in the War on Hunger," *World Today*, Vol. 22, No. 12, December 1966, pp. 529–34.

Beaglehole, E., "Cultural Factors and Social Change," *International Labor Review*, Vol. LXI, No. 5, May 1954, pp. 416–30.

Belshaw, H., "Economic Development as an Operational Problem," *Civilizations*, Vol. II, No. 2, 1952, pp. 159–66.

Chambers, F., "Interest Groups and Foreign Affairs," *Yearbook of World Affairs*, Vol. 8, 1954, pp. 220–41.

Cohen, Bernard C., "The Influence of Non-Governmental Groups on Foreign Policy Making," New York, World Peace Foundation, 1959. 26 pp.

Coult, A. D., "Unconscious Inference and Cultural Origins," *American Anthropology*, Vol. 65, No. 1, February 1963, pp. 32–35.

Cox, Robert W., "Education for Development," *International Organization*, Vol. XXII, No. L, Winter 1968, pp. 19–32.

Davis, H. B., "Imperialism and Labor: an Analysis of a Marxist View," *Science and Society*, Vol. 26, Winter 1962, pp. 26–45.

Deutsch, Karl W., "External Influences on the Internal Behaviour of States," in Farrel, R. B., ed., *Approaches to Comparative and International Politics*, Evanston, Northwestern University Press, 1966, pp. 5–26.

Dowse, Robert E., "A Functionalist Logic," *World Politics*, Vol. 18, July 1966, pp. 607–23.

Haug, Marie R., "Social and Cultural Pluralism as a Concept in Social Systems Analysis," *American Journal of Sociology*, Vol. 73, No. 3, November 1967, pp. 294–304.

Hurh, W. M., "Imitation: Its Limitations in the Process of Inter-Societal Cultural Diffusion," *International Journal of Comparative Sociology*, Vol. 10, Nos. 3–4, September and December 1969, pp. 263–85.

Kawadias, G., "Assimilation of the Scientific and Technological 'Message,'" *International Social Science Journal*, Vol. 18, No. 3, 1966, pp. 362–71.

Kunkel, John H., "Some Behavioural Aspects of the Ecological Approach to Social Organization," *American Journal of Sociology*, Vol. 73, No. 1, July 1967, pp. 12–29.

Lundsfeldt, Sven, "International Factors in Technical Assistance," *World Mental Health,* Vol. 12, No. 3, August 1960, pp. 123–29.

Maquet, M. J., "Objectivity in Anthropology," *Current Anthropology,* Vol. 5, 1964, pp. 47, 55.

McKenzie, H. I., "The Plural Society Debate, Some Comments on a Recent Contribution," *Social and Economic Studies,* Vol. 15, No. 1, March 1966, pp. 53–60.

Mead, Margaret, "The Study of National Character," in Lerner, David, and Lasswell, Harold D., eds., *The Policy Sciences,* Stanford, Stanford University Press, 1951, pp. 70–85.

———, "Crossing Boundaries in Social Science Communications," *Social Science Information,* Vol. VIII, No. 1, February 1969, pp. 7–15.

Medawar, D. P., "Anglo-Saxon Attitudes," *Encounter,* Vol. 25, No. 2, August 1965, pp. 52–58.

Mitrany, David, *A Working Peace System,* London Royal Institute of International Affairs, Post War Problems No. 1, 1943. 56 pp.

Modeleski, George, "The Corporation in World Society," *Yearbook of World Affairs,* Vol. 22, 1968, pp. 65–92.

Nath, Roger, "A Methodological Review of Cross-Cultural Management Research," *International Social Science Journal,* 20, No. 1, 1968. pp. 35–62.

Ogburn, William F., "The Hypothesis of Cultural Lag," in Parsons Talcott; Shils, Edward; Naegele, Kaspar D.; and Pittes, Jess R., eds., *Theories of Society,* Vol. II, New York, Free Press of Glencoe Inc., 1961, pp. 1270–73.

Robinson, H. J., *The Motivation and Flow of Private Foreign Investment,* Stanford Research Institute, California, 1961. 60 pp.

Robinson, James A., and Snyder, Richard C., "Decision Making in International Politics," in Kelman, Herbert C., ed., *International Behavior,* New York, Holt, Rinehart and Winston, 1966, pp. 435–63.

Robson, William A., "The Transplanting of Political Institutions and Ideas," *The Political Quarterly,* Vol. 35, No. 4, October–December 1964, pp. 410–19.

Williams, Peter, and Moyes, Adrian, *Not by Government Alone: the Role of British Non-government Organisations in the Development Decade*, London, Overseas Development Institute Ltd., 1964. 51 pp.

Willner, A. R., "The Foreign Expert in Indonesia: Problems of Adjustability and Contribution," *Economic Development and Cultural Change*, Vol. II, No. 1, April 1953, pp. 71–80.

Wilson, A. T. M., "Recruitment and Selection for Work in Foreign Cultures," *Human Relations*, Vol. 14, No. 1, 1961, pp. 3–21.

BAUXITE/ALUMINIUM INDUSTRY

SOURCES

United States Government:

Resources for Freedom, a report by the President's Materials Policy Commission, 5 vols., Washington, D.C., 1952, Vol. II, pp. 65–73.

Department of the Interior: *Minerals Yearbook*, 1964, and 1965, Vol. IV, pp. 124–27.

Department of Labor: *Technological Trends in Major American Industries*, Bulletin No. 1474, February 1956, pp. 85–90.

United Nations: (Economic Commission for Latin America), *Aspects of Development and Trade in the Commonwealth Caribbean*, Mexico, 1965, p. 97, "Bauxite and Alumina," pp. 9–15.

Commonwealth Economic Committee: *Non-Ferrous Metals*, a review of resources, production, trade, consumption, stocks and prices relating to bauxite, aluminium, copper, lead, zinc, tin, and cadmium, London, HMSO, 1963.

Anglo-American Council on Productivity: *Non-Ferrous Metals (wrought)*, London, HMSO, 1951. 96 pp.

International Metalworkers' Federation:

Annual Survey of Wages and Working Conditions, Production and Employment in Principal Branches of the Metal Industry, Geneva, 1963, 1965, and 1966, no page nos.

Steel and Aluminium Workers' Conference, 1965, *Aluminium Industry Throughout the World*, Luxemburg, 1965, no page nos.

Comparative Study on Wages and Working Conditions in Steel, Aluminum and Metallic Mineral Companies in Latin America and the Caribbean, Mexico City, 1965, no page nos.

Report of *Study Conference on Collective Bargaining in the Iron, Steel, Aluminium and Copper Industries in Latin America and Caribbean*, 1969, no page nos.

Alcan Aluminium Limited:
Jamaican Achievement, Montreal, 1962. 16 pp.
Alcan in the Caribbean, Montreal, no date (1965?). 16 pp.

Caribbean Bauxite and Mineworkers' Federation: Bauxite: *Monthly Newsletter,* February 1964 to November 1964.

BOOKS

Anderson, H. D., *Aluminum for Defense and Prosperity,* Washington, D.C., Washington Public Affairs Institute, 1951. 65 pp.

Brubaker, Sterling, *Trends in the World Aluminum Industry,* Baltimore, Resources for the Future, Johns Hopkins Press, 1967. 260 pp.

Huggins, H. D., *Aluminium in Changing Communities,* London, Andre Deutsch, in association with the Institute of Social and Economic Research, University of the West Indies, 1968. 309 pp.

Jenson, Vernon, *Nonferrous Metals Industry Unionism—1932–1953: a Story of Leadership Controversy,* Ithaca, N.Y., Cornell University Press, 1954. 328 pp.

ARTICLES AND PAMPHLETS

Aronson, Robert L., "Labour Commitment Among Jamaican Bauxite Workers: a Case Study," *Social and Economic Studies,* Vol. 10, No. 2, June 1961, pp. 156–62.

Gage, Daniel, "Aluminum Links the Pacific Coast with Jamaica," *Oregon Business Review,* Vol. 24, January 1965, pp. 1–6.

Gill, C. H. S., "Setting Up Training Schemes in a Jamaican Mining Company," in Lauwerys, Joseph A., and Scanlon, David G., eds., *Education Within Industry,* London, Evans Brothers, 1968, pp. 345–51.

Girvan, Norman, "The Caribbean Bauxite Industry," Kingston, Jamaica, *Studies in Regional Economic Integration*, Vol. 2, No. 4, Institute of Social and Economic Research, University of the West Indies, 1967. 45 pp.

Rosane, Robert E., "Mackenzie in Metamorphosis: the Emerging Need for Institutions of Social Authority in Guyana's Second Community," *International Institute for Labour Studies*, Bulletin 1, October 1966, pp. 65–79.

Reno, Philip, "Aluminum Profits and Caribbean People," *Monthly Review*, 15, October 1963, pp. 305–15.

Smith, R. A., "Aluminum Ltd., Unlimited Aluminum," *Fortune*, Vol. 50, June 1954, pp. 3 and 21.

INTERVIEWS

The following persons agreed to be interviewed in connection with this book. Titles refer to the positions which were of specific interest to the study and are not necessarily those held at the time of interview. The list is in alphabetical order with place and year of interview given for each person.

E. Anderson, Research Officer, BITU; Kingston, Jamaica, 1967.

W. Beard, Member of the International Committee of TUC, 1938–65; Geneva, Switzerland, 1965.

E. Bell, Secretary of the International Department, TUC, 1941–53; Sussex, England, 1969.

M. Berstein, Director, International Department, USWA, 1960–; Geneva, Switzerland, 1969.

Collison (Lord), Chairman, TUC General Council; Geneva, Switzerland, 1965.

C. Dunkely, Research Officer, NWU; Kingston, Jamaica, 1967.

K. Dunn, Commissioner of Labour, British Honduras, Belize; British Honduras, 1967.

H. Dunning, Official, International Department, TUC; Geneva, Switzerland, 1965.

F. Glasspole, Secretary, TUCJ and Minister of Labour (Jamaica) 1956–62; Kingston, Jamaica, 1967.

Goodwin (Dame), Member, International Committee, TUC, 1956–63; London, England, 1965.

C. Greaves Hill, Officer, Labour Department and Permanent Secretary, Minister of Labour (Jamaica) 1952–63; Kingston, Jamaica, 1967.

J. Hargreaves, Secretary, International Department, TUC; London, England, 1965.

F. Hayday, Chairman, International Committee, TUC; Brighton, England, 1965.

K. Hill, General Secretary, TUCJ, 1940–52; Kingston, Jamaica, 1967.

T. Kelly, President, NWU; Kingston, Jamaica, 1967.

C. Millard, Director, Canadian Section USWA, 1948–56; Toronto, Canada, 1968.

E. Nelson, General Secretary, BITU; Kingston, Jamaica, 1967.

R. Smith, Member, International Committee, TUC, 1962–66; Brighton, England, 1965.

N. Zonarich, International Representative, USWA, 1950–58; Washington, D.C., USA, 1968.

LIST OF ABBREVIATIONS

AF of L	American Federation of Labor
AFL-CIO	American Federation of Labor and Congress of Industrial Organizations
AIFLD	American Institute for Free Labor Development
ALA	Alliance for Labor Action
ALCAN	Aluminium Company of Canada
AWA	Aluminum Workers of America
BGLU	British Guiana Labour Union
BG&WILC	British Guiana and West Indian Labour Conference
BITU	Bustamante Industrial Trade Union
CAAWF	Carribbean Aluminium and Allied Workers' Federation
CADORIT	Caribbean Area Division of the Inter-American Regional Organization of Workers
CBMWF	Caribbean Bauxite and Mine Workers' Federation
CCLab	Caribbean Congress of Labour
CD&W	Colonial Development and Welfare Fund
CIA	Central Intelligence Agency
CIO	Congress of Industrial Organizations
CIT	Inter-American Confederation of Workers
CLASC	Latin American Confederation of Christian Trade Unions
CLC	Caribbean Labour Congress
IBRD	International Bank for Reconstruction and Development
ICFTU	International Confederation of Free Trade Unions
IFC	International Finance Corporation
IFCTU	International Federation of Christian Trade Unions
IFPAAW	International Federation of Plantation and Agricultural Workers

IFTU	International Federation of Trade Unions
ILO	International Labour Organisation International Labour Office
IMF	International Metalworkers' Federation
ISTUC	International Secretariat of National Trade Union Centers
ITF	International Transport Federation
ITS	International Trade Secretariat
IUD	Industrial Union Department
JFTU	Jamaican Federation of Trade Unions
JIC	Joint Industrial Council
JLP	Jamaica Labour Party
JWTU	Jamaican Workers' and Tradesmen's Union
NLC	National Labour Congress
NWU	National Workers Union
ORIT	Inter-American Regional Organization of Workers
PNP	People's National Party
SAWU	Sugar and Agricultural Workers' Union (Jamaica)
SMA	Sugar Manufacturers' Association
SWOC	Steel Workers' Organizing Committee
T&GWU	Transport and General Workers' Union
TUAC	Trades Union Advisory Council
TUC	Trades Union Congress (United Kingdom)
TU-Council	Trade Union Council
TUCJ	Trades Union Congress of Jamaica
TUEI	Trade Union Education Institute
UAW	United Auto Workers of America
UN	United Nations
USWA	United Steelworkers of America
UWI	University of the West Indies
WCL	World Confederation of Labour
WFTU	World Federation of Trade Unions

INDEX